WEAPONS OF WORLD WAR II

WEAPONS OF WORLD WAR II

INFANTRY WEAPONS · UNARMORED VEHICLES · ARMORED VEHICLES
ARTILLERY · SPECIAL WEAPONS · AIRCRAFT · SHIPS

ALEXANDER LÜDEKE

Bath · New York · Singapore · Hong Kong · Cologne · Delhi · Melbourne

This is a Parragon Publishing book

Copyright © 2007 Parragon Books Ltd
Queen Street House
4 Queen Street
Bath BA1 1HE, UK

Production: akapit Verlagsservice, Berlin-Saarbrücken
Project coordination and provision of illustrations: akapit Verlagsservice
Author: Alexander Lüdeke
Layout and composition: Geert Möbius, KONTUR Media Team, Bergisch Gladbach
US edition produced by: Cambridge Publishing Management Ltd
Translation: Richard Elliott, John Kelly, James Taylor
Editing: Gillian Delaforce
Proofreading: Kate Knight

ISBN: 978-1-4054-9489-2

Printed in China

CONTENTS

INTRODUCTION

The Greek philosopher Heraclitus wrote: "War is the father of all things." As terrible as the Second World War was, there is no doubt that this saying applies to its technological dimensions. The war that raged from 1939 to 1945 was an out-and-out conflict of technology. The courage, determination, and personal aptitude of the individual had only a limited ability to determine victory or defeat. What was far more important for victory was the material and, in particular, the technological advantage over the opponent.

While fighting spirit, leadership qualities, and clever tactics were repeatedly able to decide the result of individual engagements or even campaigns, it was no longer possible to win the total war in this manner. The countries engaged in this war placed their total scientific and industrial capacity at the service of the military so as not to be left behind by their opponents. Therefore the development of weapons technology accelerated in the years between 1939 and 1945 to an extent never before seen, and all the major countries engaged in the war produced weapons and vehicles in quantities and varieties that had never been seen either before or after this time. Within less than six years weapons technology progressed remarkably to an extent that would otherwise have required decades. One can find striking examples of this phenomenon in every field of military technology. While in 1939 most tanks were still fitted with cannon of 1.6 inches (40 mm) caliber or less, and most weighed not more than 15 tons (15.2 tonnes), in 1945 heavy monsters of up to 70 tons (71.1 tonnes) fitted with weapons of calibers of up to 5 inches (128 mm) ranged over the battlefields. In the infantry one can also observe a similar trend. While at the outbreak of war many soldiers went into combat with weapons that would have been familiar to their fathers in 1914–18, by 1945 modern models were in use, some of which are still produced today. The best example of this is the German MG 42 machine gun. In 1939 almost all countries still possessed biplanes, whose performance hardly differed from that of machines at the start of the 1920s. By 1945, however, aircraft driven by jet or rocket propulsion hunted in the skies at up to 600 miles per hour (965.6 km/h), and multi-engine bombers carried ten times the load of their predecessors at the start of the war. To understand the pattern of events and the outcome of this war it is also necessary to become acquainted with the dimensions

A Red Army T-34 on the advance.

of weapons technology. Without an appreciation of progress and developments in this field anyone who is interested in its history cannot review and classify all aspects of this dreadful war. This book therefore provides a comprehensive overview of the rapid progress of weapons technology and the variety of design and development from 1939 to 1945. It presents all the important and forward-looking weapons and vehicles that were in use at this time in the countries engaged in the conflict. Wherever possible details are also provided concerning the production quantities for the models in question so that their relevance can be better assessed. The countries are classified according to whether they were part of the Axis or of the Allied powers, and are listed in the order in which they entered the war. May the study of this subject lead to a clear understanding that a conflict of this kind must never be repeated. For each one of the more than 50 million sacrifices on all sides was one too many.

The Boeing B-17 Flying Fortress is, with the P-51 Mustang, one of the best-known American Second World War combat aircraft.

Russia 1943: An MG 42 machine gunner from the Grossdeutschland Division.

INFANTRY WEAPONS

MODEL 08 SEMI-AUTOMATIC PISTOL 0.3 INCH (9 MM)

The development of this pistol is closely linked with the names of two world-famous designers: Hugo Borchardt and Georg Luger. The predecessors of this weapon originated as early as the last decade of the 19th century, and various stages of development led to the 08 pistol, which in 1908 was introduced as the standard handgun of the German Imperial Army. By the end of the First World War more than 1.5 million of these weapons had been produced. After 1918 civil and military versions of this model were exported, not least on account of its excellent reputation, to many countries such as Finland, Sweden, the Netherlands, Switzerland, Portugal, Spain, Brazil, Latvia, Turkey, Iran, and the USA.

From 1930 onward the pistol was mainly manufactured by the Mauser factories in Oberndorf. Up to cessation of production in June 1942 more than

900,000 examples had been produced for the German Army (Wehrmacht) and for export. The 08 was used by the Wehrmacht, the Luftwaffe, and the Marines, and proved its worth. It was rated as accurate and reliable, but was expensive and complicated to manufacture.

Caliber:	0.35 in
Cartridge:	0.35 x 0.75 in parabellum
Muzzle velocity:	1,050 ft/s
Weight with full magazine:	2.13 lb
Magazine capacity:	8 rounds
Operational range:	55 yd

WALTHER SEMI-AUTOMATIC PISTOL MODEL P 38 0.3 INCH (9 MM)

The Wehrmacht command had recognised since the mid-1930s that the 08 could only be produced by expending vast resources in terms of material, time, and costs. The search was therefore under way for a new weapon that would supplement the 08 as a military weapon and even replace it. However, the first model put forward by the Walther weapons factory in Thuringia did not meet requirements; the third version was only introduced in 1938

Caliber:	0.35 in
Cartridge:	0.35 x 0.75 in parabellum
Muzzle velocity:	1,165 ft/s
Weight with full magazine:	1.96 lb
Magazine capacity:	8 rounds
Operational range:	55 yd

as a military sidearm named the P 38 pistol. However, it soon became clear that the P 38 was not much cheaper than

the P 08, but it was faster and no more complicated to manufacture. Since Walther could not meet the demands of the Wehrmacht alone the P 38 was also produced by other companies, such as the Mauser factories in Oberndorf. By the end of the war in 1945 more than 1.2 million P 38s had been produced. While the first models were of excellent quality and made from high-quality materials, workmanship steadily declined from 1943 onward. Nevertheless the P 38 was rated as a thoroughly good weapon with excellent characteristics. Many experimental models were produced during the war, including a short version, the P 38 k, which was originally destined for special units.

In 1957 Walther (now based in Ulm) resumed production. Named the P1, the weapon has been introduced into the Bundeswehr, police units of several of the Federal states, and into the armies of other countries.

MP 38 AND MP 40 MACHINE PISTOLS 0.3 INCH (9 MM)

Caliber:	0.35 in
Cartridge:	0.35 x 0.75 in parabellum
Muzzle velocity:	1.247 ft/s
Firing rate:	400 rounds/min
Weight with full magazine:	7.9 lb
Magazine capacity:	32 rounds
Operational range:	219 yd

This weapon, often incorrectly called the "Schmeisser MP," originated in 1938 at the request of the German Tank Corps, which, as a result of its experiences in the Spanish Civil War, was looking for a close combat weapon. Even in later models the origin of the MP 38 as a weapon for tank crews is still clear in the form of the "nose" under the barrel, which was designed to hook into firing slits, and the downward-pointing box magazine. For infantrymen who had to shoot lying down this type of magazine was a real hindrance. The designer of the weapon was not, as is often assumed, Hugo Schmeisser, but Heinrich Vollmer, who was working at the ERMA (ERfurter MAschinenfabrik) weapons factory.

In the MP 38 the wooden stock that was usual up to that time was dispensed with, and the pistol was made completely out of metal and plastic. Also the shoulder stock was foldable for the first time, to allow better handling in a small space—another indication of its origin as a weapon for the Tank Corps. The MP 38 was rated as an excellent, forward-looking design that was easy to operate, with good accuracy and stability. However, if not well maintained it tended to jam during loading, and the safety record of the pistol gave rise to criticism because of its ability to cause accidents time and again. Since the metal parts of the MP 38 were machined, the manufacturing costs were extremely high. From 1940 onward a version therefore appeared that was manufactured using sheet metal pressing technology; the MP 40. This model was also meant to remove the weak points of the MP 38, but in this it was not altogether successful. Nevertheless the MP 38 and 40 were well liked by troops, since they had significantly higher firepower than the Mauser 98 k standard carbine.

To provide a further increase in firepower the model MP 40/1 was developed with a magazine that was twice the size—i.e. with 64 rounds—but this design proved not to be effective. The MP 38/40 was never available in sufficient numbers. Even the paratrooper units were mainly equipped with the Mauser 98 k carbine. By the end of the war around 1 million MP 38/40s had been produced.

The MP 40 in Stalingrad.

44 STG 44 / MP 43 / MP 44 ASSAULT RIFLE 0.3 INCH (7.92 MM)

Caliber:	0.3 in
Cartridge:	0.3 x 1.3 in
Muzzle velocity:	2,247 ft/s
Firing rate:	500 rounds/min
Weight with full magazine:	12.1 lb
Magazine capacity:	30 rounds
Operational range:	437 yd

The StG 44 was the first rifle of its kind worldwide, and the predecessor of a whole series of assault rifles.

This weapon, designed by Hugo Schmeisser, utilized the advantages of the newly developed 0.3 x 1.3 inch (7.92 x 33 mm) short cartridge. This cartridge had in fact a lower muzzle velocity and range than conventional ammunition, but it had been found that the maximum range of conventional weapons was almost never fully utilized. More important was the firepower. Machine pistols were not a perfect solution since their pistol ammunition possessed too low a penetration capability. With the new cartridge, which weighed significantly less and was smaller than the 0.3 x 2.2 inch (7.92 x 57 mm), more ammunition could be carried; 150 cartridges weighed only 5.5 lb (2.5 kg) instead of 8.6 lb (3.9 kg). First tests were carried out from 1940 onward,

and in 1943 Albert Speer authorized mass production under the designation "MP 43." This name was chosen as a kind of camouflage, since in spite of all the positive reports Hitler had decided against the introduction of the machine carbine.

In September 1943 the first large-scale trial took place on the Eastern Front. Finally Hitler was persuaded to change his mind as a result of pleas from troops at the front—supported by Speer—and authorized production. In 1944 the designation was first altered to MP 44 and

then, apparently at Hitler's instigation, to Sturmgewehr (Assault rifle) 44, without any further modifications being made to the weapon. The MP 44 was reliable, easy to dismantle, and accurate. The recoil force was less than half the strength of that of the 98 k. In total some 424,000 rifles were produced. After the war the weapon was used by the People's Police of the German Democratic Republic and the Yugoslav Army. MP 44s have even surfaced in Africa, probably originating from Soviet stocks of appropriated weapons.

MAUSER CARBINE 98 K 0.3 INCH (7.92 MM)

The 98 k carbine was the standard weapon of the soldiers of the Wehrmacht from 1935 onward and during the whole of the Second World War. Altogether 12.8 million carbines were manufactured—of which more than 2.26 million were produced in 1944—and they were also manufactured under license in other countries. The origins of the carbine go back to the rifle that was introduced into the Imperial German Army in 1898, and which was

also the standard infantry weapon from 1914 to 1918. The main difference was a shorter barrel (thus 98 "k" for "kurz," i.e. "short"). After 1918 rifles of this type were exported across the world from the Mauser factories. In the war many different versions were built, e.g. with a target telescope, or as a launcher for rifle grenades. Because of its large stocks the 98 k continued to be used after the war, for example in Norway, Spain, and Portugal. Also the early German

Caliber:	0.3 in
Cartridge:	0.3 x 2.2 in
Muzzle velocity:	2,477 ft/s
Weight with empty magazine:	8.1–9 lb
Magazine capacity:	5 rounds
Operational range:	437 yd, max 2,187 yd

Democratic Republic and Federal Republic of Germany used such weapons in their armed forces and police units.

MG 34 UNIVERSAL MACHINE GUN MODEL 34 0.3 INCH (7.92 MM)

Caliber:	0.3 in
Cartridge:	0.3 x 2.2 in
Muzzle velocity:	2,477 ft/s
Firing rate:	800–900 rounds/min
Weight with bipod:	25.3 lb
Magazine capacity:	50 or 75 rounds drum or 300 rounds belt
Operational range (bipod):	1,312 yd

In the First World War machine guns demonstrated their devastating effect and thus their value in battle. However, the majority of the machine guns of this time were too heavy, so an attempt was made to find a new weapon that could be universally used and was also light enough to be carried by a soldier in an attack. First tests began in 1929 and continued until 1933. Officially the new machine gun was introduced as early as 1934 as the MG 34, but series production actually began only in 1936. The MG was designed to be used as a light machine gun on a bipod, as a heavy machine gun on a tripod, as a weapon in armored vehicles and bunkers, and also as an anti-aircraft weapon. The MG 34 was extremely accurate and versatile, but because of the complicated method of manufacture was expensive and time-consuming to produce. Moreover, the gun mechanisms were very sensitive, requiring a well-trained crew, and it malfunctioned if there was any lack of maintenance. For this reason the MG 34 was later supplemented and in part replaced by the MG 42. In vehicles these disadvantages were not so important, and for this reason the MG 34 remained the standard German armored vehicle machine gun until the end of the war. The armies of Axis-aligned countries such as Hungary, Italy, Slovakia, and Finland also used the MG 34.

After 1945 the MG 34 continued to be produced for some years in Czechoslovakia, both for its own army and for export (factories there had to work for the Wehrmacht during the German occupation). After the war the MG 34 could also be found in France, Israel, Vietnam, and Portugal as well as in a number of African countries. It featured in many conflicts including the war in Indochina, the Middle Eastern wars between Israel and its neighbors, and the wars in Angola and Mozambique in the mid-1970s.

MG 34 on a tripod mounting.

In the first years of the war the MG 34 was the standard machine gun for the Wehrmacht.

GERMANY

MG 42 UNIVERSAL MACHINE GUN MODEL 42 0.3 IN (7.92 MM)

The war clearly demonstrated the weaknesses of the inherently outstanding MG 34: it was not only too expensive, but also too sensitive to dirt, snow, and ice. An attempt was therefore made to simplify the production methods. However this design—called the MG 34/41—was not introduced, instead a decision was made in favor of a new design, the MG 42. As events turned out, this would become one of the best, if not indeed the best, machine gun design of all time. The MG 42 was developed under the leadership of Dr Gruner in the Grossfuss factories at Döbeln in Saxony. Dr Gruner was in fact not a weapons specialist, but rather a specialist in sheet metal pressing technology. He simply combined the

principles of other machine guns into the design of the MG 42. Instead of resource-intensive manufacture involving tight tolerances he decided in favor of the production of pressings utilizing forming and moulding technologies, and developed the gun from sheet metal pressed parts, investment castings, and plastics. This robust method of manufacture proved to be outstandingly successful in use on all fronts. Using this method of production both the number of machine tools and the number of working operations could be reduced, and thus the price of each gun was also reduced. With its extremely high rate of fire of 1,500 rounds per minute, not previously achieved by universal machine guns, the

Caliber:	0.3 in
Cartridge:	0.3 x 2.2 in
Muzzle velocity:	2,461 ft/s
Firing rate:	1,500 rounds/min
Weight with bipod:	25.5 lb
Magazine capacity:	belt with 50 or 250 rounds
Operational range (bipod):	1,312 yd

MG 42 entered into mythology on both sides of the front. The Allied soldiers feared it and used the MG 42 whenever they could get hold of it. Among the German soldiers it enjoyed a very high reputation, achieving up to 75–80% of the firepower of a section armed only with carbines.

After the war the MG 42 continued to be produced and—adapted to the NATO 0.3 x 2 inch (7.62 x 51 mm) caliber—was introduced into the Bundeswehr as the MG 1 and MG 3. The model was also used in Italy, Norway, Pakistan, Turkey, and Austria. In the former Yugoslavia

the MG 42 continued to be produced with its original 0.3 x 2 inch (7.92 x 57 mm) caliber and was used in the Balkan wars of the 1990s. Even today, more than 60 years after its debut, this weapon continues to be manufactured, which speaks eloquently for its quality.

The MG 42 proved itself, even in the mud and snow of the Eastern Front.

Russia 1943: an MG 42 machine gunner of the Grossdeutschland Division.

PANZERFAUST MODEL 30, 60, 100, 150

The Panzerfaust (meaning "armored fist") was in principle a small recoilless gun of the simplest form of construction that fired a high-caliber shaped charge projectile with an armor-piercing capability. Germany's desperate state required the availability of a more effective anti-tank weapon that was simpler to produce in large numbers than the Panzerschreck anti-tank rocket launcher. The design concept of the Panzerfaust was developed in 1941, but the first prototypes were only tested from 1943 onward. From mid-1944 onward the Panzerfaust was introduced into the Wehrmacht in various models (30 small, 30, 60, 100, 150). These types differed from each other only slightly; it was just the range that differed. The Panzerfaust was designed for one-time use only. After firing, the barrel could be thrown away, although empty barrels were often gathered up and reloaded in the factory. Operation was very simple: the soldier firing the weapon raised the sight, released the safety catch, located the target, and pressed the trigger. Thus the Panzerfaust became the ideal weapon for the poorly trained soldiers of the last phase of the war, and also for the children and old men of the Volkssturm (literally the "People's Storm"). Nevertheless use of the weapon was not without its problems. As in the case of the Panzerschreck it was inadvisable for anyone to be in the area behind the Panzerfaust when it was fired. Moreover the shaped charge very often did not explode on impact. It is no longer possible to establish exact production numbers, but the Panzerfaust was produced in very large quantities. In November 1944 alone the Wehrmacht had more than half a million at its disposal, of which more than half were fired in the same month.

Despite all its disadvantages, most of which were caused by poor quality resulting from the state of the war and lack of training, the Panzerfaust was a feared weapon. Many armored units attempted to provide their vehicles with additional protection in the form of improvised "armoring." The mode of operation of the Panzerfaust meant that rolls of wire mesh or similar were often sufficient for this purpose; these "softly" captured the slow-moving, shaped charge and triggered a premature detonation. Similar devices can be seen today on vehicles of the US and British Armies in Iraq.

Caliber of the barrel	
(Panzerfaust 30):	1.7 in
Muzzle velocity:	148 ft/s
Length:	40.6 in
Weight:	11.2 lb
Weight of explosive charge:	3.3 lb
Max. operational range:	33–44 yd
Penetration capability:	5.5 in armored steel

The Panzerfaust gave infantrymen the ability to fight against even heavy tanks with a good prospect of success.

GERMANY

PANZERSCHRECK ANTI-TANK ROCKET LAUNCHER 54 3.4 INCH (88 MM) AND 3.9 INCH (100 MM)

The Panzerschreck (which literally means "armor fear") was introduced into the Grenadier units at the start of 1944. The motive for the development of this recoilless rocket launcher to fight against tanks was the desperate position of the infantry in the face of armored attacks. The Panzerbüchsen 39 anti-tank rifles with a 0.3 inch (7.92 mm) caliber that were available at the start of the war had demonstrated a lack of capability as early as 1939. The Grenadiers were forced to use demolition charges, magnetic hollow charges, or Molotov cocktails; they even resorted to jamming anti-tank mines between the turret and deck of a tank. All these devices required the soldier to enter into the immediate vicinity of the tank, to allow it to roll over him, or even to clamber onto the vehicle. At the end of 1942 and the start of 1943 US Army rocket weapons of the Bazooka type were captured in Tunisia; these were studied with great haste and it was recognized that this weapon could provide anti-tank defense forces with an unimagined hitting power. An improved weapon, based on the Bazooka but with a greater caliber (3.4 inch/88 mm instead of 2.3 inch/60 mm), was developed; because of its shape this was first called the "Ofenrohr" ("Stovepipe") and then later the "Panzerschreck." It fired a rocket projectile with a shaped charge. In its original form the weapon still had no shield for the soldier firing the weapon; he had to wear a fireproof mask so that the exhaust from the rocket charge did not burn him. Nevertheless, this could still happen to another soldier if he was directly behind a Panzerschreck when it was being fired. A special 3.9 inch

(100 mm) version with an improved penetration capability was only manufactured in small numbers. From 1943 to mid-March 1945, 314,895 anti-tank rocket launchers 54 and more than 2.2 million charges were produced. Along with the Panzerfaust, the Panzerschreck was part of the so-called "wonder weapon program," which with the aid of a large propaganda campaign was designed to ensure that belief in the final victory remained intact.

Caliber:	3.4 in
Muzzle velocity:	427 ft/s
Length:	64.6 in
Weight:	20.94 lb
Weight of grenade:	5.29–7.28 lb
Operational range:	109–219 yd
Penetration capability (armored steel):	5.9–8.6 in at 90°

The loading procedure for the Panzerschreck: the soldier on the right introduces a rocket charge into the barrel from the rear. Wisely he is kneeling alongside, and not behind, the weapon.

FLAMETHROWER 35

Flamethrowers were used for the first time on the German side in the First World War and proved to be very successful—for the most part because of their psychological effect, since the equipment itself was heavy, difficult to handle, with a limited range, and quite dangerous for the soldier using it. If the flammable liquid tank on his back was hit this could set him alight. The Wehrmacht also used flamethrowers in the Second World War (as did the other countries engaged in the war) against bunkers, secure positions, and armored vehicles. The flamethrowers used by the Germans worked on the following principle: each flamethrower had two tanks: one for a flammable liquid, and the other for a propellant, usually nitrogen. When the valve was opened the propellant pushed the flammable liquid through the flame tube, at the front end of which it was ignited. The range was dependent on the flow rate of the nozzle, the initial velocity of the flammable liquid, and the wind direction. In turn the initial velocity was determined by the pressure in the tank and the length of hose. The first German one-man flamethrower was the Flamethrower 35. It weighed 78.9 lb (35.8 kg) and was really too heavy to use. The tank contained 3.12 gallons (11.8 liters) of flammable liquid. The jet of flame extended for 27–33 yd (2530 m). According to the length of the individual bursts up to 15 strikes could be delivered. The Flamethrower 35 was produced until 1941. Thereafter various other models (Flamethrower 40, 41, 43, 44, 46) went into production, all of which were lighter and easier to handle than the 35 version.

Weight:	78.9 lb
Propellant:	nitrogen
Quantity of flammable liquid:	3.12 gal
Number of possible strikes:	2–15
Operational range:	27–33 yd

*German soldier with
a Flamethrower 35.*

3.1 INCH (8 CM) MODEL 34 MORTAR

From 1932 onward the Rheinmetall company developed the 3.1 inch (8 cm) 34 mortar. The weapon was a smooth-barreled muzzle-loader with a weight of 125.7 lb (57 kg). The mortar consisted of the barrel with cover, bipod with aiming and elevating mechanisms, baseplate, and sight mounting. The barrel was 45 inches (1,143 mm) long, the caliber was 3.2 inches (81.4 mm). With a muzzle velocity of 564 ft/sec (172 m/sec) the heavy 7.2 lb (3.5 kg) mortar 34 shell could be fired up to 2,625 yards (2,400 m). Scatter at the maximum range was of the order of 71 yards (65 m). The first weapons were received by soldiers in 1937, and at the outbreak of war they had access to more than 3,625 pieces. When the mortar was mounted on a self-propelled carriage

(e.g. Sd.Kfz. 250/7), it was called the 67 mortar. More than 73,000 mortars of this model had been produced by March 1945. In addition the Wehrmacht used many captured mortars of French, Polish, Czech, or Russian origin.

Caliber:	3.2 in
Muzzle velocity:	564 ft/s
Length:	45 in
Weight:	125.7 lb
Weight of mortar shell:	7.2 lb
Max. operational range:	2,625 yd

A 34 mortar team takes cover while firing.

BERETTA MODEL 1938/42 MACHINE PISTOL AND VARIANTS 0.35 INCH (9 MM)

Caliber:	0.35 in
Cartridge:	0.35 x 0.75 in parabellum
Muzzle velocity:	1,214 ft/s
Firing rate:	400 rounds/min
Weight without magazine:	7.2–9.4 lb
Magazine capacity:	20 or 40 rounds
Operational range:	219 yd

the Beretta models from the First World War. The Model 38 used the 0.3 inch (9 mm) parabellum ammunition, was rated as extremely robust and was very much liked. Two different triggers allowed an uncomplicated choice between single or continuous fire. From the end of 1942 onward the 38/42 variant was

manufactured, which was designed to remove the main disadvantage of the machine pistol, namely the excessive resources required for its production. The Model 38/44 was a further simplification. Both variants were also produced for the Wehrmacht where they saw operation as the MP.738 and MP.739.

This weapon was the Italian Army's standard machine pistol during the Second World War. The Model 1938A was introduced in 1938, and variants were in production until 1975. The weapon was an ongoing development of

MANNLICHER-CARCANO REPEATING RIFLES 0.25 INCH (6.5 MM) AND 0.28 INCH (7.35 MM)

Caliber (Model 1938):	0.28 in
Cartridge:	0.28 x 2.1 in
Muzzle velocity:	2,477 ft/s
Weight with empty magazine:	6.8 lb
Magazine capacity:	6 rounds
Operational range:	656 yd

The rifles and carbines of the Mannlicher-Carcano family, used during the Second World War by the Italian armed forces in more than 15 variants, can be traced back to a rifle

Mannlicher-Carcano rifles were rated as unreliable and not particularly accurate.

introduced for the first time in 1891—the Model 1891. Fundamentally nothing had altered up to the start of the Second World War in the design of this conventionally built and manually operated weapon. The design, and in particular the 0.25 inch (6.5 mm) caliber cartridge that was developed for it, were rated as hopelessly out of date even at the beginning of the 20th century. An attempt was therefore made in 1938 to remove its worst weak spots by introducing a new 0.28 inch (7.35 mm) caliber cartridge and shortening the weapon, but this was unsuccessful. In the absence of any alternative the Italian troops had to remain equipped with 0.28 inch (7.35 mm) and 0.25 inch (6.5 mm) caliber weapons of this type until the end of the war.

NAMBU TAISHO SEMI-AUTOMATIC PISTOL MODEL 14 0.31 INCH (8 MM)

This weapon was designed by Major (later General) Nambu in the 14th year of the reign of the Emperor Taisho, hence its designation. It was the standard pistol of the Japanese armed forces from 1941 to 1945 and was issued primarily to officers. In total more than 320,000 were produced. In appearance it is somewhat similar to the German P 08, but is significantly simpler in its construction, and never achieved the reliability or quality of manufacture of the latter at any time. Moreover the Japanese 0.31 inch (8 mm) cartridge was greatly inferior to the German parabellum ammunition in all respects, and the weapon could react unpleasantly if it was not handled with care. A version with a 0.27 inch (7 mm) caliber was also manufactured. This variant, originally intended for the civil market, was issued primarily to Japanese pilots. After the defeat and the subsequent demilitarization of Japan in 1945 many Nambu pistols found their way to the USA, since returning GIs often

took weapons of this type home as souvenirs or trophies, even though it was against the regulations.

Caliber:	0.31 in
Cartridge:	0.31 x 0.85 in
Muzzle velocity:	951 ft/s
Weight with empty magazine:	2.12 lb
Magazine capacity:	8 rounds
Operational range:	55 yd

ARISAKA MODEL 99 REPEATING RIFLE AND VARIANTS 0.3 INCH (7.7 MM)

Like many other nations, the Japanese during the Second World War employed rifles and carbines that were already in use between 1914 and 1918, e.g. the Arisaka Model 38 with a 6.5 mm caliber. It had however been recognized during the Sino-Japanese War at the end of the 1930s that these rifles and their ammunition no longer satisfied requirements. In 1939 therefore a slightly modified and easier to handle 0.3 inch (7.7 mm) caliber rifle was introduced. These weapons were conventional, manual repeaters, similar to the European Mauser 98k or Mannlicher-Carcano. Although this very average design should have been the standard weapon for the Japanese troops, sufficient numbers were never produced to allow all troop units to be equipped with them. The Model 38 therefore remained in service up to 1945. Altogether more than 10 million rifles of the Arisaka type are believed to have been manufactured between 1897 and 1945.

Caliber:	0.3 in
Cartridge:	0.3 x 2.28 in
Muzzle velocity:	2,477 ft/s
Weight with empty magazine:	8.36 lb
Magazine capacity:	5 rounds
Operational range:	656 yd

LIGHT MACHINE GUN MODEL 99 0.3 INCH (7.7 MM)

Caliber:	0.3 in
Cartridge:	0.3 x 2.28 in
Muzzle velocity:	2,346 ft/s
Firing rate:	800 rounds/min
Weight with empty magazine and bipod:	22 lb
Magazine capacity:	30 rounds
Operational range:	875 yd

As was the case for the Arisaka rifles, it likewise became clear during the Sino-Japanese War that the 0.25 inch (6.5 mm) caliber ammunition used for the machine guns up to that time no longer satisfied requirements. The Model 96 light machine gun that had been introduced shortly before this war was thus already out of date. In addition this weapon had the disadvantage that the cartridges had to be greased before loading in order to guarantee trouble-free operation. In 1939 therefore a new machine gun was introduced, the Model 99 with a 0.3 inch (7.7 mm) caliber. Although it was declared to be a standard weapon it was never manufactured in sufficient numbers and older models also remained in service up to the end of the war.

The Model 99 appears to have been modeled on the Czech ZB 1926 and was likewise reliable and accurate as well as being a weapon that was highly prized by soldiers. It is believed that 100,000 were produced up to 1945.

The Model 99 was the standard light machine gun for the Japanese armed forces from 1941 to 1945.

HEAVY MACHINE GUN MODEL 92 0.3 INCH (7.7 MM)

Machine guns of this type were identical with the Taisho 3 Model of 1914 apart from the caliber (which was 0.3 inches/7.7 mm instead of 0.25 inches/6.5 mm). Externally these weapons were easily recognized by the massive cooling ribs on the barrel, although extended continuous fire was still not possible. Another disadvantage was the great weight, which made any change of firing position difficult. Also the cartridges had to be oiled before they were inserted. Malfunctions occurred if this procedure was not carried out sufficiently carefully. Nevertheless the Model 92 was the machine gun most often used by Japanese troops between 1941 and 1945.

Caliber:	0.3 in
Cartridge:	0.3 x 2.28 in
Muzzle velocity:	2,396 ft/s
Firing rate:	450 rounds/min
Weight with tripod:	121.9 lb
Magazine capacity (loading clips):	30 rounds
Operational range:	1,094 yd

The Allied forces named it the "Woodpecker" because of its stuttering tone when firing.

A Model 92 heavy machine gun on an anti-aircraft mounting

1.9 INCH (50 MM) MODEL 89 MORTAR

This weapon emerged from the need to bridge the gap between the range of thrown hand grenades and the minimum range of the larger mortars. The mortar was introduced in 1929 and at first was only issued to special units. By the start of the Second World War however it was part of standard infantry ordnance. The mortar had a 1.9 inch (50 mm) caliber, weighed only 10 lb (4.54 kg) and had a barrel length of just 10 inches (254 mm). It fired a shell weighing 1.75 lb (0.793 kg) over a maximum range of 700 yards (640 m), and could also fire the standard Japanese Model 91 hand grenade instead of a dedicated shell.

Caliber:	1.9 in
Muzzle velocity:	not known
Length:	10 in
Weight:	10 lb
Weight of mortar shell:	1.75 lb
Max. operational range:	700 yd

Since the mortar did not feature a bipod the soldier firing the weapon had to hold the barrel steady during firing. Therefore the firing procedure usually meant that the soldier firing the mortar knelt behind it. Thus the mortar acquired the nickname "Knee Mortar." Apparently some US Marines are believed to have taken this all too literally and tried to fire captured weapons with the base plate located on their knees—which inevitably resulted in broken bones. Despite its small size the mortar had a massive recoil.

MODEL MAS 1938 MACHINE PISTOL 0.3 INCH (7.65 MM)

As a consequence of the First World War the French state weapons factories began to work on the design of machine pistols from the mid-1920s onward. However it took until 1938 before any useful results were achieved. Series production started up only slowly, so that by the start of the campaign for France in 1940 only a few weapons were available. However, production continued in the unoccupied part of France after its defeat. Overall the weapon was rated as accurate, but also complicated and expensive to manufacture. Its greatest disadvantage was the poor performance of the 0.3 inch (7.65 mm) caliber ammunition, which was unable to match the 0.35 inch (9 mm) parabellum cartridge. Nevertheless the MAS 1938 continued to be used after the war.

Caliber:	0.3 in
Cartridge:	0.3 x 0.79 in
Muzzle velocity:	1,148 ft/s
Firing rate:	600 rounds/min
Weight with full magazine:	7.5 lb
Magazine capacity:	32 rounds
Operational range:	164 yd

The MAS 38 was the last manually loaded rifle in the world to be adopted by an army.

MAS 36 REPEATING RIFLE 0.29 INCH (7.5 MM)

Caliber:	0.29 in
Cartridge:	0.29 x 2.1 in
Muzzle velocity:	2,707 ft/s
Weight with empty magazine:	8.3 lb
Magazine capacity:	5 rounds
Operational range:	656 yd

In 1886 the French Army led the world when it introduced smokeless rifle ammunition in the form of the 0.3 inch (8 mm) Lebel cartridge. In the 1920s, however, this ammunition began to be dated. After a number of unsuccessful attempts a new standard cartridge with a caliber of 0.29 x 2.1 inch (7.5 x 54 mm) was introduced in 1929. Attempts to retrofit the old Lebelund Berthier rifles, which originated in the First World War and were still available in large numbers, were not successful, so development started on a new weapon, which was introduced in 1936 as the MAS 1936. However series production of this model also started only slowly. It is believed that only 250,000 were produced by May 10, 1940. The MAS 1936 was one of the last manually actuated conventional repeaters. Captured weapons were also used by German occupation troops. After 1945 the MAS 1936 continued to remain part of the equipment of the French Army for some years. Subsequently the weapon emerged in the armies of several of the former French colonies.

CHATELLERAULT LIGHT MACHINE GUN MODEL 1924/29 0.29 INCH (7.5 MM)

Caliber:	0.29 in
Cartridge:	0.29 x 2.1 in
Muzzle velocity:	2,592 ft/s
Firing rate:	550 rounds/min
Weight with empty magazine and bipod:	19.6 lb
Magazine capacity:	25 rounds
Operational range:	875 yd

In the First World War France was one of the first countries to introduce light machine guns, the majority of which were of the Chauchat Model 1915 type. Although this 0.3 inch (8 mm) caliber machine gun provided the soldiers with valuable firepower, it was anything but a mature, reliable weapon. In 1920 a contract was therefore awarded to the government weapons factory in Chatellerault to design a successor model that was to use the 0.29 inch (7.5 mm) caliber ammunition being developed at that time. The gun was modeled on the US Browning BAR M 1918. In 1924 the new machine gun entered service in the French Army. However it had the habit of sometimes exploding when in continuous fire mode. It was discovered that lower-quality steel had been used in its production, which conducted the heat away so poorly that cartridges ignited even as they were being fed in. An improved model appeared in 1929. In addition there were variants for installation in aircraft and fortifications. After the victory over France the Wehrmacht captured large stocks of the machine gun and called it the MG Model 24/29 (f). After the war the French Army continued to use it for some years.

BRANDT 3.1 INCH (81 MM) MORTAR MODEL 1927/31

In the trench warfare of the First World War a new weapon emerged: the grenade or mine launcher, otherwise known as a mortar. This mortar originated in 1927 as an improvement of the British Stokes model from the First World War. It was Edgar Brandt's masterpiece, exported to many countries and at the same time an archetype for many similar models across the world. The mortar was a simple smooth-barreled weapon that was muzzle loaded and weighed 131.6 lb (59.7 kg) together with a baseplate and bipod, on which were fitted both an elevating and traversing mechanism and also a sighting device. A shell with a maximum weight of 14.3 lb (6.5 kg) was fired out of the 50 inch (1,270 mm) long barrel with a muzzle velocity of 571 feet (174 m) per second. The maximum range was 3,117 yards (2,850 m).

Caliber:	3.1 in
Muzzle velocity:	571 ft/s
Length:	50 in
Weight:	131.6 lb
Weight of shell:	7.1 lb
Max. operational range:	3,117 yd

The design of this mortar was so accomplished that even today almost all mortars of whatever kind are descendants of the Brandt mortar.

ENFIELD REVOLVER MODEL NO. 2 MK. 1 CALIBER .380

Development of this revolver in the Enfield government weapons factory (Royal Small Arms Factory Enfield, RSA) took place at the start of the 1920s to replace the many different Webley and Enfield revolvers in the British Army that originated from the First World War and in some cases were even significantly older. The British stayed with the revolver, although most other countries developed semi-automatic pistols. The reason for this was a deeply rooted tradition as well as the indestructible properties and the great efficiency of the Webley and Enfield revolvers. Disadvantages, however, included the great weight and the

massive recoil of these older .455 caliber models (approximately 0.4 inch/11.5 mm) that required a practiced marksman. The decision was therefore made to stay with the revolver, but with a smaller caliber and less weight. The result was a compromise, since although the Enfield No. 2 was robust and required little maintenance, its stopping power was not always adequate. Nevertheless by the end of the war 380,000 revolvers of the military variant had been produced.

Caliber:	0.38in
Cartridge:	0.38in British R
Muzzle velocity:	656 ft/s
Weight unloaded:	1.7 lb
Magazine capacity:	6 rounds
Operational range:	49 yd

STEN MACHINE PISTOL 0.35 INCH (9 MM)

Caliber:	0.35 in
Cartridge:	0.35 x 0.75 in
Muzzle velocity:	1.247 ft/s
Firing rate:	500 rounds/min
Weight without magazine:	6.6 lb
Magazine capacity:	32 rounds
Operational range:	219 yd

The designation "Sten gun" was used for a series of very simply and cost-effectively constructed, but nevertheless reliable and effective, British Army machine pistols that originated in the Second World War. The name was derived from those of the two designers, R.V.

Shepperd and H.J.Turpin, who were working in the Enfield government weapons factory. The design of the pistol began in 1940 in response to the German victories on the continent when it appeared likely that the Wehrmacht would carry out an invasion of the United Kingdom in "Operation Sea Lion." What the British Army required in this situation —particularly after the heavy losses of equipment at Dunkirk—was an effective and inexpensive automatic weapon. In 1941 production began of the Sten Mk. 1, of which more than 100,000 were produced. The success of these crude and cheap-looking weapons led to a number

of improved models in the shape of Mk. 2 to Mk. 6, of which in total more than 3.5 million were manufactured. The Sten was not only standard equipment for the British armed forces during the war, but those dropped by parachute were also used by many partisan and resistance groups in occupied Europe. The greatest compliment to the potency and effectiveness of the Sten was without doubt that made by the Germans, when shortly before the end of the war they planned a replica under the pseudonyms "Gerät Potsdam" ("Potsdam equipment") and "Gerät Neumünster" ("Neumünster equipment") so that they could arm the Volkssturm effectively and cheaply. However only a few thousand were delivered by the end of the war. The original Sten machine pistol remained in use up to the 1960s in various armed forces, and was always highly prized because of its reliability and simplicity.

Sten MP Mk. 2.

LEE-ENFIELD REPEATING RIFLE 0.303 INCH (7.7 MM)

Caliber (all versions Lee-Enfield No. 4 Mk. 1):	0.303 in
Cartridge:	0.303 x 2.2 in R
Muzzle velocity:	2,444 ft/s
Weight with empty magazine:	9.08 lb
Magazine capacity:	10 rounds
Operational range:	875 yd

In the Second World War the British Army used rifles of the same type as were used in the First World War. Some of the weapons were still available from war stocks, but some were also improved versions. The original Lee-Enfield rifle was developed in 1895 and in 1902 was designated a standard weapon. At that time it was rated as one of the best rifles of its kind, particularly because of the 10 round magazine and what was a high firing rate for a manually loaded rifle. Various trial weapons were developed between the wars, but were unable to achieve acceptance for economic reasons. The large stocks of 0.303 caliber ammunition and the corresponding Lee-Enfield rifles from the First World War ensured that this type continue to be used in the form of various models. Thus it remained in service with only minimal modifications, but the designations of the various variants are confusing. Most heavily used was definitely the Type No. 4 Mk. 1, series production of which began in the 1930s and continued until 1945. Alongside special sniper models there was also a shortened version for the jungle, but the latter failed to prove itself.

BREN LIGHT MACHINE GUN MODEL 0.303 INCH (7.7 MM)

The name of this machine gun is based on the first letters of the locations "Brno" and "Enfield." Brno indicates the Czech origin of this weapon, which was designed in that country in 1933 and was based on the MG ZB v.b.26. The Bren fired the same ammunition as the Lee-Enfield rifle. In general the Bren was rated as a very reliable weapon. Particular emphasis was given to the easy changeover of the barrel, when this became overheated with continuous fire. The drawbacks were the rather heavy weight and the low rate of fire of 500 rounds/min compared with the MG 42's 1,500 rounds/min. The British 0.303 inch cartridge was also not ideal for automatic weapons, so loading jams could occur. It was therefore recommended that the curved magazine inserted on top of the weapon should be loaded with only 28 rounds instead of 30. This was, of course, inadequate for a machine gun—a belt feed would have been preferable—but this was never

Caliber:	0.303 in
Cartridge:	0.303 in R
Muzzle velocity:	2,444 ft/s
Firing rate:	500 rounds/min
Weight with empty magazine and bipod:	22.49 lb
Magazine capacity:	30 rounds
Operational range:	711 yd

introduced. During the war the gun was manufactured not only in Enfield, but also in Canada and Australia. After 1945 the Bren was retrofitted to take the NATO 0.3 x 51 inch (7.62 x 51 mm) caliber and was used by the British up to the 1990s.

The Bren was the standard light machine gun for Commonwealth troops until well after 1945.

VICKERS HEAVY MACHINE GUN MODEL 0.303 INCH (7.7 MM)

This machine gun was manufactured by Vickers from 1912 onward. It was a development of the Maxim machine gun developed in 1885 by Hiram Maxim, whose patent Vickers bought in 1896. The Vickers gun was the British Army's standard machine gun in the First World War, and from 1916 onward formed the standard armament of British and French fighter aircraft. The British standard ammunition with a 0.303 inch caliber was used for the Vickers machine gun. The cartridges usually had to be loaded by hand into the ammunition belts, which were made of material. Operation of the machine gun required six men: one fired the weapon, a second man had to feed in the ammunition belt, while the others carried ancillary equipment and looked after the ammunition logistics. The Vickers was well liked by soldiers because of its reliability and solid workmanship. As a result of its water cooling it was exceptionally well suited for continuous fire. The ammunition boxes, each holding 250 rounds, weighed 22.05 lb (10 kg). As aircraft armament the gun operated in an air-cooled mode and was fitted with an interrupter gear to provide synchronization with the propeller. There were many versions for installation in aircraft, armored vehicles, and even ships, including a 0.5 inch caliber (12.7 mm) version.

Caliber:	0.303 in
Cartridge:	0.303 in R
Muzzle velocity:	2,444 ft/s
Firing rate:	450 rounds/min
Weight with tripod:	90.98 lb
Magazine capacity:	250 rounds/belt
Max. operational range:	4,374 yd

The Vickers remained in service with the British Army until well into the 1960s.

BOYS ANTI-TANK RIFLE .55 MK. 1 MODEL

Caliber:	0.55 in
Cartridge:	0.55 in
Muzzle velocity:	2,493 ft/s
Penetration capability:	0.79 in/98 yd /90°
Weight with empty magazine and bipod:	35.9 lb
Magazine capacity:	5 rounds
Operational range: (further against armored targets)	98 yd

This rifle was developed from 1934 onward by the British weapons expert Captain Boys in response to the start of rearmament in Germany, and was introduced officially into the British armed forces in November 1937. Its penetration capability of 0.79 inches (20 mm) of armored steel at a distance of 98 yards (90 m) was already inadequate at this time. The German anti-tank rifle 39 with a 0.3 inch (7.92 mm) caliber could penetrate 1.1 inches (30 mm) at a distance of 109 yards (100 m)! Therefore an improved version (Mk. 2) was designed during the war, but this in turn was quickly overtaken by developments in vehicle armor. At the outbreak of war in 1939 the Boys was only effective to a limited extent against modern tanks, but could still be used against lightly armored scout cars or personnel carriers, and also later against light Japanese tanks. In 1940 the Germans captured quite a number of these weapons at Dunkirk and used them temporarily. In North Africa the Boys was often installed in armored vehicles by Commonwealth troops. Besides its low penetration capability further disadvantages included its great weight and heavy recoil. Nevertheless approximately 63,000 were produced up to 1942.

PIAT

Caliber of the tube:	2.9 in
Muzzle velocity:	348 ft/s
Length of tube:	39 in
Weight unloaded:	32 lb
Weight of explosive charge:	2.49 lb
Max. operational range:	27–98 in
Penetration capability: (armored steel)	2.9 in/90°

The PIAT (Projector Infantry Anti Tank) arose out of the need to equip the British troops with a more effective anti-tank weapon than the Boys anti-tank rifle—this, however, had to be light enough such that it could also be used by parachute troops. In the same manner as the Panzerfaust and the Bazooka the PIAT used the shaped charge principle to achieve the greatest possible effect on the target. Nevertheless this weapon had some particular features. Thus it functioned in principle like a crossbow, using spring tension: the projectile had a hollow tail piece fitted with vanes for stabilization, in which was the propellant charge. In the barrel were a strong spiral spring and a metal rod. When the soldier

The PIAT, introduced into service from the end of 1942, was a simple design which at the same time was heavy and difficult to handle. Nevertheless it proved itself as an anti-tank weapon and in street fighting, and continued to be used even after 1945.

firing the weapon pressed the trigger, the rod sprang forward, ejected the round, and at the same time ignited the propellant charge. In theory this process should have put the spring under tension again, but this did not always happen. Tensioning by hand was laborious, since it required a pull force of 176 lb (90 kg)!

3 INCH (76.2 MM) MORTAR

This mortar originated as an improved version of the British Stokes model from the First World War, when the British Army were planning at the end of the 1920s to improve the immediate fire support for their infantry. At first, light guns were envisaged, but for reasons of cost and weight the decision was made in favor of a mortar, 112 lb (50.8 kg) in weight, with a 3 inch (76.2 mm) caliber, which fired a 9.9 lb (4.53 kg) shell with a muzzle velocity of 650 ft/s (198 m/sec) from a 53.9 inch (1,370 mm) barrel. The maximum range of the first models was approximately 1,597 yards (1,460 m). During the war, however, it emerged that the German 3.1 inch (8 cm) mortar 34 had a significantly greater range (2,625 yd/

Caliber:	3 in
Muzzle velocity:	650 ft/s
Length:	53.9 in
Weight:	112 lb
Weight of projectile:	9.9 lb
Max. operational range:	Mk. 1: 1,597 yd Mk. 2: 2,800 yd

2,400 m). Therefore a variant was designed with a longer barrel and a projectile with a more powerful propellant charge, which brought the range up to 2,800 yards (2,560 m) (Mk. 2).

TULA-TOKAREV SEMI-AUTOMATIC PISTOL MODEL TT 1933 0.3 INCH (7.62 MM)

Caliber:	0.3 in
Cartridge:	0.3 x 0.9 in
Muzzle velocity:	1,378 ft/s
Weight with empty magazine:	1.88 lb
Magazine capacity:	8 rounds
Operational range:	55 yd

The Tokarev TT-33 was the standard pistol of the Red Army from the 1930s and in that respect was the successor to a number of older revolvers. The mechanism was based on the Browning designs. It was designed for the 0.3 inch (7.62 mm) caliber Tokarev, which was almost identical to the very powerful German 0.3 inch (7.63 mm) Mauser cartridge, which could also be fired. The weapon was rated as very robust, reliable, safe, and accurate. The TT-33 was produced up until 1952 in enormous numbers and introduced into the whole of the Eastern bloc. Some models remained in service into the 1970s. Copies of the TT-33 are also known to originate from China and Egypt, among other countries.

SHPAGIN MACHINE PISTOL MODEL PPSH 1941 0.3 INCH (7.62 MM)

The PPSh machine pistol was designed and developed by the Russian designer Georgii Shpagin. The first model appeared in 1940 and was tested together with other designs in the same year. In these tests the weapons were fired with artificially contaminated magazines and were unlubricated (to do

parts were no longer cast but manufactured from 0.07–0.19 inch- (2–5 mm) thick sheet metal, metal could be saved and production costs lowered. The most expensive parts to produce were the barrel and the drum magazine, which was taken from the earlier PPD-40 weapon. The machine pistol only had two

Caliber:	0.3 in
Cartridge:	0.3 x 0.9 in
Muzzle velocity:	1,640 ft/s
Firing rate:	900 rounds/min
Weight with full magazine:	9–11.6 lb
Magazine capacity:	35 or 71 rounds
Max. operational range:	219 yd

A PPSh with a 35-round box magazine.

this individual parts were cleaned with kerosene and rubbed dry). Moreover 5,000 rounds were fired without cleaning the machine pistol. Since it performed the best in these rigorous tests, the PPSh was introduced into the Red Army in December 1940. It was designed to be in service for a minimum of 30,000 rounds with the requirement that also afterwards the weapon should demonstrate satisfactory accuracy and reliability. When the PPSh-41 originated, sheet metal pressing procedures were not yet widely used. Nevertheless many of the machine pistol's parts were manufactured using metal pressing technology. Since most of the individual

threaded connections. In total almost 6 million of these were manufactured. The Wehrmacht thought highly of the indestructible weapon. Captured examples were not only used unofficially by soldiers, but also became part of the official armament. The designation was MP 717(r); there were also models that were retrofitted to take the 0.35 inch

(9 mm) parabellum cartridge. The PPSh was one of the best weapons of its class. Its primary advantages were its high firepower, the uncomplicated production methods, and also its indestructibility, but its great weight was a disadvantage.

MOSIN-NAGANT REPEATING RIFLE 91/30 0.3 INCH (7.62 MM)

Caliber:	0.3 in
Cartridge:	0.3 x 2.1 in R
Muzzle velocity:	2,838 ft/s
Weight with empty magazine:	9.9 lb
Magazine capacity:	5 rounds
Operational range:	656 yd

Weapons of this type were in service over seven decades in Russia and subsequently the Soviet Union. The original model was a repeating rifle designed in 1891 by Sergei Mosin and introduced into the Tsarist Army. This rifle was called the Mosin-Nagant, since the magazine had been designed by the Belgian Nagant brothers. A new 0.3 x 2.1 inch (7.62 x 54 mm) cartridge was introduced with the Mosin-Nagant. During the First World War this rifle was the standard weapon of the Russian infantry and remained so until after the Second World War; it was prized on account of its robust design and accuracy. Various versions were also introduced into many other armies in the Soviet Union. In China the M1938 carbine version and its M1944 variant were produced under license as the Type 53. Licensed versions and further developments were also produced in Czechoslovakia (the Model 54 sniper rifle) and Yugoslavia. The 0.3 x 2.1 inch (7.62 x 54 mm) R rimmed cartridge developed for this rifle has meanwhile become the oldest rifle cartridge in use in the world and is even now produced worldwide and used in modern weapons such as the Dragunov sniper rifle and heavy machine guns, primarily those made in Russia and China.

DEGTYAREV LIGHT MACHINE GUN MODEL DP 1928 AND DPM 1944 0.3 INCH (7.62 MM)

The Degtyarev DP 1928 was the standard light machine gun of the Red Army during the Second World War and thereafter. Its origin goes back to the year 1934 when the designer Degtyarev began to develop a new machine gun for the Soviet armed forces that was required to be as simple as possible, robust, cost-effective, and usable under widely varying conditions. In tests in the summer of 1927 its new design proved to be superior to all others—including foreign machine guns—and it was therefore introduced into the Red Army in 1928. Although Degtyarev's objectives had been more than achieved and the weapon was rated as reliable, light, and robust, there were still a few weak points. Thus from their experience on the Eastern Front the

Caliber:	0.3 in
Cartridge:	0.3 x 2.1 in R
Muzzle velocity:	2,756 ft/s
Firing rate:	600 rounds/min
Weight with bipod:	18.5 lb
Magazine capacity: (pan magazine):	49 (47) rounds
Operational range:	875 yd

troops complained that the bipod was too unstable, the barrel changing procedure was too complicated and the magazine was too difficult to load under battle conditions. An improved version, the Model DPM 1944, replaced the DP 1928 in production.

The DP 1928/1944 was the standard light machine gun of the Red Army during the Second World War.

MAXIM HEAVY MACHINE GUN MODEL PM 1910 0.3 INCH (7.62 MM)

As the name suggests, this veteran went into production in 1910 for the Tsarist Army. The Model PM 1910 is an improved version of the Model 1905 that in turn was based on the first successful automatic weapon ever, the Maxim machine gun. The American Hiram Maxim developed this machine gun in 1885; it was the first weapon to use the recoil gases generated during firing in an automatic loading and ejection procedure. The previously developed weapons, e.g. the Gatling or Gardener guns, were still reliant on manual operation. The British armaments company Vickers acquired the license rights from Maxim and exported these machine guns all over the world. By the start of the 20th century weapons based on the Maxim system were very widespread and found many imitators, among them the German MG 08, the French Hotchkiss, and the Vickers machine gun. The Russian PM 1910 variant was manufactured in enormous numbers up to 1942, in 1942 alone 55,258 were produced. Because of its robust design and reliability it continued to be used even after 1945. The Soviet Union gave large numbers of this machine gun to China and North Korea, where the PM 1910 (and its successors) were in use until the 1970s.

Caliber:	0.3 in
Cartridge:	0.3 x 2.1 in R
Muzzle velocity:	2,822 ft/s
Firing rate:	520 rounds/min
Weight with mounting:	99.8 lb
Magazine capacity (textile belt):	250 rounds
Operational range:	1,094 yd

The PM 1910 proved itself in 1941–1945.

DEGTYAREV-SHPAGIN MACHINE GUN DSHK 1938 0.5 INCH (12.7 MM)

This weapon is a real classic and has now been in use for more than seven decades. Its origin goes back to the year 1930 when the Red Army awarded a contract for a heavy machine gun utilizing the 0.5 x 4.2 inch (12.7 x 108 mm) cartridge to counter lightly armored and aerial targets. The designer Degtyarev therefore brought across features of his 0.3 inch (7.62 mm) DP 27 machine gun using the principle of gas pressure loading. The machine gun, designated the DK, was built from 1934 onward in small numbers, but was not satisfactory because of its low firing rate of only 360 rounds/min. To increase the firing rate, Shpagin developed a modified cartridge feed, which brought the rate of fire up to approximately 600 rounds/min. This machine gun, now named the DShK, was tested in 1938 and was accepted into the armament of the Red Army in 1939. The machine gun was not only introduced into infantry units as an infantry support and anti-aircraft machine gun, but was also used as turret armament for light tanks, and as an anti-aircraft machine gun on ships and armored trains. The first Soviet tank to receive a machine gun of this type was the IS-2 from 1943 onward. During the war the feed mechanism was modified (cartridge feed via belt boxes), the mounting was improved, the changeover of barrel was simplified, and the length of service of essential parts was raised. Overall the DShK was rated as a reliable, indestructible weapon with a high efficiency on target. After the war a modernized version was designated the DShKM 38/46. When modified as anti-aircraft armament for medium tanks the machine gun was called the DShKMT. The former Soviet Union exported weapons of this type in large numbers and even today the DShK is in service in more than 40 countries worldwide.

Caliber:	0.5 in
Cartridge:	0.5 x 4.2 in
Muzzle velocity:	2,789 ft/s
Firing rate:	600 rounds/min
Weight without mounting:	73.4 lb
Magazine capacity (metal belt):	50 rounds
Operational range:	2,187 yd

DEGTYAREV ANTI-TANK RIFLE MODEL PTRD 1941 0.57 INCH (14.5 MM)

In the Second World War the Red Army used two types of anti-tank rifles: the Degtyarev PTRD with single cartridges and the five-round, semi-automatic Simonov PTRS. Both were developed to meet the requirement to supply an anti-tank rifle using the 0.57 x 4.4 inch (14.5 x 114 mm) cartridge in the shortest possible time. Just one month later both weapons were tested, but neither one seemed to be better than the other. Therefore the Soviet armed forces introduced both weapons into active service in 1941. In contradiction to a view

widely held at that time, anti-tank rifles were not completely useless. On the battlefield a large number of only lightly armored vehicles were moving around, whose armor could easily be penetrated by an anti-tank rifle. The side armor of the early German battle tanks was also vulnerable against the anti-tank rifles of the Red Army. At first glance the PTRD appears to be a primitive weapon but in reality it is complex. The barrel moves a certain amount back into the shaft as a result of the recoil during firing, which results in the bolt rotating and unlocking. At the end of this

Caliber:	0.57 in
Cartridge:	0.57 x 4.4 in
Muzzle velocity:	3,314 ft/s
Penetration capability:	1.57 in/109 yd/90°
Weight with empty magazine and bipod:	38.1 lb
Magazine capacity:	1 round
Operational range: (further against unarmored targets)	437 yd

movement the bolt engages, while the barrel is pushed back into its initial position. This opens the breech and the empty cartridge shell is ejected. Now the soldier firing the weapon can load a new cartridge and close the breech manually.

3.23 INCH (82 MM) MORTAR MODEL PM-37

Caliber:	3.23 in
Muzzle velocity:	692 ft/s
Barrel length:	48 in
Weight:	99.2 lb
Missile weight:	6.7 lb
Max. operational range:	3,325 yd

The Red Army has always placed great value on artillery support for the infantry, and as the attempt was being made in the mid-1930s to find a support weapon that would be immediately available to the infantry units, the decision was made in favour of mortars. In 1936 the Soviet Union therefore acquired a number of French 3.2 inch (81 mm) Brandt mortars. The evaluation of these weapons was essentially positive and with a few modifications an unlicensed copy of the Brandt mortar was produced from 1937 onward. The caliber was increased to 3.23 inches (82 mm) and the Russians inserted a spring mechanism between the barrel and the bipod; in addition the aiming mechanism was improved and instead of a rectangular base plate the copies were given a round base plate.

Budapest, 1945: Soldiers of the Red Army using a 3.23 inch (82 mm) mortar in street fighting. This design was extremely successful and more than 165,000 of them were produced—with only a few modifications—by 1945. Production also continued after the Second World War. Many mortars were exported all over the world or produced under license. Even today this mortar is used in many armies with hardly any modifications.

COLT SEMI-AUTOMATIC PISTOL M 1911 A1 0.45 INCH (11.43 MM)

From its introduction in 1911 through to its replacement in 1992 by the Beretta 92 FS the Colt M 1911 was a standard weapon in the US Army. Even today its popularity is undiminished and this model is still manufactured and in use.

At the start of the 20th century the US Army, in its search for a new pistol, needed nearly five years for rigorous fundamental tests in which the new Colt, designed by Browning, distinguished itself as the best and most reliable weapon. As a result it was adopted by the army in 1911 and although Colt had reckoned on this outcome of the test series, the company needed some time in order to be able to deliver large numbers of the pistols. When the First World War broke out, across the world various other companies also produced the pistol under license. After the war a number of improvements were introduced and standardized into the Model 1911 A1. The American armed forces also went into the Second World War using this pistol.

Caliber:	0.45 in
Cartridge:	0.45 x 0.9 in ACP
Muzzle velocity:	953 ft/s
Weight with empty magazine:	2.4 lb
Magazine capacity:	7 rounds
Operational range:	55 yd

Countless weapons have been generated since 1911, including unlicenced copies made in China. Among the advantages of the Colt M 1911 are its extreme robustness, reliability, and the efficiency of the 0.45 inch (11.43 mm) bullet. At the same time, however, this results in a heavy weapon that is somewhat difficult to handle and has a really hard recoil. Many of its users are, however, happy to accept these features and consider this to be one of the best pistols in the world.

THOMPSON M1928 MACHINE PISTOL 0.45 INCH (11.43 MM)

Caliber:	0.45 in
Cartridge:	0.45 in ACP
Muzzle velocity:	919 ft/s
Firing rate:	675 rounds/min
Weight without magazine:	10.7 lb
Magazine capacity:	according to the type of magazine 20, 30, 50 or 100 rounds
Max. operational range:	219 yd

The Thompson M1928 machine pistol—also known as the "Thompson A1" or "Tommy Gun"—was developed during the First World War with contributions from the US General Thompson and was designed to be a "trench cleaner" in the trench battles. However, in the 1920s it became famous when it was used by many American gangsters, such as Al Capone. They called the Thompson the "Chicago Typewriter" and it was prized because of its superior firepower, which the police at this time had nothing to counter. Because of this feature, however, the army was also interested in the pistol and introduced it as the M1928 A1, although in significant numbers only from 1938 onward. The Thompson ran through many modifications during its military service, almost all of which were related to the reduction of production costs and times. It was finally replaced in 1944 by the M3 "grease gun." By that time more than 1.5 million of all models had been produced. The Thompson was generally prized on account of its stable platform when firing, its high quality, and firepower, but it was rated as heavy and expensive.

MODEL M3 MACHINE PISTOL CALIBER 0.45 INCH (11.43 MM) AND 0.35 INCH (9 MM)

An M3 0.45 inch (11.43 mm) caliber.

Caliber:	0.45 in
Cartridge:	0.45 in ACP
Muzzle velocity:	approx. 1.312 ft/s
Firing rate:	270 rounds/min
Weight without magazine:	8.1 lb
Magazine capacity:	box magazine 30 rounds
Max. operational range:	109 yd

The recoil-loading machine pistol M3 was also called the "grease gun" or "cake decorator." It fired the 0.45 inch caliber ACP and was developed in December 1942 by the designer George J. Hyde, who originated from Germany, to replace the Thompson machine pistol, which was expensive and complicated to manufacture. The British Sten gun and the German MP 38/40 served as the basis for the design. The M3 can only fire in fully automatic mode, and its magazine contains 30 rounds. One interesting feature of the M3 was that it could quickly be converted from 0.45 inch caliber to 0.35 inch (9 mm) parabellum, which enabled captured German ammunition to be used. As a result this weapon was also very much liked by partisans and resistance fighters. Although it was almost primitive in its construction, the M3 was extremely accurate and resistant to dirt and contamination although it sometimes had problems with the ammunition feed. This was rectified with the M3 A 1 version. After 1945 the USA exported many M3s. Overall more than 655,000 of them were believed to have been manufactured in the USA and some models were also manufactured under license in Argentina, Taiwan, and Portugal. Even In the 1990s weapons of this type could still be found in armed forces.

SPRINGFIELD SEMI-AUTOMATIC RIFLE M 1903 AND VARIANTS .30 CALIBER 0.3 INCH (7.62 MM)

The Springfield rifle was another veteran from the First World War that remained in use until 1945 and later. The reason for that was not so much the properties of the rifle—a design of high quality—but rather the lack of a modern replacement. As early as the mid-1930s the US Army planned the replacement of the M 1903 by the new M1 Garand design. But the production of this new weapon did not proceed at the required pace, so that when the USA entered the war in December 1941 large sections of the US Army continued to carry the Springfield rifle. The new units that were subsequently formed had to be equipped in the first instance with the M 1903 from storage stocks, so that the Springfield was not completely replaced, even by 1945.

Caliber:	0.3 in
Cartridge:	0.3–6 in
Muzzle velocity:	2,674 ft/s
Weight with empty magazine:	8.6 lb
Magazine capacity:	5 rounds
Operational range:	656 yd

The Springfield semi-automatic rifle.

American soldiers with a Bazooka, 1944.

At the end of 1942 the Bazooka was first used by the US Army in the battles against the German Afrikakorps in Tunisia. There some of them were captured by the Germans and after careful examination were developed into the Panzerschreck. In 1943 the Model M1A1 appeared with an improved aiming device and from 1944 onward the significantly improved M9 version appeared with a two-part light metal barrel, which greatly simplified handling. In addition to a warhead for tank fighting with a shaped charge, high explosive and phosphorus warheads were also available. Bazookas were produced in large numbers and enjoyed great popularity with the troops. The M1 can be said to be the prototype of many similar weapons that continue to be used up to the present.

BROWNING EXTRA-HEAVY MACHINE GUN M 2 AND M 2 HB 0.5 INCH (12.7 MM)

After the First World War the Type M 1917 machine gun was converted to a new 0.5 inch (12.7 mm) caliber cartridge based on captured German Mauser ammunition. This machine gun was intended for the defense of armored vehicles and aircraft and was designated the M 1921. In the mid-1930s the heavy Browning M 1921 was fitted with an air-cooled barrel and renamed the M 2 Browning, but this version tended to overheat. A heavier barrel was therefore introduced, and the M 2 HB (Heavy Barrel) that thus emerged became the standard 0.5 inch (12.7 mm) machine gun of the US armed forces and also of some of the other Allied forces. The M 2 proved to be extremely durable and became a real classic. Even today the "Fifty Cal" is to be found in the USA and another 20 countries. It found and continues to find service in aircraft and helicopters, in tanks and armored vehicles, as a heavy infantry machine gun, and also on ships. The great weight and the relatively low firing rate are the result of the use of the heavy 0.5 x 3.9 inch (12.7 x 99 mm) M 2 cartridge, which because of its enormous power of penetration and hard recoil demands a robust design. Against unprotected targets the ammunition is effective at a distance of up to 2,187 yards (2,000 m). At 547 yards (500 m) armor of up to 1.3 inches (34 mm) thickness can still be penetrated. In the newer versions of the M 2 modifications allow the barrels to be changed more quickly than in earlier variants, in which a laborious adjustment of the barrel to the shell was required. Some sources give the number of M 2s manufactured as more than 3 million. During the whole of the Second World War the air-cooled version of the M 2 was also used as aircraft armament—using either a fixed or movable mounting. The main difference from the HB version was

Caliber:	0.5 in
Cartridge:	0.5 x 3.9 in US
Muzzle velocity:	approx. 2,936 ft/s
Firing rate:	500 rounds/min
Weight without tripod:	84 lb
Magazine capacity: (metal belt in box):	110 rounds
Max. operational range:	2,187 yd

the barrel which was shortened, and also wrapped in a perforated jacket in order to improve the cooling, since no change of barrel was possible. The water-cooled versions of the M 2 were primarily used as light anti-aircraft machine guns. A tank surrounded the barrel with cooling fluid, which circulated inside the weapon.

An M 2 on a mounting used in armored vehicles.

BAZOOKA MODELS M1, M1A1 AND M9 2.36 INCH (60 MM)

Caliber:	2.3 in
Muzzle velocity:	344 ft/s
Length:	54.7 in
Weight:	12.7 lb
Weight of shell:	3.4–6.1 lb
Operational range:	219 yd
Penetration capability: (armored steel)	approx. 3.9 in/ 90°

After the entry of the USA into the war the US Army was looking for a new high-performance anti-tank weapon for the infantry. When in 1942 a test demonstration of new anti-tank rifles took place, the weapons expert Skinner was able to demonstrate in a quasi non-competitive manner his rocket weapon based on the shaped charge principle, and this outclassed all other designs. As a result a contract for production of the weapon, called the M1, was immediately awarded. Skinner's design was in principle little more than a metal barrel open at both ends that was used to fire an electrically ignited rocket projectile with a shaped charge warhead of 2.36 inches (60 mm) caliber. Nevertheless this was a revolution, since for the first time an individual soldier was provided with the possibility (for that time) of fighting successfully and at some distance against heavily armored targets. Since the propulsive jet of the rocket projectile exited rearward out of the open barrel there was no recoil, which enabled the use of a thin wall barrel and control of the weapon by an individual soldier. The soldiers christened the weapon the "Bazooka"—the name owed something to a similar looking musical instrument used by the American radio comic Bob Burns.

A Bazooka M1A1.

GARAND SEMI-AUTOMATIC RIFLE M1 0.3 INCH CALIBER (7.62 MM)

John C. Garand developed as early as the 1920s the first semi-automatic rifles, from which came the M1 in the mid-1930s. While the plan was to replace the manually loaded model M 1903 by the new model relatively quickly, this only happened completely after 1945. The M1, a reliable robust gas pressure loader, was the first semi-automatic rifle in military service and helped the US Army to achieve increased firepower. Its considerable weight was a disadvantage, but this ensured a stable platform for the weapon and a relatively low recoil that placed less load on the soldier firing the weapon. The magazine of the M1 had to be filled with special loading strips which could only be reloaded when they fell out of the weapon after the last round. This generated a characteristic noise that betrayed to the enemy that the rifleman was out of ammunition, and also where he was located. However the M1 riflemen utilized this disadvantage, in that they simulated this noise and so lured the enemy out of cover. Up to the discontinuation of production in 1957 more than 5.5 million M1 Garand rifles

Caliber:	0.3 in
Cartridge:	0.3–6 in
Muzzle velocity:	2,805 ft/s
Firing rate:	30 rounds/min
Weight unloaded:	9.6 lb
Magazine capacity:	8 rounds
Operational range:	656 yd

had been produced. After 1945 it was also used by other countries and was, for example, manufactured in Italy by Beretta under license.

M1 CARBINE SEMI-AUTOMATIC RIFLE 0.3 INCH CALIBER (7.62 MM)

Caliber:	0.3 in
Cartridge:	30 M1 Carbine
Muzzle velocity:	2,001 ft/s
Firing rate:	45 rounds/min
Weight unloaded:	5.2 lb
Magazine capacity:	15 rounds box magazine
Operational range:	273 yd

During the late 1920s the US Army decided to develop an automatic weapon for troop units that were not in service in the immediate front line. This weapon was required to be more compact than a normal rifle and more effective than a pistol or a machine pistol. Since the new M1 Garand was also being introduced at this time, this project progressed only slowly for financial reasons. In 1940, however, the position in Europe forced the USA into action and a competition was announced for an automatic infantry weapon that had to be a maximum of 5.5 lb (2.5 kg) in weight. It quickly became clear however that this requirement could not be fulfilled with existing ammunition. Thus emerged the new 30 M1 Carbine cartridge with a 0.3 inch (7.62 mm) caliber. From October 1941 production of the new weapon began under the designation of M1 Carbine. Despite the original service objective the M1 Carbine was also used in the front line and, for example, played a role in the landing of US troops in North Africa and in Normandy. Although the range and penetration force were less than for the Garand, the Carbine had a higher firing rate and a lower weight. The M1 Carbine is not dissimilar to the design of the M1 Garand. In addition to the M1 standard version there was also the model M1 A1 with a folding shoulder stock, the M2 version for continuous fire, and the M3 sniper rifle. By 1945 a total of 6,117,827 of these weapons had been manufactured.

BROWNING AUTOMATIC RIFLE LIGHT MACHINE GUN (BAR)
MODEL M 1922 AND M 1918 A1 AND A2 0.3 INCH (7.62 MM)

When the USA went into the First World War in 1917 the army was equipped with a total of 1,150 heavy machine guns and a few light machine guns. Trials with the French Chauchat machine gun were not very successful so the development of new weapons was put out to contract. The weapon designer John Moses Browning thereupon developed two different models: the heavy machine gun M 1917 and a type of light machine gun with the designation Browning Automatic Rifle (BAR), which was used by the army from September 1918.

The BAR, although a gas pressure loader, is not a machine gun in the true sense, but rather an automatic rapid-firing rifle. This is also confirmed by the magazine capacity, too small for a machine gun, of only 20 rounds, which is more suited for targeted individual rounds and short volleys than for continuous fire. A further disadvantage of the BAR was its great weight of more than 22 lb (10 kg) (loaded). The 1918 version was further developed to become the M1922. The firing rate could be adapted from 350 rounds/min to 550 rounds/min, but in practise it was only 60–80 rounds. The further improved models

Caliber:	0.3in
Cartridge:	0.3 x 6 in
Muzzle velocity:	approx. 2,805 ft/s
Firing rate:	350–550 rounds/min
Weight without magazine:	20.9 lb
Magazine capacity:	20 rounds trapezoidal magazine
Operational range:	875 yd

M 1918 A1 and M 1918 A2 (introduced in 1937 and 1940 respectively) were given barrels with thicker wall thicknesses that were better suited for continuous fire, but the magazine capacity remained the same. Although the BAR did not match the requirements of a light machine gun it was astonishingly rated as one of the most important automatic weapons in the Second World War. The various BAR models were also used in the Korean War (1950–1953) and at the start of the Vietnam War. The production of all versions of the BAR amounted to more than 350,000.

BROWNING HEAVY MACHINE GUN M 1919 A4 AND VERSIONS OF IT

Caliber:	0.3 in
Cartridge:	0.3–6 in
Muzzle velocity: approx.	2,805 ft/s
Firing rate:	500 rounds/min
Weight without tripod:	31 lb
Magazine capacity: (textile belt in box):	250 rounds
Operational range:	1,531 yd

In 1917 the weapons designer J. M. Browning built the heavy, water-cooled M 1917 machine gun that was the standard machine gun of the US Army up until the start of the Second World War. As early as 1919 a lighter weapon with air cooling for installation in aircraft and armored vehicles was developed: the M 1919. Since the BAR was not a true machine gun and the M 1917 was too heavy on account of its water cooling, these versions were further developed into the M 1919 A4 and used by the Allies in large numbers. Nevertheless

the weight of the M 1919 A4 was still too great compared with other air-cooled weapons of that time: 31 lb (14.1 kg) compared with the 22.4 lb (10.2 kg) of the Bren machine gun. Moreover it was fitted with a tripod mounting that weighed an additional 14 lb (6.35 kg). In total therefore the M 1919 A4 was almost twice

as heavy as the Bren. Also it did not always function correctly because of insufficient recoil energy. Nevertheless this machine gun was a solid design that was used by the US Army until the 1960s, and in other countries up until the end of the 1980s.

An M 1919 A4 on a mounting used in armored vehicles.

Italy, November 1944: A mortar section of the 92nd US Infantry Division fires on Wehrmacht positions. Mortars of this type were also mounted in half-track vehicles of the M3 Model, which were then designated as "M21 mortar carriers." US troops were still using this mortar during the Korean War.

FLAMETHROWER M1, M1 A1, AND M 2-2

The first American flamethrower, the M1 model, was introduced in 1942. In principle it functioned in exactly the same way as the flamethrowers of the Wehrmacht. However, the US Army used manual flamethrowers in Europe only very infrequently. More often they were used in the Pacific theater where these dreadful weapons were often the only option for breaking the fanatical resistance of Japanese troops. The greatest disadvantage of the M1 and its successor the M1 A1—which used napalm for an increased range—was the electrical ignition of the flame jet, which often failed, so that the soldier had to use his lighter to fire the weapon! The M 2-2 model, introduced from 1944 onward, used special ignition cartridges that were in a revolver-type drum at the tip of the flame tube instead of the problematical electrical ignition. Because of the risk that the soldier firing the weapon would be engulfed in flames if the flammable liquid tank was hit, the US Army and US Marines gradually replaced these weapons with flamethrowers that were installed in Sherman tanks; these moreover had a higher range and a greater flammable liquid capacity.

Weight (M1):	70 lb
Propellant:	nitrogen
Flammable liquid quantity:	4.7 gal
Number of possible flamethrows:	5
Flamethrows:	each of 2 seconds
Range:	44–49 yd

Training in the USA: a GI learns how to handle a flamethrower.

MODEL M1 3.1 INCH (81 MM) MORTAR

Caliber:	3.1 in
Muzzle velocity:	699 ft/s
Barrel length:	45.6 in
Weight:	136 lb
Shell weight:	HE: 6.8–14.9 lb
Max. operational range:	3,292 yd

As was the case for many other mortars of that time the M1 was based on the French Brandt model 1927–31. As a simple smooth-bore weapon which only fired in a high angle trajectory, the M1 was loaded from the muzzle. The projectile slipped down to the end of the barrel where it was ignited by a firing pin. Since the barrel did not have any rifling to set the shell in rotation to stabilize the flight path, the shell was stabilized by fins at the rear. In addition to a light high-explosive shrapnel shell with which ranges of more than 3,281 yards (3,000 m) were achieved, the M1 mortar also made use of special ammunition with a greater explosive force that was correspondingly heavier and therefore achieved a range of only around 1,301 yards (1,190 m). Smoke and flare shells were also available for the M1.

UNARMORED VEHICLES

HEAVY 750 CC MOTORCYCLES WITH SIDECARS
BMW R 75, ZÜNDAPP KS 750

The Wehrmacht used many different motorcycles that were divided into three categories: light (up to 350 cc), medium (up to 500 cc) and heavy (more than 500 cc). Their prime suppliers were BMW, Zündapp, and NSU. Two of the best-known machines were without doubt the BMW R 75 and Zündapp KS 750 motorcycle combinations. Both models emerged in the Fall of 1940 and were in fact intended in the first instance only for the Mediterranean region and in particular

for the Afrikakorps. They had permanently mounted, powered sidecars. In addition, they were fitted with a reverse gear. In the first instance it was also planned to use the large heavy machines to tow light ordnance for parachute troops. When towing, however, the front wheel lifted off the ground, so this idea was abandoned. Both machines were designed for three

men and were often armed with a Model 34 machine gun. They were mostly used by motorcycle units and reconnaissance units. The motorcycle combinations proved to be robust and reliable, but a machine cost around twice as much as a VW Kübelwagen. BMW manufactured in total 16,510 motorcycle combinations, while Zündapp manufactured 18,635.

A BMW R 75.

	BMW R 75	Zündapp KS 750
Empty weight:	926 lb	882 lb
Payload:	551 lb	595 lb
Dimensions in inches (length/width/height):	94.5/68.1/39.4	93.9/65.0/39.8
Engine:	BMW 2-cylinder horizontally-opposed, air-cooled, 746 cc, 26 hp	Zündapp 2-cylinder horizontally-opposed, air-cooled, 751 cc, 26 hp
Speed:	max. 58 mph	max. 59 mph
Range:	approx. 215 miles road, 170 miles cross-country	approx. 205 miles road, 165 miles cross-country
Armament:	0.31 in Model 34 machine gun on occasion	0.31 in Model 34 machine gun on occasion
Fording depth:	13.8 in	15.7 in

VW TYPE 82 "KÜBELWAGEN"

The Volkswagen Type 82 was manufactured in larger numbers than any other Wehrmacht personal transport. Its undemanding nature and reliability made it famous and well liked. In particular the air-cooling proved its worth in icy temperatures. The soldiers called it the "Kübelwagen" (literally "bucket automobile") or "Kübel" ("bucket") for short because of its bucket-type seats. From 1939 onward the Type 82 was developed by Professor Porsche on the basis of the VW Beetle. To improve its cross-country capability the ground clearance was increased to 11.4 inches (29 cm), the chassis was strengthened, the bodywork was simplified, lightened and adapted for military service. The gearbox was fitted with a limited slip differential and a lesser overall transmission ratio, and the air filter was increased in size. In this way the "Kübel" was able to get through in circumstances where few other vehicles could follow.

According to various sources either 50,000 or 55,000 vehicles had been built by 1945. The bodywork was not in fact made by VW, but by Ambi-Budd in Berlin, and then brought by train to VW for assembly. In addition to the standard version there were also trial models and special models that never went into production. In 1943 the lack of working materials led to a new variant with a wood gas generator—this could be recognized by the "bump" in the front bonnet. There were also versions that operated with brown coal, anthracite, or wood.

Empty weight:	1,654 lb
Payload:	882 lb
Dimensions in inches (length/width/height):	148.5/63.0/65.0 (with cover)
Engine:	up to March 1943: 4-cylinder horizontally-opposed, air-cooled, 985 cc, 24 hp; later: 1,131 cc, 25 hp
Speed:	max. 50 mph
Range:	250–280 miles
Armament:	0.31 in Model 3442 machine gun on occasion
Fording depth:	17.7 in

Type 82, Afrikakorps, Libya, 1942.

VW TYPE 166 "SCHWIMMWAGEN"

Although the Type 82 proved itself in service it did not have unlimited cross-country and amphibious capability. In particular reconnaissance units and pioneer units wanted a vehicle with which they did not need to make a detour around rivers or lakes. Professor Porsche therefore developed the Type 128, which had watertight tub-shaped bodywork and all-wheel drive. After only 30 had been built, however, the production of the model was terminated, since it proved to be too complex and heavy. Thus there emerged the Type 166, the bodywork of which was once again built by Ambi-Budd in Berlin. The tub of the Type 166 was without doors, welded out of steel plate and had a shape similar to that of a boat. The engine and gearbox were taken from the Type 128. The new Schwimmwagen offered space for four fully-equipped soldiers and was fitted with all-wheel drive. For travel on water a three-bladed ship's propeller was folded down into the water at the rear of the vehicle, steered by swiveling the propeller. On the Eastern Front and in the desert the Schwimmwagen proved its worth and was often used in reconnaissance units. The real advantage was, however, its cross-country capability, which was hardly inferior to that of tracked vehicles. For this reason the Schwimmwagen was a well-liked command and reconnaissance automobile. Between 1942 and 1944 around 14,300 of them were produced.

Empty weight:	2,006 lb
Payload:	959 lb
Dimensions in inches (length/width/height):	150.6/58.3/63.6 (with cover)
Engine:	4-cylinder horizontally-opposed, air-cooled, 1,131 cc, 25 hp
Speed:	max. 50 mph, in water 6 mph
Range:	approx. 325 miles
Armament:	0.31in Model 34 or Model 42 machine gun on occasion
Fording depth:	amphibious

VW TYPE 166, the "Schwimmwagen" ("SwimAutomobile").

LIGHT ALL-TERRAIN STANDARD PERSONNEL VEHICLE

Initially the Reichswehr (1919–1935) and Wehrmacht were equipped with a large number of commercial vehicles. Between 1934 and 1936 the Army Ordnance Office therefore began a simplification of its fleet of personnel vehicles. The objective was to have a standard personnel vehicle in three weight classes: light, medium, and heavy. These personnel vehicles were to display the following features: permanent all-wheel drive, limited slip differential, integral chassis, and replaceability of parts subject to wear. The light standard personnel vehicle was manufactured by BMW with a BMW 325 engine (45 hp/32.85 kW), by Hanomag

Empty weight:	3,913 lb
Payload:	937 lb (425 kg)
Dimensions in inches (length/width/height):	140.9/61.8/70.1 (with cover)
Engine:	4-cylinder petrol, water-cooled, 45–50 hp
Speed:	max. 63 mph
Range:	approx. 250 miles
Armament: as Kfz. 4:	two 0.31 in Model 34 machine guns
Fording depth:	23.6 in

Kfz. 1, light all-terrain personnel vehicle.

with the 20 b engine (50 hp/36.8 kW) and by Stöwer with the R-180-W engine or AW-2 engine (both 50 hp/36.8 kW). According to application and bodywork the vehicles received different Kfz ("vehicle") numbers; Kfz. 1 was the light personnel all-terrain vehicle, Kfz. 4 was a air protection troop vehicle fitted with a twin anti-aircraft machine gun, the Model 34. In total around 14,500 of these were built.

MEDIUM ALL-TERRAIN STANDARD PERSONNEL VEHICLE

Empty weight:	5,952 lb
Payload:	1,323 lb
Dimensions in inches (length/width/height):	174.8/66.1/68.1 (with cover)
Engine:	Opel: 6-cylinder inline, petrol, water-cooled, 3,600 cc, 68 hp; Horch: V8, 3,800 cc, 75 hp, otherwise data identical
Speed:	max. 56 mph
Range:	approx. 250 miles
Armament:	none
Fording depth:	23.6 in

The medium standard personnel vehicle was built by the Auto-Union and Opel companies. Because of the long wheelbase all such personnel vehicles in the first instance had spare wheels fitted at the side on a special support axle in order to prevent grounding. From 1940 onward, however, the vehicles were also manufactured without this feature by Auto-Union with a Horch V8 231.9 ci (3,800 cc) engine. In total some 12,000 vehicles were manufactured, and according to their duties were fitted with varying bodywork with which the Kfz. numbers were then aligned. The Kfz. 11 was the medium all-terrain personnel vehicle without a trailer coupling, the Kfz. 15 was with a trailer coupling, while Kfz. 16 and 17 were signals vehicles. The Opel engine was much more robust and simple, and was therefore preferred by the soldiers to the Horch engine. However, in the war, particularly on the Eastern Front, these vehicles proved to be too heavy and complicated.

Medium all-terrain personnel vehicle Kfz. 15 Horch, 16th infantry division (motorized).

HEAVY ALL-TERRAIN STANDARD PERSONNEL VEHICLE

The chassis of the heavy standard personnel vehicle was produced exclusively by Auto-Union, i.e. Wanderer, and was driven by a Horch engine. There were two versions: A with a total weight of 6,614 lb (3,000 kg) and B with a total weight of almost 11,023 lb (5,000 kg). According to duty the vehicles again received different identification numbers, for example, the designation Kfz. 18 as an 8-seater personnel vehicle. Others included an ambulance (Kfz. 31), a tug vehicle (Kfz. 69) for the towing of light ordnance, signals vehicles (Kfz. 81), and

Empty weight:	A: 6,614 lb, B: 11,023 lb
Payload:	1,984 lb
Dimensions in inches (length/width/height):	174.8/66.1/68.1 (with cover)
Engine:	A: Horch V8, petrol, water-cooled, 3,500 cc, 75 hp, B: 3,800 cc, 90 hp, otherwise data identical
Speed:	max. 56 mph
Range:	approx. 250 miles
Armament:	as Kfz. 70: 0.79 in anti-aircraft cannon 30/38
Fording depth:	23.6 in

Heavy all-terrain personnel vehicle Kfz. 18 Horch, 606 Artillery Regiment, Africa, 1942.

personnel carriers (Kfz. 70). The latter were sometimes fitted out as a provisional self-propelled platform for the Model 30 or Model 38 0.79 in (2 cm) anti-aircraft cannon. In the course of the war these vehicles all in all also proved to be too expensive, complicated, and heavy.

KRUPP 1.5 TON "KRUPP-TUG"

Krupp 1.5 ton truck.

Empty weight:	5,401 lb
Payload:	3,307 lb
Dimensions in inches (length/width/height):	194.9/76.8/90.6 (with cover)
Engine:	Krupp 4-cylinder horizontally opposed, M304, air-cooled, 3,308 cc, 60 hp
Speed:	max. 44 mph
Range:	approx. 250 miles road, 170 miles cross-country
Armament:	provisionally 0.79 in anti-aircraft cannon 30/38 or 1.46 in anti-tank cannon 36
Fording depth:	23.6 in

There were two versions of this vehicle: the L 2 H 43, and the L 2 H 143. The difference between the two models lay in the wheel spacing on the rear axle. The vehicles were fitted with the following types of bodywork: tug vehicle for the towing of ordnance (Kfz. 69 "Krupp Tug"), personnel vehicle (Kfz. 70), and a light searchlight vehicle (Kfz. 83). 0.79 in (2 cm) anti-aircraft cannon or 1.46 in (3.7 cm) anti-tank cannon were sometimes fitted to the Kfz. 69 thus creating provisional self-propelled platforms. The Krupp engine proved to be problematical, since it required a high octane petrol that was not always available. From 1934 to the start of 1942 around 7000 Krupp vehicles of this kind were built.

OPEL BLITZ 1.5 AND 3 TON TRUCKS

The truck that was best known and which saw the most service with the Wehrmacht, was the Opel Blitz, of which some 130,000 were supplied in various versions up to 1945, but only around 25,000 of them were the four-wheel drive 6700A military version. At that time the Opel Blitz was definitely one of the most reliable trucks. The engine was built in a modular manner, and many parts were exchangeable with the four-cylinder engine from the personnel vehicle series, which was also used in the NSU Kettenkrad. As a result of continuous development from 1931 onward the Blitz surpassed its competitors from Daimler-Benz, Borgward, or Magirus. It proved to be reliable, easy to maintain, and docile under all conditions. How highly prized it really was, was shown when Daimler-Benz was forced to manufacture it unmodified under license and to cease production of its own 3 ton range of trucks. The Opel was manufactured from July 1944 onward as the DB 701 with the standard Wehrmacht driver's cab (but without any kind of Opel identification). The Blitz was produced in many versions: as a 1.5 or 3 ton truck, with pallet, van, or bus bodywork, and with different wheelbases and types of transmission. Even a half-tracked version (the Opel Maultier [Mule]) was built. The Maultier and truck versions were occasionally armed by units with 0.79 inch (2 cm) or 1.46 inch (3.7 cm) anti-aircraft cannon and used as self-propelled gun platforms. Production of the Blitz was continued by Opel after 1945.

	1.5 ton Type 2.3–32	3 ton Type 3.6–6700A
Empty weight:	3,362 lb	7,385 lb
Payload:	3,693 lb	6,834 lb
Dimensions in inches (length/width/height):	212.6/76.4/72.6	234.3/92.1/125.2 (with cover)
Engine:	Opel 6-cylinder inline, water-cooled, 2,473 cc, 55 hp	Opel 6-cylinder inline, water-cooled, 3,600 cc, 75 hp
Speed:	max. 50 mph	max. 50 mph
Range:	approx. 215 miles road	190 miles road, 145 miles cross-country
Armament:		provisionally 0.79 in anti-aircraft cannon 30/38 or 1.46 in anti-aircraft cannon 36
Fording depth:	19.7 in	19.7 in

Opel Blitz.

HALF-TRACKED MOTORIZED TRACTION VEHICLES SD.KFZ. 6, 7, 8, 9, 10, AND 11

In the course of motorization of the Wehrmacht the Army Ordnance Office developed the concept of a range of six different motorized traction vehicle models, each of which was to possess standard design features. The individual types were divided into different groups according to their towed load capacity. The main purpose for the vehicles was to pull artillery pieces. Contracts for development and production of the models were awarded to various German manufacturers (see table).

Common to all models was the relatively long crawler track drive with large running wheels in a typical nested configuration with a drive wheel at the front. The front wheels, which were fitted with pneumatic tires, were not driven and had no brakes; they served only to provide steering, although above a certain steering angle track steering also contributed. All the motorized traction vehicles proved their worth in the war, and indeed some of them did so outstandingly well. Technically, however, they were peacetime designs that were too complex, and the variety of models was too great to withstand the tough demands of mass production under most difficult conditions. This fact was also clearly demonstrated by the designs that succeeded them in wartime—the Wehrmacht tractor and the Ost crawler tractor—which were far more primitive, but also more cost-effective.

Nevertheless an astonishing number of the motorized traction vehicles were produced. The 1 ton model served primarily as a means of pulling light anti-aircraft and anti-tank cannon, which in the course of the war were also mounted on the loading bed. Versions included the Sd.Kfz. 10/4 with a 0.79 inch (2 cm) anti-aircraft cannon and the Sd.Kfz. 10/5 with a 1.97 inch (5 cm) anti-tank cannon. The 1 ton motorized traction vehicle also formed the basis for the Sd.Kfz. 250 armored personnel carrier. The Sd.Kfz. 11 (the 3 ton model) was mainly used for pulling howitzers and rocket launchers. The chassis of this model provided the basis for the Sd.Kfz. 251 armored personnel carrier.

The 5 ton motorized traction vehicles saw little service, and were used in a similar manner to the 3 ton models.

Sd.Kfz. 7 8 ton medium motorized traction vehicle.

	Sd.Kfz. 10; 1 ton Demag	Sd.Kfz. 11; 3 ton Hanomag	Sd.Kfz. 6; 5 ton Büssing-NAG	Sd.Kfz. 7; 8 ton Krauss-Maffei	Sd.Kfz. 8; 12 ton Daimler-Benz	Sd.Kfz. 9; 18 ton Famo
Empty weight:	7,496 lb	12,236 lb	16,535 lb	21,495 lb	27,999 lb	33,510 lb
Payload:	3,307 lb	3,307 lb	3,307 lb	3,968 lb	4,409 lb	6,173 lb
Towed load:	2,205 lb	6,614 lb	11,023 lb	17,637 lb	30,865 lb	39,683 lb
Dimensions in inches (length/width/height):	187.0/76.0/63.8	218.5/78.7/84.6	9.0/89.0/98.4	269.7/92.5/103.1	289.4/98.4/109.1	324.8/102.4/112.2
Engine:	Maybach HL-42, 6-cylinder inline, water-cooled, 4,170 cc, 100 hp	Maybach HL-42, 6-cylinder inline, water-cooled, 4,170 cc, 100 hp	Maybach HL-54, 6-cylinder inline, water-cooled, 5,420 cc, 115 hp	Maybach HL-62, 6-cylinder inline, water-cooled, 6,191 cc, 140 hp	Maybach HL-85, V-12, water-cooled, 8,520 cc, 185 hp	Maybach HL-108, V-12, water-cooled, 10,830 cc, 250 hp
Speed:	max. 41 mph	max. 33 mph	max. 31 mph	max. 31 mph	max. 32 mph	max. 31 mph
Range:	190 miles road, 105 miles cross-country	150 miles road, 90 miles cross-country	195 miles road, 95 miles cross-country	155 miles road, 75 miles cross-country	155 miles road, 70 miles cross-country	150 miles road, 65 miles cross-country
Fording depth:	27.6 in	19.7 in	23.6 in	25.6 in	24.8 in	31.5 in
Number manufactured:	approx. 25,000	approx. 25,000	approx. 3,000	approx. 12,000	approx. 4,000	approx. 2,500

Sd.Kfz. 9 18 ton heavy motorized traction vehicle.

The 8 ton tractor (Sd.Kfz. 7) achieved a certain fame as the means of traction for the legendary "Acht-Acht." It also formed the basis for self-propelled gun carriages for anti-aircraft cannon. The Sd.Kfz. 8 (the 12 ton model) was intended to pull the heavier artillery pieces, such as the 5.91 inch (15 cm) howitzers and 8.27 inch (21 cm) mortars. In 1940 some were even fitted with 3.46 inch (8.8 cm) anti-aircraft cannon, but these did not prove to be successful. The largest and heaviest model, the Sd.Kfz. 9 (18 tons) was mainly used as a recovery vehicle for tanks that had become stuck. When it was a matter of recovering heavy tanks, however, three 18 tonners were required to move these vehicles, and so the Sd.Kfz 9 finally had to be replaced by recovery tanks.

Sd.Kfz. 10/4 1 ton vehicle with a Model 30 0.79 inch (2 cm) anti-aircraft cannon.

Sd.Kfz. 10 with a Model 38 1.97 inch (5 cm) anti-tank cannon.

SD.KFZ. 2 LIGHT TRACKED MOTORCYCLE NSU HK-101

NSU tracked motorcycle.

Empty weight:	2,822 lb
Payload:	717 lb
Dimensions in inches (length/width/height):	118.1/39.4/47.2
Engine:	Opel-Olympia, 4-cylinder inline, water-cooled, 1,500 cc, 36 hp
Speed:	max. 44 mph
Range:	approx. 155 miles road, 110 miles cross-country
Fording depth:	17.3 in

In 1939 the Army Ordnance Office was looking for a means of pulling smaller loads, such as the light weapons of parachute troops, mortars, or field cables. The engineer Heinrich Ernst developed a vehicle with a front wheel and controls similar to those of a motorcycle and a rear crawler track drive. Production was undertaken by NSU in Neckarsulm, and later under license by the Stöwer factory in Stettin. The first 500 were delivered from July 1940. On June 5, 1941 the vehicle was officially introduced into service as the Sd.Kfz. 2. Although particularly valuable in winter and in the mud, the tracked motorcycle was both too expensive and too complicated (with 124 lubrication points!). Further versions were the Sd.Kfz. 2/1 for field cables and the Sd.Kfz. 2/2 for heavy field cables. In total 8,733 were built by 1944.

2 TON CRAWLER TRACKED TRUCK "MAULTIER"

As a result of the very poor weather and road conditions in the Soviet Union an attempt was made to give the trucks of the German logistical support troops a better cross-country capability. A research vehicle of the Waffen-SS was requisitioned for this purpose. This vehicle featured a British Carden-Lloyd transmission that had been installed under a normal 3 ton truck. The installation of this simple crawler track drive in place of the rear axle proved to be a success and the vehicles were introduced into the Wehrmacht under the name "Maultier" ("Mule") (Sd.Kfz. 3). Later versions were produced by Opel (Type 3.6-36 S), by Klöckner-Humboldt-Deutz (Type 3000 S with a diesel engine), and by Ford (Type G 398 TS/V 3000 S). In 1942, 635 vehicles were manufactured, in 1943 around 13,000 and in 1944 another 7,310.

Some Maultiers were fitted with a 0.79 inch (2 cm) or 1.46 inch (3.7 cm) anti-aircraft cannon. 300 vehicles were provided with an armored body and acquired the Model 41 5.91 in (15 cm) rocket launcher, whose ten tubes could be swiveled through 360° (Model 42 rocket launcher), and 90 unarmed vehicles were used as ammunition carriers for the launchers. A 4.5 ton design was developed by Daimler-Benz, using the undercarriage of a Model 11 tank, and 1,480 of this heavy model were produced. The Magirus model proved to be the best

Empty weight:	8,664 lb
Payload:	4,409 lb
Dimensions in inches (length/width/height):	236.2/113.4/106.7
Engine:	Opel, 6-cylinder inline, water-cooled, 3,600 cc, 75 hp
Speed:	max. 24 mph (38 km/h)
Range:	100 miles road, 50 miles cross-country
Fording depth:	17.3 in

and most reliable Maultier because of its indestructible diesel engine.

Maultier based on the Opel Blitz.

OST CRAWLER TRACTOR RSO/01

An Ost crawler tractor with a 2.95 inch (75 mm) anti-tank cannon.

Empty weight:	7,716 lb
Payload:	3,748 lb
Towed load:	6,614 lb
Dimensions in inches (length/width/height):	174.2/78.3/99.6
Engine:	Steyr V-8, air-cooled, 3,517 cc, 70 hp
Speed:	max. 11 mph
Range:	190 miles road, 95 miles cross-country
Armament:	variants with a 2.95 in anti-tank cannon or a 2.95 in howitzer
Fording depth:	33.5 in

Since the trucks operated by the Wehrmacht were often stuck fast in the Russian mud and ice, and production of the half-tracked motorized traction vehicles was too complex, a fully tracked vehicle simple to manufacture but capable of movement under the most adverse conditions was designed: the Ost (East) crawler tractor, abbreviated to RSO.

The pattern for this design was provided by the extremely robust and reliable tracked tractors that were captured during the advance on the Eastern Front. The RSO/01 was manufactured from 1942 onward by Steyr. In 1944, because of the great need for such a vehicle, Klöckner-Humboldt-Deutz, Gräf & Stift, and Auto-Union also participated in its manufacture.

In total almost 26,000 Osts were built by the end of the war. A self-propelled gun carriage with a 2.95inch (7.5cm) anti-tank cannon was also built on the basis of the RSO, but this variant was not a success.

For mountain infantry units the Gebirge (Mountain) crawler tractor (RSG) was produced, which carried a Model 34 2.95 inch (7.5 cm) mountain howitzer.

HEAVY WEHRMACHT TRACTOR S.WS

Empty weight:	29,762 lb
Payload:	8,818 lb
Towed load:	17,637 lb
Dimensions in inches (length/width/height):	269.7/98.4/111.4
Engine:	Maybach HL-42, 6-cylinder inline, water-cooled, 4,170 cc, 100 hp
Speed:	max. 17 mph
Range:	190 miles road, 95 miles cross-country
Armament:	variant with a 1.46 in anti-aircraft cannon
Fording depth:	39.4 in

Only two different vehicles were to be built as the successors to the motorized traction vehicle (rather than the previous six), and these had to be simple and cost-effective to produce, but very robust: these were the light and heavy Wehrmacht tractors. Only prototypes were ever produced of the former, but the heavy version went into production at Büssing-NAG in the fall of 1943. Although the requirements were met, the vehicle's cruising speed had to be severely reduced, with the result that it could no longer be used in tank units, but only in infantry divisions. As variants there emerged a model with a 1.46 inch (3.7 cm) anti-aircraft cannon and a partially armored model for the supply of front-line units.

Only 825 heavy Wehrmacht tractors had been produced by March 1945.

CAMIONETTA 42 SAHARIANA SPA AS 42

These unarmored vehicles were created by SPA (at that time part of the Fiat group) especially for use in North Africa—hence the designation AS ("Africa Settentrionale," which can be approximately translated as "North Africa"). They are based on the chassis of the AB-41 armored scout car.

The vehicles were fitted with oversize tires for use on sand, together with a large fuel tank and fixtures for a large number of additional fuel cans to achieve a long range. The scout cars were mainly used by reconnaissance units and special troops, for example, for excursions behind enemy lines. The armament for the vehicles was

Empty weight:	8,708 lb
Payload:	1,764 lb
Dimensions in inches (length/width/height):	226.4/88.9/84.6
Engine:	SPA, 6-cylinder inline, petrol, 4,995 cc, water-cooled, 88 hp
Speed:	max. 50 mph
Range:	500 miles
Armament:	from a 0.31 in machine gun through to a 1.85 in anti-tank cannon
Fording depth:	23.6 in

very varied, and ranged from an 0.31 inch (8 mm) Breda machine gun, via a 0.79 inch (2 cm) Breda anti-aircraft cannon, through to a 1.85 inch (4.7 cm) anti-tank gun. 0.79 inch (2 cm) anti-tank rifles or 0.50 inch (12.7 mm) machine guns were also used among other weapons.

BEDFORD MWD 4 × 2 15 CWT 0.75 TONNER

Bedford MWD vehicles were the light trucks most frequently used by the British troops. The first pre-production models appeared in 1937. Series production was carried out during the whole of the war by Vauxhall Motors, where a total of 66,000 trucks were produced. In addition to a pallet bed version there was also a version with an enclosed body fitted with signals equipment, and a tanker variant with a capacity of 200 gallons (approximately 900 liters). In the whole 15 cwt class more than 230,000 vehicles were produced in the United Kingdom during the war. The armies of the British Empire defined the payload of their trucks in terms of hundredweight (cwt). This unit of weight corresponds to 112 English pounds (lb) or 50.8 kg. A payload of 15 cwt was therefore 1,680 lb (762 kg). Highly prized as a versatile and robust transport vehicle, Bedford MWDs continued in service with the British armed forces into the late 1950s. Light trucks of the Bedford MWD type (and countless other vehicles) were captured by the Wehrmacht in substantial numbers in France—particularly during the British retreat from Dunkirk—and also in Norway. Since the Wehrmacht was

chronically short of vehicles of all kinds captured vehicles were absorbed into its own fleet and used for as long as replacement parts were available. Sometimes conversions and adaptations of the original vehicles were even undertaken to meet German needs. The Bedford MWD also proved its worth in the service of the Wehrmacht.

A Bedford MWD.

Empty weight:	4,718 lb
Payload:	1,680 lb
Dimensions in inches (length/width/height):	172.4/78.3/90.2 (with cover)
Engine:	Bedford OHV, 6-cylinder inline, 3,518 cc, water-cooled, 72 hp
Speed:	max. 38 mph
Range:	240 miles
Fording depth:	27.6 in

BEDFORD QLD 4 × 4 3 TONNER

The Bedford QLD was the most frequently manufactured British 3 tonner. The design of the all-wheel drive vehicle began shortly after the outbreak of war and in 1941 the first trucks were delivered to units. Vauxhall in Luton built 52,245 QLDs, which were not only deployed in the British Army.

In 1942 the Soviet Union also received a number of these vehicles as part of Allied military aid. The versatile and reliable truck was used in a wide variety of roles, from acting as a tractor unit for artillery, via transport duties, through to a tanker vehicle. The weakest feature of the Bedford was its low-powered engine.

Empty weight:	21,385 lb
Payload:	6,614 lb
Dimensions in inches (length/width/height):	235.8/89.0/118.1
Engine:	Bedford OHV, 6-cylinder inline, 3,518 cc, water-cooled, 72 hp
Speed:	max. 38 mph
Range:	230 miles
Fording depth:	15.7 in

Bedford QLD.

MORRIS COMMERCIAL C 8 "QUAD" ARTILLERY TRACTOR UNIT

Empty weight:	3.7 tons
Payload:	no data
Dimensions in inches (length/width/height):	177/87/90
Engine:	Morris inline 4-cylinder, 3,600 cc, water-cooled, 70 hp
Speed:	max. 50 mph
Range:	155 miles
Fording depth:	16 in

In 1937 the Guy Motors company originally developed an artillery tractor unit for 25-pounder guns on the basis of the all-wheel drive transmission of the Morris Commercial C 8. With the outbreak of war the need for such vehicles rose sharply and Morris itself began to produce this vehicle. Later on Chevrolet Canada also manufactured a large number of the vehicles. Generally known as the "Quad," these tractor units offered sufficient space for a crew and

ammunition. Because of its 4 x 4 drive it had an extremely high towing capacity and was outstandingly good at cross-country duties. In addition the "Quads" were fitted with a winch with a 8,818 lb (4,000 kg) pulling force. Alongside

models with enclosed metal bodywork there were later some that also acquired a canvas cover. In total more than 10,000 were produced by all the manufacturers and used by the Commonwealth armed forces.

Morris Commercial C 8 "Quad."

FORD F15A 4 × 4 15-CWT 0.75-TONNER

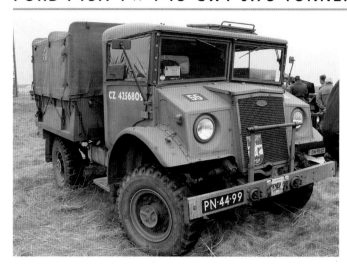

A Ford 15A with all-wheel drive

Empty weight:	5,490 lb
Payload:	1,680 lb
Dimensions in inches (length/width/height):	166.0/82.7/86.1
Engine:	Ford V-8, water-cooled, 95 hp
Speed:	max. 56 mph
Range:	220 miles
Armament:	variant with a 0.79 in anti-aircraft cannon
Fording depth:	23.6 in

During the war Canada produced more than 710,000 trucks of all kinds, which were used by the Commonwealth armed forces. Many were similar to each other, since they were manufactured in accordance with the Canadian Military Pattern (CMP). As early as 1937 planning started at Ford of Canada on a light military truck with 4 x 4 drive on the basis of a British requirements specification. A year later Chevrolet joined the planning

activities and vehicles of different classes were designed that were to have a maximum number of components in common. The result was the series of CMP trucks, which mainly differed from each other only in terms of power units. The first prototypes were subjected to rigorous testing in 1939, and series production began in 1940. The 0.75 tonners (15 cwt) built by Ford and Chevrolet were the most numerous light

trucks in this program. They were versatile, robust, and were utilized in every sector of the armed forces. Ford's 0.75 tonner appeared in the widest number of variants: the Ford 15A featured all-wheel drive, while the Ford 15 variant only had rear-wheel drive. In addition there were models that had a canvas cover over the driver's cab. Others had a metal roof. The same was true for the 0.75 tonner built by Chevrolet to the same pattern. There was also a version of the Ford 15A that had a 0.79 inch (2 cm) Polsten anti-aircraft cannon, a variant of the well-known 0.79 inch (2 cm) Oerlikon.

CHEVROLET C60L 4 × 4 3 TONNER

Chevrolet of Canada, part of the enormous General Motors group, built large numbers of standardized military vehicles during the Second World War, as did Ford of Canada. One of these CMP vehicles was the C60L. The Chevrolet differed primarily from the Ford truck of the same pattern in terms of having a different engine. For those who are not

experts, the two variants can only be distinguished from each other by the company badge, and the same is true for almost all the CMP vehicles. In total around 209,000 CMP 3 tonners were built. While they were in fact rated as under-powered and slow, they were also judged to be indestructible and reliable. Thanks to their 4 x 4 drive they were also suitable as tractor

Empty weight:	6,665 lb
Payload:	6,720 lb
Dimensions in inches (length/width/height):	223.0/82.7/89.6
Engine:	Chevrolet, 6-cylinder inline, water-cooled, 3,600 cc, 85 hp
Speed:	max. 44 mph
Range:	170 miles
Fording depth:	19.7 in

units. The payload of 3 tons could be exceeded to a considerable extent without causing any problems. Many variants were built which differed primarily in terms of their bodywork, long or short wheelbases, and drivers' cabs. As in the case of the 0.75 tonner the 3 tonners were also adapted to almost every conceivable purpose, from a pallet bed vehicle to an enclosed body forming an observation post (OP). Some of these trucks were also delivered to the Soviet Union.

GMC CCKW 2.5 TONNER

From 1939 onward the standardization program for the US Armed Forces envisaged only two different vehicles in each class. One of these vehicle classes was the 2.5 ton truck, of which more than 800,000 units were built up to 1945. The largest manufacturer was General Motors (GMC) with—according to the source—562,750 or 625,000 units, but companies like Studebaker, Reo, or International also manufactured 2.5 tonners during the war. GMC built a large number of different versions. There were chassis with short

(CCKW-352) and long wheelbases (CCKW-353), 6 x 6 or 6 x 4 transmissions, and even types with only two axles instead of the usual three. Early models featured an enclosed driver's cab, while later versions had a canvas roof. A very wide variety of bodies were placed on these different chassis, from a van body, via tanks for petrol or water, crane systems, through to bodies for workshop or fire vehicles. The most common version was, however, the one pictured here with load restraints and tarpaulins.

Empty weight:	11,949 lb
Payload:	5,512 lb
Dimensions in inches: (length/width/height)	272.8/88.0/86.6
Engine:	GMC, 6-cylinder inline, OHV, petrol, water-cooled, 4,420 cc, 90 hp
Speed:	50 mph
Range:	175 miles
Armament:	0.50 in anti-aircraft machine gun
Fording depth:	29.5 in

DUKW AMPHIBIOUS TRUCK

Empty weight:	16,314 lb
Payload:	5,512 lb
Dimensions in inches (length/width/height):	372.0/99.0/111.9
Engine:	GMC, 6-cylinder inline, OHV, petrol, water-cooled, 4,420 cc, 90 hp
Speed:	50 mph (in water 6 mph)
Range:	175 miles
Fording depth:	29.5 in

Army required a transport vehicle that could convey soldiers and material from the ships onto the beach, and also further into the interior of the country. GMC therefore developed, together with the Sparkman & Stevens boatyard, an amphibious version of the proven GMC 2.5 tonner. The DUKW was fitted

with powerful bilge pumps that enabled it to remain afloat after having been damaged by gunfire. Although of tubby appearance the DUKW was very seaworthy and proved its worth in the Pacific, and in 1944 also in Normandy. By 1945 more than 21,000 DUKWs had been built.

This vehicle, named the "Duck" on account of its military designation DUKW, was basically nothing more than a GMC 2.5 tonner with a boat-shaped hull. For its amphibious landings the US

M4 FULLY TRACKED TRACTOR UNIT

Empty weight:	31,500 lb
Payload:	37,479 lb
Dimensions in inches (length/width/height):	205.9/96.9/99.2
Engine:	6-cylinder inline, petrol, water-cooled, 210 hp
Speed:	33 mph road
Range:	175 miles road
Armament:	0.50 in M2HB anti-aircraft machine gun on occasion
Fording depth:	39.4 in

The M4 "High-Speed Tractor" was created in response to a US Army requirement for a new mobile tractor unit for heavy artillery and anti-aircraft guns, such as the M1 3.54 inch (9 cm) anti-aircraft cannon, the M2 6.1inch (15.5 cm) "Long Tom" cannon, or the M1 7.99 inch (20.3 cm) howitzer. The development of the M4 began in 1941, and was based on the chassis of the M2A1 light tank. In 1942 the new tractor unit, produced by Allis-Chalmers, received the designation M4 and was delivered to units. In addition to ten seats for the whole of the gun crew in the forward zone, the M4 also featured stowage for sufficient ammunition so that limbers were unnecessary. The engine was located in the central zone. For loading heavy shells a small crane was also fitted. A cable winch with a 13 ton pulling force was installed in the rear above the trailer coupling. Often a rotary mount was fitted on the roof of the crew cabin with a 0.5 inch (12.7 mm) anti-aircraft machine gun of the Browning M2HB type. Between 1943 and 1945 Allis-Chalmers built around 5,500 vehicles of this type, which proved themselves exceptionally well in all duties—not only on the roads but also when traveling cross-country. After the war fully tracked tractor units of this kind were delivered by the USA in the course of military aid programs to many countries, for example Brazil, Japan, Pakistan, and Yugoslavia. The newly formed Bundeswehr also profited from these supplies, and until the start of the 1960s used a number of M4s to pull its heavy guns.

The M4 fully tracked tractor unit.

M29 WEASEL

Originally this crawler vehicle was developed for special units that were to attack factories in Norway in which the Nazis were producing "heavy water" (deuterium), which was required for the construction of atomic bombs. Since it was thought that the troops would have to overcome snow and ice, the decision was made to equip them with a new vehicle. On May 17, 1942 Studebaker received the contract, and only 34 days later the first prototype was produced, but this did not immediately fulfill all requirements. Therefore modifications were undertaken on two prototypes, but shortly thereafter the planned attack was abandoned. Nevertheless the US Army recognized the potential of the vehicle, named the "Weasel," and equipped mountain troops and pioneer units with it. The M29 served primarily for the transport of supplies and wounded. In remote regions such as Alaska, Greenland, or Iceland M29s were also used for rescue duties. While early production models were designated the M28, the main production model was the M29. Although even the basic version could float it was very difficult to steer in the water. Therefore an amphibious version was generated, the M29C, with a boat-shaped front end, buoyancy aids, and a cable winch. In total Studebaker built around 15,124 vehicles between 1942 and 1945. After the war the M29 continued to be used by the US armed forces and in the civilian sector it was used for polar exploration. The last M29s were in service up until the 1980s in Norway, in other words, in the terrain for which they had been developed.

Empty weight:	4,081 lb
Payload:	1,202 lb
Dimensions in inches (length/width/height):	125.7/67.2/60.0
Engine:	Studebaker, 6-cylinder inline, petrol, water-cooled, 75 hp
Speed:	36 mph
Range:	155 miles
Fording depth:	31.5 in

The M29 "Weasel" of the US Army.

ARMORED VEHICLES

LIGHT ARMORED CARS SD.KFZ. 221, 222, 223

Sd.Kfz. 223 of the 15th Panzer Division, Libya, 1942.

	Sd.Kfz. 223 Ausführung B
Combat weight:	4.8 tons
Crew:	3
Dimensions in inches (length, width, height):	189/77/71; height with antenna: 81
Engine:	Horch V8 gas, water-cooled, 3,823 cc, 81 hp
Power/weight ratio:	15.3 hp/ton
Max. speed:	50 mph road
Range:	175 miles road 125 miles cross-country
Armament:	1 x 0.3 in MG 34 machine gun
Armor:	0.3–0.6 in, later up to 1.2 in
Fording depth:	24 in

The Wehrmacht used a whole series of armored cars based on the same chassis. Sd.Kfz. 221—armed at first with no more than an MG 34—was brought into service in 1936. From 1942 onward, it was equipped with the 1.1 inch (2.8 cm) Panzerbüchse anti-tank rifle. These light reconnaissance vehicles consisted in essence of an armored superstructure with a rotating turret mounted on a traditional chassis. In addition to an MG 34, Sd.Kfz. 222 also mounted a 0.8 inch (2 cm) KwK cannon and had a larger turret. The Sd.Kfz. 223 was a Sd.Kfz. 221 with a large, conspicuous frame antenna and high-performance radio system. Vehicles of this series were deployed in the armored car units of the reconnaissance battalions, mostly in teams made up of gun and radio vehicles. Sd.Kfz. 220 and 261, known officially as "small armored communications vehicles" were turretless, unarmed versions of Sd.Kfz. 223. They carried a full set of radio equipment and were used mainly at headquarters and in armored communications companies. All models remained in service up to the end of the war and were based on good if somewhat over-complicated designs. In Russia their role was eventually taken over by special half-track vehicles. Altogether 2,118 vehicles were built.

HEAVY ARMORED CARS SD.KFZ. 231 AND 232 (6-WHEEL)

	Sd.Kfz. 231 Type G31 (Büssing-NAG)
Combat weight:	6.3 tons
Crew:	4
Dimensions in inches (length, width, height):	180/72/89; height with antenna: 114
Engine:	Büssing-NAG Type G inline 4-cylinder gas, water-cooled, 3,920 cc, 60 hp
Power/weight ratio:	9.5 hp/ton
Max. speed:	40 mph road
Range:	160 miles road, 85 miles cross-country
Armament:	1 x 0.8 in KwK 30 cannon 1 x 0.3 in MG 34 machine gun
Armor:	0.3–0.6 in
Fording depth:	20 in

Sd.Kfz. 232 (6-wheel) with bedstead antenna.

These heavy armored cars comprised an armor-plated superstructure and rotating turret mounted on a regular commercial truck chassis. Starting in the early 1930s, three different companies (Daimler-Benz, Büssing, and Magirus) manufactured versions of this vehicle which varied slightly from one another. None of them had all-wheel drive and their cross-country capability was therefore limited. They were no longer used on the front after 1940. Sd.Kfz. 231 (6-wheel) was the so-called Kanonenwagen (gun vehicle) while the Sd.Kfz. 232 (6-wheel) was equipped with a radio and large bedstead antenna. Small numbers were also produced of another model, the Sd.Kfz. 263, which served as a command vehicle and had a high superstructure in place of a turret. An unusual feature of all the different versions was that they had duplicate front and rear controls. In total 928 6-wheel reconnaissance vehicles were built.

HEAVY ARMORED CARS SD.KFZ. 231 AND 232 (8-WHEEL)

Sd.Kfz. 232
(8-wheel).

	Sd.Kfz. 232
Combat weight:	9.7 tons
Crew:	4
Dimensions in inches (length, width, height):	230/87/92; height with antenna: 114
Engine:	Büssing-NAG Type L 8V-GS V8 gas, water-cooled, 8,360 cc, 180 hp
Power/weight ratio:	18.6 hp/ton
Max. speed:	53 mph road
Range:	185 miles road, 100 miles cross-country
Armament:	1 x 0.8 in KwK 30 cannon, 1 x 0.3 in MG 34 machine gun
Armor:	0.3–0.6 in; later 1.2 in
Fording depth:	39 in

Army command soon became aware of the limitations of the 6-wheel reconnaissance vehicles and awarded contracts for a successor as early as 1934. Büssing-NAG delivered the first of the new vehicles to the Wehrmacht in 1937. Because they were designed to perform the same role as the 6-wheel versions, the new models were again named "Sd.Kfz. 231" and "Sd.Kfz. 232." They were the best models of their day with the greatest cross-country capability. This was only achieved, however, at the expense of an extremely complex chassis with all-wheel drive and steering. They were also relatively large and high—something of a disadvantage for a reconnaissance vehicle. Like their 6-wheel predecessors, the 8-wheel versions also had front and rear controls. Because of their size, they proved to be relatively vulnerable during the war and were therefore fitted with an anti-tank-gun shield mounted some distance in front of the vehicle's nose. The thickness of the front armor was later increased to 1.2 inch (30 mm). In addition to the two main versions there was also a command vehicle (Sd.Kfz. 263) with a high superstructure as well as a support variant (Sd.Kfz. 233) with an open turret and short 3 inch (7.5 cm) StuK L/24 assault gun. By the time production finally ceased in 1942 1,235 had been built.

HEAVY ARMORED CAR SD.KFZ. 234 PUMA

Although the first generation of 8-wheel reconnaissance vehicles had been relatively successful, they also had a number of major drawbacks, not least the

	Sd.Kfz. 234/2
Combat weight:	12.9 tons
Crew:	4
Dimensions in inches (length, width, height):	236/92/94
Engine:	Tatra 103 V12 diesel, air-cooled, 14825cc, 210 hp
Power/weight ratio:	16.5 hp/ton
Max. speed:	56 mph road
Range:	560 miles road, 375 miles cross-country
Armament:	1 x 2 in KwK 39 cannon 1 x 0.3 in MG 34 (or MG 42) machine gun
Armor:	0.3–1.2 in
Fording depth:	39 in

risers that supported the large frame antenna and the vehicles' limited off-road range. Büssing-NAG therefore designed a vehicle with a monocoque hull that dispensed with the frame antenna, thereby reducing the height. It also featured a new Tatra air-cooled diesel engine and large fuel tanks which extended the range to 560 miles (900 km), a decision taken with North Africa and the Russian steppes in mind. The new vehicle, named the Sd.Kfz. 234, went into production in 1943 in four different versions: the Sd.Kfz. 234/1 had a turret similar to the Sd.Kfz. 222 with a 2 cm KwK cannon, the Sd.Kfz. 234/2 had the same turret as the Leopard light tank and the 2 inch (5 cm) KwK cannon, the Sd.Kfz. 234/3 had a short 3 inch (7.5 cm) StuK 24 assault gun mounted in its open, fixed turret while the Sd.Kfz. 234/4 mounted the long 3 inch (7.5 cm) Pak 40 L/46. Technically, these vehicles were way ahead of their time and were to influence the development of reconnaissance vehicles for years to come. Around 1,000 units were manufactured.

Sd.Kfz. 234/2.

LIGHT ARMORED PERSONNEL CARRIER SD.KFZ. 250

	Sd.Kfz. 250/1
Combat weight:	6.3 tons
Crew:	2 + 4
Dimensions in inches (length, width, height):	179/77/65 (without machine gun shield)
Engine:	Maybach HL 42 TRKM inline 6-cylinder, water-cooled, 4,170 cc, 100 hp
Power/weight ratio:	15.9 hp/ton
Max. speed:	40 mph road
Range:	215 miles road, 125 miles cross-country
Armament:	2 x 0.3 in MG 34 or 42 machine guns
Armor:	0.3–0.5 in
Fording depth:	27 in

Sd.Kfz. 250/1 of the Grossdeutschland Division, Eastern Front.

The Blitzkrieg concept was based largely on swift, deep tank advances with infantry support. The Wehrmacht was the first army in the world to develop special armored personnel carriers that enabled the infantry to keep pace with the tanks. This strategy required all kinds of additional support vehicles, which were based on the same chassis. The army's light armored personnel carriers were based on the chassis of the 1 ton tractor and were manufactured in a wide range of variants. The basic model was the Sd.Kfz. 250/1, a simple troop carrier often used by platoon or company sergeants and equipped with a machine gun. There were also radio/command vehicles with or without a frame antenna

(e.g. Rommel's Sd.Kfz. 250/3, known as the "Greif") and armored artillery observation vehicles with binocular periscope and other special equipment (Sd.Kfz. 250/5). So-called *Kanonenwagen* (gun vehicles) were intended to provide the mechanized infantry with supporting fire and were equipped with either the 1.5 inch (3.7 cm) Pak (Sd.Kfz. 250/10) or 3 inch (7.5 cm) StuK 24 (Sd.Kfz. 250/8). The Sd.Kfz. 250/9 was a special reconnaissance variant and was fitted with the Sd.Kfz. 222 turret and a 0.8 inch (2 cm) KwK cannon. There were also mortar carriers and

ammunition transporters based on the Sd.Kfz. 250. In 1943 the vehicle's complex angular hull was greatly simplified in order to make production easier. The Sd.Kfz. 252, an ammunition transporter also based on the light armored personnel carrier, had a closed, foreshortened superstructure and—like the observation variant Sd.Kfz. 253—was assigned to assault gun units. All the vehicles in this series proved outstandingly successful and were highly valued by the army. By 1945 around 7,500 units had been built.

Sd.Kfz. 250/3.

MEDIUM ARMORED PERSONNEL CARRIER SD.KFZ. 251

This medium armored personnel carrier was based on the chassis of the 3 ton (3 tonne) tractor and had in common with it a front axle that was neither powered nor equipped with brakes and served solely to steer the vehicle. A chain brake came into play during extreme steering maneuvers, however. The first vehicles were supplied to the army in 1939 and received a baptism of fire in the Polish campaign. Like the light armored personnel carrier, the medium personnel carrier was manufactured in a wide range of variants. There were 22 officially designated models. The basic model (Sd.Kfz. 251/1) was a ten-man troop carrier and was armed with two machine guns. The numerous special versions included radio, command, ambulance, engineers', ammmunition, and artillery observation vehicles. There was great variety in the

vehicles' armaments too. The Sd.Kfz. 251/10 was often fitted out as a platoon leader's vehicle with the 1.5 inch (3.7 cm) Pak anti-tank gun and the Sd.Kfz. 251/9, in its role as provider of supporting fire, with the short 7.5 cm StuK assault gun. From the end of 1944 the 3 inch (7.5 cm) StuK 40 was also fitted in one model (Sd.Kfz. 251/22). Other variants of the medium armored personnel carrier included mortar carriers, rocket launchers, flamethrowers, and self-propelled anti-aircraft guns (such as the Sd.Kfz. 251/21 equipped with the 0.6 inch (1.5 cm) Drilling 151 MG). The hull underwent minor modifications a number of times during the war and was greatly simplified in 1944. The medium armored personnel carrier proved extremely successful on all fronts and pretty well represented a new generation of armored vehicle. Wherever

German troops were to be found, the Sd.Kfz. 251 could be found alongside them and in this respect the vehicle could be said to have been a defining feature of the Wehrmacht. By 1945 around 16,000 medium armored personnel carriers had been built.

Sd.Kfz. 251/1	
Combat weight:	9.4 tons
Crew:	2 + 10
Dimensions in inches (length, width, height):	228/79/69 (without machine gun shield)
Engine:	Maybach HL 42 TRKM inline 6-cylinder, water-cooled, 4,170 cc, 100 hp
Power/weight ratio:	10.7 hp/ton
Max. speed:	33 mph road
Range:	200 miles road, 110 miles cross-country
Armament:	2 x 0.3 in MG 34 or 42 machine guns
Armor:	0.3–0.4 in
Fording depth:	20 in

Sd.Kfz. 251/1 Ausf. A, 1941, 5th Panzer Division.

Sd.Kfz. 251/1 Ausf. C, SS Totenkopf Mechanized Infantry Division, Russia, 1943.

PANZER I SD.KFZ. 101

Panzer Command Vehicle I, 11th Panzer Division, Tula, 1941.

	Pz.Kpfw. I Ausführung A
Combat weight:	5.9 tons
Crew:	2
Dimensions in inches (length, width, height):	158/79/68
Engine:	Krupp 4-cylinder boxer gas, air-cooled, 3,460 cc, 60 hp
Power/weight ratio:	17.7 hp/ton
Max. speed:	23 mph
Range:	125 miles road, 85 miles cross-country
Armament:	2 x 0.3 in machine guns
Armor:	0.2–0.5 in
Fording depth:	24 in

Panzer I Ausf. A, 5th Panzer Regiment, Libya 1941.

Germany was prohibited under the Treaty of Versailles from building armored vehicles but this did not stop the National Socialists from embarking upon a secret program of tank design and construction after they seized power in 1933. A number of prototypes of a new tank—referred to initially, for reasons of secrecy, as a Landwirtschaftlicher Schlepper (agricultural towing vehicle) before being renamed "Panzerkampf-wagen I"—were tested as early as 1934. The new tank's armament consisted solely of two 0.3 inch (7.92 mm) machine guns mounted in a rotating turret. Ausf. A was powered by a 60 hp engine which was upgraded to 100 hp in Ausf. B. The later version was also extended by some 16 inches (40 cm). Although its firepower was relatively modest, Panzer I was used in the Polish and French campaigns. After the Battle of France it was withdrawn from the front line but remained in service for the whole of the war either as a special variant of one kind or another, or as a training tank. One of the Wehrmacht's first self-propelled guns was based on Panzer I. The 15 cm SIG-33 heavy infantry gun—complete with wheels and carriage—was mounted on a Panzer I hull and the whole structure covered with armor plating. Another Panzer I variant that pointed the way forward was the tank command vehicle that facilitated the mobile command of tank battles for the first time. Attempts were also made to build a Panzer I direct infantry support vehicle by equipping the basic design with armor 3.1 inch (80 mm) thick but this idea never progressed beyond the prototype stage. Around 2,800 Panzer Is of all types were built between 1934 and 1939.

SIG-33 heavy infantry gun mounted on a Panzer I.

PANZER II SD.KFZ. 121

Like Panzer I, Panzer II was initially regarded as a stopgap that would have to do until the Panzers III and IV were ready. Krupp, Henschel, and MAN developed proposals for a 10 ton tank designated for reasons of secrecy the "Landwirtschaftlicher Schlepper 100." Army command decided in favor of the MAN version and the first vehicles were delivered to the Wehrmacht in 1935. The earliest versions, which were only produced in small numbers, had a chassis with six small road wheels fitted to a single arm. Only with Ausf. A did the Panzer II adopt its final form with five medium-sized wheels. This design continued to be used for versions B, C, and F, which differed only in terms of their armor. Versions D and E were equipped with a Christie-type suspension with four large wheels and a more powerful engine. They were capable of up to 34 mph (55 km/h) and were intended as fast fighting vehicles. Although the Panzer II was well made, its armor and armament were considered inadequate. It nevertheless remained in service as a battle tank until 1941; after this it was used mainly in a reconnaissance role. Ausf. L was developed specifically as a reconnaissance tank although only a few were actually built. Flamethrowers (the "Flamingo") and submergible versions for the planned invasion of the United

Panzer II Ausf. B, 6th Panzer Regiment, September 1938.

Kingdom were also based on the Panzer II design. Far better known and more successful than these, however, were the self-propelled anti-tank and artillery guns Marder and Wespe.

	Pz.Kpfw. II Ausführung C
Combat weight:	10.5 tons
Crew:	3
Dimensions in inches (length, width, height):	189/90/79
Engine:	Maybach HL 62 TRM inline 6-cylinder gas, air-cooled, 6190cc, 140 hp
Power/weight ratio:	13.3 hp/ton
Max. speed:	25 mph road, 12 mph cross-country
Range:	93 miles road, 62 miles cross-country
Armament:	0.8 in KwK 30 cannon, 1 x 0.3 in MG 34 machine gun
Armor:	0.2–1.2 in
Fording depth:	36 in

Panzer II Ausf. C, 8th Panzer Regiment, Libya, 1941.

Panzer II Ausf. C, 7th Panzer Division.

PANZER 35(T) ŠKODA LT 35

This tank was built by Škoda in Czechoslovakia in the 1930s and was introduced into the Czech armed forces in 1936. Following the annexation of Czechoslovakia in 1938, numerous Czech tanks fell into the Wehrmacht's hands including this model. The Škoda Model LT 35 mounted a 1.5 inch (3.7 cm) gun and proved extremely reliable. Named "Panzerkampfwagen 35(t)" by the Wehrmacht, it was at least as good as the Panzer II and played an important part in the equipping of the German tank divisions. The (t) in its new name stood for "tschechisch" (Czech). The tag (f) was used for captured French weapons, (r) for Russian weapons etc. Although its armor

plating was riveted, which to some extent impaired its fighting strength, the general quality of the 35(t)'s construction was outstanding. The drive sprocket was located at the rear in order to create more space in the crew compartment. The gears and steering were driven by compressed air in an attempt to make the driver's job easier. On the Eastern Front in winter, however, this system proved extremely temperamental and the compressed air was replaced by mechanical components. The tank's suspension was extremely well designed and the lifespan of the tracks was almost 4,500 miles (7,000 km). The Panzer 35(t) was integrated into German tank

	Pz.Kpfw. 35(t)
Combat weight:	12.1 tons
Crew:	4
Dimensions in inches (length, width, height):	183/89/92
Engine:	Škoda inline 4-cylinder gas, water-cooled, 8,620 cc, 115 hp
Power/weight ratio:	9.5 hp/ton
Max. speed:	21 mph road
Range:	120 miles road, 75 miles cross-country
Armament:	1.5 in Škoda cannon, 2 x 0.3 in MG 34 machine guns
Armor:	0.6–1 in
Fording depth:	30 in

divisions and was used in Poland and France as well as on the Eastern Front as late as 1942, by which time it was considered obsolete. The remaining vehicles were converted into recovery tanks or towing vehicles. The Wehrmacht had brought around 300 LT 35s into service. Before the Second World War, Škoda had supplied a number of tanks of this type to Romania, which deployed them alongside the Wehrmacht in Russia. Having thoroughly overhauled the Škoda design, Hungary started to build its own version of it, the Turan, in a range of different models in 1940.

Panzer 35(t).

A Škoda R-2 of the 1st Romanian Panzer Division, Eastern Front, November 1942.

PANZER 38(T) PRAGA TNHP-S LT 38

	Pz.Kpfw. 38(t)
Combat weight:	11.6 tons
Crew:	4
Dimensions in inches (length, width, height):	183/89/92
Engine:	Praga inline 6-cylinder gas, water-cooled, 7,754 cc, 125 hp
Power/weight ratio:	10.8 hp/ton
Max. speed:	26 mph road
Range:	150 miles road, 100 miles cross-country
Armament:	1.5 in cannon, 2 x 0.3 in MG 34 machine guns
Armor:	0.6–1 in; later up to 2 in
Fording depth:	35 in

A Panzer 38(t) on the advance in the West in 1940.

The second Czech tank to be adopted by the Wehrmacht was the LT 38, made by CKD. These vehicles were trialled from May 1939 onward and proved significantly superior to Germany's Panzers I and II. The Army Ordnance Department therefore ordered that production continue and the manufacturer's name was changed to "Böhmisch-Mährische-Maschinenfabrik" (BMM). By the start of the war the army had taken receipt of 98 vehicles, which were given the official designation Panzer 38(t) Ausführung A. The tanks carried 90 rounds for their 1.5 inch (3.7 cm) KwK 38(t) L/48 cannon. With a muzzle velocity of 2,430 feet (740 m) per second, this weapon was capable of penetrating armor plating up to 1.4 inches (35 mm) thick from a distance of around a third of a mile (500 m). The 38(t)'s armor was very weak, however, and, like that of the 35(t), riveted, which meant that if the vehicle were hit, the rivets would turn into dangerous projectiles and explode into the interior of the vehicle. Four large road wheels benefited from simple but effective leaf spring suspension that ensured good handling. The vehicle was well designed and proved extremely reliable and versatile. Later versions B, C, and D differed only in minor details. Versions E and F were given additional 25-mm-thick riveted armor at the front. The final version, Ausf. G, remained in production until 1942. Ausf. S was an export version supplied to Hungary (102 units), Slovakia (69 units), Romania (50 units), and Bulgaria (10 units). Sweden had ordered 92 vehicles from CKD which were not supplied (the Wehrmacht took delivery of them instead). In December 1942, however, Sweden was granted the right to manufacture the tank under license. In 1943, 70 units of a 38 reconnaissance tank based on the 38(t) were built. This involved fitting the turret of the Sd.Kfz. 222 onto the unmodified 38(t) hull and equipping it with a 2 cm KwK 38 cannon and MG 42 machine gun. A far more familiar sight was the numerous self-propelled guns based on the 38(t), which played an important role for the Wehrmacht. The German forces employed around 1,500 38(t)s although they no longer used them as battle tanks after 1942.

A Panzer 38(t) Ausf. E, 8th Panzer Division, 1941.

PANZER III SD.KFZ. 141

	Pz.Kpfw. III Ausführung J
Combat weight:	24.6 tons
Crew:	5
Dimensions in inches (length, width, height):	219/116/99 (length without gun barrel)
Engine:	Maybach HL 120 TRM V12 gas, water-cooled, 11,870 cc, 300 hp
Power/weight ratio:	12.2 hp/ton
Max. speed:	25 mph road, 12 mph cross-country
Range:	85 miles road, 55 miles cross-country
Armament:	2 in KwK 39 L/60 cannon, 2 x 0.3 in MG 34 machine guns
Armor:	0.7–2 in
Fording depth:	39 in

A Panzer III Ausf. F in Russia in Winter 1941.

The Panzer III was intended as a standard battle tank and for logistical reasons (the infantry was already using the 1.5 inch (3.7 cm) Pak anti-tank gun) was initially to have been equipped with a 1.5 inch (3.7 cm) KwK cannon. Leading generals such as General Guderian, however, wanted a 2 inch (5 cm) gun. In 1935, development contracts were

awarded to MAN, Daimler-Benz, Rhein-metall, and Krupp and in 1936 the Daimler-Benz design emerged victorious. The first models (Ausf. A to D) were used mainly to test different kinds of running gear. Only with Ausf. E in 1939 did the Panzer III assume its typical appearance with six medium-sized wheels. Although the tank was reasonably well made, it suffered from

the outset from inadequate weaponry. This became particularly apparent in 1940 and so later models were equipped with more powerful guns (the 2 inch (5 cm) L/42 and later the L/60). The thickness of armor was also steadily increased (1.2 inches (30 mm) maximum for Ausf. E; 2.8 inches (70 mm) maximum for Ausf. L). Ultimately the tank was fitted with a spaced turret girdle and side skirts. The final production model was Ausf. N, which mounted a short 3 inch (7.5 cm) KwK L/24. Compared to the Panzer IV, which had similar dimensions, the Panzer III was always underarmed. The size of its turret ring prohibited it from being fitted with the long 3 inch (7.5 cm) KwK, which would have been necessary against the T-34 from 1943. Nevertheless, with its advanced design (five-man crew, radio equipment, torsion bar suspension), the Panzer III was forward-looking and effective in combat. From 1942, however, it could no longer be relied upon to be the match of any opponent and was clearly inferior to the T-34 or KV-1. In addition to the command and flamethrower versions, an amphibious model was made for Operation Sea Lion. By 1943 around 5,700 Panzer IIIs of all variants had been built although many of these were assault guns based on the Panzer III chassis. The Russians also found that (captured) Panzer IIIs made a useful base for an assault gun (e.g. the SU-76i).

A Panzer III Ausf. N, Kursk, July 1943.

A Panzer III Ausf. J with 2 in (5 cm) KwK L/60 cannon, "Wiking" Panzer Division, 1942.

PANZER IV SD.KFZ. 161

A Panzer IV Ausf. D1, Hungarian Panzer Division "Don 09," 1942.

Panzer IVs wore a coating of Zimmerit paste to impede magnetic charges. With Ausf. J (April 1944 to the end of the war) it was decided to sacrifice the electric turret traversing gear in order to make room for an additional fuel tank, which extended the vehicle's range to around 160 miles (260 km). From September 1944, skirts of wire mesh were commonly used in order to save weight. The Panzer IV remained a serious battlefield opponent through to the end of the war—not a bad outcome for a design that dated back to 1934. There were also ammunition transporter, bridgelaying, and recovery variants as well as a series of self-propelled guns. Around 9,200 Panzer IV units were produced. In addition to the Wehrmacht, the tank was used by Germany's allies as well as by a number of neutral states. The last Panzer IVs in service were probably those deployed in 1973 by Syria, which had bought them cheaply from the Soviet Union's stock of captured tanks.

The Panzer IV was initially conceived as a heavy support vehicle. During the course of the war, however, it became the backbone of the German tank fleet. Development was begun by Krupp in 1934. The first 35 units of the 19 ton Ausf. A, equipped with a 3 inch (7.5 cm) KwK L/24, two machine guns, and 0.6 inch (14.5 mm) armor all over, were delivered by 1938. The Panzer IV had pretty well found its final form with this first version because no significant modifications were undertaken during the war other than the upgrading of its gun and armor.

From the middle of 1942, Ausf. F2 was equipped with the 2 inch (7.5 cm) KwK-40 L/43 and its armor was reinforced through the addition of 1.2 inch (30mm)-thick plates on the nose and at the front of the turret, finally producing a match for the T-34. Ausf. G mounted the even better KwK-40 L/48. Ausf. H (May 1943 onward), was given reinforced turret roof armor, 3.1 inch (80mm)-thick front armor, side skirts to protect it from anti-tank rifles and hollow charge projectiles and wider tracks for use in the snow and mud of the East. From September 1943 onward,

	Pz.Kpfw. IV Ausführung H
Combat weight:	27.6 tons
Crew:	5
Dimensions in inches (length, width, height):	233/113/105 without barrel or skirts; 276/132/105 with barrel and skirts
Engine:	Maybach HL 120 TRM V12 gas, water-cooled, 11,870 cc, 300 hp
Power/weight ratio:	11.3 hp/ton
Max. speed:	24 mph road, 10 mph cross-country
Range:	110 miles road, 75 cross-country
Armament:	3 in KwK 40 L/48 cannon 2 x 0.3 in MG 34 machine guns
Armor:	0.4–3.1 in; skirts 0.2 in
Fording depth:	47 in

A Panzer IV H of an assault gun unit on the Eastern Front.

GERMANY

PANZER V SD.KFZ. 171 (PANTHER)

A Panzer V Ausf. D1, "Das Reich" Panzer Battalion.

A Panzer V Ausf. D2, 9th Panzer Regiment ("Hohenstaufen"), Normandy, 1944.

	Pz.Kpfw. V Ausführung D
Combat weight:	50.1 tons
Crew:	5
Dimensions in inches (length, width, height):	270/129/122 without without barrel or skirts; 340/129/122 with barrel and skirts
Engine:	Maybach HL 230 P30 V12 gas, water-cooled, 23,880 cc, 700 hp
Power/weight ratio:	13.9 hp/ton
Max. speed:	29 mph road, 15 mph cross-country
Range:	100 miles road, 60 miles cross-country
Armament:	3 in KwK 42 L/70 cannon, 2–3 x 0.3 in MG 34 machine guns
Armor:	1–3.9 in
Fording depth:	67 in

The development of the Panther was largely influenced by the emergence of the Soviet T-34, which set new standards in tank construction. The Army Ordnance Department contracted MAN and Daimler-Benz to develop a 34.4 ton (35 tonne) tank with the same outstanding properties as the T-34: a ballistically effective shape (providing effective shot deflection), powerful weaponry, and good maneuverability. The MAN design was chosen and the tank went into production at the end of 1942. The Panther had its debut at the Battle of Kursk (Operation Citadel)—albeit without success as the first Panthers were still suffering from teething problems as a result of having been sent into battle prematurely.

Their gearboxes and running gear failed and many broke down before they had even reached the front. Once these defects had been rectified, the Panther went on to become one of the best, if not the best tank of the Second World War. It combined firepower, effective armor, and maneuverability and was justifiably feared by opposing tank crews. Its 7.5 cm KwK L/70 could pierce the armor of almost any tank at around two-thirds of a mile (1 km). Even the Panther had its defects, however: its turret traversing gear was so weak that the turret would not rotate if the tank was on a slope; its engine had a lifetime of little more that 600 miles (1,000 km); the side and rear armor was relatively thin—only frontally did the tank offer first-class protection—which was why Panzer IVs were often deployed to protect the flanks. Another problem was the shape of the gun mantlet: hits were known to have ricocheted off it and penetrated the roof of the hull. In addition to battle tank versions D, A, and G, a number of special recovery Panthers were also built because the usual 20 ton (18 tonne) towing machines were not powerful enough to tow either Panthers or Tigers. By the end of the war around 6,000 Panthers had been built. The French army continued to use captured Panthers for some time afterward.

A Panther on difficult terrain. Despite weighing 50 tons (45,000 kg), the tank was extremely maneuverable.

JAGDPANTHER 8.8 CM TANK DESTROYER SD.KFZ. 173

After a number of attempts to use the excellent but unwieldy 3.5 inch (8.8 cm) Pak 43 in a variety of self-propelled guns, resulting in vehicles such as the Nashorn and Elefant, the decision was finally taken to mount the anti-tank gun on the chassis of the highly successful Panther tank. The first prototype was unveiled in October 1943. At the beginning of 1944, the new fighting vehicle was given the name "Jagdpanther" at Hitler's suggestion, and went into production at MIAG in February. By the end of the war just 382 Jagdpanthers had been built. The Jagdpanther was extremely mobile and well armored with sloped armor that was

The Jagdpanther's sloping sides are particularly conspicuous from the front.

Combat weight:	50.7 tons
Crew:	5
Dimensions in inches (length, width, height):	270/129/107 without barrel or skirts; 388/135/107 with barrel and skirts
Engine:	Maybach HL 230 P30 V12 gas, water-cooled, 23,880 cc, 700 hp
Power/weight ratio:	13.8 hp/ton
Max. speed:	30 mph road, 15 mph cross-country
Range:	95 miles road, 60 miles cross-country
Armament:	3.5 in Pak 43/3 L/71 anti-tank gun, 0.3 in MG 34 machine gun
Armor:	0.7–3.1 in
Fording depth:	59 in

A Jagdpanther with the Panzer Training Division, Uelzen area, March 1945.

highly effective from a ballistics point of view. Like other German assault guns and tank destroyers, however, the vehicle had to be pointing in the approximate direction of the target because the gun had a very limited traverse. The superstructure was roomy and Krupp was therefore commissioned to design an upgraded version with a 0.5 inch (12.8 cm) Pak. The combination of 3.5 inch (8.8 cm) Pak and Panther chassis proved extremely successful. The gun was capable of destroying any Allied tank in existence and the chassis was mobile and robust. As a result the vehicle was loved by its crews and feared by the Allies. The Jagdpanther is widely regarded as a "masterpiece" of middle-period tank design.

A Jagdpanther in the Tank Museum, Münster, Germany.

PANZER VI TIGER SD.KFZ. 181

	Pz.Kpfw. VI Ausführung E
Combat weight:	60.1 tons
Crew:	5
Dimensions in inches (length, width, height):	237/140/113 without barrel or skirts; 324/147/113 with barrel and skirts
Engine:	Maybach HL 230 P45 V12 gas, water-cooled, 21,353 cc, 700 hp
Power/weight ratio:	11.1 hp/ton
Max. speed:	24 mph road, 12 mph cross-country
Range:	55 miles road, 35 miles cross-country
Armament:	3.5 in KwK-36 L/56, 2 x 0.3 in MG 34 machine guns
Armor:	1–4.3 in
Fording depth:	47 in; first units capable of submerging to a depth of 157 in

A Sturmtiger assault gun of the Sturmmörser (mortar) Company 1002 in the Ardennes, winter 1944–45.

A Tiger Ausf. E, 101st Heavy SS Panzer Battalion, Normandy, 1944.

A Tiger Ausf. H1, 503rd Heavy Panzer Battalion, Rostov, 1943.

Experience of the Battle of France in 1940 and the appearance of the T-34 and KV-1 confirmed the Wehrmacht's urgent need for a heavy tank. In 1941, therefore, the Army Ordnance Department commissioned Porsche and Henschel to develop an appropriate vehicle. Both firms turned to designs and prototypes they had been working on since 1937. The Porsche design proved too technically complex; Henschel's was more conventional and was chosen for production. Confident that his design would be selected, however, Professor Porsche had already manufactured 90 chassis, which were later turned into the Elefant tank destroyer. Henschel's design was heavily armored but did not share the T-34's innovative sloping design. The turret was made by Krupp and was equipped with an 3.5 inch (8.8 cm) gun based on the legendary 3.5 inch (8.8 cm) anti-aircraft gun. This gave the new tank, which by now had been named the Tiger, the ability to penetrate the armor of any opponent. Production began in 1942 and the first Tigers were sent to North Africa and the Eastern Front in late summer. As a consequence of the hasty development process, the tank was mechanically unreliable and furthermore the right

battlefield tactics had yet to be devised for the 60-ton (61-tonne) colossus. Once these weaknesses were rectified, the Tiger began to be greatly feared by the enemy. Although it was not sloped, the thickness of its armor (3.9in/100 mm at the front and 3.1in/80 mm at the sides) meant it could withstand most shells. The Tiger was therefore capable of taking extremely heavy punishment and still penetrating the armor of a T-34/76 a mile (over 1.5 km) away with its 3.5 inch (8.8 cm) KwK 36.

When properly deployed, the Tiger dominated battlefields on both the Eastern and Western fronts. In 1944, for example, a single Tiger destroyed 25 Allied tanks, holding up an entire division before being hit itself. But the mighty Tiger also had its weak points. Its great weight was the cause of numerous

difficulties—there were many bridges it could not cross, for example. Its width was also a problem because narrow transport tracks had to be fitted (a slow and laborious process) before it could be loaded onto railroad trucks. In heavy mud or freezing snow its interleaved running gear had a tendency to become blocked. One Tiger variant was a tractor designed specifically to tow other Tigers. Another was the so-called "Sturmtiger," whose turret was replaced with an armor-plated superstructure accommodating a 15 inch (38 cm) rocket mortar, although only 18 of these were built. Production of the Tiger came to a halt in August 1944 after only 1,350 or so had been built—not many when one stops to consider the legendary reputation the tank had acquired.

TIGER (P) TANK DESTROYER SD.KFZ.184 (FERDINAND/ELEFANT)

	Jagdpanzer Tiger (P) Ferdinand
Combat weight:	75 tons
Crew:	6
Dimensions in inches (length, width, height):	268/135/117
Engine:	2 x Maybach HL 120 TRM/ 112 V12 gas, water-cooled, 11,870 cc, 300 hp
Power/weight ratio:	7.0 hp/ton
Max. speed:	12 mph road
Range:	80 miles road, 55 miles cross-country
Armament:	3.5 in Pak 43/2 L/71 anti-tank gun
Armor:	sides and rear 3.1 in front 7.9 in
Fording depth:	39 in

A Ferdinand tank destroyer with its long 3.5 inch (8.8 cm) Pak 43.

After losing out to the Henschel Tiger design, an alternative use was sought for the chassis units that had already been manufactured by Porsche. Back in 1942, Hitler had called for an armored fighting vehicle capable of mounting the 3.5 inch (8.8 cm) KwK L/71 and in September 1942 a vehicle of this type was commissioned based on the Porsche Tiger. In February 1943, Hitler ordered that the weapon be delivered as soon as possible. The Jagdpanzer Tiger (P) Sd.Kfz. 184 adopted the Porsche Tiger's running gear unchanged. The fighting compartment with its fixed superstructure up to 7.9 inch (200 mm) thick was located at the rear with the engine in the middle. The vehicle had an interesting drive system which offered a number of distinct advantages from a mechanical and constructional point of view: two Maybach HL 120 TRM tank engines powered generators that delivered current to electric motors that drove the sprockets positioned at the front of the vehicle. The tank had a powerful gun and thick armor, making it extremely heavy and slow. Another disadvantage was that it had no means of defending itself against infantry attack, not even a machine gun. Ninety vehicles were produced in total. This tank destroyer, initially named the "Ferdinand,"

first saw combat at the Battle of Kursk in 1943. The 90 Ferdinands deployed there are thought to have knocked out over 500 enemy tanks but they in turn broke down by the dozen. Only 48 vehicles remained after the battle and nearly all were damaged. Following this débâcle, they were recalled for modifications and finally fitted with a machine gun and turret hatch. Their name was changed to "Elefant" and from this point on they saw battle mainly in Italy, where they impressed when used defensively as a kind of mobile bunker. Essentially, however, the vehicle was too heavy, slow, and unreliable.

A Tiger on the Eastern Front in winter 1943.

An Elefant tank destroyer with modified front machine gun.

TIGER II SD.KFZ. 182

A "King Tiger" with Henschel turret. 502nd Heavy Panzer Division, Ardennes, winter 1944–45.

Pz.Kpfw. VI B (Henschel turret)	
Combat weight:	76.8 tons
Crew:	5
Dimensions in inches (length, width, height):	286/142/122 without barrel or skirts: 405/148/122 with barrel and skirts
Engine:	Maybach HL 230 P30 V12 gas, water-cooled, 23,889 cc, 700 hp
Power/weight ratio:	9.0 hp/ton
Max. speed:	24 mph road, 11 mph cross-country
Range:	75 miles road, 50 miles cross-country
Armament:	3.5 in KwK 43 L/71, 2 x 0.3 in MG 34 machine guns
Armor:	1.6–7.3 in
Fording depth:	63 in

Although production of the Tiger had only just started, the Army Ordnance Department immediately commissioned designs for a successor with a ballistically more efficient shape that would be equipped with the 3.5 inch (8.8 cm) KwK 43. Once again Porsche and Henschel were in competition and once again, Professor Porsche was so sure of victory that he started production of the tank turret before waiting for the decision. The Army Ordnance Department, meanwhile, preferred yet again the Henschel design. The Porsche turrets were incorporated into the first 50 Henschel vehicles, which went into production in December 1943. Nicknamed the "King Tiger" or "Royal Tiger" by the Allies, the Tiger II featured near-indestructible sloped armor and one of the most powerful tank guns of the Second World War. It was also, however, extremely heavy. Its engine was under constant strain, rendering the vehicle ponderous and mechanically unreliable. The Maybach power plant consumed over 400 gallons (1,514 l) of valuable gasoline for every 100 miles (161 km) of terrain it covered. By 1944–45 the necessary fuel was often simply not available. Most Tiger IIs were put out of action not by enemy hits but by engine failure or a shortage of gas. In spite of this—or perhaps because of it—the tank acquired a legendary reputation for its firepower and the strength of its armor. By the end of the war only 485 Tiger IIs had been built.

JAGDTIGER TANK DESTROYER SD.KFZ. 186

Jagdtiger Ausführung B	
Combat weight:	79.4 tons
Crew:	5
Dimensions in inches (length, width, height):	307/142/116; length with barrel: 419
Engine:	Maybach HL 230 P30 V12 gas, water-cooled, 23,889 cc, 700 hp
Power/weight ratio:	8.9 hp/ton
Max. speed:	22 mph road, 10 mph cross-country
Range:	75 miles road, 50 miles cross-country
Armament:	5 in Pak 44 L/55 anti-tank gun, 2 x 0.3 in MG 34 machine guns
Armor:	1.2–9.8 in
Fording depth:	69 in

A Jagdtiger with the 653rd Heavy Tank Destroyer Battalion, Westphalia, April 1945

The Tiger II also provided the basis for a tank destroyer with a fixed superstructure and limited field of fire. Contracts for this vehicle were awarded in February 1943 and the initial prototype was completed by the Nibelungen Works in April 1944. The first Jagdtigers were delivered to the army in November 1944. Professor Porsche was again involved and the first two vehicles were provided with running gear of his design. This system did not prove successful, however, and was replaced by the Henschel-designed Tiger II running gear. The Jagdtiger was designed to be able to deal effectively with even the heaviest Allied tank, from a long distance. Its 5 inch (12.8 cm) Pak 44 was indeed up to the task. With a muzzle velocity of over 3,000 feet (920 m) per second, its 62.4-pound (28.3 kg) tank shell was capable of penetrating 170 mm of armor from nearly two miles (3,000 m) away. Unsurprisingly, the ammunition was very heavy and charge and shell had to be loaded separately each time, resulting in a low rate of fire. The Jagdtiger's solid 9.8 inch (250 mm) frontal armor made it almost invulnerable to attack from this angle although its sides and rear, where the armor was just 3.1 inches (80 mm) thick, were highly susceptible. The weight of this armor made the tank extremely heavy. Its engine and gears were constantly under strain and consequently the Jagdtiger was often out of action. Because of its great weight it was seldom used as a Jagdpanzer (literally "hunter tank") but rather in an infantry support role. The tank was unpopular with its crews and only 74 of them were built.

PANZERJÄGER I (SELF-PROPELLED GUN BASED ON PANZER I AUSF. B)

Panzerjäger I, LAH Division, France, 1942.

	Panzerjäger I
Combat weight:	7 tons
Crew:	3
Dimensions in inches (length, width, height):	174/73/89
Engine:	Maybach NL-38 TRKM inline 6-cylinder gas, water-cooled, 3,790 cc, 100 hp
Power/weight ratio:	14.1 hp/ton
Max. speed:	25 mph road
Range:	110 miles road, 80 miles cross-country
Armament:	1.9 in Pak 36(t) L43 anti-tank gun
Armor:	0.2–0.6 in
Fording depth:	24 in

The 4.7 cm Pak (t) self-propelled gun—Panzerjäger I—was the first in a long series of self-propelled guns designed specifically for use against tanks. It had become clear as early as 1939 that the Panzer I was ineffective in this role. In order to be able to continue using its chassis, the Czech 1.9 inch (4.7 cm) Pak L/43, an outstanding anti-tank gun for its day, was mounted on the hull of the Pz.Kpfw. I Ausf. B. The gun was protected on three sides by an armor-plated superstructure up to 0.6 inches (14.5 mm) thick but was left open at the back. Alkett in Berlin converted 132 Panzer I Ausf. Bs into tank destroyers. There was no question of converting Ausf. A because of its inadequate engine performance and small size. The Panzerjäger I proved extremely effective on the battlefields of France, North Africa, and during the first phase of the Russian campaign. Before long, however, its fighting power was inadequate in the Soviet Union. Against the newer T-34 and KV-1 the 4.7 cm Pak was simply too weak. It was unable to provide protection for German tanks and therefore began to be withdrawn in 1942. The Panzerjäger I continued to be highly successful in Africa, however, until 1943.

BISON HEAVY INFANTRY GUN   SD.KFZ 138/1

	Bison Ausführung H
Combat weight:	14 tons
Crew:	5
Dimensions in inches (length, width, height):	192/85/97; length with barrel: 220
Engine:	Praga inline 6-cylinder gas, water-cooled, 7,754 cc, 125 hp
Power/weight ratio:	8.9 hp/ton
Max. speed:	22 mph road
Range:	130 miles road, 85 miles cross-country
Armament:	5.9 in SIG-33
Armor:	0.4–1.6 in
Fording depth:	35 in

Another vehicle built on the chassis of the reliable and resilient Panzer 38 (t) was the Bison self-propelled gun, which mounted a 5.9 inch (15 cm) heavy infantry gun. These vehicles were not intended as tank destroyers but were designed to provide mobile artillery support. There were two versions of the Bison (also known as the "Grille"). Like the Marder III, the engine was positioned either at the back (Ausf. H) or in the middle (Ausf. M). In total 370 units were built between 1942 and 1944.

A Bison Ausf. H from an unknown unit, Russia, 1944.

MARDER I, II, AND III TANK DESTROYERS

Germany's invasion of the Soviet Union in 1941 and in particular the appearance of the T-34 highlighted the Wehrmacht's urgent need for anti-tank vehicles. As production was already running at capacity and it took time to develop new vehicles, a decision was taken to follow the example of Panzerjäger I and equip a quantity of out-of-date chassis with high-performance, heavy anti-tank guns. The Marder tank destroyers used three different chassis and were designated Marder I, II, and III. When they had invaded France in 1940, German troops had captured around 300 so-called Lorraine tractors, small supply vehicles with a front-mounted engine. Little attention was paid to them initially. It was only with developments in the East that their existence was remembered. On his own initiative, one Hauptmann Becker, an artillery captain and engineer stationed in France, had equipped his battery with self-propelled guns made by members of the unit from British Mark VIs. Hitler had been so impressed that a production unit named "Baustab Becker" was formed with the task of developing an appropriate use for the captured French vehicles. An order was duly issued on August 25, 1942 for the construction of a light tank destroyer to be named Marder I. It was initially planned to convert around 160 of the French tractors. 60 were to be turned into anti-tank vehicles with a 3 inch (7.5 cm) Pak 40/1 L/46 and the rest into self-propelled artillery guns with 4.1 inch (10.5 cm) and 5.9 inch (15 cm) howitzers.

When other Lorraine tractors became available, they too were fed into the program. The vehicle's running gear was highly durable.

	Marder II Sd.Kfz. 132	Marder III Sd.Kfz. 139
Combat weight:	12.7 tons	11.9 tons
Crew:	4	4
Dimensions in inches (length, width, height):	183/91/102; length with barrel: 222	192/85/98; length with barrel: 230
Engine:	Maybach HL 62 TRM, inline 6-cylinder gas, water-cooled, 6,190 cc, 140 hp	Praga inline 6-cylinder gas, water-cooled, 7,754 cc, 125 hp
Power/weight ratio:	11.0 hp/ton	10.5 hp/ton
Max. speed:	34 mph road	26 mph road
Range:	95 miles road, 60 miles cross-country	150 miles road, 100 miles cross-country
Armament:	3 in Pak 36(r) L/51,1	3 in Pak 36(r) L/51,1
Armor:	0.6–1.2 in	0.4–2in
Fording depth:	33 in	35 in

A Marder, based on the chassis of the Lorraine tractor, with 3 inch (7.5 cm) Pak 40.

A Marder II with 3 inch (7.5 cm) Pak 40.

811 Marder IIs were built. They performed their role as tank destroyers extremely well thanks to their excellent firepower.

Marder III Ausf. H with 3 inch (7.5 cm) Pak 40 (seen from above).

Both the tank destroyers and the artillery vehicles were fitted with a box-shaped superstructure made of armor plating up to 0.4 inches (12 mm) thick. The anti-tank vehicle weighed just over 9 tons (8 tonnes). Its Delahaye 103TT inline 6-cylinder engine was capable of powering it to a top speed of 24 miles per hour (38 km/h) and it had a range of 93 miles (150 km). 184 vehicles were converted from 1942 onward, almost all of which remained in France. Only a few found their way to Italy or the Eastern Front as and when their units were redeployed. Together with other improvised armored anti-tank vehicles based on captured French vehicles, these self-propelled guns were named Marder I. Most Marder Is were involved in the Battle of Normandy from mid-1944 onward and were lost in the fighting.

The Marder II was based on the chassis of the Panzer II. Initially it was equipped mainly with the 3 inch (7.62 cm) Pak 36(r) or a 3 inch (7.62 cm) field gun captured in Russia; later with the German Pak 40 L/46. To start with, versions D and E of the Panzer II, the so-called *Schnellkampfwagen* ("fast fighting vehicle") were converted—185 in total—including 30 that had previously been converted to Flamingo (Flammpanzer II) flamethrowers. The turret and the rest of the Panzer II's superstructure were removed in order to make room for the centrally positioned anti-tank gun, which was then surrounded by a box-like guard up to 14.5 mm thick (Sd.Kfz. 132). Once all the available Panzer II Ausf. Ds and Es had been converted, it was the turn of Ausf. F, which meant a further 50 Marder IIs could then be produced. Following the great success of the weapon on the Eastern Front, new orders were received and versions A, B, C, and F of the Panzer II were also converted. These differed slightly in appearance to the earlier Marder II model and were designated Sd.Kfz. 131.

The Marder III self-propelled gun was based on the Panzer 38(t) chassis and was produced in greater numbers (1,143) than either of the other two Marders. The first version (Panzerjäger 38(t) Sd.Kfz. 139, Marder III) appeared in March 1942 and was equipped with the Russian 3 inch (7.62 cm) anti-tank gun mounted on the upper part of the hull and protected only by a small guard. 344 guns of this version were produced. The next version (Sd.Kfz. 138, Marder III Ausf. H) had a 3 inch (7.5 cm) Pak 40 with a special 0.4 inch (10 mm)-thick guard that was far more substantial than that of the first version. These first models were slightly top-heavy, however, and in the next version (Sd.Kfz. 138, Marder III Ausf. M) the engine was therefore shifted to the middle of the vehicle and the fighting compartment moved to the back. This resulted in a far better-balanced vehicle with a larger fighting compartment. The main armament and the thickness of the armor remained the same. Changes to the engine, however, boosted output to 150 hp. Between 1942 and 1944 418 Ausf. Hs and 381 Ausf. Ms were manufactured.

Marder III Ausf. H of a tank destroyer battalion with the 9th Panzer Division, Kursk, July 1943.

GERMANY

STUG III ASSAULT GUN SD.KFZ. 142

The German Blitzkrieg concept was based on rapid advances by Panzer divisions accompanied by mechanized infantry. As tanks were not generally available to them, the infantry needed to have their own armored vehicles. Back in 1935, General von Manstein had therefore called for an infantry support vehicle. In June 1936 Daimler-Benz was awarded the contract to develop a vehicle of this type mounting a 3 inch (7.5 cm) gun. Daimler based its designs on the Panzer III, which was already in production. In order to reduce height, the vehicle was given a fixed superstructure (in place of a turret)

	StuG III Ausf. D Sd.Kfz. 142	StuG 40 Ausf. G Sd.Kfz. 142/1
Combat weight:	24.5 tons	26.3 tons
Crew:	4	4
Dimensions in inches (length, width, height):	213/116/777	219/116/85; with barrel and skirts: 267/134/85
Engine:	Maybach HL 120 TRM, V12 gas, water-cooled, 11,870 cc, 300 hp	Maybach HL 120 TRM V12 gas, water-cooled, 11,870 cc, 300 hp
Power/weight ratio:	12.2 hp/ton	11.3 hp/ton
Max. speed:	25 mph road, 12 mph cross-country	24 mph road, 12 mph cross- country
Range:	85 miles road, 55 miles cross-country	80 miles road, 55 miles cross-country
Armament:	3 in StuK L/24	3 in StuK 40 L/48, 1 x 0.3 in MG 34
Armor:	0.7–2 in	0.7–3.1 in; skirts: 0.2 in
Fording depth:	31 in	31 in

A StuG III Ausf. G with "Saukopf" gun mantlet.

accommodating a 3 inch (7.5 cm) L/24 assault gun. This was based on the almost unchanged chassis of the Panzer III. The first prototypes were built by Alkett in 1937 and were extensively tested. Production of the StuG III Ausf. A (Sd.Kfz. 142), based on Pz.Kpfw III Ausf. F, began in January 1940. The Panzer III hull was adapted to the StuG III and the frontal armor was increased in thickness from 1.2 inches (30 mm) to 2 inches (50 mm). The engine and running gear remained identical to those of Panzer II Ausf. F, however. The first StuGs were tested in combat in France and proved extremely successful, whereupon they went into large-scale production.

734 units were built of versions B to E, which differed only in small details. Originally intended simply to provide support for infantry attacks, StuGs

began to be used in increasing numbers in a tank destroyer role. Because of its low muzzle velocity, however, the 3 inch (7.5 cm) StuK L/24 was not powerful enough to fight tanks effectively and so Ausf. F was upgunned to the StuK 40 L/43. This significantly improved its firepower

and gave it the capability to knock out targets at a greater distance. With Ausf. F, the vehicle's code number changed to Sd.Kfz. 142/1 and the StuG III was often referred to as the StuG 40 after its new gun. Once 300 or so Ausf. F vehicles had been built, this version was upgraded again and renamed the F/8. In addition to changes to the upper part of the body, the vehicle was also equipped with the 3 inch (7.5 cm) StuK 40 L/48, which was capable of penetrating 3.3 inches (85 mm) of armor plating at a distance of over 1,000 yards (1,000 m) with a 60° angle of impact. The thickness of the frontal armor was increased from 2 inches (50 mm) to 3.1 inches (80 mm). Many vehicles of the earlier versions were later refitted with the long-barreled StuK 40. From 1943 onward the StuG III was equipped with side skirts as protection against anti-tank rifles and hollow charge projectiles. The last version of the StuG III, and also the one

A StuG III Ausf. D of the 243rd StuG Battalion.

StuG 40, SS StuG Battalion, LAH Division.

1944, 1,114 of these vehicles had been built. StuG III Ausf. G continued to be produced right up to the end of the war, long after production of the Panzer III had ceased. The StuG III proved exceptionally successful and by the end of the war had become the Wehrmacht's most important armored fighting vehicle despite its origins as a compromise solution. Its main advantages were its low cost due to its lack of a turret and the fact that unlike the Panzer III it was able to accommodate the long-barreled 3 inch (75 mm) gun. In addition to the Wehrmacht, some of Germany's allies also used StuG IIIs and Finland was still using them several years after the war. The Soviets also used captured StuG IIIs and converted a number of them to take their 3 inch (7.62 cm) gun. A total of 7,900 StuG III versions F and G were built.

manufactured in the largest numbers, Ausf. G, went into production in December 1942. Its armor was strengthened again and it was equipped with a new cylindrical hatch. A folding machine gun shield now became standard. In February a cast pig's head mantlet, designed to provide better protection, was introduced, replacing the previous bolted-on box mantlet. Early StuG Ausf. Gs were also equipped with three smoke grenade launchers on either side. Protective track skirts also became standard as did Zimmerit paste coating. In 1942, the 4.1 inch (10.5 cm) assault howitzer was also successfully combined with the StuG III and went into production as the "Sturmhaubitze 42." By the end of

STUIG 33 INFANTRY ASSAULT GUN ON PANZER III CHASSIS

The StuIG 33 was already in planning by mid-1941 but the first task was to develop an armored superstructure capable of accommodating the 5.9 inch (15 cm) SIG-33 heavy infantry gun. This was the third attempt to produce a mobile version of the SIG-33 as the gun had already been mounted on Panzer I and II chassis. In mid-September 1942 an order was issued to fit a number of existing assault guns with the new superstructure and SIG-33. Different sources place the number of StuIGs produced at either 12 or 24. These vehicles mounting a heavy infantry gun and therefore belonging to the armored artillery were used in direct combat against fixed targets such as bunkers or buildings. Their guns were set up for direct fire and could only be raised by 25°. All the vehicles produced were sent to the Eastern Front in 1942 and most are thought to have been lost at Stalingrad.

Combat weight:	24.2 tons
Crew:	5
Dimensions in inches (length, width, height):	217/116/91
Engine:	Maybach HL 120 TRM V12 gas, water-cooled, 11,870 cc, 300 hp
Power/weight ratio:	12.2 hp/ton
Max. speed:	24 mph road, 12 mph cross-country
Range:	85 miles road, 55 miles cross-country
Armament:	5.9 in SIG-33 L/11, 1 x 0.3 in MG 34 machine gun
Armor:	0.7–3.1 in
Fording depth:	31 in

A SIG-33 on a Pz.Kpfw. III chassis, Russia, fall 1942.

STUG IV ASSAULT GUN SD.KFZ. 163

	Pz.Kpfw. IV Ausf. H
Combat weight:	25.4 tons
Crew:	5
Dimensions in inches (length, width, height)	233/114/87 without barrel or skirts 264/132/87 with barrel and skirts
Engine:	Maybach HL 120 TRM V12 gas, water-cooled, 11,870 cc, 300 hp
Power/weight ratio:	10.9 hp/ton
Max. speed:	24 mph road, 10 mph cross-country
Range:	110 miles road, 75 miles cross-country
Armament:	3 in StuK 40 L/48, 2 x 0.3 in MG 34 machine guns
Armor:	0.4–3.1 in; skirts 0.2 in
Fording depth:	47 in

A StuG IV photographed at the Krupp works in Essen in September 1944.

The StuG IV was basically a StuG III mounted on a Panzer IV chassis, albeit with somewhat improved armor. The first experiments with this combination took place in 1943, when it was intended as an interim solution pending the development of a dedicated tank destroyer—the Jagdpanzer IV. At the end of 1943, however, the factory where the Panzer III chassis (on which the StuG III was based) was being built, was so badly bombed that production ground almost completely to a halt. Hitler personally ordered part of the Panzer IV production to be switched to the manufacture of assault guns and Krupp converted its Panzer IV production line accordingly. Like the StuG III, the StuG IV proved extremely successful and a total of 1,500 were built.

STURMPANZER IV ASSAULT TANK SD.KFZ. 166 (BRUMMBÄR)

	Brummbär – early model
Combat weight:	31.1 tons
Crew:	5
Dimensions in inches (length, width, height)	230/113/99 without skirts; 132 width with skirts
Engine:	Maybach HL 120 TRM V12 gas, water-cooled, 11,870 cc, 300 hp
Power/weight ratio:	9.6 hp/ton
Max. speed:	24 mph road, 10 mph cross-country
Range:	110 miles road, 75 miles cross-country
Armament:	5.9 in StuH 43 L/12
Armor:	0.4–3.9 in; skirts 0.2 in
Fording depth:	47 in

An early version of the Sturmpanzer IV Brummbär.

This vehicle was developed jointly by Alkett and Krupp in mid-1942. Alkett manufactured the superstructure while Krupp's role was to modify its Panzer IV chassis. Like the StuG III, the Brummbär was intended mainly for urban combat and use against fortifications. It was based on the Panzer IV chassis and mounted a 5.9 inch (15 cm) assault howitzer set in a heavily armored superstructure (up to 3.9 inches (100 mm) thick at the front and 2 inches (50 mm) at the sides). At first this was its only armament but combat experience revealed that a machine gun was essential against infantry attack. Subsequent vehicles were therefore equipped with an MG 34 on a ball mount. Skirts and Zimmerit coating were standard. The Panzer IV chassis was put under excessive strain by the vehicle's considerable weight, however. The first vehicles were delivered in 1943 to the 216th Sturmpanzer Battalion and 17 were lost at Kursk during Operation Citadel in July 1943. By the end of 1944 around 300 Sturmpanzer IVs had been built.

JAGDPANZER IV TANK DESTROYER SD.KFZ. 162

A Jagdpanzer IV/70 of the 116th Panzer Division, Wesel, spring 1945.

	Jagdpanzer IV Ausf. F
Combat weight:	26.7 tons
Crew:	4–5
Dimensions in inches (length, width, height):	232/114/73; 270/125/73 with barrel and skirts
Engine:	Maybach HL 120 TRM V12 gas, water-cooled, 11,870 cc, 300 hp
Power/weight ratio:	11.3 hp/ton
Max. speed:	24 mph road, 10 mph cross-country
Range:	120 miles road, 80 miles cross-country
Armament:	3 in Pak L/48 anti-tank gun, 1 x 0.3 in MG 34 machine gun
Armor:	0.4–3.1 in; skirts 0.2 in
Fording depth:	39 in

From 1941, assault guns started being used increasingly as tank destroyers, a role for which they had not been intended. Even though they were very low-slung, their angular superstructures presented ample opportunities to enemy gunners. In 1943, Vomag in Plauen began designing a purpose-built tank destroyer to replace the StuG III. The new vehicle was to have as low a silhouette as possible as well as a ballistically optimized shape. Hitler was shown a wooden model in May 1943 and was greatly impressed by the vehicle's low profile. The first production vehicles left the factory five months later.

The Jagdpanzer IV was a modified StuG IV with sloping, shot-deflecting sides and a 3 inch (7.5 cm) Pak L/48 with "pig's head" mantlet. The original 3.1 inch (80 mm)-thick frontal armor had to be reduced to 2.4 inches (60 mm) to improve handling (this version was named the Panzer 39).

Another variant, the Jagdpanzer IV/70 (V) was equipped with the 3 inch (7.5 cm) Pak L/70 (similar to the Panther's main armament). This gun possessed enormous penetrating power but also made the vehicle very top-heavy and therefore hard to steer. As a result it acquired the nickname "Guderian's Duck." Alkett also manufactured a Jagdpanzer IV with the L/70 gun. This was a stopgap solution and unlike the Vomag-produced vehicles, its superstructure looked improvised, as if it had simply been dropped onto the lower half. This is because unmodified Panzer IV chassis were used. This vehicle was delivered to the Wehrmacht as the Jagdpanzer IV/70 (A). By the time production ceased, around 1,800 Jagdpanzer IVs had been built.

The Jagdpanzer IV/70 seen from above.

Prototype of the Jagdpanzer IV/70 (A).

JAGDPANZER 38(T) TANK DESTROYER (HETZER)

Although the Marder tank destroyers were very successful, they also had a number of disadvantages such as their extremely thin frontal and side armor and complete lack of armor plating on top and behind, which made them highly vulnerable to artillery and air attack. General Guderian is credited with the idea of developing a tank destroyer based on the Panzer 38(t) that would be completely enclosed like the assault guns. The Army Ordnance Department awarded contracts for the development of such a vehicle in May 1943. A modified version of the 3 inch (7.5 cm) Pak 39 L/48 was chosen to be the main armament. This version had an advanced recoil brake that rendered a muzzle brake superfluous. In order to cope better with the weight of the vehicle, which had increased to 17-plus tons (16,000 kg), broader, stronger tracks were fitted and every last bit of power squeezed out of what was originally a 125 hp engine. To secure the vehicle against infantry attack, a remote-controlled machine gun, which could swivel through 360°, was mounted on the roof. The Hetzer's shape was outstanding from a ballistics point of view as the all-round sloping sides ensured maximum shot deflection. The dimensions of the tank were also extremely advantageous—to the chagrin of its crews, who literally had to squeeze themselves into it. The first vehicles were delivered in May 1944. Initially BMM was

the sole manufacturer but in September 1944 it was joined by Škoda.

The Hetzer was one of the best German tank destroyers of the war. It was small and therefore easy to conceal and benefited from good firepower and armor. In actual fact the Hetzer was supposed to replace the Marder but due to production delays and high losses, this objective was never achieved. On April 1, 1945, 627 Hetzers were still operational, making it Germany's most important armored vehicle after the StuG III during the final months of the war. Even during the very last month of the

Combat weight:	17.6 tons
Crew:	4
Dimensions in inches (length, width, height):	192/104/5; length with barrel: 247
Engine:	Praga inline 6-cylinder gas, water-cooled, 7,754 cc, 160 hp
Power/weight ratio:	9.0 hp/ton
Max. speed:	26 mph road
Range:	160 miles road, 105 miles cross-country
Armament:	3 in Pak 39 L/48 anti-tank gun, 1 x 0.3 in MG 42 machine gun
Armor:	0.3–2.4 in
Fording depth:	39 in

A Hetzer with an independent tank destroyer unit, Western Front, winter 1944–45.

war, 121 Hetzers were built and delivered to the army and a few were even delivered to the Hungarian Army. In total, 1,500 vehicles were manufactured including flamethrower and recovery variants. After the war, Škoda continued

making Hetzers for the Czech Army. Switzerland bought 158 vehicles, which remained in service under the name G13 until 1970.

The front view shows how far to the right of center the main 3 inch (7.5 cm) gun was set.

Rear view of the same vehicle. Both pictures taken at the BMM works, late summer 1944.

WESPE MOTORIZED HOWITZER SD.KFZ.124

Wespe motorized howitzer, 10th Panzer Division ("Frundsberg"), France, 1944.

Combat weight:	13 tons
Crew:	5
Dimensions in inches (length, width, height):	189/90/91
Engine:	Maybach HL 62 TRM inline 6-cylinder gas, water-cooled, 6,190 cc, 140 hp
Power/weight ratio:	11.8 hp/ton
Max. speed:	26 mph road
Range:	85 miles road, 55 miles cross-country
Armament:	4.1 in light FH 18/2 L/28, 1 x 0.3 in MG 34 or 42 machine gun
Armor:	0.4–0.8 in
Fording depth:	31 in

The German Blitzkrieg strategy was predicated upon rapid tank advances accompanied by artillery support. In order to provide this, the Wehrmacht developed a series of self-propelled artillery guns that proved successful to differing degrees. One of the best known of these guns, and the one produced in the greatest numbers, was the Wespe, which was based on the chassis of the Panzer II and mounted a 4.1 inch (10.5 cm) light field howitzer. Alkett, MAN, and Rheinmetall-Borsig began work on its development in 1942 and soon after it went into full-scale production at the Famo factory in Warsaw. The Wespe was based on new as well as refitted Panzer II chassis. Famo built 683 of these guns up to 1944. The Wespe's ammunition storage capacity was very small (40 rounds) and so a further 158 weaponless ammunition carriers were built that were capable of carrying a further 90 rounds. If a Wespe were lost, its howitzer could be removed and mounted onto an ammunition carrier, creating a "new" Wespe. The armor plating of the Wespe's superstructure was only 0.4 inches (10–12 mm) thick and open-topped while its hull armor was between 0.6 inches (15 mm) and 0.8 inches (20 mm) thick. As the vehicle was not generally deployed directly on the front, this was not normally a problem. The Wespe was used by the armored artillery battalions of the Panzer and mechanized infantry divisions. Units generally consisted of two Wespe batteries made up of six Wespe self-propelled guns and an ammunition carrier.

HUMMEL MOTORIZED HOWITZER SD.KFZ. 165

The strategy of mobile tank warfare pursued by the Wehrmacht during the early years of the war meant that the artillery had to be able to keep pace with the tank units. This led to the development of self-propelled guns based on more or less suitable chassis. Geschützwagen III/IV, based on the Panzer IV chassis, was an attempt to create a common base vehicle for a range of self-propelled artillery guns. The engine was moved forward in order to make room for a large fighting compartment at the rear. On top and at the rear the vehicle's armor was poor, but it should be remembered that the designs were completed at a time when the Luftwaffe still possessed air superiority and attacks from enemy bombers were relatively uncommon. During the first few years of the war, troops sometimes even found open-topped vehicles an advantage because of the better all-round vision they afforded. The version of the Geschützwagen III/IV with the heavy 18-caliber 5.9 inch (15 cm) field howitzer was named the "Hummel" (bumblebee). As it could only carry 18 rounds of spare ammunition, an unarmed ammunition transporter was also developed. The Hummel first saw action in mid-1943 on the Eastern Front and remained in service with the artillery battalions of the Panzer Division through to the end of the war. The Hummel proved extremely successful and 666 self-propelled howitzers and 150 ammunition transporters were built in total.

Combat weight:	25.9 tons
Crew:	6–7
Dimensions in inches (length, width, height):	244/116/116;
with barrel:	263
Engine:	Maybach HL 120 TRM V12 gas, water-cooled, 11,870 cc, 300 hp
Power/weight ratio:	11.6 hp/ton
Max. speed:	25 mph road, 12 mph cross-country
Range:	155 miles road, 100 miles cross-country
Armament:	5.9 in heavy FH 18 L/30, 1 x 0.3 in MG 34 machine gun
Armor:	0.4–0.8 in
Fording depth:	31 in

Hummel motorized howitzer with the artillery regiment of the Grossdeutschland Division, Eastern Front, 1944.

NASHORN TANK DESTROYER SD.KFZ. 164

The tremendously powerful 3.5 inch (8.8 cm) Pak 43 suffered from the major disadvantage of being highly immobile on the battlefield. Its weight of 4.4 tons (4,000 kg) meant that changes of position could only be effected with the help of a towing vehicle. The idea arose at a relatively early stage, therefore, of turning the weapon into a self-propelled unit. The vehicle onto which it was mounted was the Geschützwagen III/IV, a Panzer IV with the engine shifted to the front, which was intended as the basis for a range of artillery guns including the Hummel motorized howitzer. Alkett was contracted to develop a prototype in February 1942. Chassis and superstructure (493 units)

were manufactured by Deutsche Eisenwerke. Deliveries of the new vehicle, whose official designation was the "8.8 cm Pak 43 L/71 auf Fahrgestell Panzerkampfwagen III/IV(Sf)," started in November 1942. After the first few units had rolled off the production line, the main gun was substituted with the improved Pak 43/1. In February 1944, Hitler commanded that the name of all vehicles equipped with the Pak 43/1 be changed from "Hornisse" (hornet) to "Nashorn" (rhinoceros) because he thought the original sounded too harmless.

Although the vehicle was highly effective on the battlefield and was considered a successful design, it presented a number of disadvantages,

Combat weight:	26.5 tons
Crew:	4–5
Dimensions in inches (length, width, height):	244/116/116; with barrel: 332
Engine:	Maybach HL 120 TRM V12 gas, water-cooled, 11,870 cc, 300 hp
Power/weight ratio:	11.3 hp/ton
Max. speed:	25 mph road, 12 mph cross-country
Range:	155 miles road, 100 miles cross-country
Armament:	3.5 in Pak 43/1 L/71 anti-tank gun, 1 x 0.3 in MG 34 machine gun
Armor:	0.4–1.2 in
Fording depth:	31 in

among them its thin armor and high silhouette. Furthermore it was open to the top and rear and offered no protection against air or infantry attack. Units equipped with Nashorn tank destroyers nonetheless achieved astounding successes—especially when operating from well-prepared positions and when they were able to rely on the power and range of the Pak 43/1. There are reports of Nashorns hitting Soviet T-34s from a distance of almost a mile (1.6 km) with such force that the entire turret was torn from the hull. Nashorn tank destroyers remained in service right through to the end of the war. Shortly before hostilities ended, a Nashorn became the only German fighting vehicle to knock out a US M26 Pershing tank.

A Nashorn from an unknown unit, Eastern Front, March 1945.

Note the long-barreled 3.5 inch (8.8 cm) Pak 43/1, which gave the Nashorn enormous firepower.

112

FLAKPANZER IV ANTI-AIRCRAFT TANKS (MÖBELWAGEN, WIRBELWIND, AND OSTWIND)

	Flakpanzer IV Wirbelwind
Combat weight:	24.2 tons
Crew:	5
Dimensions in inches (length, width, height):	233/114/109
Engine:	Maybach HL 120 TRM/112 V12 gas, water-cooled, 11,870 cc, 310 hp
Power/weight ratio:	12.8 hp/ton
Max. speed:	25 mph road, 12 mph cross-country
Range:	110 miles road, 75 miles cross-country
Armament:	0.8 in Flak Vierling anti-aircraft gun, 1 x 0.3 in MG 34 machine gun
Armor:	Hull 0.4–3.1 in, turret 0.6 in all round
Fording depth:	31 in

A Wirbelwind Flakpanzer equipped with a quadruple 0.8 inch (2 cm) Vierling 38.

An Ostwind Flakpanzer IV.

A Flakpanzer I of the 614th Flak Battalion, Stalingrad, January 1943.

As air superiority increasingly slipped away from the Luftwaffe, another method had to be found of protecting the Panzer force from air attack. While élite troops such as the Waffen-SS, Grossdeutschland Division and others already had self-propelled flak guns at their disposal during the early years of the war, these were mostly part-armored or unarmored vehicles. The first, highly provisional, anti-aircraft tanks (based on the Panzer I) had appeared shortly after the Battle of France, albeit without all-round protection. They took the form of a 0.8 inch (2 cm) Flak 38 gun mounted on the hull of a withdrawn Panzer I. 24 of these vehicles were built and proved successful in spite of appearances. The last of them were lost at the Battle of Stalingrad. Further conversions were not undertaken until October 1943, when Hitler approved the

conversion of 150 Panzer 38(t)s into anti-aircraft tanks with a 2 cm Flak 38. It soon transpired that their firepower was inadequate. In order to accommodate a 0.8 inch (2 cm) Flak Vierling (quadruple) or 1.5 inch (3.7 cm) Flak, a bigger chassis was needed and attention turned to the Panzer IV. The early prototypes were equipped with a 2 cm Vierling but the version that went into production, in March 1944, had a 1.5 inch (3.7 cm) Flak 43 (240 units). The anti-aircraft gun was mounted on the hull of the tank and surrounded by high side walls made of 0.8-inch (20-mm)-thick steel which had to be folded down when in operation, thereby exposing the crew to enemy fire. The "Wirbelwind" was an improved version with a 0.8 inch (2 cm) Vierling in a turret made of 0.6 inch (16 mm) plates. For reasons of fire control, however, the turret was left open at the

top. 105 Wirbelwinds were created from damaged Panzer IVs. The version named "Ostwind" mounted a 1.5 inch (3.7 cm) Flak 43 in a turret similar to that of the Wirbelwind. Forty-three of these were obtained through conversion. During the last few months of the war a number of other prototypes and variants were developed. These included an Ostwind variant with the 1.5 inch (3.7 cm) Zwilling (double) anti-aircraft gun, a model named the "Kugelblitz" (lightning) based on the Panzer IV or Panzer 38(t) which mounted a 1.2 inch (3 cm) Flak Zwilling 103/38 in a fully enclosed turret and the "Zerstörer 45" which was equipped with a 3 cm Flak Vierling 103/38 in a Wirbelwind turret. The armaments ranged from a 0.8 inch (2 cm) Flak Vierling 151/20 via a 1.5 inch (3.7 cm) Flak Zwilling 44 to a 2.2 inch (5.5 cm) Zwilling.

AB 40 AND 41 ARMORED SCOUT CARS

The AB 40 and 41 armored cars came into being as the result of an invitation for tenders to build an armored vehicle that could be used both by the Italian police in the African colonies and by the Italian cavalry units. The requirements were: four-wheel drive and steering, steering wheels fore and aft to enable the vehicle to be driven in both directions, and good cross-country capability. It was initially intended that the vehicle should carry a machine gun only. All these criteria were met by the AB 40, which appeared in mid-1940. After a small number of units had rolled off the production line, experiments were conducted with a new turret and a 0.8 inch (2 cm) cannon in place of the twin 0.3 inch (8 mm) machine guns in order to increase firepower. These experiments proved successful and production was switched to the new version, which was named the AB41. Many AB 40s were converted. This armored car was a high-performance

*An Autoblinda AB 41
in North Africa.*

Combat weight:	8.3 tons
Crew:	4
Dimensions in inches (length, width, height):	205/76/98
Engine:	SPA inline 6-cylinder gas, water-cooled, 4,995 cc, 88 hp
Power/weight ratio:	10.6 hp/ton
Max. speed:	48 mph road
Range:	250 miles road
Armament:	0.8 in Breda M 35 cannon, 2 x 0.3 in Breda machine guns
Armor:	hull: 0.2–3.5 in; turret: max. 0.7 in
Fording depth:	24 in

vehicle that was very advanced for its day but plagued by steering problems that were never rectified. A number of vehicles also had an anti-aircraft machine gun mounted on the turret. A special conversion kit enabled the AB 41 to travel on rails, a feature used in the Balkans. The AB 41 was also employed extensively by

Italian troops in North Africa. A command and reconnaissance version was produced in small numbers. Models AB 42 and 43 had a new, flatter turret and L/32 cannon but had only been produced in small numbers by the time Italy surrendered in September 1943. The Wehrmacht also used captured vehicles of this type.

LIGHT TANKS CV 33 AND CV 35

	CV 33
Combat weight:	3.8 tons
Crew:	2
Dimensions in inches (length, width, height):	124/55/50
Engine:	SPA CV 3 inline 4-cylinder gas, water-cooled, 43 hp
Power/weight ratio:	11.3 hp/ton
Max. speed:	26 mph road
Range:	80 miles road
Armament:	0.3 in Fiat M18/36 twin MG
Armor:	0.2–0.5 in

A CV 33 of the 67th Bersaglieri Regiment, North Africa, 1940.

During the late 1920s and early 1930s, the two-man light tank made by British firm Carden-Loyd had been extremely popular due to its reasonable price. Italy also acquired two Carden-Loyd Mk VIs, along with the rights to manufacture them under license. Following a number of alterations, the outcome was the CV 33. Series I was equipped with a water-cooled 0.2 inch (6.5 mm) machine gun that proved so

catastrophic that it was soon replaced by a 3.5 inch (88 mm) Fiat 18/35 twin machine gun (Series II). Other changes subsequently made included modifications to the superstructure and upgrading to a 0.5 inch (13.2 mm) machine gun. This new version was named the CV 35. CV 33s and 35s were used in the Spanish Civil War and later in Greece, Africa, and the Soviet Union and turned into death traps for their crews

wherever they came up against serious opposition. Although this had already become apparent in Spain, the vehicles were only withdrawn after the disastrous experiences in Russia. After 1943 the Wehrmacht also deployed a number of captured vehicles of this type.

TANK M 13/40

An Ansaldo-FIAT M13/40.

	M13/40
Combat weight:	15.4 tons
Crew:	4
Dimensions in inches (length, width, height):	194/87/94
Engine:	SPA 8 TM 40 V8 diesel, water-cooled, 125 hp
Power/weight ratio:	8.0 hp/ton
Max. speed:	20 mph road
Range:	125 miles road
Armament:	1.9 in L/32 cannon in turret, 1 x coaxial 0.3 in MG, 1 x 0.3 in twin MG at the front of the hull
Armor:	0.2–1.7 in, turret: max. 0.7 in
Fording depth:	no details

The M13/40 was Italy's main tank of the Second World War. Its predecessor, the M 11/39, failed to convince due to its cumbersome shape, deficient running gear and 1.5 inch (3.7 cm) cannon mounted in the hull rather than in the turret. Fewer than 100 M11/39s were built and nearly all of them were lost in North Africa. The M13/40 had better running gear, mounted a powerful 1.9 inch (4.7 cm) cannon based on Germany's 1.9 inch (4.7 cm) Pak and had better armor. All in all it was in no way inferior to other countries' tanks of the same period but neither could it be called an outstanding vehicle. In 1941 the M13/40's

gun was capable of penetrating the armor of most British tanks and had a greater range than the British 2-pounder. The Commonwealth troops in North Africa redeployed every M 13/40 they conquered and had at times over 100 vehicles at their disposal. Two further tanks featuring minor changes were based on the same chassis: the M 14/41

was equipped with a more powerful engine capable of producing 145 hp and the M15/42 was given thicker armor. Around 2,000 of these tanks were built as well as a series of assault guns based on the same chassis.

American GIs examine a captured M 13/40 in Tunisia in 1943. Note the sandbags positioned in front of the driver, intended to provide additional protection.

ASSAULT GUNS M 40 DA 75/18, 75/34, AND 105/25

Semovente da 75/18	
Combat weight:	18.7 tons
Crew:	4
Dimensions in inches (length, width, height):	194/87/71
Engine:	SPA 8 TMA 40 V8 diesel, water-cooled, 145 hp
Power/weight ratio:	7.7 hp/ton
Max. speed:	19 mph road
Range:	125 miles road
Armament:	3 in L/18 cannon, 1 x 0.2 in MG
Armor:	0.2–2.8 in

Italy built a series of assault guns ("semovente") inspired by Germany's StuG III and based on the chassis of the M 13–15 vehicles. The prototype of the first version, based on the chassis of the M 13/40 with a 3 inch (7.5 cm) L/18 cannon mounted in a fixed superstructure, was unveiled in February 1941. This assault gun first saw combat in North Africa in 1942 and proved extremely successful; 222 of them were built. Version 75/34, based on the M 15/42 and mounting a 3 inch (7.5 cm) L/34 cannon, appeared at the end of 1942 but did not go into large-scale production until April 1943. By the time of the ceasefire on September 8, 1943, 192 of them had been built. The most powerful version, some 250 of which were made, was the 105/25, a 4.1 inch (10.5 cm) howitzer mounted on a widened M 15/42 chassis. After Italy's surrender in September 1943, German troops took possession of all the semovente-type guns they could lay their hands on and—as the factory was located within the area they controlled—ensured that production continued under the name Sturmgeschütz M 43/05/25.

Semovente M 40 75/18.

SELF-PROPELLED GUN M 41 DA 90/53

These Italian self-propelled guns came into being as a result of experiences gained on the Eastern Front. The emergence of the T-34 and KV-1 pressed home the need for a mobile anti-tank weapon with good penetrating power. Italy's best available gun was the 3.5 inch (9 cm) L/53 anti-aircraft gun. Ansaldo therefore modified the M 14/41 tank, shifting the engine to the middle and removing the upper hull. The excellent 3.5 inch (9 cm) gun was mounted on the back of the vehicle behind a large shield. The first prototype was ready by March 5, 1942 and series production began the following month although

Assault gun M 41 90/53.

Combat weight:	18.5 tons
Crew:	4
Dimensions in inches (length, width, height):	208/89/89
Engine:	SPA 15 TM 41 V8 diesel, water-cooled, 145 hp
Power/weight ratio:	7.8 hp/ton
Max. speed:	22 mph road
Range:	125 miles road
Armament:	3.5 in L/53 gun, 1 x 0.2 in MG
Armor:	0.2–1.2 in

this comprised only 30 guns. As the vehicle could only carry six rounds of spare ammunition, it had to be accompanied in the field by special ammunition transporters. Its biggest drawback, however, was that there was no protection for the crew, who simply had to stand behind the vehicle.

TYPE 2 KA-MI

Type 2 Ka-Mi.

Combat weight (with pontoons):	12.5 tons
Crew:	4–5
Dimensions in inches (length, width, height):	292/110/92
Engine:	Mitsubishi inline 6-cylinder diesel, air-cooled, 120 hp
Power/weight ratio:	9.6 hp/ton
Max. speed:	23 mph road 6 mph water
Range:	125 miles road, 60 water
Armament:	1.5 in Type 94 cannon, 2 x 0.3 in MG
Armor:	0.4–0.5 in
Fording depth:	amphibious

The Japanese army started conducting experiments with amphibious tanks as early as 1928. In 1940 the program was taken over by the navy as the tanks were intended for use by the marines. A whole series of amphibious vehicles was developed, of which Type 2 was produced in the largest numbers. Entering service in 1942, Type 2 had many components in common with Type 95 but was equipped with a brand new watertight hull. Buoyancy was provided by two large pontoons attached to the front and rear which were discarded on dry land. In the water the vehicle was powered by two propellers and steered by two rudders controlled from the turret by the tank commander. These vehicles were ideal for attacking small islands and atolls in the Pacific and were initially successful. When Japan was forced onto the defensive, however, and heavy US tanks were brought into play, these lightly armed and lightly armored tanks stood no chance. Japanese sources place the number of Type 2s built at 184.

TYPE 97 TE-KE

This light tank was unveiled in 1937 and went into large-scale production for the Imperial Japanese Army in 1938. The Te-Ke was initially intended as a reconnaissance vehicle but was also frequently used in an infantry support role, which was only successful if the enemy had few or ideally no anti-tank weapons. As with Type 95, the commander of this tank was the sole occupant of the turret and was overstretched as a result. In spite of these disadvantages, Type 97 was one of Japan's most important tanks and remained in service throughout the war. Although it was used successfully in China, it stood no chance against the US Army's M3s and M4s. It is interesting to note that US tanks switched during the course of the war from using anti-tank shells to using high explosive shells against Japanese fighting vehicles. Because of the tanks' very thin armor, anti-tank shells generally passed straight through them causing little damage unless they happened to hit a vital component or crew member. There was also an armored ammunition transporter (with armored trailer) based on the Type 97.

Combat weight:	5.2 tons
Crew:	2
Dimensions in inches (length, width, height):	145/71/70
Engine:	Ikega inline 4-cylinder diesel, air-cooled, 65 hp
Power/weight ratio:	12.4 hp/ton
Max. speed:	26 mph road
Range:	155 miles road
Armament:	1.5 in Type 94 cannon or 1 x 0.3 in MG in turret
Armor:	0.2–0.6 in

Type 97 Te-Ke.

TYPE 95 HA-GO

Combat weight:	8.1 tons
Crew:	3
Dimensions in inches (length, width, height):	172/81/86
Engine:	Mitsubishi inline 6-cylinder diesel, air-cooled, 120 hp
Power/weight ratio:	14.7 hp/ton
Max. speed:	28 mph road
Range:	155 miles road
Armament:	1.5 in Type 94 cannon, 1 x 0.2 in MG or 2 x 0.3 in MG
Armor:	0.23–0.5 in

Type 95 Ha-Go.

The prototype of this light tank was built by Mitsubishi in 1934. At that time it was at least as good as the tanks of any other country but by the outbreak of war in December 1941 it was completely out of date. The driver and machine gunner sat at the front of the hull while the tank commander occupied the turret alone. He had to command the vehicle and aim, load, and fire the main gun. In a later model he also had to operate a turret machine gun, which was asking too much even of the most capable tank commanders. Type 95 tanks first saw combat in the war against China and remained in service throughout the Second World War. The Japanese tactic was to use them solely for infantry support and from the end of 1941 they were deployed mostly in small groups on the numerous occupied islands of the Pacific. Their armor only provided protection against hand-held weapons, with the result that they were an easy target for Allied anti-tank guns and fighting vehicles. On the plus side, they were agile and reliable. By 1945, 2,375 of these tanks had been built, making Type 95 Japan's most important tank of the war.

Type 95s of the 16th Tank Regiment on Marcus Island (US Navy).

A Type 95 Ha-Go captured by the US marines on Guam.

TYPE 89B OTSU

Although not much heavier and barely any larger than Type 95, Type 89B qualified as a medium tank because of its 2.2 inch (5.7 cm) gun. The design of its predecessor, the Type 89, introduced in 1929, had been based on imported British Vickers Mark C tanks. When Type 89's gasoline engine was replaced by a Mitsubishi diesel engine in 1934, this new version was named Type 89B. In this form the vehicle became Japan's standard medium tank during the late 1930s and was still in service in 1941–42. By this time, though, it was completely out of date. Like all Japanese tanks, Type 89B had been intended merely to provide infantry

Type 89 Otsu.

Combat weight:	12.7 tons
Crew:	4
Dimensions in inches (length, width, height):	169/85/87
Engine:	Mitsubishi inline 6-cylinder diesel, air-cooled, 120 hp
Power/weight ratio:	9.5 hp/ton
Max. speed:	17 mph road
Range:	125 miles road
Armament:	2.2 in Type 90 cannon, 2 x 0.2 in MG
Armor:	0.4–0.7 in

support but even this was only possible against poorly equipped opponents. Its thin armor made it extremely vulnerable and in addition it was slow and not especially maneuverable. After 1942, Type 89B tanks were no longer used at the front. Around 400 Type 89 and 89B tanks were built.

TYPE 97 CHI-HA

Combat weight:	16.5 tons
Crew:	4
Dimensions in inches (length, width, height):	217/92/88
Engine:	Mitsubishi V12 diesel, air-cooled, 170 hp
Power/weight ratio:	10.2 hp/ton
Max. speed:	24 mph road
Range:	130 miles road
Armament:	2.2 in Type 90 cannon, 2 x 0.3 in MG
Armor:	0.3–1.0 in

The Type 97 Chi-Ha was the Japanese Army's standard medium tank during the Second World War. Its predecessor, Type 89, had shown as early as 1936 that it was no longer a match for enemy tanks. The armaments industry was therefore invited to draw up proposals for a successor. Mitsubishi won the contract and its tank went into large-scale production (in which other companies were later involved) in 1938. The driver and machine gunner sat at the front of the hull while the main gunner and tank commander occupied the turret. The running gear was well designed and performed respectably. Although more modern than other Japanese tanks, Type 97, like its predecessors, was intended primarily for an infantry support role. Its short-barreled 2.2 inch (5.7 cm) cannon was not particularly effective against tanks and its armor was still too thin, a fact that came to light during the 1939 border incidents with Soviet troops in Manchuria. A special version of the Type 97 Shinhoto Chi-Ha was therefore developed specifically for an anti-tank role. This variant had a new turret equipped with a long 1.9 inch (4.7 cm) gun with good penetrating power but did not enter service until 1942. Also based on Type 97 were recovery and bridgelaying tanks as well as self-propelled guns mounting weapons of up to 15 cm cal. Taking into account all the variants, 2,208 Type 97s were built.

Type 97 Shinhoto Chi-Ha with the long 1.9 inch (4.7 cm) cannon.

TK3 TANKETTE

In 1929 Poland bought a British Carden-Loyd Mk. IV tank and used it to develop a series of "tankettes" or light tanks. These vehicles, which generally had a crew of two, were small, maneuverable, and normally armed with no more than a machine gun. Following various open-topped versions such as the TK1 and TK2, production began in 1931 of a fully enclosed model, the TK3, of which around 300 were made. When it became clear in 1939 that this machine was vastly inferior to most other tanks, attempts were made to improve its firepower. Shortly before

Combat weight:	2.7 tons
Crew:	2
Dimensions in inches (length, width, height):	102/70/52
Engine:	Ford Model A, inline 4-cylinder, water-cooled, 40 hp
Power/weight ratio:	14.9 hp/ton
Max. speed:	28 mph road
Range:	125 miles road
Armament:	1 x 0.3 in MG
Armor:	0.2 in–0.4 in
Fording depth:	16 in

A Polish TK3.

the war a number of vehicles were upgraded to a 5 inch (2 cm) anti-tank gun but this did little to improve their chances against the Wehrmacht. All surviving TK3s were re-equipped by the Wehrmacht with the French Hotchkiss 0.4 in (9 mm) M/1914 and used for security duties.

7TP

Combat weight:	10.9 tons
Crew:	3
Dimensions in inches (length, width, height):	198/95/85
Engine:	Saurer diesel, air-cooled, 110 hp
Power/weight ratio:	10 hp/ton
Max. speed:	20 mph
Range:	100 miles road, 75 miles cross-country
Armament:	1.5 in Bofors cannon, 1 x 0.3 in MG
Armor:	0.2–0.7 in (some up to 1.6 in)
Fording depth:	28 in

The 7TP was a match for German tanks in 1939 but was defeated by their superior numbers.

At the beginning of the 1930s, Poland bought 50 Vickers 6-tonners, in its day a highly modern and successful tank, from British armaments manufacturer Vickers-Armstrong. From this it developed the 7TP, 169 of which were built between 1934 and 1939. The 7TP was the first European tank to be given a diesel engine and was a respectable enough machine for its day. The first versions (7TP dw) had twin turrets each equipped with a 0.3 inch (7.92 mm) Browning machine gun while later models had a single turret with a Swedish 1.5 inch (3.7 cm) Bofors cannon and coaxial 0.3 inch (7.92 mm) machine gun. Unusual for the time was not only the diesel engine but also the fact that most of the tanks were equipped with radio. Shortly before the outbreak of war a more heavily armored version was designed (up to 1.6 inches/40 mm at the front) but it did not progress beyond prototype stage. The 7TP fought bravely against the German invaders and was only overwhelmed by the Wehrmacht's superior numbers. The Wehrmacht used the surviving vehicles as training vehicles and for security duties under the designation Kampfpanzer 7TP(p).

PANHARD AMD 178 ARMORED CAR

In 1940, France's main armored vehicle was the Panhard AMD 178. Work began on its design in the mid-1930s and it was a first-class vehicle in its day. Although its armor was riveted, which meant that in the event of a hit, rivets would fly through the fighting compartment like bullets, the AMD 178 had many interesting and innovative features, for example a second, rear-facing driver who could take control in the event of danger in order to avoid the vehicle having to turn round. The engine was an unusual two-stroke model with rotary rather than poppet valves. In addition to a version armed with a 1 inch (2.5 cm) cannon, there was also an unarmed radio car and a version armed with only 0.3 inch

(7.5 mm) twin machine guns. Around 300 AMD 178s had been built by the time of France's defeat. The Wehrmacht re-equipped 190 or so with German radios and in some cases frame antennae for use as reconnaissance vehicles with the designation P 204(f). Others were fitted with railroad wheels for use as rail patrol vehicles. A few AMD 178s escaped capture by the enemy and were taken to the unoccupied zone, but when the Wehrmacht also occupied Vichy France, they were taken over directly by the Wehrmacht. The German Army

Panhard AMD 178.

valued the Panhard highly and regarded it as a very worthwhile addition to its reconnaissance units. Following liberation in 1944, production of the AMD 178 was immediately resumed by Panhard.

Combat weight:	9.3 tons
Crew:	4
Dimensions in inches (length, width, height):	189/79/90
Engine:	Panhard inline 4-cylinder gas, water-cooled, 6,330 cc, 105 hp
Power/weight ratio:	11.2 hp/ton
Max. speed:	45 mph road
Range:	205 miles road, 75 miles cross-country
Armament:	1 in cannon, 1 x 0.3 in MG
Armor:	7–20 mm
Fording depth:	24 in

RENAULT UE CHENILLETTE

The Renault UE was an armored supply vehicle. During the early 1930s the French army pursued a vigorous policy of mechanization which included armored vehicles to supply troops at the front. Renault took the Carden-Loyd running gear as the starting point for the UE, which went into large-scale production in 1931. The two-man crew sat next to each other under a hemispherical head guard with observation slits which could be

folded away. The engine was positioned between the driver and co-driver. At the rear was a tilting loading platform that enabled the cargo to be unloaded without the crew having to leave the vehicle. Renault also developed an armored tracked trailer that could also run on wheels. UE supply tractors were sometimes used to tow light anti-tank and anti-aircraft guns but were generally unarmed themselves. The Wehrmacht captured around 1,200 of these vehicles and used some of them as supply vehicles and towing machines (for the

1.5 inch/3.7 cm Pak, for example) but also turned a number of them into self-propelled guns and weapon carriers. With the 1.5 inch (3.7 cm) Pak mounted on the vehicle, the only protection available to the gunner was the gun shield. Many other vehicles were converted for security duties through the addition of a machine gun. In 1944, Rommel ordered the remaining UE supply tractors to be fitted with platforms for cal. 28 or 12.6 inch (32 cm) grenade launchers positioned on the sides of the vehicle or mounted on the hull.

Renault UE Chenillette.

Empty weight:	3 tons
Crew:	2
Useful load:	880 lb
Trailer load:	1,102 lb
Dimensions in inches (length, width, height):	106/67/41
Engine:	Renault inline 4-cylinder gas, water-cooled, 2,120 cc, 38 hp
Max. speed:	21 mph road
Range:	80 miles road, 35 miles cross-country
Armament:	see text
Armor:	0.4 in all round
Fording depth:	16 inches

LORRAINE 37 L

Empty weight:	6.2 tons
Crew:	2
Useful load:	1,786 lb
Trailer load:	1,764 lb
Dimensions in inches (length, width, height):	165/62/49
Engine:	Delahaye 135 inline 6-cylinder gas, water-cooled, 3556cc, 70 hp
Max. speed:	22 mph road
Range:	85 miles road
Armament:	see text
Armor:	0.2–0.4 in
Fording depth:	28 in

The crew of the 37 L sat at the front, the engine compartment was located in the middle, and at the rear there was a relatively large load area. As with the UE, the vehicle could be unloaded without the crew having to leave it. The 37 L also had an armored trailer that could be used for transporting fuel. By the time of France's defeat, 432 of the 37 Ls had been built. The Wehrmacht took over some 300 of them, quickly realizing that their rear load area and centrally positioned engine made them ideal for conversion into self-propelled guns, first with the 3 inch (7.5 cm) Pak 40 (see p.78) and later with the 4.1 inch (10.5 cm) and 5.9 inch (15 cm) howitzers. Although these conversions strained the 37 L's chassis to its limits, its basic construction was so solid that these self-propelled guns were still highly successful.

A Lorraine 37 tracked tractor with armored trailer.

This vehicle went into production in 1937 as a successor to the Renault UE. By 1940 it had still by no means replaced its predecessor in the supply vehicle role, however.

RENAULT FT-17

In 1917, after France's first tanks had failed to deliver the anticipated results, Renault unveiled a new light tank whose design was to become the model for all later armored vehicles. The driver sat at the front of the hull, the turret and commander were located in the middle, and the engine compartment was at the back. The FT-17 also had the honor of being the first tank whose main armament was housed in a turret with 360° traverse. Despite these features it was a child of its time and essentially just an armor-plated box and feeble engine mounted on an underdeveloped chassis. In 1918, however (by which time some 3,000 units had been built by Renault and a number of other manufacturers), it was one of the best tanks around and production continued after the war in order to satisfy the demand from abroad. Numerous countries bought the FT-17 after 1918 and used it to build up tank divisions. Accordingly there was a wide range of variants from models mounting a 3 inch (7.5 cm) anti-tank gun to radio vehicles, bridgelaying tanks, and searchlight tanks. In France there were still 2,500 FT-17s in service as late as May 1940, although only 500 were with front-line

Combat weight:	7.7 tons
Crew:	2
Dimensions in inches (length, width, height):	161/68/91
Engine:	Renault inline 4-cylinder gas, water-cooled, 4,500 cc, 35 hp
Power/weight ratio:	4.5 hp/ton
Max. speed:	5 mph road
Range:	25 miles road
Armament:	1.5 in cannon or 2 x 0.3 in MG (numerous variants)
Armor:	0.2–0.8 in
Fording depth:	20 in

units. By this time, however, the Renaults were completely antiquated and stood no chance against the Wehrmacht's tanks. A large number of captured tanks were redesignated 17/18 R(f) and used by the Germans for security duties. A number of FT-17 turrets were also incorporated into German fortifications on the Atlantic coast. The deployment of FT-17s by the Germans during the Battle of Paris in 1944 should probably be seen as an act of desperation.

An F-17 captured by the Wehrmacht.

RENAULT R-35

R-35.

In 1934 the French Army called upon a number of manufacturers to develop a successor to the Renault FT-17. The winning design was Renault's R-35 and in May 1935 an order was placed for 300 vehicles. By June 1940 a total of 1,600 R-35s had been built. Like its predecessor the FT-17, the R-35 was intended mainly to provide infantry support. The hull was reasonably well armored for its day (up to 40 mm at the front) and constructed of cast sections screwed together. The driver sat at the front and the commander occupied the turret by himself. The main armament, a short 1.5 inch (3.7 cm) M 1918 cannon, was almost completely ineffectual against tanks. A number of R-35s were therefore equipped with the longer-barreled 1.5 inch (3.7 cm) L/33. Although the running gear was thoroughly efficient, the poor power/weight ratio (just 7.6 hp/ton) meant the tank was too slow. The first vehicles lacked radio. A variant named the AMX-40 or R-40 boasted new running gear with 12 small road wheels and tracks of the same type as Char B but it was only produced in small numbers. It is interesting to note that the turret of the R-35 was identical to that of the H-35/38/39. The R-35 was well suited to its role as an infantry support vehicle but by 1940 this whole strategy was out of date. Large numbers of R-35s were overwhelmed and captured by the German forces. The approximately 800 captured vehicles were designated Pz.Kpfw. 35 R(f) and used for security duties, fighting partisans, as towing machines, and as the basis for a range of self-propelled guns.

Combat weight:	10.8 tons
Crew:	2
Dimensions in inches (length, width, height):	165/73/83
Engine:	Renault inline 4-cylinder gas, water-cooled, 5,878 cc, 82 hp
Power/weight ratio:	7.6 hp/ton
Max. speed:	12 mph road
Range:	85 miles road
Armament:	1.5 in M 1918 L/21 cannon, 1 x 0.3 in coaxial MG
Armor:	max. 1.8 in
Fording depth:	20 in

HOTCHKISS H-35, H-38, AND H-39

The Hotchkiss H-35 came into being as a result of the same call for tenders for an infantry tank as that which led to the R-35. The H-35 was rejected by the infantry, however, as its mobility was even worse than the R-35's. Weighing 12.7 tons (11,500 kg), the H-35 had only a 75 hp engine. Ironically, the armored cavalry showed an interest in the tank and so it found a use after all. Its armor was 1.4 inches (34 mm) thick and it was equipped with the same gun as the R-35. The armor at the front of its turret was up to 1.8 inches (45 mm) thick. Around 400 H-35s were built before production switched to the H-38 in 1938. The new version had a modified hull and was equipped with a 120 hp engine producing a maximum speed of 23 mph. The version equipped with the longer-barreled 1.5 inch (3.7 cm) L/33 cannon, which was better suited for use against German tanks, was named the H-39. By June 1940 a total of 1,080 of the three versions had been built. The H-38 and H-39 (and with certain reservations the H-35) were good tanks for the time but the two-man crews greatly restricted their combat effectiveness. Tanks of this type were captured by the Wehrmacht in large numbers and designated Panzerkampfwagen 35, 38, and 39 H(f). In addition to the occupation forces in France, most Panzer units in the Balkans, Greece, and Norway also used Hotchkiss tanks.

	H-39
Combat weight:	13.3 tons
Crew:	2
Dimensions in inches (length, width, height):	166/73/84
Engine:	Hotchkiss inline 6-cylinder gas, water-cooled, 5,976 cc, 120 hp
Power/weight ratio:	7.6 hp/ton)
Max. speed:	23 mph road, 10 mph cross-country
Range:	93 miles road, 56 miles cross-country
Armament:	1.5 in SA 38 L/33 cannon 1 x 3 in coaxial MG
Armor:	max. 1.8 in
Fording depth:	20 in

An H-39 with 1.5 inch (3.7 cm) L/33 from an unknown unit.

SOMUA S-35

In 1940 the S-35 was undoubtedly France's best tank. A disadvantage, however, was its one-man turret, which considerably reduced its combat effectiveness. Another factor that prevented the S-35 from fulfilling its potential was the French doctrine of only using tanks in small groups for infantry support. At the beginning of the 1930s the French armored cavalry called for a new medium tank and in 1935 chose the prototype developed by Somua, which went into production the following year. The S-35 was a well-armored vehicle (hull max. 1.4 inch/35 mm); turret max 2.2 inch/55 mm) equipped with an outstanding gun, the 1.9 inch (4.7 cm) SA 35 L/32. Its hull consisted of three cast steel sections screwed together. The driver

In 1940 the S-35 was one of the best tanks in existence.

and radio operator sat together at the front of the hull while the commander occupied the turret. The engine was located at the rear. An improved version with a 220 hp engine was ready in 1940 but was only built in small numbers. The prototype of an assault gun with a 3 inch (7.5 cm) cannon mounted in its hull was developed the same year but France's defeat put an end to the experiment. At

the beginning of the Battle of France in May 1940 over 418 S-35s were in service with the French Army. The Wehrmacht adopted 297 of them, which were used mainly in secondary theatres of war.

	S-35
Combat weight:	21.5 tons
Crew:	3
Dimensions in inches (length, width, height):	212/83/103
Engine:	Somua V8 gas, water-cooled, 12,700 cc, 190 hp
Power/weight ratio:	8.8 hp/ton
Max. speed:	28 mph road, 23 mph cross-country
Range:	160 miles road, 80 miles cross-country
Armament:	1.9 in SA 35 L/32 cannon, 1 x 3 in coaxial MG
Armor:	max. 2.2 in
Fording depth:	28 in

CHAR B-1 BIS

Combat weight:	35.3 tons
Crew:	4
Dimensions in inches (length, width, height):	251/98/110
Engine:	Renault inline 6-cylinder gas, water-cooled, 16,500 cc, 300 hp
Power/weight ratio:	8.5 hp/ton
Max. speed:	16 mph road
Range:	85 miles road, 60 miles cross-country
Armament:	1 x 1.9 in SA 34 L/32 cannon (turret), 1 x 3 in coaxial MG 1 x 3 in cannon and 1 x 0.3 in MG in the hull
Armor:	max. 2.4 in
Fording depth:	30 in

The B-1 could withstand all German anti-tank weapons. Only the 3.5 inch (8.8 cm)   *anti-aircraft gun stood any chance at all against it.*

Char B-1 bis, whose armor was 2.4 in (60 mm) in places, could not be penetrated by the German 1.5 in (3.7 cm) Pak and even German tanks had to hope for lucky hits. Only the 3.5 inch (8.8 cm) anti-aircraft gun was capable of piercing its steel plates. In 1940 around 400 B-1s were

in service on the French side. The origins of the vehicle go back to the late 1920s when the French Army commissioned a heavy tank. Char B was equipped with a short-barreled 3 inch (7.5 cm) L/17 cannon and twin machine guns all mounted in the hull. The cannon had no horizontal traverse capability and had to be aimed by adjusting the position of the entire vehicle. To assist with this process, Char B was equipped with hydrostatic steering mechanism. Another set of twin machine guns was mounted in the turret. After just 35 vehicles, production switched to version B-1 bis, which was equipped with a

more powerful engine, thicker armor, and a turret-mounted 1.9 inch (4.7 cm) cannon in addition to the hull-mounted 3 inch (7.5 cm) gun. The Wehrmacht used large numbers of captured tanks of this type as training vehicles. In 1941–42 around 60 vehicles were converted to flamethrower tanks and deployed on the Eastern Front. The conversion involved replacing the hull-mounted 3 inch (7.5 cm) gun with a fire tube. The turret, with its 1.9 inch (4.7 cm) cannon, was retained. A tank containing enough flamethrower oil for up to 200 jets of flame was located at the rear of the hull.

DAIMLER DINGO SCOUT CAR

This Daimler armored car was designed by BSA in 1937 and went into production as the Daimler Dingo in 1939 following Daimler's takeover of BSA. The Dingo was a small, relatively lightly armored four-wheel drive vehicle whose only armament was a Bren machine gun mounted in front of the driver. It was, however, very fast and maneuverable and furthermore relatively inconspicuous thanks to its compact form—not bad qualities for a reconnaissance vehicle. The Dingo experienced considerable success with the armed forces of the Commonwealth countries and was manufactured in large numbers. By 1945, Daimler/BSA and Humber had built a total of 6,626 Dingos. In Canada the

Combat weight:	3.4 tons
Crew:	2
Dimensions in inches (length, width, height):	125/67/59
Engine:	Daimler inline 6-cylinder gas, water-cooled, 2,500 cc, 60 hp
Power/weight ratio:	17.9 hp/ton
Max. speed:	55 mph road
Range:	200 miles road
Armament:	1 x 0.3 in MG
Armor:	max. 1.2 in
Fording depth:	24 in

The Daimler Dingo's compact form is seen clearly here.

design was adopted and reworked by Ford, resulting in the Lynx, which was heavier and more strongly armored as well as being fitted with a more powerful Ford engine. Ford's Canadian production ran to some 3,255 vehicles. The Dingo remained in service until the 1950s. The Italians captured a few Dingos in North Africa and were so impressed that an almost identical copy, called the Lince, was produced by Lancia.

DAIMLER MK. 1 ARMORED CAR

There was no concealing the Daimler Mk. 1's kinship with the Dingo: both were short vehicles with an almost quadratic wheel arrangement and an angular superstructure. What was new in the Mk. 1 was its monocoque hull that helped to save weight and reduce the height of the car. The vehicle was equipped with a radio, servo-steering, and a pre-selector gearbox. The original plan was to mount either two 0.3 inch (7.7 mm) machine guns or one 0.5 inch (12.7 mm) and one 0.3 inch (7.7 mm) machine guns in the turret. Initial combat experience led to the fitting of a 2-pounder and a 0.3 inch (7.92 mm) machine gun on a parallel axis. The first vehicles were delivered to the British Army in 1941 and were used in all of the main theatres of the Second World War.

The Daimler Mk. 1 was a reliable and maneuverable vehicle and was popular as a result. During the final phase of the war, however, its 2-pounder gun was no longer adequate as it could only shoot anti-tank shells. Taking into account all the different variants, 2,700 vehicles were built. After the war the Daimler Mk. 1 continued to be used until the late 1950s.

Daimler Mk. 1

Combat weight:	8.4 tons
Crew:	3
Dimensions in inches (length, width, height):	156/96/88
Engine:	Daimler inline 6-cylinder gas, water-cooled, 4,500 cc, 95 hp
Power/weight ratio:	11.3 hp/ton
Max. speed:	50 mph road
Range:	205 miles road
Armament:	2-pounder cannon in turret, 1 x 0.3 in coaxial Besa MG
Armor:	max. 1.2 in
Fording depth:	24 in

HUMBER MK. 1 ARMORED CAR

In terms of numbers (5,600 built), the Humber was one of the British Army's most important fighting vehicles of the Second World War. Its design was derived from a vehicle built by Guy in 1939 based on the chassis of the Guy artillery tractor. 101 of these earlier vehicles had been built and most had been lost in France in 1940. As Guy was operating at full capacity producing tractors, Humber took over the design and developed it further. The Humber Mk.1 was based on the 4 x 4 chassis of Rootes' Karrier tractor and its superstructure was a modified version of the original design constructed of welded steel plate. The crew compartment was organized in the traditional way with the driver at the front, gunner and commander in the turret and the engine, separated from the crew by a fireproof bulkhead, at the rear. The armament was relatively light and so later models were

Humber Mk. 1.

upgunned to a 1.5 in (3.7 cm) cannon mounted in a three-man turret. An anti-aircraft version with a 0.3 inch (7.92 mm) quadruple machine gun entered service in 1943–44 but was unsuccessful due to its small caliber. Humber armored cars were used by nearly all the Commonwealth armies and a slightly modified version known as the "Fox" was

built in Canada by GM. Humber armored cars continued to be used by the British Army until the late 1950s.

Combat weight:	7.5 tons
Crew:	3
Dimensions in inches (length, width, height):	180/86/94
Engine:	Rootes inline 6-cylinder gas, water-cooled, 90 hp
Power/weight ratio:	11.9 hp/ton
Max. speed:	45 mph road
Range:	250 miles road
Armament:	1 x 0.6 in Besa MG in turret, 1 x 0.3 in coaxial Besa MG, 1 x 0.3 in Bren anti-aircraft MG
Armor:	max. 0.6 in
Fording depth:	30 in

UNIVERSAL CARRIER (BREN CARRIER)

Combat weight:	4.4 tons
Crew:	2 + 3
Dimensions in inches (length, width, height):	148/83/63
Engine:	Ford inline V8 gas, water-cooled, 85 hp
Power/weight ratio:	19.1 hp/ton
Max. speed:	32 mph road
Range:	160 miles road
Armament:	1 x 0.3 in Bren MG and/or A 0.6 in Boys anti-tank rifle
Armor:	0.2–0.5 in
Fording depth:	20 in

The Bren Carrier was used extensively by Allied troops.

These vehicles were a development of the Mk. VI Vickers/Carden-Loyd light tank of the late 1920s. The Universal Carrier was designed to transport a machine gun unit along with its weapons and ammunition safely through enemy infantry fire to its intended position. It was essentially an open-topped sheet-steel box with engine and running gear, and was extremely robust as a result. The driver sat at the front with a machine gunner by his side. The engine was

positioned behind them, in the middle of the vehicle, and to either side of the engine were the load areas (for soldiers, weapons, ammunition, or supplies). As the vehicle was frequently used to transport units with Bren machine guns, it came to be known popularly as the Bren Carrier. The first Universal Carrier entered service in 1939. The most common version had three road wheels on each side but there was also a larger version with four wheels on each side that could transport up to nine men. Universal Carriers proved to be extremely flexible. There were countless

adaptations and modifications, some of them executed by the field troops themselves. The Universal Carrier was built by numerous manufacturers throughout the Commonwealth and by 1945 over 84,000 (including all variants) had been produced. Many vehicles were also supplied to Russia under the Lend-Lease program. In 1940 the Wehrmacht captured large numbers of Universal Carriers in France and adopted them as the Br 731(e) armored machine gun carrier as well as using them as anti-tank and supply vehicles and for security duties.

VICKERS MARK VI

During the late 1920s and early 1930s, Vickers built a whole series of light tanks using Carden-Loyd or Horstmann running gear. The Vickers Mark VI, which first appeared in 1941, was the last of the series. It was equipped with a radio and a new, larger turret. The driver sat at the front of the hull on the left next to an 88 hp engine that made the light vehicle extremely nimble. The turret, containing the gunner and 0.5 inch (12.7 mm) and 0.3 inch (7.7 mm) machine guns, was located at the rear. At the outbreak of the Second World War the Vickers Mark VI B was the standard light tank of the British Army and remained in service until 1941. Model VI C was equipped with the more powerful 0.6 inch (15 mm) Besa machine gun but this could not alter the simple fact that the tank was underarmed. The Wehrmacht captured a large number of Vickers Mark VI tanks in France in 1940 and also encountered them in North

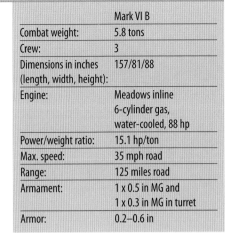

A Vickers Mk. VI, Tobruk, spring 1942.

	Mark VI B
Combat weight:	5.8 tons
Crew:	3
Dimensions in inches (length, width, height):	157/81/88
Engine:	Meadows inline 6-cylinder gas, water-cooled, 88 hp
Power/weight ratio:	15.1 hp/ton
Max. speed:	35 mph road
Range:	125 miles road
Armament:	1 x 0.5 in MG and 1 x 0.3 in MG in turret
Armor:	0.2–0.6 in

Africa, Greece, and Crete. In France, Baukommando Becker converted 20 of the captured vehicles into 4.1 inch (10.5 cm) and 0.6 inch (15 cm) self-propelled howitzers and a similar number into armored ammunition carriers and observation tanks which proved successful on the Eastern Front.

INFANTRY TANK MK. I MATILDA

Combat weight:	12.3 tons
Crew:	2
Dimensions in inches (length, width, height):	191/90/73
Engine:	Ford V8 gas, water-cooled, 3,600 cc, 70 hp
Power/weight ratio:	5.7 hp/ton
Max. speed:	8 mph road
Range:	80 miles road
Armament:	1 x 0.5 in MG or 1 x 0.3 in MG in turret
Armor:	0.5–2.4 in
Fording depth	28 in

Infantry Tank Mk I Matilda.

The British doctrine regarding the use of tanks before and during the war provided for two main types: slow, heavily armored infantry tanks and fast, relatively lightly armored cruisers. The Mk. I Matilda was the first infantry support tank to be built under this approach—and proved a complete failure. In order to keep costs down, designer Sir John Carden was forced to limit the tank to the bare essentials. The result was a two-man vehicle with a top road speed of just 8 mph (13 km/h), which meant it could be overtaken by a runner. The insubstantial armament, consisting of one turret-mounted machine gun, was completely useless. Nevertheless the General Staff accepted the vehicle in April 1937 and it went into production. The tank's shortcomings had been noted, however, and it was therefore regarded as a temporary solution. By 1940 a total of 139 Matildas had been produced, all of which were lost in France. Their sole plus point was their heavy armor of up to 2.4 inches (60 mm) at the front, which could not be penetrated by Germany's 1.5 inch (3.7 cm) Pak. The Wehrmacht, which used all other captured tanks for its own purposes, could find no use for these.

INFANTRY TANK MK. II MATILDA II A12

	Matilda II Mk. III
Combat weight:	29.7 tons
Crew:	4
Dimensions in inches (length, width, height):	221/102/99
Engine:	2 Leyland 6-cylinder diesel, water-cooled, combined 190 hp
Power/weight ratio:	6.3 hp/ton
Max. speed:	15 mph road, 8 mph cross-country
Range:	90 miles road, 55 miles cross-country
Armament:	2-pounder cannon in turret, 1 x 0.3 in coaxial Besa MG
Armor:	0.8–3 in
Fording depth	36 in

A Matilda II Mk. III of the 7th Royal Tank Regiment, Libya, 1941.

These vehicles are painted in a typical camouflage scheme of dark gray, sky blue, and sand colors.

A Soviet Matilda II from an unknown unit, 1942

It had become clear to the British General Staff even before completion of the trials of the Matilda I prototype, that a better vehicle was needed for the infantry tank role and contracts were therefore awarded for the development of a new machine. This resulted in the Matilda II, whose prototype was unveiled in 1938. This tank was unusually heavily armored for its day (nose up to 3 in/78 mm, sides 2 in/65 mm, turret 3 in/75 mm all round) and was equipped with a turret-mounted 2-pounder with coaxial machine gun. Although still not particularly fast, it was twice as fast as the Matilda I. The vehicle's cast steel construction was problematic, however, as production had to be entrusted to foundries and locomotive builders with little experience of manufacturing fighting vehicles and the

required production levels were never achieved.

As a result there were only 24 Matilda IIs in operation in France in 1940, although even this small number posed enormous problems to the German troops. Their armor could not be penetrated by German tanks or anti-tank guns and only the 3.5 inch (8.8 cm) anti-aircraft gun stood any chance against them. The Matilda's 2-pounder, on the other hand, was capable of piercing the armor of any enemy tank from some distance. In North Africa too the Matilda (the tank's popular name) initially notched up a number of major successes against the Italians, acquiring the nickname "Queen of the Desert" in the process. When Rommel's Afrikakorps turned up in Libya with the 3.5 inch (8.8 cm) anti-aircraft gun in mid-

1941, however, the tables were turned. Attempts to equip the Matilda with a 6-lb gun failed because of the small diameter of the turret ring. The tank was last used as a battle tank in Western Europe/North Africa at the second Battle of El Alamein in July 1942. After that it was converted for special tasks such as mine-clearing. No major modifications were undertaken during the lifetime of the tank. The engine output was increased slightly from 174 hp to 190 hp and one variant was given a 3.1 inch (7.8 cm) turret-mounted howitzer. As part of the Lend-Lease program, the Soviet Union received around 1,000 of the 3,000 or so Matilda tanks built by the time production ceased in mid-1943 and these played an important role on the Eastern Front.

INFANTRY TANK MK. III VALENTINE

Between 1939 and 1944 8,275 Valentines were built in the United Kingdom and Canada, which meant that it was manufactured in greater numbers than any other British tank in the Second World War. It was designed by Vickers and shared many components with the A10 cruiser. The prototype was shown to the War Office on February 14, 1938, Valentine's Day, hence the tank's name. Large-scale production began in 1939 and the first vehicles were delivered to the army in May 1940.

The Valentine had good defensive armor for an infantry tank but was slow and armed with only a 2-pounder. The tank entered service with the British Army in North Africa in 1941 and remained in service until 1945, earning itself a good reputation for its robustness and reliability. The main problem with it was its small turret, which provided just enough room for two men and a 2-pounder. When the vehicle was upgunned to a 2.2 inch (5.7 cm) and then to a 3 inch (7.5 cm) cannon, however, space became extremely tight. Many tank commanders preferred the confinement of a three-man turret because there was simply too much to do in a two-man turret: command the tank, operate the radio, load the main weapon, and maintain an overview of the battlefield. They were not helped in the latter by the fact that they only had a single periscope. The Valentine was extremely adaptable and went through 11 versions with guns ranging from 1.6 inches (4 cm) to 3 inches (7.5 cm) and a number of different engines. In addition there were also various self-propelled guns and special variants such as bridgelayers and amphibious tanks. The best-known self-propelled gun based on the Valentine was without doubt the "Archer" tank destroyer, which mounted a 17-pound anti-tank gun. Interestingly this gun, which had a limited traverse and was mounted on an armored superstructure, did not point forwards but faced the rear. As the Archer

	Valentine Mk. I
Combat weight:	17.9 tons
Crew:	3
Dimensions in inches (length, width, height):	213/103/89
Engine:	AEC inline 6-cylinder, water-cooled, 9,600 cc, 135 hp
Power/weight ratio:	7.5 hp/ton
Max. speed:	15 mph road, 9 mph cross-country
Range:	85 miles road, 50 miles cross-country
Armament:	2-pounder cannon in turret, 1 x 0.3 in coaxial Besa MG
Armor:	0.3–2.6 in
Fording depth	35 in

was designed to make surprise attacks and then withdraw, this orientation meant it was already facing in the right direction for its retreat. Canada and the United Kingdom supplied the Soviet Union with 2,690 Valentine tanks under the Lend-Lease program. The Soviets valued the tanks highly and praised their reliable engines and robust running gear. Nevertheless they found the 2-pound guns of the early models too weak and equipped some of the vehicles with Russian-made 0.3 inch (7.62 mm) cannon. Germany's Afrikakorps captured a number of Valentines in North Africa and used them until the lack of spare parts meant they could no longer be repaired.

A Valentine Mk. I of the 8th Royal Tank Regiment, Bardia, Libya, January 1942.

INFANTRY TANK MK. IV CHURCHILL A22

A Churchill Mk. IV.

Churchill Mk. VII	
Combat weight:	44.8 tons
Crew:	5
Dimensions in inches (length, width, height):	297/128/98
Engine:	Bedford twin-six, water-cooled, 21,100 cc, 350 hp
Power/weight ratio:	7.8 hp/ton
Max. speed:	15 mph road, 8 mph cross-country
Range:	90 miles road, 50 miles cross-country
Armament:	1 x 3 in cannon in turret, 2 x 0.3 in Besa MGs (one coaxial and one in the hull), 1 x 0.3 in Bren anti-aircraft MG
Armor:	0.7–5.9 in
Fording depth	40 in

Work on the design of a successor to the Matilda II (designated the A22) was begun by Vauxhall in mid-1940. The war was raging, most British tanks had been lost in France, and replacements were urgently needed. Design time was in short supply and Vauxhall therefore turned to the designs for the A20, which had been developed on the assumption that the war would be fought in a similar way to the First World War, in other words positionally with trenches and fortifications. The Churchill therefore possessed tracks that ran around the entire height of the hull in order to enable it to cross wide trenches. The first prototypes rolled out of the factory barely a year later, in July 1941, and large-scale production began shortly afterwards. The time pressure under which the Churchill was produced meant problems were inevitable. The engine, in essence two linked side-mounted Bedford truck engines, gave continual trouble and neither the steering nor the gearbox had been adequately developed. Furthermore a 2-pounder (4 cm) gun capable of firing only anti-tank shells (not high explosive shells) was inadequate, but at the time it was all that was available. For this reason some of the early vehicles were also fitted with a hull-mounted 3 inch (7.62 cm) howitzer although this was of only limited use because of its minimal traverse. The Mk. III, however, was equipped with the more effective

6-pound (5.7 cm) gun, significantly improving the Churchill's combat effectiveness. In North Africa a number of Mk. IVs were fitted with the Sherman tank's 2.2 inch (5.7 cm) gun (Mk IV NA 75). From Mk VI onwards, Churchill tanks mounted a 3 inch (7.5 cm) gun as standard. The Churchill was first deployed at the Dieppe landings in August 1942

and was used widely and with considerable success in North Africa, Italy, and later France. Its heavy armor and robust running gear helped it to survive even severe damage and rough terrain. Because of its wide, roomy hull and strong running gear, the tank was ideal for a range of special uses (see p.109). By 1945 a total of 5,460 Churchills had been built.

A Churchill Mk. VII of the British 34th Armoured Brigade in northern France, September 1944.

A Churchill Mk. IV in Tunisia, 1943.

CRUISER MARK I A9

An A9 captured by the Italians in October 1940.

Combat weight:	14.3 tons
Crew:	6
Dimensions in inches (length, width, height):	228/98/104
Engine:	AEC inline 6-cylinder, water-cooled, 9,600 cc, 150 hp
Power/weight ratio:	10.4 hp/ton
Max. speed:	25 mph road, 15 mph cross-country
Range:	150 miles road
Armament:	2-pounder cannon in turret, 1 x 0.3 in coaxial Vickers MG, 2 x 0.3 in Vickers MG in small turrets
Armor:	0.2–0.5 in
Fording depth	31 in

France, June 1940: a destroyed A9.

The first in Britain's series of fast cruisers was the Mark 1 A9. This vehicle was designed by Vickers-Armstrong under tight financial constraints in the mid-1930s and was far too lightly armored to be effective in combat. Unusually, it had two machine gun turrets to the left and right of the driver, each housing a 0.3 inch (7.7 mm) MG. Because they were so cramped, however, these turrets often became death traps for the gunners. At the time the Mark I went into production, its hydraulic turret traversing gear was extremely advanced, as was a ventilation system for the fighting compartment. The running gear was robust and capable of coping with rough terrain and was later used in slightly modified form on the Valentine. The A9 was not a success, however, and production was cancelled after just 125 had been manufactured. The last A9 was used in North Africa.

CRUISER MARK II A10

Combat weight:	15.9 tons
Crew:	5
Dimensions in inches (length, width, height):	220/100/104
Engine:	AEC inline 6-cylinder, water-cooled, 9,600 cc, 150 hp
Power/weight ratio:	9.4 hp/ton
Max. speed:	16 mph road, 8 mph cross-country
Range:	150 miles road
Armament:	2-pounder cannon in turret, 1 x 0.3 in coaxial Vickers MG
Armor:	0.3–1.2 in
Fording depth	31 in

Cruiser Mark II A10.

The A10 was originally intended as an infantry tank version of the A9 but was too lightly armored for that role. Instead it was reclassified as a heavy cruiser, a role for which it was also unsuited as it was too slow. Expectations were therefore that the A10 would meet with no more success than the A9. Although the two pointless machine gun turrets had been removed, the upper part of the tank still presented too many shell traps. 175 A10s were produced and first saw combat in France in 1940, where a number of them fell into German hands. The remainder were used in North Africa where they achieved initial success against the Italians but were completely outclassed when the Afrikakorps arrived.

CRUISER MARK VI CRUSADER

A Crusader Mk. I of the British 7th Armoured Division, North Africa, 1941.

	Crusader Mk. III
Combat weight:	22.1 tons
Crew:	3
Dimensions in inches (length, width, height):	236/104/88
Engine:	Nuffield Liberty V12 water-cooled, 340 hp
Power/weight ratio:	15.3 hp/ton
Max. speed:	27 mph road, 15 mph cross-country
Range:	200 miles road
Armament:	6-pounder cannon in turret, 1 x 0.3 in coaxial Besa MG
Armor:	0.2–2 in
Fording depth:	39 in

A Crusader Mk. III of the British 6th Armoured Division, Tunisia, early 1943.

Having soon become clear that the running gear of types A9 and A10 could not cope with the speed required of a cruiser tank, alternatives were sought. In the USA, engineer Walter Christie had been experimenting during the 1920s and 1930s with a new kind of running gear that allowed for high speeds while delivering excellent all-terrain capability. "Christie suspension" used large, rubber-rimmed road wheels and a suspension system housed in the hull. Of the first tank produced using this system (the Mark III A13 cruiser), only 65 were built. Far more successful was the Mark VI cruiser, the Crusader, which went on to become the most important British tank of the desert war. The newly founded Nuffield Mechanization and Aero began to develop a cruiser tank with Christie suspension and powered by its Liberty airplane engine. Dating back to the First World War, this engine had proved

its worth and most importantly was extremely powerful. Even though its output was cut back from 400 to 340 hp, this was enough to make the vehicle extremely fast. The Crusader's armament consisted initially of a turret-mounted 2-pounder with coaxial machine gun and a second machine gun in a separate turret located at the front of the tank next to the driver. This machine gun turret was often removed in the field and was dropped altogether for Mk. II. Mk. III, meanwhile, was equipped with the outstanding 6-pounder (5.7 cm gun).

The new tank received its baptism of fire in North Africa in June 1941 but more tanks were lost to mechanical failure than to enemy fire. The problems were caused not by the engine or running gear but by the cooling system and air filter. The engine was often restored to its original 400 hp by the troops, enabling the tank to reach 40 mph (64 km/h). The Christie

suspension was able to cope well with speeds of this kind but the lifespan of the engine was shortened. Crusader III, equipped with the 6-pounder, which required a larger but flatter turret, came on the scene in mid-1942. Crusaders remained the most important British tank until the end of the North African campaign, after which they were quickly replaced by US vehicles as their thin armor and inability to take a gun any bigger than the 6-pounder meant they rapidly became obsolete from 1943. Special versions such as anti-aircraft guns and artillery tractors remained in service until the end of the war, however. Including all the different versions, around 5,300 Crusaders were built.

CRUISER MARK VIII CROMWELL

	Cromwell Mk. IV
Combat weight:	30.8 tons
Crew:	5
Dimensions in inches (length, width, height):	253/120/112
Engine:	Rolls-Royce Meteor V12, water-cooled, 27,000 cc, 600 hp
Power/weight ratio:	19.5 hp/ton
Max. speed:	32 mph road, 18 mph cross-country
Range:	175 miles road
Armament:	3 in cannon in turret, 1 x 0.3 in coaxial Besa MG, 1 x 0.3 in MG in hull (some vehicles)
Armor:	0.3–3 in
Fording depth	48 in

In 1941 the British General Staff drew up a list of specifications for a heavy tank as previous models had failed to convince in terms of protection and firepower. Among other things, the new tank was to have 2.8 inch (70 mm)-thick armor and a 2.2 inch (5.7 cm) gun. Nuffield and Leyland each submitted a design. Nuffield's design was to be powered by a Liberty engine, Leyland's by a Meteor. The Meteor was a variant of the famous Rolls-Royce Merlin engine that powered the Royal Air Force's Spitfires, Hurricanes, and Lancasters. Nuffield was awarded the contract without having built a prototype. Its "Cavalier" was a complete failure, however, and could only

be used for training purposes. As a result, Leyland's design was resurrected and went into production as the "Centaur," initially with a Liberty power plant as no Meteor engines had yet been delivered. When the Meteor engines finally arrived, the tank's name was changed to "Cromwell." As the British Army had had unfortunate experiences regarding the reliability of its tanks, the Cromwell was intensively tested before being issued. As a result, the first production models were not available until the beginning of 1943. In the meantime the General Staff demanded a 0.3 inch (7.5 mm) gun instead of a 0.2 inch (5.7 mm) gun, resulting in further delays. The Rolls-Royce Meteor engine and Merrit-Brown gearbox proved an outstanding choice as the engine was both powerful and reliable. Its 600 hp made the vehicle extremely fast with a top speed of 40 mph (64 km/h). However, this put the running gear under such strain (on open country in particular) that when the Mk. IV came out, its

maximum speed was restricted to 32 mph (52 km/h). In 1943 and 1944 the Cromwell was only used for training, and it first saw combat at the D-Day landings in 1944.

The Cromwell proved its worth and remained Britain's most important tank up to the end of the war. Above all it was exceptionally fast and maneuverable. Compared to German tanks, however, it was still too lightly armed and armored, despite the armor of later models being increased to a maximum 4 inches (102 mm). Furthermore, although the tank did not appear until 1943, its shape was far less sophisticated than that of the T-34 or the Panther. Had the Cromwell been available in the North African desert in 1942, it would no doubt have achieved a better record of success. As things were, it was slightly behind the times, yet remained in service with the British Army until 1950. In total, 4,500 vehicles of all variants were built.

A Cromwell Mk. IV of the British 7th Armoured Division, Normandy, July 1944.

The Cromwell was fast and maneuverable but still undergunned.

HOBART'S FUNNIES

*M4 Sherman
Duplex Drive DD.*

Sherman Duplex Drive DD

This was a set of equipment to convert a Sherman tank into an amphibious tank. Buoyancy was provided by a collapsible canvas skirt while forward thrust was provided by two propellers connected to the engine. However, rough seas on June 8, 1944 caused some of the converted tanks to fill with water and sink with the loss of their crews.

Sherman Amphibian Exhaust Device

The US Army went down a different route, making its Shermans watertight and equipping them with long air supply/exhaust shafts designed to enable them to wade ashore through deep water.

It was clear to the Allied planners that the success of the Normandy invasion would depend on the speed with which the coastal fortifications and obstacles could be overcome. As a result of the Dieppe experience, the British and Canadians in particular had been forced to recognize that the first wave of assault troops would require the support of armored vehicles to eliminate bunkers and pockets of resistance but also to provide covering fire while the troops overcame the defensive structures erected by the Germans.

A whole "menagerie" of extremely curious but effective armored vehicles was developed from the ideas of Major General Hobart. These vehicles came to be known as "Hobart's Funnies."

*M4 Sherman AED (Sherman
Amphibian Exhaust Device).*

Sherman Dozer.

Sherman Dozer

A much-used piece of equipment was a Sherman tank fitted with a bulldozer blade which could clear obstacles of all kinds out the way. It proved particularly useful in clearing hedges in Normandy. A whole series of sappers' vehicles (Armoured Vehicle Royal Engineers or AVRE) was developed around the Churchill tank. In addition to the variants described here, there was a tank armed with an 11 in (29 cm) mortar for use against bunkers plus explosive charge layers, assault bridges, mine-clearing tanks, and fascine carriers whose function was to fill in anti-tank ditches.

Sherman Crab

A Sherman mine-clearing tank. This vehicle was equipped with a mine flail, a rotating cylinder to which weighted chains were attached that thrashed the ground, detonating any unexploded mines.

AVRE Bobbin

The purpose of this device mounted on a Churchill chassis was to lay a canvas strip 10 ft (3 m) wide over the beach in order to prevent heavy vehicles from sinking into soft sand.

AVRE Bridgelayer

This bridgelaying tank carried a bridge 30 ft (9 m) long with a load-bearing capacity of 66 tons (60,000 kg) that could be laid hydraulically.

Churchill Bobbin.

Churchill Bridgelayer.

Sherman Crab mine-clearing tank.

BISHOP

Combat weight:	19.3 tons
Crew:	4
Dimensions in inches (length, width, height):	218/104/113
Engine:	AEC inline 6-cylinder diesel, water-cooled, 9,600 cc, 131 hp
Power/weight ratio:	6.7 hp/ton
Max. speed:	15 mph road, 9 mph cross-country
Range:	90 miles road, 55 miles cross-country
Armament:	25-pounder cannon, 1 x 0.3 in Bren MG
Armor:	0.3–2.4 in hull, superstructure 0.5–2 in
Fording depth	35 in

A Bishop from an unknown unit, Libya, 1942.

The fast and fluid style of warfare that was being conducted in North Africa highlighted Britain's need for a self-propelled artillery gun capable of following quickly behind the tank units. Such a vehicle, based on the Valentine infantry tank, was designed at great haste and given the name "Bishop." A large, angular superstructure housed a 25-pound gun, the standard weapon of the British field artillery. A major disadvantage was that the barrel could only be raised a maximum of 15°—a disastrously small angle for an anti-tank howitzer because it reduced the maximum range by half! To counteract this, the vehicles were often driven onto earth ramps in an attempt to achieve a greater angle of elevation. The Bishop was first used at the Second Battle of El Alamein in 1942 and only remained in service until the end of 1943. Due to its low speed (typical of the Valentine) and the narrow vertical traverse capability of the 25-pounder, the Bishop was unable to perform its intended role and was replaced by better self-propelled guns such as the Sexton and the Priest. Sources place the number of Bishops produced at either 100 or 150.

SEXTON

Although Sexton self-propelled howitzers were built in Canada, the British Army was their main user.

Combat weight:	28 tons
Crew:	6
Dimensions in inches (length, width, height):	241/107/96
Engine:	Continental R975-4 9-cylinder radial engine, air-cooled, 484 hp
Power/weight ratio:	17 hp/ton
Max. speed:	25 mph road
Range:	180 miles road
Armament:	25-pounder cannon, 2 x 0.3 in Bren MG
Armor:	max. 1 in
Fording depth	39 in

In 1942, Great Britain received its first delivery of matériel from the USA including the M7 Priest self-propelled gun. The M7 proved highly effective in North Africa and was vastly superior to the Bishop. Its only disadvantage was that the US vehicle was equipped with a 4.1 inch (10.5 cm) howitzer whereas the standard caliber of the Commonwealth field artillery was 0.3 inches (8.8 mm) (the 25-pounder). In order to avoid supply problems arising from the use of non-standard ammunition, the British General Staff called for a similar vehicle fitted with a 25-pound gun. The M7 was based on the hull and running gear of the M3 medium battle tank, a modified version of which (with a turret-mounted 1.6 inch (4 cm) gun instead of a 3 inch (7.5 cm) weapon housed in a casemate on one side) was built in Canada as the Ram. The Canadians therefore used the Ram as the basis for a self-propelled gun similar to the M7 mounting a 25-pounder. This vehicle was named the Sexton. Between 1943 and 1945 Montreal Locomotive Works produced a total of 2,150 Sextons, an extremely useful self-propelled howitzer that remained in service in Britain into the 1950s.

BA-10 ARMORED CAR

A BA-10 from an unknown unit, Maikop, early 1942.

Combat weight:	5.7 tons
Crew:	4
Dimensions in inches (length, width, height):	183/81/87
Engine:	GAZ M1 inline 4-cylinder, water-cooled, 3,300 cc, 50 hp
Power/weight ratio:	8.8 hp/ton
Max. speed:	34 mph road
Range:	185 miles road
Armament:	1.8 in cannon, 1 x 0.3 in coaxial MG, 1 x hull-mounted 0.3 in MG
Armor:	0.2–0.6 in
Fording depth	24 in

The BA-10 was the last in a long line of Soviet 6-wheel armored cars whose development had begun in 1930 and which were based on the regular GAZ truck chassis. The BA-10 entered service in 1938 and was heavily armed for an armored car of the day. Its 1.8 inch (4.5 cm) cannon was more powerful than the armament of most German tanks of that time. This car, which remained in production until 1941, was the standard vehicle of the Russian reconnaissance units at the time of the German attack on the Soviet Union and was also used by independent tank brigades. In addition to an amphibious variant, there were also ammunition transporters, and an ambulance version. The BA-10 remained in service with the Red Army until the beginning of 1943, when it was finally withdrawn. In 1941 the Wehrmacht captured a large number of BA-10s which were renamed the BA-10(r) and used for security duties and in an anti-resistance role.

BA-64 ARMORED CAR

Combat weight:	2.6 tons
Crew:	2
Dimensions in inches (length, width, height):	144/60/75
Engine:	GAZ MM inline 4-cylinder, water-cooled, 3,300 cc, 54 hp
Power/weight ratio:	20.4 hp/ton
Max. speed:	50 mph road
Range:	375 miles road
Armament:	generally 1 x turret-mounted 0.3 in DT MG,
Armor:	0.5 in

BA-64 armored car.

This small, light scout and liaison car entered service with the reconnaissance units of the Red Army in 1942. It was based on the chassis of the GAZ-64 jeep and its angular superstructure was strongly influenced by the design of Germany's light armored cars. There were versions with or without radio as well as a variant armed with a 12.7 mm machine gun. In the field, 0.6 inch (14.5 mm) anti-tank rifles or captured German 0.8 inch (2 cm) autocannon were sometimes fitted. The BA-64ZhD was a special railcar version for patrolling the railroads. Taking into account all the variants, 3,500 BA-64s were built. The vehicle continued to be used after the war, for example by the North Koreans in the Korean War. The *Volkspolizei* and NVA (People's Army) of the newly created German Democratic Republic were also issued with second-hand BA-64s as start-up equipment.

T-60

	T-60 Model 1941
Combat weight:	6 tons
Crew:	2
Dimensions in inches (length, width, height):	161/93/69
Engine:	GAZ 202 inline 6-cylinder, water-cooled, 3,300 cc, 70 hp
Power/weight ratio:	11.5 hp/ton
Max. speed:	29 mph road, 12 mph cross-country
Range:	380 miles road, 195 miles cross-country
Armament:	0.8 in ShVAK cannon, 1 x 0.3 in coaxial MG
Armor:	0.3–1.4 in
Fording depth	34 in

A T-60 M 1941 of the 3rd Guards Tank Brigade, Kalinin Front, 1942.

In the summer of 1941 the Red Army lost a vast number of armored vehicles and was forced to acknowledge that some models were simply not up to the task. A means of producing large numbers of tanks quickly was sought and attention was focused on the light tank. As the T-40 (a light amphibious tank armed with only a machine gun) stood little chance of survival in combat due to its minimal armor, it was decided to use the same basic model to create a new and better tank. The new tank was to be more strongly armed and armored than its predecessor and it was decided it no longer needed to be amphibious. The resulting T-60 was intended initially to be equipped with a 1.5 inch (3.7 cm) cannon but its turret proved too small. A powerful 0.8 inch (2 cm) weapon was therefore developed that would have the same penetrating power as the 1.5 inch (3.7 cm) gun. Under the pressure of war, this all happened extremely quickly and the T-60 went into production in November 1941. The following year saw the introduction of an improved version with thicker armor. Most T-60s were issued to reconnaissance units or used to provide direct infantry support. As soon as the T-70 became available, the T-60s were converted for use as tractors or carriers for the Katyusha BM-8 rocket launcher (Stalin's Organ). 6,292 T-60s were built in total.

T-70

T-70 M 1942 from an unknown unit, winter 1942–43.

	T-70 Model 1942
Combat weight:	11 tons
Crew:	2
Dimensions in inches (length, width, height):	183/97/80
Engine:	2 GAZ 202 inline 6-cylinder, water-cooled, 3,300 cc, combined 140 hp
Power/weight ratio:	11.5 hp/ton
Max. speed:	32 mph road, 12 mph cross-country
Range:	280 miles road, 110 miles cross-country
Armament:	1 x 1.8 in L/46 cannon, 1 x 0.3 in coaxial MG
Armor:	0.4–2.4 in
Fording depth	35 in

Just a few months after the T-60 was delivered to the army, production began of the T-70, intended as its replacement, and for almost a year production of the two models ran in parallel. The T-70 was better armored and was equipped with a gun based on the 1.8 inch (45 mm) anti-tank gun. As the weight had nearly doubled, the new tank was powered by two heavy truck engines. While the T-70 could be seen as an advance, its combat effectiveness was limited, not least because of its two-man crew. As the Soviets could not afford to be too fussy in 1942, the T-70 went ahead; it enabled units that would otherwise have had no fighting vehicles at all to be equipped with light tanks. In September 1943 a new version was introduced with stronger armor and a modified turret design, but production of the T-70 nevertheless ceased in October of that year. Its running gear continued to be used in modified form on the SU-76 assault gun.

T-26

Thousands of T-26s were destroyed in summer 1941.   An earlier T-26 with two machine gun turrets.

	T-26 C
Combat weight:	10.6 tons
Crew:	3
Dimensions in inches (length, width, height):	192/95/79
Engine:	GAZ T-26 inline 6-cylinder, water-cooled, 90 hp
Power/weight ratio:	8.5 hp/ton
Max. speed:	20 mph road, 7.5 mph cross-country
Range:	214 miles road, 109 miles cross-country
Armament:	1 x turret-mounted 1.8 in L/46 cannon with coaxial 0.3 in MG, 1 x hull-mounted 0.3 in MG
Armor:	0.2–0.6 in
Fording depth	31 in

After acquiring two Vickers 6-ton tanks along with a license to manufacture them, the Soviet Union initiated production of the T-26 in 1931. The first version, the T-26 A, had two adjacent machine gun turrets. Following experiments with a 1.5 inch (3.7 cm) weapon, a new version (the T-26 B), fitted with a 1.8 inch (4.5 cm) L/46 cannon, was introduced in 1933. 1937 saw the start of production of the T-26 C, which had a new, slightly conical turret and was equipped with radio. Two flamethrowers (OT-130 and OT-133) were also developed

and produced in large numbers. Many other variants (including bridgelaying tanks, command tanks, and self-propelled guns) were manufactured in small volumes. The T-26 was intended mainly for infantry support and reconnaissance roles. Following combat experience many vehicles were fitted with additional armor. At the time of the German invasion, the T-26 fleet, though still comparatively well armed, was aging and had inadequate armor. Thousands were destroyed by the Germans, abandoned by their crews and then either captured or blown up by the

Wehrmacht. As PzKpfw. T-26(r) they were reused only for security and anti-resistance duties. Between 1931 and 1941 around 14,000 T-26s of all versions were produced.

T-28

	T-28 M
Combat weight:	35 tons
Crew:	6
Dimensions in inches (length, width, height):	293/110/111
Engine:	M 17L V12 gas, water-cooled, 46,900 cc, 500 hp
Power/weight ratio:	14.1 hp/ton
Max. speed:	23 mph road, 8 mph cross-country
Range:	150 miles road
Armament:	0.3 in L/26 cannon and 1–2 x 0.3 in MG in main turret, 2 x 0.3 in MG in small turrets to the left and right of the driver
Armor:	0.6–3.1 in
Fording depth	31 in

T-28 M 1934.

In August 1933, the prototype of the T-28 was presented as a defense-busting tank. It possessed good climbing and trench-crossing capability and was

equipped with two machine gun turrets positioned toward the front of the hull. All vehicles had radio and were fitted with a smokescreen device. The first models mounted a short 0.3 inch (7.62 cm) L/16.5 cannon that was later replaced by the longer L/26. In Manchuria and during the Winter War against Finland, it became clear that the T-28's armor (up to 1.6 inches/40 mm thick) was inadequate.

A new version was therefore developed (the T-28 M) with 3.1 inch (80 mm) armor at the front and 1.6 inch (40 mm) armor at the sides and rear. Although this increased its weight by a good 4 tons (4,064 kg), it did not affect the tank's mobility and the T-28 acquired a reputation when it was involved in breaking through the Mannerheim Line in Finland in 1940. Around 600 T-28s were built in total.

T-34

The Russian T-34 was without doubt one of the best and most successful tanks of the Second World War. It successfully combined the three main requirements of a tank—mobility, protection (armor), and firepower. The story of the T-34 began in 1937 with the systematic development of the BT series. The seldom used option of driving on road wheels was dispensed with and all-round sloped armor was introduced for maximum shot deflection. The T-34 was arrived at in spring 1940 via the

Disposable spare fuel tanks gave the T-34/85 an extensive range.

A T-34 M 1943 captured and reused by the Wehrmacht.

	T-34/76 Model 1943	T-34/85
Combat weight:	29.2 tons	35 tons
Crew:	4	4–5
Dimensions in inches (length, width, height):	240/118/104; length with barrel: 266	240/118/104; length with barrel: 319
Engine:	V-2 43 V12 diesel, water-cooled, 38,900 cc, 500 hp	V-2 34 V12 diesel, water-cooled, 38,900 cc, 500 hp
Power/weight ratio:	16.9 hp/ton	14.1 hp/ton
Max. speed:	34 mph road, 15 mph cross-country	31 mph road, 12 mph cross-country
Range:	170 miles road, 130 miles cross-country	185 miles road, 150 miles cross-country
Armament:	3 in F-34 L/41 cannon in turret, 1 x 0.3 in coaxial MG, 1 x hull-mounted 0.3 in MG	3.3 in L/51.5 cannon in turret, 1 x coaxial 0.3 in MG, 1 x hull-mounted 0.3 in MG
Armor:	0.5–2.8 in	0.9–3.5 in
Fording depth:	51 in	51 in

prototype A-20 and the T-32. Its broad tracks ensured low ground pressure, allowing the vehicle to cope well with mud and snow. A powerful 500 hp diesel engine and improved Christie suspension increased mobility and reduced the risk of fire as diesel is less inflammable than gasoline. The vehicles built in 1940 still mounted a short 3 inch (7.62 cm) L-11 L/30 cannon while the 1941 model was equipped with the more powerful F-34 L/41.

When the Wehrmacht encountered the T-34 for the first time in summer 1941, it had a massive shock. All its anti-tank weapons and tank guns were rendered ineffectual at a stroke. The only German gun that could beat the new Soviet tank was the 3.5 inch (8.8 cm) anti-aircraft gun. As a result the 1.5 inch (3.7 cm) 35/36 Pak earned itself the derisory nickname das Heeresanklopfgerät (meaning roughly the "army's door-knocking device"). Naturally the T-34 was not without its weak points. Its transmission, for example, caused continual problems and many of the T-34s that fell into German hands had simply been abandoned because of gearbox damage. The tank only had a two-man turret, which increased the burden on the commander and restricted combat effectiveness, particularly during the early part of the war when crews were relatively inexperienced. To start with the T-34 had no radio and was therefore at a tactical disadvantage to the Wehrmacht.

As production progressed, numerous modifications were made. The most

T-34/76 M 1942 of the 129th Motorized Brigade.

important was carried out in fall 1943, when an anti-tank gun based on the outstanding 3.3 inch (8.5 cm) anti-aircraft gun and housed in a new cast-steel turret was successfully mounted on the tank. This was necessary if the T-34 was to match the German Panther or Tiger tanks, which had revealed themselves to be superior to the T-34/76. The new version benefited from thicker armor and its 3.3 inch (8.5 cm) gun could penetrate tank armor 3.9 inches (100 mm) thick at 1,100 yards (1,000 m). There was also, at last, space for three men in the turret, albeit in almost unbearably cramped conditions. The T-34 became the standard tank of the Red Army and was produced in vast numbers. It is thought that by the end of 1945, 55,000 vehicles had been built, of which 19,430 were T-34/85s.

At the beginning of the war in the east, the Wehrmacht captured a large number of T-34s and thereafter continued to get its hands on a few examples here and there. Whenever the German anti-tank units saw a T-34 they tended to fire first and only look later to see whether the tank bore a German cross; so these captured vehicles were never systematically incorporated into the Wehrmacht's equipment as deployment on the battlefield was fraught with danger. Often the turrets were removed and the vehicles were used as improvised recovery tanks. Production continued for a while after 1945 and for a long time the T-34 remained the standard tank of the Soviet Union and its allies. It was also exported to third world countries in large numbers, where it was often used in combat, e.g. in Korea, Vietnam, the wars of the Middle East, and many African conflicts. T-34s were even used in the fighting in Yugoslavia in the 1990s.

The T-34/76 M 1943 had a modified turret with command hatch.

The T-34/85 had a cast-steel turret and a 3.3 inch (8.5 cm) L/51 gun.

T-35

On paper and on parade, the T-35 appeared a mighty, unbeatable weapon. With its five turrets, three cannon, six machine guns, and enormous size, it looked more like a battleship than a tank. In reality, it was a complete failure as it was too slow, mechanically unreliable, and too thinly armored. Furthermore, T-35 tank commanders were completely overstretched, having five turrets and ten men to coordinate. The first prototype of the T-35 was unveiled in 1933 and, like the T-28, was intended as a heavy defense-busting tank. The vehicle's weaknesses had become apparent during the Winter War against Finland in 1939–40 yet this did not prevent it being sent into battle in 1941. Most T-35s either failed to reach the front due to mechanical failure or were very quickly destroyed due to the enormous target they presented to the enemy. They were last used during the Battle of Moscow in winter 1941, by which time the Red Army had long had significantly better heavy tanks at its disposal. Only 60 or so T-35s were built.

	T-35 M
Combat weight:	55.1 tons
Crew:	11
Dimensions in inches (length, width, height):	383/126/135
Engine:	M 17M V12 gas, water-cooled, 46,900 cc, 500 hp
Power/weight ratio:	9.1 hp/ton
Max. speed:	19 mph road, 8 mph cross-country
Range:	95 miles road
Armament:	3 in L/16 cannon and 2 x 0.3 in MG in main turret, 1 x 1.8 in L/46 cannon in each secondary turret, 1 x 0.3 in MG in two MG turrets
Armor:	0.4–1.2 in
Fording depth	47 in

A T-35 Model 1935.

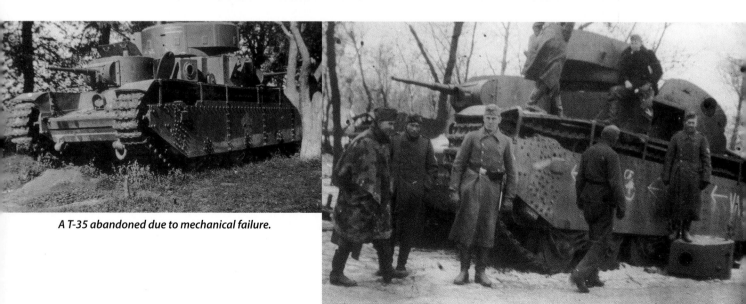

A T-35 abandoned due to mechanical failure.

A destroyed T-35 always attracted interest due to its size.

BT-5 AND BT-7

Although highly mobile, BT-7s were thinly armored and therefore vulnerable.

BT is the abbreviation of the Russian for "fast tank." The BT-7 was the last of a long line of fast tanks designed during the 1930s. Each of the tanks in the series had Christie suspension (the Soviets had purchased a tank of this kind in the USA in 1930) and could be driven either on tracks or on their road wheels (carrying their tracks with them). The rear set of road wheels was powered and the front set was steerable, which gave the vehicle the appearance of a regular wheeled vehicle. The removing and replacing of the tracks was, however, a laborious, time-consuming process and fast driving

without tracks was in any case only possible on road. As a result, this option was often neglected. The BT-5 went into production at the end of 1932 and in addition to good mobility, possessed a first-class gun, the 1.8 inch (4.5 cm) L/46 cannon. Unfortunately it was thinly armored with riveted plates and the rivets had a tendency to fly around under fire. Externally the BT-7 bore a strong resemblance to the BT-5 but had a new turret, new transmission, a more powerful (500 hp) engine, and stronger, welded armor. These tanks were intended to push forward swiftly and break through or

circumvent enemy lines, spreading confusion in their wake. For this they needed mobile covering fire, which the BT-5A was designed to provide with its 7.62 mm howitzer. Vehicles of the BT series were deployed in the Spanish Civil War, Manchuria, Finland, and the Second World War, and large numbers were lost in 1941. Rather than incorporating captured BT tanks into their tank divisions, the Wehrmacht used them only for security duties behind their line of advance. Around 5,000 BT-5s and 2,700 BT-7s were built.

	BT-7
Combat weight:	15.3 tons
Crew:	3
Dimensions in inches (length, width, height):	223/90/95
Engine:	M 17T V12 gas, water-cooled, 46,900 cc, 500 hp
Power/weight ratio:	32.7 hp/ton
Max. speed: on wheels:	45 mph
on tracks:	33 mph
Range: road (wheels):	455 miles
road (tracks):	265 miles
Armament:	1.8 in L/46 cannon and 1 x 3 in coaxial MG in turret, 1 x 0.3 in MG in rear of turret (some vehicles)
Armor:	0.4–0.9 in
Fording depth	47 in

Summer 1941: Wehrmacht soldiers inspect a BT-5

SOVIET UNION

KV-1 AND KV-2

Development of the KV-1 (named after the Soviet defense minister of the day, Kliment Voroshilov) started at the beginning of 1939. It was intended to replace the heavy multi-turreted tanks T-28 and T-35. In order to save weight, it was of more conventional design than its predecessors and yet had thicker armor. Indeed its front and side armor of 4.3 inch (110 mm) and 0.3 inch (75 mm) respectively were sensational for 1939. Its armament consisted of the same 0.3 inch (7.62 mm) cannon as the T-34. KV-1 went into production in February 1940 and was immediately put through its paces in the Winter War against Finland. During the breakthrough of the Mannerheim Line not a single KV-1 was destroyed while numerous T-28s and T-35s were knocked out. There were, however, a number of mechanical problems that required a reworking of the design. The political situation in Europe did not permit this, however, and so large-scale production went ahead in spite of the mechanical defects.

By the time of the German invasion of the Soviet Union, 636 KV-1s had already entered service and gave the Wehrmacht a nasty surprise. Tanks and anti-tank guns were helpless against them and even the 3.5 inch (8.8 cm) anti-aircraft experienced

	KV-1 Model 1941	KV-2
Combat weight:	52.4 tons	57.3 tons
Crew:	5	6
Dimensions in inches (length, width, height):	246/130/107	246/130/138; length with barrel: 288
engine:	V-2-K V12 diesel, water-cooled, 38,900 cc, 600 hp	V-2-K V12 diesel, water-cooled, 38,900 cc, 600 hp
Power/weight ratio:	11.4 hp/ton	10.4 hp/ton
Max. speed:	19 mph road, 12 mph cross-country	16 mph road, 9 mph cross-country
Range:	155 miles road	155 miles road
Armament:	3 in F-34 L/41 cannon in turret, 1 x 0.3 in coaxial MG 2 x 0.3 in MG (rear of turret and hull-mounted)	6 in M 1938/40 L/20 howitzer in turret, 1 x 0.3 in, coaxial MG, 2 x 0.3 in MG (rear of turret and hull-mounted)
Armor:	1.2–4.3 in	1.2–4.3 in
Fording depth:	59 in	59 in

occasional difficulties defeating this colossus. Until the arrival of the Tiger in 1942, the KV-1 remained the best protected and probably the most powerful tank in the world.

To support the KV-1 units, a version was developed that mounted a 5 inch (15.2 cm) howitzer in an enormous, ungainly turret: the KV-2. Although this version was also extremely effective in combat, its turret presented the enemy with an easy target and the vehicle itself was not fast enough. Production was not resumed after the Wehrmacht captured the factory where the KV-2 was made.

Although still comparatively well armored, the KV-1 experienced difficulties when the Panther and Tiger arrived on the scene as its 3 inch (7.62 cm) gun was no longer powerful enough to penetrate their armor. From mid-1943, therefore, the 3.5 inch (8.5 cm) anti-aircraft gun was set in a cast-steel turret and mounted on the hull of the KV-1. This version was known as the KV-85 but it, in turn, became obsolete with the introduction of the T-34/85, which mounted the same armament. Development then continued with the JS-1 and JS-2. By fall 1943 around 3,000 KV-1s and KV-2s had been built, and 130 KV-85s.

The design of the KV-1 proved less successful than that of the T-34.

A KV-1 of the 235th Motorized Brigade, Stalingrad, September 1942.

A KV-2 M 1940.

The high turret of the KV-2 provided the enemy with an easy target.

JS-2

Combat weight:	51 tons
Crew:	4
Dimensions in inches (length, width, height):	267/132/108
Engine:	V-2-IS V12 diesel, water-cooled, 38,900 cc, 600 hp
Power/weight ratio:	10.2 hp/ton
Max. speed:	23 mph road, 12 mph cross-country
Range:	155 miles road, 95 miles cross-country
Armament:	4.8 in D-25 L/43 cannon in turret and coaxial 0.3 in MG, 1 x 0.3 in MG at rear of turret, 1 x 4.8 in DShK anti-aircraft MG
Armor:	0.7–5.2 in
Fording depth	51 in

heavy tank with the same weapon as a medium tank, however, and some prototypes were therefore fitted with a 4 inch (10 cm) cannon. When a means of equipping the tank with a 4.8 inch (12.2 cm) weapon was finally found, this became the preferred variant. Production of the IS-1 ended after only 100 vehicles and the new, more heavily armed model with a larger turret went into production at the end of 1943. Many IS-1s were later converted to IS-2s. The new tank was first used in combat in February 1944. Its 4.8 inch (12.2 cm) gun was able to destroy

Panthers and Tigers with ease but the tank was not without certain drawbacks. The crew compartment was extremely cramped and because shot and cartridge had to be loaded separately, the rate of fire was slow. Another problem was that because it was very light for a heavy tank, its armor was far from invulnerable. The next stage of development was therefore the IS-3, a mighty weapon of which only a very small number had entered service by the end of the war. Approximately 3,800 IS-2s were built altogether.

An IS-2 from an unknown unit, Berlin, May 1945.

The IS heavy battle tanks, named after Joseph (Iosif) Stalin, were based on the KV series. The IS-1 was introduced in Fall 1943 and mounted the same 3.5 inch (8.5 cm) gun as the T-34/85 and SU-85. It did not really make sense to equip a

SU-76

Combat weight:	12.3 tons
Crew:	4
Dimensions in inches (length, width, height):	196/108/87
Engine:	two GAZ 202 inline 6-cylinder engines, water-cooled, 3,300 cc, 140 hp
Power/weight ratio:	11.3 hp/ton
Max. speed:	27 mph road, 12 mph cross-country
Range:	165 miles road, 85 miles cross-country
Armament:	7.62 cm ZIS-3 cannon
Armor:	0.4–1.4 in
Fording depth	35 in

SU-76M.

The SU-76 was a highly successful attempt to find an alternative use for the chassis of the T-70 light tank, which was aging rapidly. The hull was widened and the running gear lengthened through the addition of one wheel. The

engine was located in the middle and an open-topped fighting compartment, housing the renowned ZIS-3 7.6 cm field gun, positioned at the back. These vehicles were first issued to the troops at the end of 1942 but were highly prone to mechanical breakdown, which meant the design had to be reworked. The new version went into production as the SU-76M in May 1943 and large numbers (12,671 SU-76s in total) were built. The

vehicle was extremely flexible and was used in a mobile artillery support role both as a tank destroyer and as a self-propelled howitzer. It was also frequently used as an assault gun for direct infantry support despite being inadequately armored for this function. The ZSU-37 anti-aircraft tank, which mounted a 1.5 inch (3.7 cm) gun, shared the same chassis but was built in smaller numbers.

SU-122

SU-122.

Combat weight:	34.1 tons
Crew:	4–5
Dimensions in inches (length, width, height):	234/118/91; length with barrel: 273
Engine:	V-2 34 V12 diesel, water-cooled, 38,900 cc, 500 hp
Power/weight ratio:	14.6 hp/ton
Max. speed:	34 mph road, 15 mph cross-country
Range:	185 miles road, 125 miles cross-country
Armament:	4.8 in M-30 L/23 howitzer
Armor:	0.6–1.8 in, mantlet up to 2.8 in
Fording depth	51 in

The SU-122 was the Soviet Union's first assault gun of the Second World War. Its development began in summer 1942 under the name SU-35, when a solid box-shaped superstructure with all-round sloped armor was mounted on the chassis of the T-34. Its armament was a front-mounted 4.8 inch (12.2 cm) M-30 howitzer with limited traverse. Due to its low muzzle velocity, the howitzer was not particularly well suited to fighting enemy tanks and even a specially developed hollow charge failed to convince. The vehicle was effective in an infantry support role, however, and useful for bombarding fortifications. From the end of 1943 its role was increasingly taken over by the even more effective SU-152. As the Red Army particularly wanted a tank destroyer, development continued with the SU-85 and SU-100. By March 1945 a total of 1,148 SU-122s had been built.

SU-85 AND SU-100

In 1943 the Soviets needed to find a way of destroying the new German Panther and Tiger tanks, which neither the T-34/76 nor the SU-122 was capable of defeating. In order to save time, they took the hull of the SU-122 and equipped it with the 3.3 inch (8.5 cm) anti-aircraft gun. The use of existing components speeded up the development time and reduced costs. The first prototype was ready in August 1943 and by the end of the year, 750 SU-85s had rolled off the production line. The introduction of the T-34/85 with the same 3.3 inch (8.5 cm) weapon rendered the SU-85 superfluous, however, and production only ran until September 1944. By that time, 2,000 SU-85s had been built. Its successor was the SU-100, which was introduced the same month. The main difference between the two was the SU-100's new and powerful 4 inch (10 cm) gun. This had originally been a naval weapon and its size meant the command hatch had to jut out over the sloped right-hand side of the superstructure. The mantlet was also different from that of the SU-85.

	SU-85	SU-100
Combat weight:	32.6 tons	34.8 tons
Crew:	4	4
Dimensions in inches (length, width, height):	116/118/96; length with barrel: 321	116/118/89; length with barrel: 372
Engine:	V-2 34 V12 diesel, water-cooled, 38,900 cc, 500 hp	V-2 34 V12 diesel, water-cooled, 38,900 cc, 500 hp
Power/weight ratio:	15.3 hp/ton	14.3 hp/ton
Max. speed:	34 mph road, 15 mph cross-country	31 mph road, 12 mph cross-country
Range:	185 miles road, 125 miles cross-country	185 miles road, 125 miles cross-country
Armament:	3.3 in D-5S L/53 cannon	4 in D-10S L/56 cannon
Armor:	0.6–1.8 in, mantlet up to 3 in	0.8–2.1 in, mantlet up to 3 in
Fording depth:	51 in	51 in

An SU-85 from an unknown unit, Berlin, 1945.

The first vehicles reached the units at the beginning of 1945 and proved extremely successful. Production ceased in June 1945, by which time 1,675 SU-100s had been built.

SU-152

Combat weight:	50.2 tons
Crew:	5
Dimensions in inches (length, width, height):	246/130/96; length with barrel: 352
Engine:	V-2 K V12 diesel, water-cooled, 38,900 cc, 600 hp
Power/weight ratio:	11.9 hp/ton
Max. speed:	25 mph road, 12 mph cross-country
Range:	155 miles road
Armament:	6 in ML-20 L/32.3 cannon-howitzer
Armor:	1.5–3 in
Fording depth	59 in

SU-152.

At the end of 1942, the Soviet high command called for a powerfully armed and armored self-propelled gun for use against fortifications and heavy tanks. The first prototype, which was based on the KV-1, was ready in February 1943. The designers had mounted a 6 inch (15.2 cm) ML-20 cannon-howitzer in an angular fixed superstructure. This gun fired a 108 pound (48.8 kg) anti-tank shell which was thought capable of destroying any tank in existence. The SU-152 had its first major combat deployment at the Battle of Kursk in July 1943, where it was believed to have destroyed 12 Tigers and seven Ferdinands. Production ceased after production of the KV-1 chassis ended, by which time 704 SU-152s had been built.

The SU-152 was based on the chassis of the KV-1.

ISU-122 AND ISU-152

ISU-122.

ISU-152.

As the SU-152 had proved so successful in combat, it was decided to build a similar vehicle based on the IS-2 chassis. Although the superstructure of the ISU-152 was higher and more angular, it bore a strong resemblance to the SU-152. As production of the ML-20 howitzer could not keep up with demand, a further version was produced. The ISU-122 was intended mainly as a tank destroyer and mounted the 4.8 inch (12.2 cm) A-19 and later the D-25. In other respects there was hardly any difference between the two models. The main drawback of all three versions (SU-152, ISU-152, and ISU-122) was the extremely scarce storage space for shells and low rate of fire of 2–3 shots per minute dictated by the two-part ammunition. Spare ammunition was often carried on the engine cover—potentially highly dangerous in combat situations. These vehicles were nevertheless extremely effective thanks to their enormous firepower and remained in service with the Red Army long after 1945. By the time production ceased in 1945, 4,075 ISU-122s and ISU-152s had been built.

	ISU-152
Combat weight:	46.1 tons
Crew:	4
Dimensions in inches (length, width, height):	267/132/106;
length with barrel:	356
Engine:	V-2 IS V12 diesel, water-cooled, 38,900 cc, 600 hp
Power/weight ratio:	13.1 hp/ton
Max. speed:	23 mph road, 12 mph cross-country
Range:	135 miles road, 60 miles cross-country
Armament:	6 in ML-20 L/32.3 cannon-howitzer, 1 x 0.5 in DShK anti-aircraft MG
Armor:	0.7–4.3 in
Fording depth	51 in

M3A1 SCOUT CAR

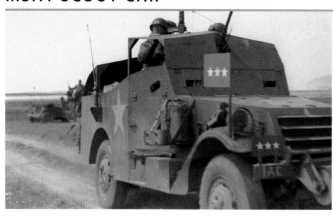

General Patton's M3 command vehicle.

Combat weight:	6.2 tons
Crew:	8
Dimensions in inches (length, width, height):	221/80/83
Engine:	Hercules JXD inline 6-cylinder gas, water-cooled, 87 hp
Power/weight ratio:	14.2 hp/ton
Max. speed:	55 mph road
Range:	250 miles road
Armament:	1 x 12.7 mm Browning M2HB MG (sometimes supplemented by 1 x 7.62 cm M1919A4 MG)
Armor:	0.2–4.8 in
Fording depth	28 in

The M3 was developed by the White Motor Company in 1938 and was adopted by the US Army as the M3A1 in 1939. The M3A1 was based on a commercial truck chassis and was open-topped. A Browning M2 machine gun was mounted on a rail which ran around the open fighting compartment and a cylindrical roller was fitted to the front of the vehicle to prevent it getting bogged down in difficult terrain. The bullet-proof windscreen could be covered by a 4.8 inch (12.7 mm)-thick armor plate. The M3A1 was used only rarely by the US Army and British forces as a scout car, serving more commonly as a personnel transporter or command vehicle (General Patton's, for example) or being used for patrol duties in conquered territory. There was also an ambulance variant. Many of the 20,918 vehicles built by 1944 went to the Soviet Union and to the French units reconstituted after June 1944.

M8 GREYHOUND ARMORED CAR

Combat weight:	8.5 tons
Crew:	4
Dimensions in inches (length, width, height):	197/100/88
Engine:	Hercules JXD inline 6-cylinder gas, water-cooled, 110 hp
Power/weight ratio:	13.2 hp/ton
Max. speed:	55 mph road
Range:	285 miles road
Armament:	1 x 1.5 in M6 L/56 cannon, 1 x 0.3 in M1919A4 coaxial MG, 1 x 4.8 in Browning M2HB anti-aircraft MG
Armor:	0.1–0.7 in
Fording depth	24 in

An M8 of the 2nd Cavalry Division, Belgium, winter 1944–45.

The M8.

This vehicle was originally developed as a tank destroyer. By the time it was ready for production in 1942, however, its 1.5 in (3.7 cm) cannon was no longer effective against tanks and so it was adopted by the army as the M8 armored car. The open-topped turret was manually operated. A 4.8 inch (12.7 mm) anti-aircraft gun was often mounted on a rail that ran around the perimeter of the turret. The first M8s had no floor armor and later vehicles were fitted with only 0.1 inch (3 mm)-thick steel plate. This inadequate floor armor was the most significant drawback of a vehicle that otherwise convinced with its reliability, good off-road capability, and robustness. The M8 had its baptism of fire in Italy in 1943. The British also used it and gave it the nickname "Greyhound." The same year a personnel transporter and command vehicle (the M20) was based on the M8 with the turret removed and with benches fitted in the open fighting compartment. By 1945 Ford had manufactured 11,667 M8s and 3,791 M20s.

M24 CHAFFEE

Combat weight:	20.2 tons
Crew:	4–5
Dimensions in inches (length, width, height):	196/116/96; length with barrel: 216
Engine:	Cadillac Twin, comprising two V8 water-cooled gas engines, combined 220 hp
Power/weight ratio:	11.1 hp/ton
Max. speed:	35 mph road, 24 mph cross-country
Range:	100 miles road
Armament:	3 in M6 cannon in turret, 1 x 3 in coaxial M1919A4 MG and 1 x hull-mounted M1919A4 MG, 1 x 0.5 in anti-aircraft MG
Armor:	0.4–1.5 in
Fording depth	79 in with waterproofing; 39 in without

The M24 remained in service in a number of countries (including Norway and Portugal) until recently—albeit in modernized form.

In April 1943, work began on the designs for a new light tank to replace the M3 and M5. The first prototypes were ready by October of that year and the US Department of Defense placed an order for 1,000 vehicles and then 5,000 even before testing had finished. The first tanks, named the M24 Chaffee (after US General Adna R. Chaffee), were delivered to Europe in November 1944. The Chaffee was probably the first modern light tank and had a well-designed hull with sloped surfaces all round for maximum shot deflection. Four years before this, its 3 inch (7.5 cm) gun would have been used to arm a heavy tank. The M24 was, however, fast and relatively small—good characteristics for a reconnaissance vehicle. Although around 4,400 tanks were built by 1940, only a fraction of them entered service. Most were still with training units in Europe at the end of the war; after 1945 the Chaffee was exported to many different countries and was used in the wars in Korea and Indochina.

An M24 of the US 8th Armored Division, Rheinberg, March 1945.

HALF-TRACK VEHICLES M2, M3, M5, AND VARIANTS

By the beginning of 1940, a range of half-track vehicles had been designed and tested in the US, most importantly by the White Motor Company. Two main types emerged. Both were based on a commercial truck chassis and the slightly modified armored superstructure of the White M3A1 scout car. The M2 was intended as a reconnaissance and towing vehicle and had no rear doors. The M3, which had a slightly elongated superstructure and rear doors, was designed mainly as a personnel carrier. Version M4 was built to carry an 81 mm mortar along with crew and ammunition. All the vehicles were open-topped and were equipped with one or two 0.3 inch (7.62 mm) or 0.5 inch (12.7 mm) machine guns. In bad weather the fighting compartment could be covered by a hood but there was no protection against artillery fire or air attack. Shortly after the US Army placed its order, it became clear that White would not be able to manufacture the necessary number of vehicles itself and so the Autocar and Diamond T companies were brought in to help. Later they were joined by International Harvester, which manufactured what were essentially the same half tracks with minor modifications under the names M5 and M9. To all intents and purposes, these vehicles represented the Allied counterpart to the German Sd.Kfz. 251 and found a similarly diverse range of uses. They also formed

	M3
Combat weight:	10 tons
Crew:	3 + 10–12
Dimensions in inches (length, width, height):	243/87/89
Engine:	White 160AX inline 6-cylinder gas, water-cooled, 147 hp
Power/weight ratio:	15 hp/ton
Max. speed:	45 mph road
Range:	195 miles road
Armament:	1 x 0.5 in Browning M2HB MG and/or 1 x 0.3 in M1919A4 MG
Armor:	0.2–0.6 in
Fording depth	28 in

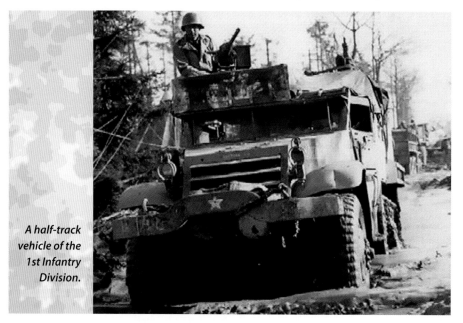

A half-track vehicle of the 1st Infantry Division.

the basis for a number of self-propelled artillery and anti-aircraft guns for which weapons ranging from 2 inch (5.7 cm) to 4.1 inch (10.5 cm) were mounted behind guards on the open fighting compartment or special anti-aircraft mounts fitted that held twin or quadruple 0.5 inch (12.7 mm) machine guns. US half-track vehicles were extensively used not only by the USA but by all the other Allies as well. Under the Lend-Lease agreement, thousands were also supplied to the Soviet Union, which developed its own variants. The career of these vehicles did not end in 1945 as excess US stocks were exported all over the world.

The M17 was based on the M5 chassis but fitted with a Maxson M45 quadruple 0.5 inch (12.7 mm) gun mount. From 1944 onward, the Soviet Union was supplied with around 1,000 of these anti-aircraft vehicles, which also proved highly effective against ground targets.

An M3 half track.

*The M2 is easy to identify from its slightly shortened superstructure.
The Soviet Union received its first consignment of US half tracks,
most of which were used on the Southern Front as reconnaissance
vehicles or artillery tractors, in winter 1943–44.*

M3 AND M5 STUART

An M3 Stuart I of the Royal Irish Hussars, 7th Armoured Division, North Africa, November 1941.

BELLEMAN

T.28037

In 1940, events in Europe forced the US Army to recognize that its light tanks were out of date and a decision was taken to modernize the M2. In July 1940 the designs for an improved model with heavier armor were accepted and large-scale production began of what now became the M3 in mid-1941. Initially the tank was only riveted (it was later welded) and had a 250 hp radial aero engine that made the light M3 wonderfully fast for the time. This engine was always in short supply, however, as it was also used by the aircraft industry and some M3s were given a diesel engine instead. Also highly innovative was the main armament's gyroscopic stabilization system designed to improve accuracy, the first use of such technology anywhere in the world. By contrast, the two machine guns mounted on the side of the hull seemed rather anachronistic. During the course of production, modifications were undertaken to the turret and hull and these side-mounted machine guns were dropped. From version M3A3 onwards,

the tank was fitted with a continuous sloped (rather than stepped) glacis plate. The M3 underwent its baptism of fire against Rommel in North Africa. The British had been supplied with a number

of M3s under the Lend-Lease agreement and valued the reliability and speed of this tank (whose official British Army name was the "Stuart") so highly that they nicknamed it "Honey."

	M3	M5
Combat weight:	13.7 tons	16.5 tons
Crew:	4	4
Dimensions in inches (length, width, height):	178/88/99	171/91/89
Engine:	Continental W-670 7-cylinder radial, gas, air-cooled, 250 hp	Cadillac Twin, comprising two V8 gas engines, water-cooled, combined 242 hp
Power/weight ratio:	18.5 hp/ton	14.6 hp/ton
Max. speed:	36 mph road, 20 mph cross-country	36 mph road, 19 mph cross-country
Range:	75 miles road	100 miles road
Armament:	31.5 in M6 L/56 cannon (turret), 1 x 0.3 in coaxial M1919A4 MG 2 x 0.3 in hull-mounted MG 1 x 0.3 in MG on turret	1.5 in M6 L/56 cannon, 1 x 0.3 in coaxial M1919A4 MG 1 x 0.3 in M1919A4 MG on turret
Armor:	0.4–2 in	0.5–2.6 in
Fording depth:	35 in	35 in

The ongoing shortage of Continental engines led to the M3 being fitted with a new power plant comprising twin auto-engines and a commercially available automatic gearbox. The new drive system worked well and after further modifications to the turret and hull, the new version went into production in spring 1942 as the M5. Large-scale production only began with the end of the M3 program in fall 1943, however.

The M5 Stuart remained in service with the Allies until the end of the war, proving highly effective as a reconnaissance vehicle and with the US cavalry units. Although undergunned and extremely lightly armored, it was nevertheless reliable and fast. A variant of the M5 known as the M8 mounted a short 3 inch

(7.5 cm) howitzer in an open turret. Soviet and French units were supplied with large numbers of the 24,522 Stuart tanks of all versions that were built.

Although its official British designation was the "Stuart," the troops were so smitten with the M3 that they nicknamed it "Honey."

An M5A1 Stuart in the Yad la-Shiryon Museum, Israel.

M3 LEE AND GRANT

	M3 Grant Mk I
Combat weight:	30.8 tons
Crew:	6
Dimensions in inches (length, width, height):	222/107/119
Engine:	Continental R-975 EC2, 9-cylinder radial, gas, air-cooled, 340 hp
Power/weight ratio:	11.4 hp/ton
Max. speed:	26 mph road, 16 mph cross-country
Range:	105 miles road
Armament:	3 in M2 or M3 L/31 in a sponson on the right of the hull, 1.5 in M5 or M6 L/56 cannon in the turret, 1 x 0.3 in M1919A4 coaxial MG, 2 x 0.3 in MGs in the hull
Armor:	0.4–2 in
Fording depth	39 in

An M3A1 Lee from an unknown Red Army unit, Caucasus, mid-1942.

In 1940 it became clear that the US medium M2 tank, armed with only a 1.5 inch (3.7 cm) turret-mounted gun, was out of date. In order to save time, its replacement was based on the same chassis. It had a modified hull with a 3 inch (7.5 cm) gun with limited traverse mounted in the front right of the superstructure. There was also a turret housing a 1.5 inch (3.7 cm) cannon and coaxial machine gun and in addition the commander had his own small turret and 0.3 inch (7.62 mm) machine gun. The M3 was intended as an interim solution pending the introduction of the M4, which was yet to be designed. Large-scale production of the M3 began in August 1941 and continued until December 1942, during which time 6,258 M3s of all types were built. Most M3s had riveted hulls and a 9-cylinder radial aero engine. The M3 was built by a number of manufacturers, however, and so there was a variety of finishes. The machine gun turret was dropped in later models. As its own industry was at full stretch, the British government purchased US tanks including the M3 medium tank, which was fitted at its request with a new, larger turret equipped with radio (the machine gun turret was removed). This vehicle was designated the M3 Grant I and was shipped to the British Army in North Africa from early 1942 onwards. Standard M3s, named the M3 Lee (Grant and Lee were American Civil War generals) were shipped direct to the United Kingdom.

Both models earned themselves a good reputation in the desert in 1942 and proved popular with the troops. They were not without certain shortcomings, however, including the limited field of fire of the main gun, their height, and their awkward design with vertical sides and numerous shell traps. From 1943 the M3 rapidly began to show its age and was replaced in North Africa and Europe by the M4. In Asia and the Pacific, meanwhile, the M3 remained in service until the end of the war. Around 1,400 M3s were supplied to the Soviet Union under the Lend-Lease agreement. The robust chassis of the M3 also served as a basis for a number of self-propelled guns including the M7, M12, and British-Canadian Sexton.

GIs of the 1st Armored Division taking a break in front of their M3 in Tunisia, November 23, 1942.

An M3 Grant Mk. I of the British 7th Armoured Division, El Alamein, 1942.

An M3 at a US Army training ground in 1942.

M 12

Combat weight:	29.4 tons
Crew:	6
Dimensions in inches (length, width, height):	265/105/106
Engine:	Continental R-975 EC2, 9-cylinder radial, gas, air-cooled, 340 hp
Power/weight ratio:	11.4 hp/ton
Max. speed:	24 mph road, 16 mph cross-country
Range:	135 miles road
Armament:	6.1 in M1918M1 howitzer
Armor:	0.4–2.5 in
Fording depth	47 in

In June 1941, contracts were awarded for development of a self-propelled carriage for the 6.1 inch (15.5 cm) M1918 gun based on the M3. The resulting prototype (the T6 GMC) was subsequently rejected, though, as the army saw no need for a weapon of its type. The Ordnance Department nevertheless ordered 100 vehicles for evaluation purposes and production of the M12 began in August 1942. The reorganization of the M3 hull involved the engine being moved to the middle and the fighting compartment being shifted to the rear. As a result the gun crew were unprotected, although at least in theory this was not a problem as the M12 was intended as a long-distance artillery piece. It was not until 1944, after the Normandy landings, that the US Army showed any further interest in the M12 and 75 units were overhauled and shipped to Europe, where they performed extremely well as artillery weapons. The M12 could only carry ten rounds and had to be accompanied at all times by an M30 transporter (an unarmed M12) that carried the gun crew and spare ammunition.

An M12 with the apposite name "Adolph's Assassin."

M4 SHERMAN

The M4 Sherman was probably the most important and versatile Allied tank of the Second World War. Work started on the designs for a successor to the medium M3 in August 1940, just a short while after the M3's designs were approved. The fundamental requirement for the new tank was a 3 inch (7.5 cm) gun with gyroscopic stabilization in a turret with a 360° traverse. In order to save time, the M4 was designed in such a way that as many M3 components as possible could be used in it. Thus the running gear, lower hull, tracks, and initially the power plant were the same. The first prototype was unveiled in fall 1941 and production (which continued until the end of the war) began at the beginning of 1942. No less than 12 different manufacturers produced a bewildering number of versions and special variants. The main difference could be observed in the hull, which was either cast steel, displaying a rounded shape, or welded and more angular. A wide range of different engines was also fitted after it transpired that the radial engine of the first few vehicles would not be available in the required numbers. The arming of the tank with the 3 inch (7.5 cm) M3 gun gave rise to a lot of criticism and from 1944 a 3 inch (7.6 cm) weapon was fitted in a new turret. The British, who also used large numbers of Shermans, created their own, better-armed version of the tank named the Firefly, by equipping it with their outstanding 17-pounder (3 inch (7.62 cm) gun). These two versions finally enabled the Allies to fight Germany's heavy tanks at long range. On the negative side, early M4s had a reputation of catching fire easily and to remedy this, the ammunition in later models was stowed in special water-jacketed bins. The M4's armor was also steadily improved during the course of production.

The main version during the final months of the war was the M4A3E8 (HVSS), which had the long-barreled 3 inch (7.6 cm) cannon and a new suspension system with horizontal instead of the previous vertical volute springs. For direct infantry support there was a variant armed with a 4.1 inch (10.5 cm) howitzer while the M4A3E2 Jumbo was an assault tank with armor up to 5.9 inches (152 mm) thick. There was also a large number of special versions including flamethrower, recovery, bridgelaying, and mine-clearing tanks, a rocket launcher, artillery tractors, flail tanks, and even amphibious tanks.

The M4 was first used in combat at El Alamein in North Africa in 1942. From then on it could be found wherever Allied troops were deployed. Around 2,000 Shermans were also supplied to the Soviet Union under the Lend-Lease program, although the Red Army was far from happy with the tank and considered

	M4A2
Combat weight:	34.6 tons
Crew:	5
Dimensions in inches (length, width, height):	232/105/108
Engine:	GM 6-71 6046 V12 diesel, water-cooled, 420 hp
Power/weight ratio:	12.1 hp/ton
Max. speed:	25 mph road, 17 mph cross-country
Range:	155 miles road
Armament:	3 in M3 L/40 cannon (turret), coaxial and hull-mounted M1919A4 machine guns, 1 x 0.5 in anti-aircraft machine gun
Armor:	0.5–4.1 in
Fording depth	39 in

An M4A3E8 (HVSS) Sherman of the US 11th Armored Division, Rhine, March 1945.

The M4A3E8 with the long-barreled 3 inch (7.62 cm) cannon was substantially more powerful than the version with the short 3 inch (7.62 mm) gun.

An M7 of the US
7th Armored
Division, Ardennes,
December 1944.

The same tank seen
from above.

An M7 in action during
the Korean War.

LVT (A) TRACKED LANDING VEHICLE

During the Second World War the USA developed a whole series of armored and unarmored amphibious transporters and fighting vehicles known as LVTs ("Landing Vehicle Tracked"). They were based on a pre-war design for an amphibious tracked vehicle for use in disaster areas which was designed to be propelled in the water by its tracks.

The first vehicles (LVT1) deployed by the US Marine Corps were unarmored, which soon proved impractical in a combat zone. An armed and armored version, the LVT1 (A) was therefore developed (the "A" standing for "armored"). LVT2 (A) was an armored personnel carrier that could carry up to 25 marines or the equivalent load. One disadvantage was the centrally positioned engine. Models LTV3 and LTV4 were equipped with engines positioned to the side and at the front respectively, which kept the rear free for a loading ramp. There was also a variant of each model equipped with a tank turret and a 1.5 inch (3.7 cm) cannon or 3 inch (7.5 cm) howitzer that was designed to provide supporting fire. LTVs in service with the British Army were used in the crossing of the Rhine in 1945. Including all the different versions, 18,322 LVTs were built.

	LVT2 (A)
Combat weight:	16 tons
Crew:	3 + 25
Dimensions in inches (length, width, height):	313/128/98
Engine:	Wright W-670 7-cylinder radial, gas, air-cooled, 250 hp
Power/weight ratio:	15.9 hp/ton
Max. speed:	20 mph road, 7 mph water
Range:	150 miles road, 100 miles water
Armament:	1 x 0.5 in M2HB MG, 2 x 0.3 in M1919A4 MGs
Armor:	max. 0.5 in
Fording depth	amphibious

A USMC LVT4.

A US Marines LVT (A)-4, Iwo Jima, 1945.

*LVT (A) 2: Kwajalein Atoll,
February 1945.*

ARTILLERY

1.5 INCH (3.7 CM) PAK ANTI-TANK CANNON 35/36

Caliber:	1.5 in
Combat weight:	958 lb
Barrel length:	L/45 (65 in)
Elevation:	−5° to +25°
Traverse:	60°
Ammunition type and weight:	Armor piercing (AP): 1.5 lb; High velocity armor piercing/Armor piercing composite rigid (HVAP/APCR): 0.8 lb; High explosive (HE): 1.4 lb; Super caliber hollow charge (SCHC): 18.7 lb
Muzzle velocity:	AP: 2,533 ft/s; HVAP/APCR: 3,433 ft/s
Effective range:	2,000 ft
Maximum penetration (armor steel):	AP: 1.9 in/1,667 ft/90°; HVAP/APCR: 2.2 in/1,667 ft/30°

A 1.5 inch (3.7 cm) Pak 36 in an Afrikakorps anti-tank unit.

At the beginning of the war in September 1939, the Pak (*Panzer-AbwehrKanone*) 35/36 was the standard anti-tank cannon of the Wehrmacht. The cannon, developed by Rheinmetall (Rhine Metal), had been tried and tested in the Spanish Civil War (1936–39) and it was introduced into the anti-tank companies of the Wehrmacht in large numbers. At the start of September 1939 there were 11,200 of them. As it was small, the weapon was easy to disguise and to maneuver, two important attributes for an anti-tank cannon. Yet as early as the 1940 campaign on the Western Front, the troops had dubbed it the "Heeresanklopfgerät," literally, an "army door-knocker," since it was no longer

effective against the medium-sized and heavy French and British tanks. The 3.5 inch (8.8 cm) anti-aircraft gun frequently had to be deployed for anti-tank fire instead of the anti-tank cannon. Although it was clear by late 1940 at the latest that the 35/36 anti-tank cannon was outdated, a large number were still in service for the Soviet offensive of 1941, where their inadequacy was again dramatically exposed. The 1.5 inch (3.5 cm) weapon was still effective against the Russian T-26 or BT-7 tanks, but against the new T-34, KW-1, and KW-2 it made no impact at all. The introduction of a new type of ammunition with a wolfram core (the Panzergranate 40) increased its armor-piercing effectiveness, but this was still

insufficient. So the Stielgranate 41, a high-caliber shell with a stabilizing tail plane, was introduced in February 1942. These shells were 29 inches (738 mm) long and 6 inches (159 mm) in diameter and carried a hollow charge with 5 lb (2.3 kg) of explosive. The shell was inserted in the muzzle and could penetrate up to c.7 inches (180 mm) of armor steel, but because of the cannon's limited muzzle velocity of 367 ft/s (110 m/s), the enemy tank had to be within 667 ft (200 m). Production was finally halted in March 1942, after 14,459 anti-tank cannon had been manufactured, but it was still deployed, for example, as an auxiliary weapon on Sd.Kfz. 250 and 251 half-track vehicles, until 1945.

The 1.5 inch (3.7 cm) Pak being deployed in Russia. This became obsolete when the T-34 tank was introduced.

2 INCH (5 CM) PAK 38 ANTI-TANK CANNON

Caliber:	2 in
Combat weight:	2,172 lb
Barrel length:	L/60 (177 in)
Elevation:	−8° to +27°
Traverse:	65°
Ammunition type and weight:	AP: 4.5 lb; HVAP/APCR: 2.2 lb; HE: 4.3 lb;
Muzzle velocity:	AP: 2,743 ft/s; HVAP/APCR: 3,993 ft/s
Effective range:	8,333 ft
Maximum penetration (armor steel):	AP: 3.1 in/1,667 ft/90°; HVAP/APCR: 4.7 in/1,667 ft/90°

A 2 inch (5 cm) Pak 38 of the Afrikakorps.

As early as 1935, Rheinmetall began developing a 2 inch (5 cm) anti-tank cannon, but the Pak 37 version was unconvincing. To improve its muzzle velocity, it was fitted with a longer barrel (L/60) and called the Pak 38. After the end of the 1940 campaign on the Western Front, the new anti-tank cannon was put into action, where it was deployed by individual anti-tank platoons, and its maximum range was approximately 31,300 ft (around 9,400 m). Its protective plate was interestingly constructed, consisting of two 0.15 inch (4 mm) armor plates 1 inch (25 mm) apart. Firing ammunition with a hard wolfram core (APCR) the Pak 38 was an effective weapon, but the lack of wolfram severely restricted its use, and with normal armor-piercing ammunition the cannon was not always effective against the new Soviet tanks. So a shell with a stabilizing tailplane was also developed and in March 1943, it was approved by the German Weapons Office as the Stielgranate 42. The shell weighed around 30 lb (13.5 kg) and had a hollow charge of 5 lb (2.3kg), which could penetrate 7 inches (180 mm) of armor steel. Because the Pak 38 was very heavy, it was usually towed by a 1 ton tractor or actually mounted on it, making a makeshift but effective self-propelled anti-tank cannon. Variants of the Pak 38 were even installed in aircraft, and in total over 9,500 were produced.

A 2 inch (5 cm) Pak 38 on a 1 tonne (c.1 ton) artillery tractor.

An artillery tractor towing a 2 inch (5 cm) Pak 38 in the Russian winter.

3 INCH (7.5 CM) PAK 40 ANTI-TANK CANNON

The 3 inch (7.5 cm) Pak was introduced in February 1942. Initially, only 15 were produced per month, although at the time a cannon that was effective against the T-34, KW-1, and KW-2 was badly needed. The Pak 40 was an effective weapon, but its excessive weight was one of the reasons why towed artillery was eventually withdrawn from the battlefield. Weighing just under 3,140 lb (1,425 kg), the cannon could only be moved with difficulty by teams of men, so they had to be placed on vehicles. In addition, on account of its weight, it had a tendency to get stuck in Russian mud, and as a result many were left behind when the Wehrmacht retreated as of 1943. Nevertheless, increased weight was the price that had to be paid to manufacture cannon that could penetrate ever tougher tank armor. Consequently, the Pak 40 was often deployed as a self-propelled cannon, for example, on various Marder anti-tank vehicles, and was also installed in 8-wheel scout cars, half-track vehicles, and even in aircraft.

Caliber:	3 in
Combat weight:	3,139 lb
Barrel length:	L/46 (136 in)
Elevation:	−5° to +22°
Traverse:	65°
Ammunition type and weight:	AP: 15 lb; HVAP/APCR: 9 lb; HE: 12.6 lb
Muzzle velocity:	AP: 2,650 ft/s; HVAP/APCR: 3,300 ft/s; HE: 1,850 ft/s
Effective range:	AP: 8,350 ft; HE: 25,350 ft
Maximum penetration (armor steel):	AP: 5.2 in/ 1,650 ft/90°; HVAP/ APCR: 6.1 in/1,650 ft/90°

The Pak 40 was the most deployed anti-tank cannon in the Wehrmacht in the second half of the Second World War.

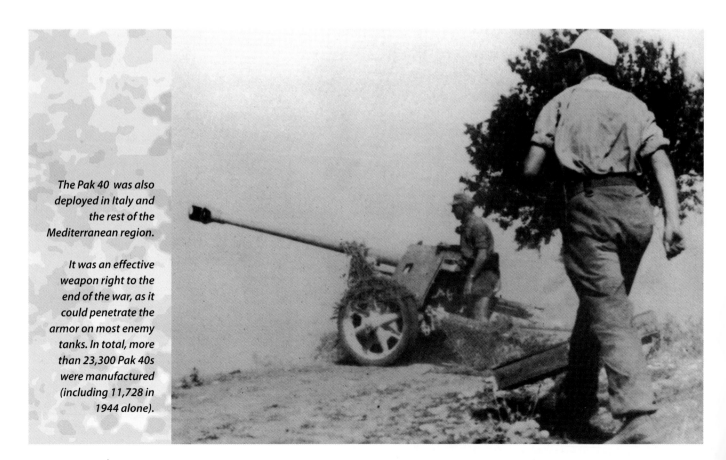

The Pak 40 was also deployed in Italy and the rest of the Mediterranean region.

It was an effective weapon right to the end of the war, as it could penetrate the armor on most enemy tanks. In total, more than 23,300 Pak 40s were manufactured (including 11,728 in 1944 alone).

3.5 INCH (8.8 CM) PAK 43 AND 43/41 ANTI-TANK CANNON

The 3.5 inch (8.8 cm) Pak 43.

Caliber:	3.5 in
Combat weight:	Pak 43: 8,040 lb;
	Pak 43/41: 9,648 lb
Barrel length:	L/71 (260 in)
Elevation:	−8° to +40° (Pak 43);
	−8° to +38°
Traverse:	360° (Pak 43); 56° (Pak 43/41)
Ammunition type and weight:	AP: 22.5 lb;
	HVAP/APCR: 16.1 lb;
	HE: 20.5 lb
Muzzle velocity:	AP: 3,333 ft/s; HVAP/
	APCR: 3,767 ft/s; HE: 2,500 ft/s
Effective range:	AP: 13,333 ft;
	HE: 51,000 ft
Maximum penetration (armor steel):	AP: 7.5 in/
	3,350 ft/90°; HVAP/APCR:
	1 in/1,650 ft/90° HVAP/APCR:
	2.2 in/1,650 ft/30°

The Pak 43 was designed by Krupp and was actually conceived as a prototype in competition with Rheinmetall's 3.5 inch (8.8 cm) Flak 41. Nevertheless, it was accepted by the German Weapons Office as an anti-tank cannon. The weapon had a new type of cross-shaped gunmount, which meant that the cannon could be rotated 360°. But it was also expensive and complicated, which meant that it was not put into action until February 1944. The barrels of the 3.5 inch (8.8 cm) Pak 43 were also mounted on the gun mount of the light Feldhaubitze 18 howitzer to make a less expensive and more readily available cannon: the 3.5 inch (8.8 cm) Pak 43/41. The first of these cannon were ready in February 1943, and they were manufactured until April 1944. Because the cannon was so tall, it was known as the "Scheunentor," or barn door. The exceptionally large gun mount made the cannon very unwieldy, but it was extremely effective at penetrating tank armor and was feared by enemy tank personnel. The cannon was also deployed as a self-propelled weapon, as in Nashorn and Elefant anti-tank vehicles. The KwK 43 L/71, which was installed in the Königstiger and Jagdpanther, for example, was a variant of the Pak 43. 3,500 Pak 43s were produced in total.

LEIG 18 3 INCH (7.5 CM) LIGHT INFANTRY CANNON

The 3 inch (7.5 cm) LeIG 18 infantry support cannon on the Eastern Front.

Caliber:	3 in
Combat weight:	880 lb
Barrel length:	L/11.2 (35 in)
Elevation:	−10° to +35°
Traverse:	12°
Ammunition type and weight:	HE: 13.2 lb
Muzzle velocity:	HE: 733 ft/s
Maximum range:	11,250 ft

The LeIG 18 3 inch (7.5 cm) Light Infantry Cannon was developed as early as 1927. It had a tipping breechblock and a simple box trail gunmount, and it was meant to be horse-drawn. So it initially had wooden wheels, which were later replaced by steel wheels with rubber tires. The weapon was introduced in 1932, and at the beginning of the war, 2,933 were available. Two different versions, which could be separated into partial loads, were also developed for mountain divisions and paratroops. In total, almost 12,000 of all the different versions of the LeIG were produced.

LEFH 18 AND LEFH 18M 4.1 INCH (10.5 CM) LIGHT FIELD HOWITZER

The LEFH 18 light field howitzer was the Wehrmacht Artillery Division's standard weapon. Rheinmetall had designed it as early as 1929, but it was not introduced until 1935. Although it was solidly constructed, with modern elements such as a split-trail gun mount and a hydropneumatic reloading system, the LEFH 18 still had old-fashioned wooden or steel wheels, as it was designed to be horse-drawn. The modernized version, the LEFH 18M, which was designed to be transported by a motorized vehicle, had a muzzle brake, and with better ammunition its range was increased to 41,085 ft (12,325m). Both models were deployed right to the end of the war and were always bound together in batteries of four cannon apiece. The LEFH 18 was effective when aimed directly at tanks and other moving targets, and this howitzer could also be found on self-propelled gun carriages like the Wasp. In total, 6,986 LEFH 18 howitzers were manufactured, and it was in service in some countries' armies even after 1945 (Yugoslavia, Czechoslovakia, Chile, Argentina, Austria, Sweden, and Portugal).

A 4.1 inch (10.5 cm) LeFH 18 light field howitzer in the Afrikakorps.

Caliber:	4.1 in
Combat weight:	4,372 lb
Barrel length:	L/28 (116 in)
Elevation:	−5° to +42°
Traverse:	56°
Ammunition type and weight:	HE: 32.6 lb; AP: 30.8 lb; HC: 27.1 lb
Muzzle velocity:	HE: 1,565 ft/s
Maximum range:	35,585 ft

SIG 33 5.9 INCH (15 CM) INFANTRY HEAVY FIELD CANNON

Caliber:	5.9 in
Combat weight:	3,855 lb
Barrel length:	L/11.3 (66 in)
Elevation:	−0° to +75°
Traverse:	11°
Ammunition type and weight:	HE: 63.4 lb; HC: 54.2 lb; SCHC: 118.9 lb
Muzzle velocity:	HE: 800 ft/s; SCHC: 350 ft/s
Maximum range:	HE: 15,665 ft; SCHC: 3,350 ft

A SIG heavy infantry support cannon with 5.9 inch (15 cm) caliber.

As early as 1927 the Rheinmetall company had begun developing a 5.9 inch (15 cm) infantry support gun. The result, a 149.1 mm (5.9 inch) caliber weapon, was introduced in 1933 as the SIG 33 infantry heavy field cannon. In 1939, 410 of these cannon were in service. From July 1942 onward, super caliber shells were produced for the SIG 33, 300 mm (11.8 inch) caliber shells which contained 59 lb (27 kg) of explosive each. Overall, this cannon's design was robust and effective, but it was really too heavy for the infantry. 4,565 SIG 33 cannon were manufactured in total, before production ceased in March 1945.

SFH 18 AND SFH 18M 5.9 INCH (15 CM) HEAVY FIELD HOWITZER

Caliber:	5.9 in
Combat weight:	12,141 lb
Barrel length:	L/29.6 (175 in)
Elevation:	−3° to +45°
Traverse:	64°
Ammunition type and weight:	HE: 95.8 lb; AP: 32.2 lb; HC: 55.1 lb
Muzzle velocity:	HE: 2,065 ft/s
Maximum range:	44,417 ft

The 5.9 inch (15 cm) SFH 18 heavy infantry support cannon.

The SFH 18 5.9 inch (15 cm) heavy field howitzer was manufactured jointly by Krupp, who made the gun mount, and Rheinmetall, who made the barrel, and was introduced in 1934. In 1939, the Wehrmacht had 1,353 SFH 18s. A new version with a muzzle brake, called the SFH 18M, was introduced in 1943. This howitzer was too heavy to be horse-drawn and it had a limited range—especially compared to the Russian ML-20 6 inch (15.2 cm) howitzer, which had a range of 57,650 ft (17,300 m). So the world's first rocket-propelled shells were developed for the SFH 18, which had a range of well over 63,000 ft (up to 19,000 m) but were not very accurate and rapidly wore out the barrel. After the war, some of these howitzers were put into service and partially modernized by Albania, Bulgaria, Portugal, and Czechoslovakia.

THE MRS 18 8.3 INCH (21 CM) MORTAR

Caliber:	8.3 in
Combat weight:	36,784 lb
Barrel length:	L/29.3 (242 in)
Elevation:	0° to +70°
Traverse:	16°
Ammunition types and weights:	HE: 249 lb; CP: 425 lb
Muzzle velocity:	HE: 1,885 ft/s
Maximum effective range:	HE: 55,650 ft
Maximum penetration (CP):	87 in

Introduced in 1939, the MRS 18 8.3 inch (21 cm) mortar was intended to replace a 8.3 inch (21 cm) mortar that dated back to 1916, but the latter remained in service until 1942. When the war broke out, 27 MRS 18 mortars were in service, with 8,300 rounds of ammunition. Because it was designed as siege artillery, it had concrete piercing shells, called Röchling shells, to destroy bunkers. It was also extremely heavy and had to be transported in two parts. In total, 711 of these mortars were manufactured.

The 8.3 inch (12 cm) SFH 18 heavy field howitzer.

0.8 INCH (2 CM) FLAK 30 ANTI-AIRCRAFT GUN

The 0.8 inch (2 cm) Flak 30 was developed by Rheinmetall and introduced in 1934 as an improved version of the 0.8 inch (2 cm) MG C/30 L machine gun. Ammunition was inserted on the left side from a 20-cartridge anti-aircraft magazine. The lower gun mount consisted of a triangular steel frame that could be mounted on the 51 special trailer. In theory it could fire 280 rounds per minute, but in practice it managed closer to 120 rounds per minute. It took a team of eight men to operate this weapon: one to move it into place, one to aim it, one to find the range, and five gunners who constantly had to supply more ammunition and change overheated barrels. The 0.8 inch (2 cm) Flak 30 was first deployed in the Spanish Civil War, where two batteries were in service from 1936. During the Second World War, it was deployed mostly in light anti-aircraft companies, which had 12 guns each on the front line and 16 each in Germany. To make the gun more mobile,

it was mounted on various self-propelled gun carriages, such as the Sd.Kfz. 10/4. It was also mounted on Maultier half-track vehicles or, as a makeshift measure, on trucks or large cars. Until production ceased in March 1945, more than 147,000 Flak 30 and 38 guns were manufactured.

A 0.8 inch (2 cm) Flak 30 anti-aircraft gun on its trailer.

Caliber:	0.8 in
Combat weight:	1,020 lb
Barrel length:	91 in
Elevation:	−12° to +90°
Traverse:	360°
Ammunition type and weight:	HE-I: 0.3 lb
Muzzle velocity:	3,300 ft/s
Rate of fire:	280 rpm (theoretically)
Maximum range:	16,000 ft
Maximum effective range (vertical):	12,350 ft

0.8 INCH (2 CM) FLAK 38 ANTI-AIRCRAFT GUN

Caliber:	0.8 in
Combat weight:	892 lb
Barrel length:	89 in
Elevation:	−20° to +90°
Traverse:	360°
Ammunition type and weight:	HE-I: 0.3 lb
Muzzle velocity:	3,300 ft/s
Rate of fire:	450 rpm (theoretically)
Maximum range:	16,000 ft
Maximum effective range (vertical):	12,350 ft

The Flak 38 was introduced in 1938 as an improved version of the Flak 30—it weighed less at 991 pound (450 kg), and had a higher theoretical rate of fire, 450 rpm (rounds per minute). A net was set up around the weapon to catch empty cartridges and protect those standing nearby, and it was transported on the 51 special trailer. It is also worth mentioning the 0.8 inch (2 cm) Flak 38 four-gun mount, theoretically capable of firing

1,800 rpm, which was conceived by the German Navy (Kriegsmarine) but was frequently deployed also by the Wehrmacht and the Luftwaffe. Its ballistic effectiveness was the same as that of the 0.8 inch (2 cm) Flak 38. The first of the four-gun mounts was delivered in May 1940, with two foot pedals to select which guns to fire. When one of the levers was operated, only two guns (one left, and one right) could fire while the others could be reloaded, and if both pedals were pressed, all four guns would fire. A shield could be attached to protect the soldiers operating the gun. Flak 38s were transported either on the 52 special trailer or motorized, mounted on various half-track vehicles (the Sd.Kfz 6/1 and Sd. Kfz. 7/1) or tank chassis. The single-gun and four-gun mounts were also deployed in tank platoons.

A 0.8 inch (2 cm) Flak 38 four-gun mount being moved into position.

1.5 INCH (3.7 CM) FLAK 36 ANTI-AIRCRAFT GUN

Caliber:	1.5 in
Combat weight:	3,419 lb
Barrel length:	143 in
Elevation:	−8° to +85°
Traverse:	360°
Ammunition type and weight:	HE-I: 1.4 lb
Muzzle velocity:	2,735 ft/s
Rate of fire:	160 rpm (theoretically)
Maximum range:	21,650 ft
Maximum effective range (vertical):	16,000 ft

The 1.5 inch (3.7 cm) Flak 36 anti-aircraft gun on a Maultier (Mule) half-track vehicle.

The 1.5 inch (3.7 cm) Flak 18, which had originally been introduced in the Wehrmacht, used a complicated and expensive four-wheel gun carriage, but most importantly, it was too heavy. To overcome this problem, it was mounted instead on a single-axle trailer, which reduced its weight by around 440 lb (200 kg), with no loss of ballistic effectiveness. The new weapon was called the 1.5 inch (3.7 cm) Flak 36 which first used a simple Type 36 visor. Weapons using the 40 flak visor were designated Flak 37s. Like the 0.8 inch (3.7 cm) Flak, 1.5 inch (3.7 cm) anti-aircraft guns were frequently mounted on self-propelled gun carriages to increase their mobility. Guns of this type were deployed throughout the war in all branches of service, and they proved their effectiveness not only as anti-aircraft guns, but also in combat on the ground. By the end of the war, 15,170 Flak 36s and 37s had been manufactured.

1.5 INCH (3.7 CM) FLAK 43 ANTI-AIRCRAFT GUN

Caliber:	1.5 in
Combat weight:	3,066 lb
Barrel length:	130 in
Elevation:	−7.5° to +90°
Traverse:	360°
Ammunition type and weight:	HE-I: 1.4 lb
Muzzle velocity:	2,735 ft/s
Rate of fire:	150 rpm (theoretically)
Maximum range:	21,650 ft
Maximum effective range (vertical):	16,000 ft

The 3.7 cm (1.5 inch) Flak 43 was another improved anti-aircraft gun: its weight was reduced to 3,066 lb (1.392 kg), yet its rate of fire was increased. The soldiers operating the gun were protected by a splinter-proof shield, and the gun's ballistic effectiveness matched that of the 1.5 inch (3.7 cm) Flak 36. The first of these guns were delivered in February 1944. There was also a twin-gun unit whose barrels were, unusually, arranged one above the other, rather than next to each other. This version weighed about 2,780 kg and its actual rate of fire was around 300 rpm. For use on ships, the Flak 43 was mounted on a LM-42 triple-axle double gun carriage.

Until production ceased in 1945, 6,103 Flak 43s were manufactured.

A 1.5 inch (3.7) Flak 43 two-gun mount.

3.5 INCH (8.8 CM) FLAK 18 AND 36 ANTI-AIRCRAFT GUNS

The legendary "Eight-Eight" was introduced as the Flak 18 in the Wehrmacht in 1933. The terms of the 1919 Treaty of Versailles prevented Germany from developing or manufacturing her own heavy anti-aircraft gun, so engineers from Krupp went to Bofors, the Swedish arms manufacturer, to use their expertise, and the preliminary designs for the Flak 18 were produced in Sweden. As a rule, Wehrmacht weapons were designated according to the year in which they were first manufactured, or the year in which they were introduced in the army. To maintain secrecy, however, all weapons developed after the 1919 ban had the model number 18. The original Flak 18 had a barrel made up of one part, but because barrel wear was particularly severe near the chamber, a three-part barrel was introduced for the Flak 36, which could only be replaced with the same specific parts. A version with improved communication between the controls and the gun was designated the Flak 37.

The "Eight-Eight" was first deployed in the Spanish Civil War, and was later deployed in every branch of the German military and on every front in the Second World War. It did not gain its legendary reputation in its intended role as an anti-aircraft gun, but mostly in combat on the ground, particularly in anti-tank deployment. In the early years of the war, the 3.5 inch (8.8 cm) Flak was often the only weapon to make any impact against heavy tanks, and the Allies were afraid of its firepower: the "Eight-Eight" could easily destroy armored targets from around 4,000 ft (1,800 m) away. Nevertheless, it had two disadvantages: it was tall and relatively heavy.

Caliber:	3.5 in
Combat weight:	10,976 lb
Barrel length:	L/56 (194 in)
Elevation:	−3° to +85°
Traverse:	360°
Ammunition type and weight:	HE: 20.7 lb; AP: 22.5 lb
Muzzle velocity:	2,735 ft/s
Maximum penetration (armor steel):	4.2 in/ 3,350 ft/30°
Maximum range:	48,650 ft
Effective range (vertical):	26,650 ft— Max: 35,350 ft

The legendary "Eight-Eight" being reloaded.

In the summer of 1944, more than 10,000 3.5 inch (8.8 cm) anti-aircraft guns were in service. In October that year alone, these guns fired more than 3.1 million rounds. Its importance is also reflected in the fact that one-third of all gun barrels manufactured in Germany in 1944 were made for "Eight-Eights." The British and Americans also deployed "Eight-Eights" which they had seized from the Germans. A total of 20,754 3.5 inch (8.8 cm) anti-aircraft guns in this series were manufactured.

A 3.5 inch (8.8 cm) Flak 18 anti-aircraft gun being prepared for deployment.

A 3.5 inch (8.8 cm) Flak 36 anti-aircraft gun being deployed to protect an industrial site in the Ruhr.

3.5 INCH (8.8 CM) FLAK 41 ANTI-AIRCRAFT GUN

Caliber:	3.5 in
Combat weight:	17,181 lb
Barrel length:	L/74 (258 in)
Elevation:	−3° to +90°
Traverse:	360°
Ammunition type and weight:	HE: 20.7 lb
Muzzle velocity:	3,335 ft/s
Maximum Penetration (armor steel):	
	7.6 in/3,335 ft/90°;
	5 in/6,670 ft/90°
Max effective range:	35,585 ft

To cope with the increasing flying altitudes of enemy aircraft, the Luftwaffe invited tenders for a new 3.5 inch (8.8 cm) caliber anti-aircraft gun, and Rheinmetall's bid was successful. Much of the Flak 41 was completely new: it used a different kind of ammunition from previous models (though the caliber was the same), and it had a longer barrel, a different gun mount, and an electronic detonation device. It was unveiled in 1941 but was not deployed until two years later.

The Flak 41 was even more effective than the 18, 36, or 37. Not only could it shoot higher, it could also shoot faster: up to 25 rpm. Yet it was also much more complicated and expensive to manufacture and maintain, and the ammunition cartridges continually

Krupp built an experimental self-propelled anti-aircraft gun carriage in 1941, the "experimental heavy anti-aircraft car" with the 3.5 inch (8.8 cm) Flak 41 anti-aircraft gun.

jammed the barrel. There were significantly fewer Flak 41s manufactured than earlier models.

The 3.5 inch (8.8 cm) Flak 41 anti-aircraft gun.

A 3.5 inch (8.8 cm) Flak 41 anti-aircraft gun on a special platform.

The 3.5 inch (8.8 cm) Flak 41 anti-aircraft gun.

An early 3.5 inch (8.8 cm) Flak 41 anti-aircraft gun with a cross-shaped gun mount.

4.1 INCH (10.5 CM) FLAK 38 ANTI-AIRCRAFT GUN

The 4.1 inch (10.5 cm) Flak 38 was originally developed for the German Navy, but in 1933 the order came from the Army Weapons Office to convert it for use in the army and the air force. It was very advanced for its time, with many new features, including a pivoting gun mount, an electrically-powered aiming device, and an automatic reloading facility. Until 1939, four of these guns were delivered per month. They had some technical glitches, as the electrical systems did not work perfectly. So in 1939 various aspects of the gun, especially the electrical installations, were changed, and the improved weapons were called

Caliber:	4.1 in
Combat weight:	22,520 lb
Barrel length:	L/63.3 (262 in)
Elevation:	−3° to +85°
Traverse:	360°
Ammunition type and weight:	HE: 32.6 lb
Muzzle velocity:	2,935 ft/s
Maximum range:	58,350 ft
Effective range:	31,500 ft—Max: 40,350 ft

the 4.1 inch (10.5 cm) Flak 39. In 1944, 2,068 versions of both types were deployed by the army, and 3,755 were manufactured in total.

A 4.1 inch (10.5 cm) Flak 38 anti-aircraft gun.

5 INCH (12.8 CM) FLAK 40 ANTI-AIRCRAFT GUN

Caliber:	5 in
Combat weight:	39,648 lb
Barrel length:	L/61.2 (308 in)
Elevation:	−3° to +88°
Traverse:	360°
Ammunition type and weight:	HE: 57.3 lb
Muzzle velocity:	2,935 ft/s
Maximum range:	69,650 ft
Effective range:	35,600 ft—Max: 49,350 ft

In 1936 Rheinmetall received the order to develop the 5 inch (12.8 cm) Flak 40, but it was not introduced in the Wehrmacht until 1941. It was equipped with an electric aiming device and an automatic reloading facility. Early versions could be transported in two parts, though later versions were transported in one piece on the 220 special trailer, but because of the gun's weight, it was generally installed in one place or transported on rail gun carriages. So in 1944 there were six mobile Flak 40s, 242 Flak 40 installations, and 201 Flak 40s deployed on rail gun carriages. The 5 inch (12.8 cm) anti-aircraft gun proved to be an excellent weapon, but its limitations were exposed in the heavy Allied attacks of late 1944. It was manufactured until the end of the war, and in total 1,129 were produced.

Each ring round the barrel of this 5 inch (12.8 cm) Flak 40 anti-aircraft gun stands for one aircraft shot down.

8.3 INCH (21 CM) K 12 (E) RAIL CANNON

The 8.3 inch (21 cm) K 12 (E) rail cannon.

The army deployed a number of different rail cannon with calibers varying from 6.7 inch (17 cm) to 31.5 inch (80 cm), but only in very small numbers, and they had a very limited impact on the course of the war. Technically, however, some of them were real masterpieces. One of them, based on the famous Paris cannon of the First World War, was the 8.3 inch (21 cm) K 12 (E) cannon, whose maximum range of over 383,000 ft (around 115,000 m) was the greatest of all the weapons of the Second World War

and is still very reputable today. The first of these cannon types was put into service in March 1939, and a second, the 4.7 inch (12 cm) K 12 N, was produced in July 1940. Since neither cannon had any traverse (they could only be pointed straight ahead), they either had to be mounted on revolving platforms, or the gun carriage had to be placed on a circular track. In the entire Second World War, the 701 Artillery Battery, which deployed these cannon, fired precisely 83 shots! Certainly, the money and

Caliber:	8.3 in
Combat weight:	678,400 lb
Barrel length:	L/158.5 (1,311 in)
Elevation:	−25° to +55°
Traverse:	0°
Ammunition type and weight:	HE: 236.8 lb
Muzzle velocity:	5,000 ft/s
Maximum range:	HE: 383,000 ft

effort that went into the construction, production, and deployment of these cannon could have been spent more wisely in other areas. But in spite of their limited practical use, they are still masterpieces of engineering.

A 8.3 inch (21 cm) rail cannon on the French coast fires at a target on the other side of the English Channel. Photo taken from the German Army magazine, **Signal.**

31.5 INCH (80 CM) DORA AND GUSTAV RAIL CANNON

These two giant 31.5 inch (80 cm) cannon were ordered by the Wehrmacht High Command in 1937, with a view to destroying the fortifications on the Maginot Line in Alsace. Gustav was named after Gustav Krupp von Bohlen und Halbach, senior partner in the Krupp company, while Dora was named after the wife of the engineer in charge of the project. Both of these cannon were completed too late for their intended purposes, so they were deployed on the Eastern Front instead. They were the largest cannon the world had ever (or has ever) seen, and had to be transported in several pieces, then assembled, and mounted on a prepared emplacement. To assemble and disassemble each cannon, its emplacement and all the necessary tracks, took around 4,000 men! Each cannon was defended against air strikes by an entire anti-aircraft regiment, as well as being protected against attacks by Soviet partisans by a guard regiment. Because neither cannon had any traverse, the tracks had to be laid down in a circle, and the cannon had to be aimed by shunting it round the track. To do so, Krupp developed two purpose-built V188 diesel locomotives, and the cannon could

be aimed while in motion by electric motors built into the gun carriage. As with all German rail cannon since the First World War Paris cannon, the shell cartridges were stored in a specially acclimatized car to keep the temperature of the nitroglycerin powder explosive at around 15°C. This was to optimize its combustion, and to make the latter as controllable as possible.

Of the two cannon, Gustav was the only one to see active service. It was deployed in the siege of Sebastopol in the Soviet Union in 1942, where it fired a total of 48 shots. The penetrative power of its huge 31.5 inch (80 cm) shells, which weighed 7.1 kg each, was enough to destroy an ammunitions dump protected by 100 ft (30 m) of rock. Dora was never deployed, and at the end of the war a third cannon was still being built. There were also plans for rocket-propelled shells that could reach targets more than 90 miles away. After the end of the war, the US Army found the remains of two of the three cannon in Grafenwöhr: they had been exploded so that they would not fall into enemy hands intact. The other cannon fell into Soviet hands in Auerswalde, Saxony, also partially

destroyed. The parts which had remained intact and some of the wreckage were analyzed by Soviet experts—it is not known what happened to the rest of the cannon. Again, Dora and Gustav were technical masterpieces, but they were basically a waste of materials, technological expertise, and manpower.

Caliber:	31.5 in
Combat weight:	2,973,550 lb
Barrel length:	L/41 (1,290 in)
Elevation:	−10° to +65°
Traverse:	0°
Ammunition type and weight:	HE: 10,575 lb; CP: 15,640 lb
Muzzle velocity:	HE: 2,735 ft/s; CP: 2,365 ft/s
Maximum range:	HE: 156,650 ft; CP: 126,650 ft
Maximum penetration (concrete):	395 in

Dora, the 31.5 inch (80cm) rail cannon.

1.9 INCH (4.7 CM) M 35 ANTI-TANK CANNON

This 1.9 inch (4.7 cm) anti-tank cannon was originally designed by the Austrian firm Böhler and sold on the international market. So as well as Austria, the Italians and the Dutch also had this weapon. The Italians manufactured it under license as the 47/32 M 35 and deployed it as both an anti-tank and an infantry cannon. In fact, so many were manufactured in Italy that in effect it was

A 1.9 inch (4.7 cm) M 35 anti-tank cannon.

virtually an Italian weapon, though it was produced in Austria until September 1940. After the German annexation of Austria in 1938 (the *Anschluss*), the Wehrmacht took charge of all 330 Pak M 35 cannon manufactured until 1940, calling it the Pak 35/36 (ö), but almost all were sold to Italy in February 1941. The Italians mounted it on self-propelled gun carriages based on the Sahariana all-terrain vehicle, and it was also adapted as a tank weapon.

Caliber:	1.9 in
Combat weight:	610 lb
Barrel length:	L/32 (60 in)
Elevation:	−15° to +56°
Traverse:	62°
Ammunition type and weight:	AP: 3.2 lb; HEAT: 5.2 lb
Muzzle velocity:	AP: 2,100 ft/s; 835 ft/s
Maximum range:	HE: 23,350 ft
Maximum penetration (armor steel):	P: 1.7 in/ 1,650 ft/90°

3 INCH (7.5 CM) 75/18 M 35 HOWITZER

Caliber:	3 in
Combat weight:	2,425 lb
Barrel length:	L/18.3 (62 in)
Elevation:	−10° to +45°
Traverse:	50°
Ammunition type and weight:	HE: 13.9 lb
Muzzle velocity:	HE: 13,350 ft/s
Maximum range:	HE: 31,350 ft

The Italians always emphasized the importance of equipping their Alpini (mountain divisions) with good modern equipment. So in 1934, to replace the old Škoda weapons of the First World War, they produced the 75/18 M 34 mountain

howitzer. It could be disassembled quickly and easily, which meant that it could be transported by the "Mule" half track in the mountains. A new howitzer based on this model was produced for the field divisions in 1935. It was easier to assemble, while having the same ballistic properties as the earlier model. The newer version was also exported to Portugal in 1940, and a number of these howitzers

were exchanged for raw materials with some South American states. The M 35 proved to be a good modern weapon, and it was also acquired and deployed by the Wehrmacht in 1943 as the 3 inch (7.5 cm) leFh 255 (i).

The 3 inch (7.5 cm) 75/18 howitzer.

0.8 INCH (2 CM) BREDA MODEL 35 ANTI-AIRCRAFT GUN

As indicated by its name, this anti-aircraft gun was introduced in the Italian Army in 1935. It was intended both as an anti-aircraft gun and for combat on the ground, and it had vizors for both applications. It had a particularly interesting loading mechanism: a metal strip with 12 rounds was inserted in one side and came out of the other with the spent cartridges. Anti-aircraft guns of this kind were also

Caliber:	0.8 in
Combat weight:	676 lb
Barrel length:	L/65 (51 ins)
Elevation:	−5° to +80°
Traverse:	360°
Ammunition type and weight:	HE: 0.3 lb
Muzzle velocity:	2,800 ft/s
Rate of fire:	230 rpm
Maximum effective range (vertical):	HE: 8,650 ft

The 0.8 inch (2 cm) Breda M 35 anti-aircraft gun.

deployed in all-terrain vehicles such as the Sahariana. From 1943 until the end of the war, the Wehrmacht deployed the 0.8 inch (2 cm) Model 35; initially they were acquired from the Italians, while later they were produced by Breda under German supervision.

3.5 INCH (9 CM) 90/53 ANTI-AIRCRAFT GUN

Caliber:	3.5 in
Combat weight:	13,745 lb
Barrel length:	L/52.6 (186 in)
Elevation:	−2° to +85°
Traverse:	360°
Ammunition type and weight:	HE: 22.8 lb
Muzzle velocity:	HE: 2,765 ft/s
Maximum effective range (vertical):	HE: 35,000 ft

The 3.5 inch (9 cm) anti-aircraft gun was solidly and intelligently constructed, and it was the most effective of all the Italian anti-aircraft guns in the Second World War, comparing favorably with any of its contemporary counterparts. It was developed and produced by Ansaldo, and the first guns of this kind were ready for deployment in 1939. It was deployed by the Italian Army not only as an anti-aircraft gun, but also as an anti-tank cannon, and in coast batteries. As an anti-aircraft gun and an anti-tank cannon, it compared favorably with the legendary German 3.5 inch (8.8 cm) anti-aircraft gun. A number of 3.5 inch (9 cm) anti-aircraft

guns were also installed in trucks and tanks to create self-propelled artillery weapons. In total, 1,087 guns of this type were ordered, but by July 1943 only 539 had been delivered. Then the Ansaldo factories were taken over by the Germans and all 3.5 inch (9 cm) anti-aircraft guns subsequently manufactured were for the

Wehrmacht. These guns were mostly used to defend northern Italian industrial sites against bombing raids and were known as the 3.5 inch (9 cm) Flak 309/I (i). British forces also seized a number of these guns on their march through Italy and deployed them in defense of the ports they occupied.

The Italian 3.5 inch (9 cm) 90/53 anti-aircraft gun.

2.8 INCH (7 CM) TYPE 92 INFANTRY CANNON

Caliber:	2.8 in
Combat weight:	468 lb
Barrel length:	L/11.3 (31 in)
Elevation:	−8° to +70°
Traverse:	45°
Ammunition type and weight:	HE: 8.7 lb
Muzzle velocity:	HE: 657 ft/s
Maximum range	HE: 9,350 ft

A Japanese 2.8 inch (7 cm) Type 92 cannon subsequently deployed by the Chinese in the Korean War.

This cannon, introduced in 1932, was the Japanese Army's standard infantry support cannon during the Second World War, and each infantry battalion had two of them. Because it could be aimed so high, it could be used both as a cannon with a straight trajectory, and as a mortar with a curved trajectory. Because it was very light and could be divided into small parts, it was easy to transport, which was a significant advantage in Asian jungle warfare. After 1945 weapons of this kind were used by Chinese and Korean troops well into the 1950s.

5.9 INCH (15 CM) TYPE 96 HOWITZER

Caliber:	5.9 in
Combat weight:	9,120 lb
Barrel length:	L/23.6 (139 in)
Elevation:	−5° to +65°
Traverse:	30°
Ammunition type and weight:	HE: 68.9 lb
Muzzle velocity:	HE: 1,800 ft/s
Maximum range	HE: 39,650 ft

Although only a small number of weapons of this type (440) were produced, compared to Western equivalents, it was the main weapon deployed by Japanese heavy artillery batteries from 1941–1945. Compared to other Japanese artillery cannon, this was a very modern weapon, and it was always meant to be transported by motor vehicles. It was first deployed in the Second Sino-Japanese War from 1937 onwards, and was very popular with the Japanese artillery troops, who rated it very highly.

The 5.9 inch (15 cm) Type 96 howitzer.

3 INCH (7.5 CM) MODEL 1897 CANNON

This was the predecessor of all modern rapid fire cannon, and it was a world leader when introduced in the French Army in the late 19th century. In the First World War, it was the French artillery's standard cannon and was exported in large numbers after 1918 to Poland, Romania, Portugal, and Greece, among other countries. More than 17,000 of these cannon are thought to have been manufactured, and in 1940 the French still had a large number of them. After its first encounters with the Russian T-34 and KW-1 tanks, the Wehrmacht based its makeshift 3 inch (7.5 cm) Pak 97/38 on the Model 1897 cannon it had seized in France and Poland, adding muzzle brakes to the original barrels and placing them on the gun mount of the 2 inch (5 cm) Pak 38. It is believed that around 700 of these cannon were assembled. At first, the Wehrmacht loaded them with ammunition left over by the French and the Poles, but this proved to be ineffective. Only special hollow charge shells (known as HEAT) made sufficient impact.

	Model 1897	97/38 anti-tank gun
Caliber:	3 in	3 in
Combat weight:	2,555 lb	2,621 lb
Barrel length:	L/36 (106 in)	L/36 (106 in)
Elevation:	−11° to +18°	−8° to +18°
Traverse:	6°	60°
Ammunition type and weight:	HE: 11.5 lb; FRAG: 15.9 lb	AP: 15 lb; HEAT: 10.6 lb
Muzzle velocity:	HE: 1,947 ft/s; FRAG: 1,763 ft/s	AP: 1,900 ft/s; HEAT: 1,500 ft/s
Maximum effective range (vertical):	HE: 28,350 ft	28,350 ft
Maximum penetration (armor steel):	N/A	AP: 2.3 in/3,350 ft/60°; HEAT: 3.5 in/any distance/60°

The 3 inch (7.5 cm) M 1897 was the first truly modern cannon.

1 INCH (2.5 CM) HOTCHKISS MODEL 38/39 ANTI-AIRCRAFT GUN

Caliber:	1 in
Combat weight:	1,773 lb
Barrel length:	L/60 (59 in)
Elevation:	−3° to +110°
Traverse:	360°
Ammunition type and weight:	HE: 0.6 lb; AP: 0.1 lb
Muzzle velocity:	HE: 3,000 ft/s
Maximum effective range (vertical):	HE: 8,350 ft
Maximum penetration (armor steel):	AP: 1.4 in/ 1,665 ft/90°

A 1 inch (2.5 cm) Hotchkiss M 39 anti-aircraft gun in firing position.

This anti-aircraft gun was produced by Hotchkiss, the French arms manufacturer, from 1938 onward, and a later model with an improved gun mount was known as the M 39. It was used both as an anti-aircraft gun and as an anti-tank cannon, and its armor-piercing shells were effective for their time. Only around 1,000 anti-aircraft guns of this type were produced, and after France's defeat in 1940, the Wehrmacht seized and deployed most of them, renaming them the 1 inch (2.5 cm) Flak Hotchkiss 38/39 (f).

3 INCH (7.5 CM) MODEL 1930 AND 1936 ANTI-AIRCRAFT GUNS

	Model 1930	Model 1936
Caliber:	3 in	3 in
Combat weight:	8,370 lb	9,031 lb
Barrel length:	L/45 (133 in)	L/45 (133 in)
Elevation:	+1° to +70°	+1° to +70°
Traverse:	360°	360°
Ammunition type and weight:	N/A	N/A
Muzzle velocity:	2,335 ft/s	2,700 ft/s
Maximum effective range (vertical):	26,650 ft	27,350 ft

A 3 inch (7.5 cm) M 30 anti-aircraft gun.

Before 1940 France produced a number of different types of 3 inch (7.5 cm) anti-aircraft guns. Just three types of First World War anti-aircraft gun were still in service after 1918, but they were extensively modified to create a number of different new models. Most of them had their barrels modernized by Schneider, but at least five completely new types were manufactured and put into service before 1940. Because there were many different sorts of anti-aircraft gun but only a modest number of each, the French anti-aircraft divisions were relatively disorganized, so the cannon were not very wisely deployed. Nevertheless, because they were equally effective, these two relatively modern models were selected for further deployment by the Wehrmacht and renamed the 3 inch (7.5 cm) Flak M 30 (f) and M 36 (f).

A German anti-aircraft battery with French 3 inch (7.5 cm) M 36 anti-aircraft cannon on the northern French coast.

1.6 INCH (4 CM) 2-POUNDER ANTI-TANK CANNON

When it first appeared in 1936, the British 2-pounder anti-tank cannon was undoubtedly the best of its kind. It had an innovative gun mount which gave it 360° traverse (it could be aimed in all directions), a useful property in anti-tank combat. It did, however, have one disadvantage: it did not have any high explosive (HE) ammunition. Since most British tanks were equipped with this weapon until 1942, this was a serious problem. Nevertheless, when it was first deployed, in the campaign on the Western Front in 1940, it had no trouble dealing with the German tanks, but it was revised in 1941. To make up for the huge

Caliber:	1.6 in
Combat weight:	1,756 lb
Barrel length:	L/52 (82 in)
Elevation:	−5° to +23°
Traverse:	360°
Ammunition type and weight:	AP: 2 lb
Muzzle velocity:	AP: 2,693 ft/s
Maximum effective range	AP: 3,350 ft
Maximum penetration (armor steel):	
	AP: 1.7 in/3,350 ft/60°

material losses of the British retreat from France in 1940, including 500 of this type alone, new 2-pounder cannon were built, even though a 6-pounder anti-tank cannon was already being developed. When the British encountered Rommel's Afrikakorps in North Africa from 1941–1942, this decision was vindicated.

The British 2-pounder anti-tank cannon with its crew.

2.2 INCH (5.7 CM) 6-POUNDER ANTI-TANK CANNON

Caliber:	2.4 in
Combat weight:	2,520 lb
Barrel length:	L/45 (101 in)
Elevation:	−5° to +15°
Traverse:	90°
Ammunition type and weight:	AP: 6 lb;
	APDS: 3.24 lb
Muzzle velocity:	AP: 2,737 ft/s;
	APDS: 4,117 ft/s
Effective range	AP: 5,000 ft—
	Maximum: 15,350 ft
Maximum penetration (armor steel):	
	AP: 2.9 in/3,350 ft/60°/
	APDS: 5.7 in/3,350 ft/60°

Although it was already being designed in 1938, the 6-pounder anti-tank cannon was not ready for production until late 1941. Nevertheless, it was a great success, and highly rated by the troops. It was not only produced under license in the USA, but was also used by some British tanks. The 6-pounder cannon fired high explosive shells (which had finally been developed) and high velocity armor-piercing (HVAP) shells (known in Britain as APCR, or "armor-piercing composite rigid" shells), and in 1944 it was the first cannon in the world to fire armor-piercing,

discarding sabot (APDS) shells, which greatly increased its penetrative power. Although toward the end of the war, the 6-pounder anti-tank cannon had trouble destroying German Panther and Royal Tiger tanks head-on, even with this new ammunition, it remained in the arsenal of the British Army until the mid-1960s. As well as various models with or without a muzzle brake, and with different barrel lengths, there was an interesting version with an automatic reloading facility installed in the De Havilland Mosquito fighter aircraft. The American M1 anti-tank cannon was based on the British 6-pounder cannon and was the US Army's standard anti-tank weapon from late 1943 onwards. The most significant difference between the two cannon was that the US version had a slightly longer barrel, yet it was slightly less effective than its British counterpart.

The 6-pounder anti-tank cannon.

3 INCH (7.62 CM) 17-POUNDER ANTI-TANK CANNON

Caliber:	3 in
Combat weight:	4,619 lb
Barrel length:	L/60 (180 in)
Elevation:	−6° to +16.5°
Traverse:	60°
Ammunition type and weight:	AP: 16 lb;
	APDS: 7.6 lb; HE: 15.4 lb
Muzzle velocity:	AP: 2,947 ft/s;
	APDS: 4,010 ft/s;
	HE: 2,920 ft/s
Maximum range	HE: 30,485 ft
Maximum penetration (armor steel):	
	AP: 4.3 in/3,350 ft/60°;
	APDS: 9.1 in/3,350 ft/60°

The British 17-pounder anti-tank cannon proved to be one of the best cannon of its kind, capable of dealing with practically every kind of tank, not least because of its newly designed armor-piercing, discarding sabot (APDS) ammunition. In 1942 the first models were provisionally mounted on the same gun carriages as the 25-pounder howitzers, so that they could be deployed as soon as possible in the North African campaign against the German Tiger tanks, but regular models were mounted on heavy split trail gun mounts, which represented this weapon's only disadvantage, as it was almost impossible to move it without a motor vehicle. The 17-pounder cannon was also used as a self-propelled weapon (the Archer), and was deployed both as an anti-tank weapon (on the Wolverine) and on the Sherman Firefly and Centurion tanks.

The 17-pounder anti-tank cannon.

3.4 INCH (8.76 CM) 25-POUNDER FIELD CANNON

Built from 1938 onward, the 25-pounder was the standard field cannon of all the Commonwealth forces in the war. Around 12,000 of these cannon were manufactured until the end of the war, and it was still in many states' arsenals after 1945. It was called the "25-pounder" because of the approximate weight of its ammunition, and was extremely successful. It was also very popular with the troops, as it was reliable and did not suffer from technical glitches. In his memoirs, one Canadian artillerist describes how in 1944 his battery of 25-pounders in Normandy would often keep firing for so long that the barrels would start "glowing red!" This cannon had different models (or "marks") of gun mount, barrel, and barrel cradle, arranged in various configurations, and was one of the first weapons that could be deployed both as a cannon and as a howitzer. The

Caliber:	3.4 in
Combat weight:	3,965 lb
Barrel length:	L/31 (107 in)
Elevation:	−5° to +45°
Traverse:	360°
Ammunition type and weight:	HE: 16.2 lb;
	AP: 19.8 lb
Muzzle velocity:	HE: 1,727 ft/s
Maximum range	HE: 40,850 ft

box trail gun mount looked conservative but was well designed. It allowed the cannon to be aimed high as a howitzer, and it had a disk at the base that could be lowered to the ground, which enabled gunners quickly to turn the cannon round 360°, a very useful property in anti-tank combat. The versatility of the 25-pounder also made it an excellent self-propelled weapon. It was deployed by the British in the North African campaign on special truck loading platforms and was fired over the driver's cab. It was also installed in the Bishop and Sexton self-propelled artillery weapons. The latter, which was open-topped, was built in larger numbers than any other British self-propelled artillery weapon.

The British 25-pounder field cannon.

5.5 INCH (14 CM) MK. 2 FIELD CANNON

Caliber:	5.5 in
Combat weight:	13,634 lb
Barrel length:	L/31 (107 in)
Elevation:	−5° to +45°
Traverse:	60°
Ammunition type and weight:	HE: 100 lb
Muzzle velocity:	HE: 1,723 ft/s
Maximum range	HE: 49,375 ft

As it became increasingly likely that war would break out in Europe, the British Army came under more and more pressure to replace its outdated 4.5 inch (11.4 cm) and 5 inch (12.7 cm) cannon

and howitzers. In early 1939 a new cannon in the same class was ordered. It was first introduced in the army in May 1942, and it was deployed in the African campaign against Rommel's troops. At first, its range was disappointing, and only

the introduction of a new shell, which was around 20 lb (9 kg) lighter, improved its range to an acceptable level. Yet it remained in the British Army armory until the 1980s, and is still part of the arsenals of South Africa, Pakistan, and New Zealand.

The 5.5 inch (14 cm) Mark 2 Field Cannon.

3.7 INCH (9.4 CM) MK.1 ANTI-AIRCRAFT GUN

Caliber:	3.7 in
Combat weight:	20,520 lb
Barrel length:	L/50 (185 in)
Elevation:	−6° to +80°
Traverse:	360°
Ammunition type and weight:	HE: 30 lb
Muzzle velocity:	2,640 ft/s
Maximum range	HE: 62,650 ft
Maximum effective range (vertical):	HE: 32,515 ft

The 3.7 inch (9.4 cm) gun was the British Army's standard heavy anti-aircraft gun throughout the Second World War. Its development had begun in the early 1930s, but it did not go into production until 1937—only just in time to produce large numbers for the outbreak of war. This gun had many innovative features, such as remote fire control. Only reloading had to be done

manually. Yet this made it difficult to aim the gun for combat on the ground, which meant that, unlike the German "Eight-Eight", it was not easy to use the gun to attack tanks. From 1943, an

automatic reloading mechanism was introduced, increasing its rate of fire from 25 to 30 rpm.

A British 3.7 inch (9.4 cm) anti-aircraft gun seized by the German Army at Dunkirk in 1940.

1.8 INCH (4.5 CM) MODEL 1937 ANTI-TANK CANNON

When the Red Army was in need of a modern anti-tank weapon in the 1930s, the Soviet Union still enjoyed close economic ties with the German Third Reich, enabling it to acquire some Rheinmetall 1.5 inch (3.7 cm) anti-tank cannon. The Russians studied these weapons, made a few alterations (a larger caliber, different sights), and produced the 1.89 inch (4.5 cm) Model 32, which still had wooden wheels and no suspension. The main variant, the Model 1937, had modern rubber tires and suspension. During the Winter War against Finland (1939–40), the Finns seized hundreds of these cannon and deployed them themselves. In June 1941 it was the Red Army's standard anti-tank cannon, but like the German 1.5 inch (3.7 cm) anti-tank cannon, it was no longer effective. So a new version was introduced in 1942 with a longer barrel (L/68.6, or 3,087 mm). Anti-tank cannon of both types were also acquired by the Wehrmacht, which renamed them the 1.8 inch (4.5 cm) Pak 184 (r). The Model 1942 remained in the Red Army arsenal after the end of the war, and according to Russian sources, 56,742 cannon of these types were produced in total.

Caliber:	1.8 in
Combat weight:	936 lb
Barrel length:	L/46 (81 in)
Elevation:	−5° to +25°
Traverse:	60°
Ammunition type and weight:	AP: 3.1 lb; HE: 4.7 lb
Muzzle velocity:	AP: 2,533 ft/s; HE: 1,133 ft/s
Effective range	HE: 62,650 ft
Maximum penetration (armor steel):	AP: 1.4 in/1,665 ft/60°

The 1.8 inch (4.5 cm) Model 1937 anti-tank cannon.

2.2 INCH (5.7 CM) ZIS-2 MODEL 1943 ANTI-TANK CANNON

Because they could foresee that the 1.8 inch (4.5 cm) anti-tank cannon would soon become obsolete, the Russians began developing a new 2.2 inch (5.7 cm) anti-tank cannon in 1940, but technical difficulties halted its introduction into the Red Army until June 15, 1943. Production was halted in 1949, after 13,400 had been manufactured. They were very effective weapons, and could penetrate the armor of most German combat vehicles, particularly when they started firing high velocity armor-piercing (HVAP) ammunition. The ZIS-2 was also

Caliber:	2.4 in
Combat weight:	2,753 lb
Barrel length:	L/73 (164 in)
Elevation:	−5° to +25°
Traverse:	54°
Ammunition type and weight:	AP: 3.1 lb; APCR: 3.9 lb
Muzzle velocity:	AP: 3,300 ft/s; APCR: 4,233 ft/s
Maximum effective range	6,650 ft
Maximum penetration (armor steel):	AP: 3.1 in/3,350 ft/90° APCR: 4.1 in/3,350 ft/90°

installed in the M-3 half-track vehicle, creating the SU-57 self propelled artillery weapon, and in some T-34 tanks, creating the T-34/57 variant. Some cannon of this type were seized by the Wehrmacht, which renamed them the Pak 208 (r) and deployed them with some success.

A Russian 2.2 inch (5.7 cm) ZIS-2 anti-tank cannon.

3 INCH (7.62 CM) ZIS-3 MODEL 1936, 1939, AND 1942 FIELD CANNON

3 inch (7.62 cm) caliber field cannon were the Red Army artillery's standard weapons, and they were deployed both as anti-tank cannon and in many situations as non-precise weapons. The original Model 1936 (of which a total of 2,844 were manufactured) was judged by the Red Army to be too heavy, so a lighter version with a shortened barrel and altered recoil system went into production in 1939. In total, 9,812 new variant weapons were manufactured. Because the cannon had a relatively high muzzle velocity and produced a distinctive sound when fired, the German soldiers nicknamed it the "Ratsch-Bumm." After invading Russia, the Wehrmacht seized huge numbers of these cannon and their ammunition, renaming them the 3 inch (7.62) Pak 36 (r) and Pak 39 (r). Because the Germans did not have comparable anti-tank cannon, they produced their own ammunition for the

Russian cannon, achieving even better results than the Russians. They also armed the Marder self-propelled artillery weapon with both types of Russian cannon. In order to offset their terrible losses in the first months of the German invasion, the 3 inch (7.6 cm) ZIS-3 field cannon was first produced in 1942. It was far lighter than previous models, and could be produced quickly and cost-effectively. Hence, there were a lot of

similarities between the ZIS-2 and ZIS-3 gun carriages. The ZIS-3 was one of the main artillery weapons for the Soviet Union and its allies in the Second World War, and it was also installed in the SU-76 as a self-propelled artillery weapon. Until 1945 49,016 units of this versatile and effective weapon were produced, and it remained in production after the war, being manufactured both in the Soviet Union and under license in other countries, including China. Large numbers of ZIS-3 cannon were also exported, and a number of countries in the developing world still have them in their arsenals.

	Model 1936	Model 1939	Model 1942
Caliber:	3 in	3 in	3 in
Combat weight:	3,568 lb	3,238 lb	2,458 lb
Barrel length:	L/51.1 (153 in)	L/42 (126 in)	L/42.6 (128 in)
Elevation:	−6° to +43°	−6° to +45°	−5° to +37°
Traverse:	57°	57°	54°
Ammunition type and weight:	HE: 13.9 lb; AP: 13.9 lb	HE: 13.7 lb; AP: 13.9 lb	HE: 13.9 lb; AP: 13.9 lb; HEAT: 8.7 lb
Muzzle velocity:	HE: 2,333 ft/s	HE: 2,207 ft/s	HE: 2,267 ft/s
Maximum effective range:	HE: 45,400 ft	HE: 44,300 ft	HE: 44,300 ft

The M 1939 3 inch (7.62 cm) field cannon.

A 3 inch (7.62 cm) ZIS-3 being towed by a Dodge WC-51, which the Soviet Union received as part of its hiring and loaning agreement with the USA.

4.8 INCH (12.2 CM) M-30 MODEL 1938 HOWITZER

The M-30 howitzer was produced from 1938 onwards, hence its designation. Like most other Soviet cannon, it was noted for being very resilient. It was mounted on the T-34 tank chassis to create the SU-122 self-propelled artillery weapon. Because of its own shortage of similar weapons, the Wehrmacht also deployed this howitzer, renaming it the 4.8 inch (12.2 cm) 396 (r) heavy field howitzer. Until 1945, 17,526 of these howitzers were manufactured, and cannon of the same sort were still deployed for decades after the war. China also produced large numbers of these weapons under license after 1945, calling them the 54 and 54-1.

Caliber:	4.8 in
Combat weight:	5,396 lb
Barrel length:	L/23 (110 in)
Elevation:	−3° to +65.5°
Traverse:	49°
Ammunition type and weight:	HE: 47.9 lb; HEAT: 29.1 lb
Muzzle velocity:	HE: 1,717 ft/s
Maximum range	HE: 39,350 ft
Maximum penetration (armor steel):	HEAT: 7.9 in/667 ft/90°

The 4.8 inch (12.2 cm) M-30 howitzer.

The ZIS-3 was the Red Army's standard artillery weapon.

6 INCH (15.2 CM) D-1 MODEL 1943 HOWITZER

To simplify production and reduce weight, this howitzer was manufactured in a special way, which gained popularity in the Soviet Union during the course of the war. The barrel of the 6 inch (15.2 cm) Model 1938 was connected to the strengthened split trail gun mount of the 4.8 inch (12.2 cm) M-30 howitzer. To function properly, this combination needed a large muzzle

Caliber:	6 in
Combat weight:	7,930 lb
Barrel length:	L/24.6 (165 in)
Elevation:	−3° to +65.5°
Traverse:	35°
Ammunition type and weight:	HE: 88.1 lb
Muzzle velocity:	HE: 1,693 ft/s
Maximum range	HE: 1,693 ft/s

brake to reduce recoil and avoid overstretching the smaller gun mount, but it made an effective howitzer, which weighed around half a ton (and more than half a metric tonne) less than its predecessor. From 1943–45, 1,404 D-1 type howitzers were manufactured, and production continued after the war. In fact, it was still a common weapon in Eastern Bloc countries and Soviet allies in the developing world until the 1990s.

The 6 inch (15.2 cm) D-1 howitzer.

6 INCH (15.2 CM) ML-20 MODEL 1937 CANNON-HOWITZER

Caliber:	6 in
Combat weight:	15,700 lb
Barrel length:	L/32.3 (194 in)
Elevation:	−2° to +65.5°
Traverse:	58°
Ammunition type and weight:	HE: 95.9 lb; AP: 107 lb
Muzzle velocity:	2,183 ft/s
Maximum range	57,500 ft
Maximum penetration (armor steel):	
	AP: 4.9 in/3,350 ft/90°

weapon and was produced in large numbers (around 7,000 until 1945) for a heavy cannon. At the beginning of the campaign on the Eastern Front in June 1941, 2,800 of these cannon were ready for deployment, but the Wehrmacht seized 974 of these highly rated weapons, renaming them 6 inch (15.2 cm) 433/1 (r) cannon-howitzers. In fact, they were deployed so often that the Germans manufactured special ammunition for them. The ML-20 was also installed in the SU-152 and JSU-152 self-propelled artillery weapons, and in the Eastern Bloc the last examples of these cannon-howitzers were only taken out of service in the 1980s.

This weapon was designed in the mid-1930s to replace outdated cannon. It was one of the first cannon-howitzers, in that it could fire ammunition in a straight or a curved trajectory. The earliest version of this weapon was first produced in 1937, and although it had metal wheels, it did not yet have rubber tires. Further alterations were made over time—for example, the barrel was lengthened from L/29 to L/32.3. Among this howitzer's distinctive features were its "horns," coil springs on either side of the barrel to offset its weight. The cannon-howitzer was the Red Army artillery corps' standard

The 6 inch (15.2 cm) ML-20 cannon-howitzer.

8 INCH (20.3 CM) B-4 M 1931 HOWITZER

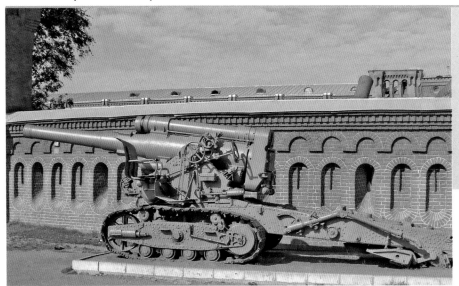

Caliber:	8 in
Combat weight:	34,802 lb
Barrel length:	L/22 (176 in)
Elevation:	−0° to +60°
Traverse:	8°
Ammunition type and weight:	HE: 220.1 lb; CP: 322 lb
Muzzle velocity:	HE: 1,910 ft/s
Maximum range	HE: 53,350 ft
Maximum penetration (concrete):	CP: 39 in

The 8 inch (20.3 cm) B-4 M 1931 howitzer.

More units of this 8 inch (20.3 cm) howitzer were manufactured by the Soviet Union than of any other heavy artillery cannon in the entire Second World War. While no more than a few dozen other weapons with calibers ranging from 8 inch (20.3 cm) to 12 inch (30.5 cm) were produced before 1941, 944 of the two main variants of this howitzer, the B-4 and B 4 M (which had a new four-wheel gun carriage), were manufactured. Howitzers of this type were used by front line artillery, and they were designed especially for sieges, so they had special concrete-piercing (CP) shells. To transport it over Russian roads in typically difficult conditions more easily, the gun carriage had chain tracks around its wheels. At the start of the Russian campaign, German troops seized a number of these howitzers, including 27 of both types in Dubno in June 1941, renaming them the 8 inch (20.3 cm) 503/1 (r) and 503/2 (r) howitzers and subsequently deploying them. By March 1944, however, the Wehrmacht only had three left.

1.5 INCH (3.7 CM) MODEL 1939 ANTI-AIRCRAFT GUN

Caliber:	1.5 in
Combat weight:	4,626 lb
Barrel length:	L/74 (107 in)
Elevation:	−5° to +85°
Traverse:	360°
Ammunition type and weight:	HE: 1.6 lb; AP: 1.7 lb
Muzzle velocity:	HE: 2,933 ft/s
Rate of fire:	180 rpm (theoretically)
Maximum range	28,000 ft
Maximum penetration (vertical):	13,350 ft

A 1.5 inch (3.7 cm) M 39 (r) anti-aircraft gun being deployed by the German Army.

The development of this 1.5 inch (3.7 cm) anti-aircraft gun began in 1938. It was based on designs from the 1930s by the Swedish manufacturer Bofors, as is very clear from its appearance, and the first 15 guns were produced in 1939, the same year in which it was introduced in the Red Army as the 1.5 inch (37 mm) 61 K Model 1939. Around 19,000 of them were produced from 1939 to 1946, and the gun was still in service in the 1960s as one of the Wehrmacht's earliest weapons. A naval version of this gun was also produced in large numbers, and almost all the ships in the Soviet Navy had them until well into the 1950s.

SOVIET UNION

3 INCH (7.6 CM) MODEL 1931 AND 1938 ANTI-AIRCRAFT GUN

A 3 inch (7.62 cm) M 1938 anti-aircraft gun.

Caliber:	3 in
Combat weight:	8,039 lb
Barrel length:	L/55 (165 in)
Elevation:	−3° to +82°
Traverse:	360°
Ammunition type and weight:	HE: 13.9 lb
Muzzle velocity:	HE: 2,717 ft/s
Maximum effective range (vertical):	HE: 25,000 ft
Maximum penetration (armor steel):	
	AP: 2.7 in/3,350 ft/90°

The design of this Soviet anti-aircraft gun was based on the Bofors 3 inch (7.5 cm) Model 1925, and Rheinmetall designs for an anti-aircraft gun of the same dimensions. The earliest examples of this gun only had a single-axle, two-wheeled gun carriage, but because this proved to be impractical for a heavy anti-aircraft gun, the Model 1938 was introduced with an improved, four-wheel gun carriage and minor alterations to the gun itself. At the beginning of the German campaign on the Eastern Front, these anti-aircraft guns were one of the mainstays of the Red Army, but large numbers of them were seized by the Germans, who renamed them the Flak 31 (r) and 38 (r). They were frequently deployed as part of Germany's home defense or supplied to Germany's allies. When the Russian ammunition ran out, the guns were converted to fire 3.5 inch (8.8 cm) ammunition. Until production was halted in 1939, 4,781 of these guns were manufactured.

3.3 INCH (8.5 CM) MODEL 1939 ANTI-AIRCRAFT GUN

Caliber:	3.3 in
Combat weight:	6,733 lb
Barrel length:	L/52 (176 in)
Elevation:	−2° to +82°
Traverse:	360°
Ammunition type and weight:	HE: 20.3 lb; AP: 20.3 lb
Muzzle velocity:	HE: 2,667 ft/s
Maximum effective range (vertical):	HE: 25,350 ft
Maximum penetration (armor steel):	
	AP: 2.8 in/3,350 ft/60°

The 3.3 inch (8.5 cm) anti-aircraft gun was one of the best and most versatile of all the Soviet guns and cannon, which themselves were generally effective weapons. Although it did not particularly stand out when it first appeared in 1939, it was a neatly and intelligently designed gun. Right from the outset, it was designed for combat on the ground as well as anti-aircraft fire, and was equipped with appropriate ammunition and sights for both. In fact, when the Soviets needed an effective anti-tank weapon during the war, it provided an excellent basis for the weapons in the T-34/85 and the SU-85. The Wehrmacht deployed this gun as the 3.3 inch (8.5 cm) Flak M 39 (r) until it ran out of Russian ammunition, after which many guns of this type were fitted with new chambers and barrels to fire 3.5 inch (3.5 cm) ammunition. Some of these guns were given to the Finnish Army. Until 1945, 13,422 of these anti-aircraft guns were manufactured, and it remained in the arsenals of almost all the Eastern Bloc countries until the 1970s.

The 3.3 inch (8.5 cm) M 1939 anti-aircraft gun.

1.5 INCH (3.7 CM) M3 ANTI-TANK CANNON

Caliber:	1.5 in
Combat weight:	911 lb
Barrel length:	L/56.6 (82 in)
Elevation:	−10° to +15°
Traverse:	60°
Ammunition type and weight:	AP: 1.9 lb;
	HE: 1.9 lb; FRAG: 1.6 lb
Muzzle velocity:	2,540 ft/s
Effective range	AP: 1,650 ft—
	HE Max: 29,000 ft
Maximum penetration (armor steel):	
	AP: 2.1 in/1,667 ft/60°

This cannon was introduced in 1937, and it was the US armed forces' standard anti-aircraft gun when America entered the war in December 1941. But the M3 was already dated by then, and production was stopped in late 1943, when the 2.2 inch (5.7 cm) M1 anti-aircraft gun was introduced. Nevertheless, the M3 was deployed in the Pacific until the end of the war, as Japanese tanks were only lightly armored. The gun's light weight was a major advantage in jungle warfare, as it did not have to be towed by a motor vehicle, and M3s were particularly effective when firing fragmenting ammunition (FRAG) against Japanese infantry attacks. It also used the same ammunition as the M5 and M6 tank cannon.

*The 1.5 inch (3.7 cm)
M3 anti-tank cannon...*

3 INCH (7.62 CM) M5 ANTI-TANK CANNON

Development of this anti-tank cannon began in 1940. It was based on the M3 anti-aircraft gun of the same caliber, and it had the same gun carriage as the 4.1 inch (10.5 cm) M2 howitzer. The first prototypes were already complete in late 1941, but the US Army decided that, because of the gun's weight, it would be more sensible to deploy it as a self-propelled weapon. This project (which would finally produce the M-10 anti-tank vehicle) progressed relatively slowly, so the first M5s were not ready for serial production until late 1942. The M5 was a solid design and was deployed until the end of the war, but it could not replace the 2.2 inch (5.7 cm) anti-tank cannon.

Caliber:	3 in
Combat weight:	4,868 lb
Barrel length:	L/50 (150 in)
Elevation:	−5° to +20°
Traverse:	45°
Ammunition type and weight:	AP: 15 lb
Muzzle velocity:	2,640 ft/s
Effective range	AP: 6,650 ft
Maximum penetration (armor steel):	
	AP: 2.8 in/3,350 ft/60°

*...and the 3 inch (7.62 cm)
M5 anti-tank cannon.*

3.5 INCH (9 CM) M1 ANTI-AIRCRAFT GUN

The M1 was built to replace the proven but dated 3 inch (7.6 cm) M3 anti-aircraft gun, whose range was no longer sufficient to hit modern fighter aircraft flying at high altitudes. So work began on a design for this 3.5 inch (9 cm) anti-aircraft gun in 1938 and it was introduced in the US Army in May 1941. It was a well-designed weapon with many modern features, such as remote control for gun

Caliber:	3.5 in
Combat weight:	18,982 lb
Barrel length:	L/52.5 (186 in)
Elevation:	−0° to +80°
Traverse:	360°
Ammunition type and weight:	HE: 23.8 lb
Muzzle velocity:	2,743 ft/s
Effective range (vertical):	HE: 34,350 ft— Max: 40,165 ft

elevation and traverse, and a spring-loaded rammer to make reloading easier and increase the firing rate. Unfortunately, the rammer proved to be faulty, and it was often removed by artillerists. Nevertheless, the M1 remained the standard US anti-aircraft gun long after the end of the war.

A US Army M-1 anti-aircraft installation on Okinawa.

3 INCH (7.5 CM) M1A1 AND M8 PACK-HOWITZER

Caliber:	3 in
Combat weight:	1,338 lb
Barrel length:	L/16 (47 in)
Elevation:	−5° to +45°
Traverse:	6°
Ammunition type and weight:	HE: 14 lb
Muzzle velocity:	HE: 1,270 ft/s
Maximum range:	HE: 29,265 ft

This weapon was developed as early as 1927 but not produced in large numbers until the war broke out. It was originally intended for mountain divisions, as well as other divisions which needed a light but effective howitzer which could be transported by teams of men or pack animals (hence the term "pack-howitzer"). To make transportation easier, it was possible to dismantle the gun and carry it in six separate parts, the heaviest of which weighed just 220 lb (100 kg), and it took a trained team just three minutes to assemble the gun.

The 3 inch (7.5 cm) M8 pack-howitzer.

A modern version with metal wheels and rubber tires, called the M8, was introduced in 1936 especially for paratroopers, and in that form it remained in the US and British armed forces' arsenals until the 1960s.

USA

4.1 INCH (10.5 CM) M2 A1 HOWITZER

The 4.1 inch (10.5 cm) M2 A1 howitzer was the US Army artillery divisions' standard weapon in the Second World War and beyond. Although the earliest models of this weapon were produced as early as 1928, large-scale serial production began only in early 1941. This robust, resilient weapon had a split trail gun mount, a hydro-pneumatic recoil system, and single piece ammunition (the shell and its cartridge were loaded together). When deployed as an anti-tank weapon, it was also loaded with hollow charge ammunition.

Caliber:	4.1 in
Combat weight:	4,471 lb
Barrel length:	L/22 (91 in)
Elevation:	−5° to +66°
Traverse:	46°
Ammunition type and weight:	HE: 33 lb
Muzzle velocity:	HE: 1,573 ft/s
Maximum range:	HE: 37,350 ft

The 4.1 inch (10.5 cm) M2 A1 howitzer.

After 1945 the M2 A1 was renamed the M101 and exported in large numbers. It has been put into service in 67 countries, and it is still in some of their arsenals. Because of this howitzer's widespread use in the West, its ammunition has become almost standard for its caliber.

An M2 A1 battery in firing position.

An M2 A1 howitzer firing on German positions, France, August 1944.

USA

6.1 INCH (15.5 CM) M1 HOWITZER

The 6.1 inch (15.5 cm) M1 howitzer being deployed.

Caliber:	6.1 in
Combat weight:	12,687 lb
Barrel length:	L/23.4 (143 in)
Elevation:	−2° to +63°
Traverse:	49°
Ammunition type and weight:	HE: 94.6 lb
Muzzle velocity:	HE: 1,880 ft/s
Maximum range:	HE: 48,650 ft

The 6.1 inch (15.5 cm) M1 howitzer was one of a new generation of American artillery weapons introduced in the early 1940s. Work began on its design in 1940, and the first of these howitzers were delivered to the US armed forces in 1941. The M1 howitzer was a very modern design for its time: it was designed to be transported by a motor vehicle, which was by no means the norm in 1940. Even the Wehrmacht, one of the best equipped armies in the world in 1940, still had a large number of horse-drawn cannon at the time. The split trail gun mount had only a small protective shield, but it was very robust and could take heavy loads, and it had a spring on either side of the barrel to keep it level. Wherever the US Army was fighting in the war, the 6.1 inch (15.5 cm) M1 howitzer was there, and over 6,000 were manufactured until 1945. After the war it was renamed the M114 and exported to over 40 countries. Almost every US ally after 1945 received this howitzer; it is still in frequent use today, and some arms companies are still prepared to modernize it.

6.1 INCH (15.5 CM) M2 "LONG TOM" CANNON

The M2 cannon was nicknamed "Long Tom" on account of its long barrel, and it was based on the French 6.1 inch (15.5 cm) cannon which the US Army had deployed in the First World War. Since the Americans were very impressed by the cannon's effectiveness, they designed their own version in the 1930s, but it did not go into production until 1941. The M1 was very large and heavy, but it was also a very powerful and accurate weapon. Nevertheless, it had one other disadvantage: the breech lock did not always close completely, which could cause accidents. The improved M2 version became the US Army's standard weapon and proved to be one of the very best cannon of its kind; it was still used by the US Army and its allies after the war. It had an eight-wheel gun mount on account of its weight, but its wheels could be raised while firing, so

Caliber:	6.1 in
Combat weight:	30,573 lb
Barrel length:	L/45 (274 in)
Elevation:	−1.5° to +63°
Traverse:	60°
Ammunition type and weight:	HE: 200 lb
Muzzle velocity:	HE: 2,843 ft/s
Maximum range:	HE: 77,400 ft

that the weapon rested directly on the gun carriage, improving its stability and accuracy.

The 6.1 inch (15.5 cm) M2 "Long Tom" cannon.

8 INCH (20.3 CM) M1 HOWITZER

Along with the 6.1 inch (15.5 cm) M2 cannon, this was the US Army's standard artillery weapon in the final stages of the war, and both weapons used the same eight-wheel gun carriage and two-wheel limber. Development began as early as 1939 but progressed very slowly because of technical difficulties, and the first howitzers of this type were only delivered to the army

Caliber:	8 in
Combat weight:	295,991 lb
Barrel length:	L/25 (200 in)
Elevation:	−2° to +65°
Traverse:	60°
Ammunition type and weight:	HE: 200 lb
Muzzle velocity:	HE: 1,983 ft/s
Maximum range:	HE: 56,650 ft

in January 1944. Although its heavy shells, which weighed 200 lb (90.72 kg) each, had a devastating effect on its targets, the 8 inch (20.3 cm) howitzer was never as accurate as the 6.1 inch (15.5 cm) M2 cannon.

The 8 inch (20.3 cm) M1 howitzer in firing position.

The 8 inch (20.3 cm) M1 howitzer being deployed in Korea.

Like the 6.1 inch (15.5 cm) howitzer, this remained in the arsenals of the USA and its allies for many years after the war. During the Cold War, the Americans even developed nuclear shells for it.

0.8 INCH (2 CM) OERLIKON ANTI-AIRCRAFT GUN

This weapon was similar to the 1.6 inch (4 cm) Bofors, and it was deployed by practically every country involved in the war. It was originally designed in 1914 by Reinhold Becker, and the Swiss company Semag obtained the patent and the production rights in 1919. Later, Oerlikon took over Semag, developing the weapon further and selling it on the international market. It was manufactured under license in numerous countries (with some alterations), and was probably produced in larger numbers than any other anti-aircraft gun in the Second World War. The USA alone produced 124,735 and over 1 billion rounds of ammunition. Moreover, while there are no exact figures for the United Kingdom and the Commonwealth, they had over 55,000 of these guns in service in May 1945, although some of these came from the USA.

The Oerlikon was a reliable, robust, and simple design, and it was easy to maintain. It was also successful: 32 per cent of all Japanese aircraft shot down by US forces between December 1941 and September 1944 were hit by Oerlikon guns. Nevertheless, from late 1944 onward the Allies began to replace it with the 1.6 inch (4 cm) Bofors, which had a more destructive impact on its targets, thus reducing the possibility of lethal kamikaze attacks. The Wehrmacht and Navy also deployed the Oerlikon, renaming it the 0.8 inch (2 cm) Flak 28/29. Different versions were also developed for deployment in aircraft and armored vehicles, and a very simple, inexpensive version was designed in Poland in 1939. The plans for the Polish gun were brought to England before the Germans occupied Poland, and it went into production as the "Polsten gun." Even today the Oerlikon can be found in many countries' arsenals—an astonishing fact for an anti-aircraft gun which originated in 1914.

Caliber:	0.8 in
Combat weight (excluding gun carriage):	150 lb
Barrel length:	L/70 (55 in)
Elevation:	−10° to +90°
Traverse:	360°
Ammunition type and weight:	HE-I: 0.3 lb
Muzzle velocity:	2,783 ft/s
Rate of fire:	450 rpm (theoretically)
Maximum range:	14,650 ft
Maximum vertical range:	10,165 ft

The 0.8 inch (2 cm) Oerlikon in a two-gun mount with twin drum magazines.

*An Oerlikon 0.8 inch (2 cm) anti-aircraft gun mounted on an American **Gato**-class submarine.*

1.6 INCH (4 CM) BOFORS L/60 ANTI-AIRCRAFT GUN

This 1.6 inch (4 cm) anti-aircraft gun, manufactured by Bofors, the Swedish arms manufacturer, was one of the most produced anti-aircraft weapons of all time, deployed by practically all the countries involved in the Second World War. There was, however, very little relation between the original Bofors design and the weapons actually produced, as they were manufactured under license with some major alterations. The origins of this weapon can be traced back to a 1918 Bofors design, which Bofors (partly under the auspices of Krupp) significantly altered and improved. The first prototype appeared in 1933, but the 1936 version, which had been altered further, was the first to go into serial production. Before 1939 Bofors exported this weapon to numerous European countries and gave them the rights to manufacture it under license. The British Army ordered the first 100 Bofors anti-aircraft guns in 1937 and was very satisfied with them, so the British obtained the rights to manufacture them under license. There are no exact figures for the number of air-cooled Bofors anti-aircraft guns manufactured in the Commonwealth countries until 1945, but the estimated figure is around 2,800. The British Royal Navy also deployed this gun on almost all its ships, albeit a specially developed water-cooled version. The US Army and Navy also deployed Bofors weapons, but the guns manufactured in the USA were significantly altered to make

them more suitable for rapid mass production. The original design required a lot of hand tooling, and it was expensive and complicated to produce, as was the ammunition. The US Navy installed single-gun, two-gun and four-gun mounts on almost all their ships from mid-1942 onward. Until the end of the war, a total of 39,200 water-cooled Bofors guns were manufactured.

The Bofors anti-aircraft gun proved to be a reliable, robust weapon, but towards

Caliber:	1.6 in
Combat weight (ex gun carriage):	4,363 lb
Barrel length:	L/56.25 (89 in)
Elevation:	−5° to +90°
Traverse:	360°
Ammunition type and weight:	HE: 2 lb; AP: 2 lb
Muzzle velocity:	HE: 2,763 ft/s–2,936 ft/s
Rate of fire:	120 rpm
Maximum vertical range:	22,667 ft–24,000 ft, depending on the model
Maximum penetration	AP: 1.2 in/6,000 ft/90°

An improvised self-propelled anti-aircraft gun carriage with a 1.6 inch (4 cm) Bofors gun.

the end of the war in the Pacific, the explosive power of its 1.6 inch (4 cm) shells was not always sufficient to prevent determined kamikaze attacks. This is why the US Navy decided to introduce the 3 inch (7.6) anti-aircraft gun after the war. The Wehrmacht and Navy, particularly the latter, also deployed Bofors guns which they had seized in Poland, Norway, and

the Netherlands—a large number also fell into German hands after Britain's retreat from Dunkirk—and a limited number were produced for the Wehrmacht under license by the Norwegian firm Konsberg. The Japanese also seized some British Bofors guns in early 1942, before using them as the basis for their own 1.6 inch (4 cm) Type 5 anti-aircraft gun.

A Bofors gun in a Wehrmacht anti-aircraft division.

A light 1.6 inch (4 cm) Bofors anti-aircraft gun being deployed by the Wehrmacht on the Atlantic coast.

SPECIAL WEAPONS

THE REMOTE-CONTROLLED DEMOLITION CARRIER

	Goliath (Carburetor)	Borgward IV "A" Version
Combat weight:	793 lb	7,599 lb
Crew:	None	None
Dimensions (length/width/height):	63 in/ 33 in/ 24 in	132 in/ 71 in/ 49 in
Engine:	Zündapp 2-cylinder, air-cooled gasoline engine, 703 cc, 12.5 hp	Borgward 4-cylinder in-gasoline engine, 49 hp
Maximum speed:	6 mph road	25 mph road
Range:	4.3 miles road	74.5 miles road
Weaponry:	165 lb explosive	991 lb explosive
Armor:	N/A	Max. 0.8 in

The Goliath demolition carrier.

The Wehrmacht used two types of remote-controlled demolition vehicle: the Borgward IV and the Goliath. The Borgward model was initially designed as an ammunition carrier and later intended as a mine detector. But because most of the vehicles were destroyed and were too expensive for this task, they were converted for use as demolition carriers. The first of these were accepted by the German Weapons Office in April 1942 and put into service that same year in November. The vehicle carried a payload of 991 lb (450 kg), which it released by remote control as soon as it had reached its target. Then the vehicle was withdrawn by remote control, and the payload exploded. Until June 1943, when it was replaced by the improved Versions B and

C, a total of 613 Version A vehicles were produced, and 565 of the later versions were manufactured. There were also attempts to equip Borgward vehicles with cameras to make it easier to control them at longer ranges, but these were still unsuccessful at the end of the war. In early 1945 some Borgward vehicles were converted into remote-controlled anti-tank vehicles and deployed mostly in defense of Berlin.

The Goliath was significantly smaller than the Borgward and was delivered to the army in April 1942. These vehicles were wire-controlled and exploded on impact with their targets. Their electric motors were too expensive, so a new petrol-powered version was developed, but until 1944, 2,650 of the electric

vehicles were produced nevertheless. The first version to be powered by a Zündapp petrol engine was delivered in April 1943, and in total 4,594 of these were manufactured. A larger model which could carry 220 lb (100 kg) of explosive was first produced in November 1944, and a total of 325 were manufactured, but all the Goliaths were vulnerable and difficult to handle, and their payloads were too small. The huge number of both versions on March 1, 1944—2,527 with electric motors and 3,797 petrol engines—shows how ineffectual a weapon it was. Nevertheless, the designs of both the Borgward IV and the Goliath were way ahead of their time—the technology available at the time just was not advanced enough.

The Borgward IV demolition carrier.

NEBELWERFER 41 AND 42 "SMOKE LAUNCHERS"

	1941 Model	1942 Model
Caliber:	5.9 in	8.3 in
Combat weight:	1,696 lb	2,423 lb
Barrel length:	51 in	51 in
Rocket length:	37 in	50 in
Rocket weight:	75 lb	242 lb
Warhead:	HE: 6.2 lb	HE: 63 lb
Muzzle velocity:	1,133 ft/s	1,067 ft/s
Maximum range:	22,350 ft	26,150 ft

A 42 Nebelwerfer in the Grossdeutschland Division.

According to the conditions of the Treaty of Versailles, Germany was forbidden to develop heavy artillery weapons, but there was no mention of rockets. So as early as 1931 the Germans began research into rocket technology, including rocket-propelled chemical weapons. This was, of course, top secret, so the weapons were known as Nebelwerfer "smoke launchers" and the troops deploying them were known as "smoke troops," which has caused plenty of confusion. During the war the Wehrmacht used a large number of artillery weapons firing rocket-propelled ammunition, but the Nebelwerfer was the best known. The 5.9 inch (15 cm) weapon had six barrels arranged in a circle, mounted on the same gun mount as the 1.5 inch (3.7 cm) anti-tank cannon, and all six barrels could be fired within six seconds. Each projectile had a rocket engine at the front which weighed 14.3 lb

(6.5 kg), firing through 26 diagonally attached jets which produced the necessary rifling (or spin), and the 6.2 lb (2.8 kg) payload was located in the rear, achieving a more powerful explosion and increasing fragmentation on impact. The first of these weapons were produced in March 1940.

The launcher was also mounted on armored half-track vehicles (Sd.Kfz. 4/1 Maultier, or Mule), its configuration was altered, and the number of barrels was increased to ten. But the 8.3 inch (21 cm) 42 smoke launcher had even greater firepower—in fact, it had considerably more, with five 51.2 inch (130 cm) barrels, bound together and placed on the same gun mount as the 5.9 inch

(15 cm) launcher. All five projectiles could be fired within eight seconds, and 5.9 inch (15 cm) ammunition could also be fired through removable rails inserted in the barrels. It also had fewer jets (22) to rifle the projectiles than the earlier model. The 8.3 inch (21 cm) 42 Nebelwerfer was produced from March 1942 until the end of the war, and in total 6,009 of the 41 model and 1,487 of the 42 model were produced for the army. 17,678 launcher barrels and 21,000 projectiles were also delivered to the Luftwaffe, which installed the barrels under the wings of twin-engine fighter planes and deployed them to attack bomber groups.

The 42 Nebelwerfer, mounted on the partially armored chassis of the Maultier (Mule) half-track vehicle.

GERMANY

HENSCHEL HS 293

The Henschel Hs 293 was a radio-controlled glide bomb which was mainly deployed against ships from 1939 to 1945. It was based on the SC 500 high explosive bomb, which had wings, a tail, a navigation system, and a Walther rocket engine slung beneath its base. After it was released from a carrier aircraft (such as the Do 217, the He 177, or the Fw 200), the rocket would fire for ten seconds, then the weapon would glide the rest of the way. At the rear of the missile, there was a light installation which made it easier for the gunner to observe it at all times of day. Although the bomb was radio-controlled, work began on a wire control system, which would have made it immune to radio interference, but it was never put into service. A version with a camera installed in its nose to aid navigation was also developed, without ever being put into serial production. In tests it was found to be 90% accurate, but its accuracy fell to around 50% in combat.

The Hs 293 was first deployed on August 25, 1943. Two days later it sank the British corvette HMS *Egret*, and it would prove to be the most effective guided weapon in the war, destroying numerous destroyers and trading ships, though it lacked sufficient penetrating power to harm cruisers or battleships. In the East and in Normandy it was also deployed against targets on the ground, such as bridges. At least 1,200 Hs 293 bombs were fired until 1945, but toward the end of the war, the Allies discovered the radio frequencies used to steer these weapons, and by causing interference they greatly reduced its effectiveness.

Launch weight:	2,148 lb
Length/wingspan:	12.7 ft/ 10.7 ft
Engine:	Walther HWK 109-507 rocket engine with 590 kp thrust
Maximum speed:	590 mph
Launch altitude:	1,350–6,650 ft
Range:	1.9–11.2 miles
Weaponry:	705–1,100 lb warhead

An Hs 293 under a Do 217 E-5 in the 100th German Bomber Wing.

An Hs 293 seized by the US Air Force.

Controls for the Hs 293 FuG 203 (Kehl III).

RUHRSTAHL SD 1400 "FRITZ X"

Launch weight:	3,458 lb
Dimensions (Length/wingspan):	12.1 ft/ 4.5 ft
Engine:	None
Maximum falling speed:	933 ft/s
Minimum launch altitude:	13,350 ft
Range:	30,000 ft
Weaponry:	705 lb warhead

"Fritz X" being examined.

This radio-controlled bomb, generally known as "Fritz X" for short, was developed in the early 1940s by Max Kramer at the Ruhrstahl (Ruhr Steel) company, and it was intended primarily to destroy heavily armored naval targets.

The Fritz X was based on the standard Type SD 1400 armor-piercing bomb, but it had superior aerodynamics, four small wings with a wingspan of 1.35 m, and a tail. To control it after it had been fired, the gunner had to be above his target, which meant that, unfortunately, the carrier aircraft often had to fly over it.

The Fritz X was put into service on August 29, 1943, and its greatest success came less than two weeks later, on September 9. After the truce between the Italians and the Allies, the Italian fleet was on its way to Malta to surrender to the Allies. To prevent this, 12 Type Do 217

aircraft from the 100th Bomber Regiment took off, each carrying a Fritz X. The Italian battleship *Roma* was hit several times, the fires exploded its ammunition, and it sank with 1,455 men on board.

Later in the war, Fritz X bombs sank the British cruiser HMS *Spartan*, the British destroyer HMS *Janus*, and the *Newfoundland* hospital ship. It also inflicted severe damage on numerous other ships, including the British battleship HMS *Warspite*, which was hit three times by Fritz X bombs and reached Malta only with great difficulty,

and the USS *Savannah* suffered a similar fate. Around 2,000 Fritz X bombs were manufactured, but only around 200 were ever deployed in battle. Because the carrier aircraft had to fly over their targets, and the bombs could not change direction abruptly, bomber groups equipped with Fritz X bombs suffered heavy losses.

The Ruhrstahl SD 1400 "Fritz X."

FIESELER FI 103 V1

The V1—or, to be more precise, the FI 103—was essentially a primitive cruise missile, with less refined navigation than its modern counterparts. On July 25, 1942, Fieseler received an order for an automatically steered flying bomb. It was to be powered by the newly developed Pulso-Schubrohr, a simple jet engine, and to keep it secret the project was called "FZG 76," "FZG" meaning "*Flakzielgerät*," or "flak-aiming device." For propaganda purposes, it was dubbed the "V1," or "*Vergeltungswaffe* 1," literally "retaliation weapon 1," shortly before being put into service. The VI was constructed like an aircraft, and its jet engine was located above the fuselage and achieved a

maximum thrust of 335 kp. It was steered by an autopilot using a weighted pendulum and a gyromagnetic compass, and its range was determined by an unpowered propeller on its nose, which cut off the fuel supply to the engine after a specific number of revolutions. It took only 280 working hours to manufacture a V1, which meant that it could be produced in large numbers. The V1 was launched either from launching ramps on the ground, which each used a 2.2 inch (55 m) long catapult with a 6° angle of elevation, or mid-air from carrier aircraft.

The V1 was first deployed on August 16, 1944, and more than 9,300 V1s were launched within the next 80 days, with London and other south-east English towns their primary targets, though Liège and Antwerp, Belgium, were also targeted (by 3,141 and 8,696 V1s respectively). Around 2,000 of these launches failed immediately after take off on account of technical failures, while 25% of the remainder were destroyed by fighter aircraft, and another 25% were shot down by anti-aircraft fire or intercepted by balloon barrages. British fighter pilots used a particularly effective tactic against the V1, aligning one of their wings just beneath one of the V1's wings then

Launch weight:	6,189 lb
Dimensions (Length/wingspan):	26.4 ft/ 19 ft
Engine:	Argus As 014 Pulso jet engine with 335 kp thrust
Maximum speed:	388 mph
Minimum altitude:	N/A
Range:	215 miles
Weaponry:	1,872 lb warhead

rolling away, thus confusing its navigation system and making it crash.

Towards the end of the war, there were also plans to deploy the V1 as a guided missile against Allied bombers. For these plans, which went under the name "Reichenberg," it was to be converted into a manned version, the Fi 103/R 3, but none of these suicide bombs was ever deployed. As early as 1945, before Germany's surrender, V1s which had come into British possession, with related technical documents, were shipped to the USA, where Ford and Republic Aircraft produced a V1 copy, called the JB 2, in very little time. Though intended for deployment against Japan, it was only ever used for test purposes.

The big disadvantage for fixed launching sites was that they were easy for bombers to destroy, and many launching platforms were lost after the Allies landed in Normandy. Hence, carrier aircraft were increasingly deployed instead, and the V1 was launched from the Heinkel He-111 H-22. It was first fired on July 7, 1944, and the last V1 rocket was fired on January 15, 1945. In total, 80 carrier aircraft were lost, and approximately 1,600 V1s were launched, but only around 50% of them reached London.

PEENEMÜNDE AGGREGAT A4 V2

A V2 is prepared for launch on its Meilerwagen transporter. Until March 27, 1945, a total of 5,500 A4s were fired, of which around 2,000 struck the Greater London area, and 1,600 struck Antwerp. Other targets included Brussels, Liège, Paris, and the bridge at Remagen: 11 rockets were fired at the latter, but not one of them hit it.

Launch weight:	28,249 lb
Dimensions (length/wingspan):	46.8 ft/ 11.9 ft
Engine:	Rocket engine with 27,500 kp
Maximum speed:	5,000 ft/s—or Mach 5
Maximum altitude:	50 miles
Range:	Initially 199 lb, later 236 miles
Weaponry:	2,148 lb

The V2 was first deployed on September 7, 1944. Its forerunner was presented to Hitler in March 1939 at the Peenemünde Rocket Research institute on the German island of Usedom, and he ordered the institute to develop the prototype into a deployable long-range rocket. The A4 was not, however, ready for production until July 1943. After bombing raids on the institute, production continued in an underground factory in Nordhausen. Both to create the tunnel system for this factory and to build the V2, the Germans relied heavily on forced laborers from concentration camps. 60,000 prisoners, many of whom died of starvation, cold, or disease, were used.

Production of the weapon now known as the V2 began in October 1943, and in January 1944 the first rockets could be delivered, but almost none were of sufficient quality to be deployed. It was impossible to steer the rocket, its range could only be roughly determined, and it was often several miles off target. This meant that it could only be deployed as a terror weapon. Initially, around 500 V2 rockets were produced per month, but the intention was to increase this figure to 900. When considering these figures, however, we must bear in mind that around 6% of all V2s exploded immediately upon being launched, and a further 60% were too defective to be deployed without further improvements.

After the fixed launch installations were hit by Allied air strikes, the V2s were launched from mobile ramps. Each mobile launch group consisted of 25 special vehicles, which traveled only by night to avoid being attacked from the air, and the rockets were launched in wooded areas, protecting them from both the wind and enemy aircraft.

There were many projects based on the V2, such as a two-stage version, with a range of over 3,400 miles (5,500 km), and a manned kamikaze model. There were also plans to attack New York, firing a V2 from an underwater container towed by a submarine.

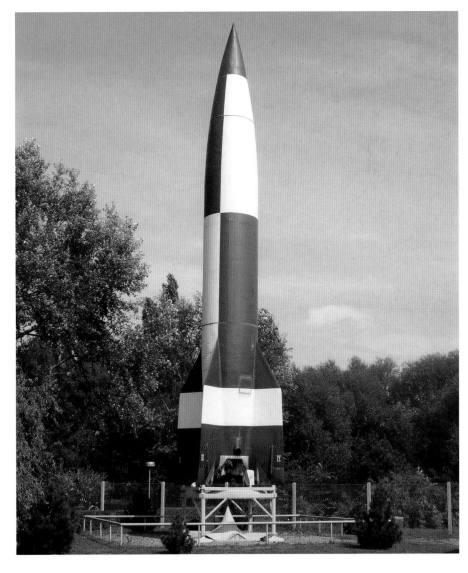

MXY-7 OHKA

The Yokosuka MXY-7 Ohka was a rocket-propelled aircraft designed especially for kamikaze attacks. The prototype's maiden flight took place in September 1944, and serial production began in the same year. To build these machines, the Japanese used as little important raw material as possible, and the aircraft's construction was very simple. There were four different models in total, the main difference between them being their propulsion. Normally the Ohka was carried under the fuselage of a Mitsubishi G4M until the target was within close range, when it was released. The pilot would then try to glide as close to the target as possible, before firing the rockets and striking the target. Because of its high terminal velocity, it was almost impossible to intercept the Ohka once it had been fired, but the weapon enjoyed little success, as the carrier aircraft could easily be attacked, as could the Ohka when it was gliding. In addition, to steer the Ohka once the rockets had been fired, the pilot needed to be relatively experienced. Nevertheless, at least one US destroyer was sunk by this weapon, which the American soldiers nicknamed the "Baka," which means something like "idiot" in Japanese.

Crew:	1 man
Launch weight:	4,718 lb
Length/wingspan:	20.1 ft/ 17.7 ft
Engine:	Solid propulsion charge rocket engine with 800 kp thrust
Maximum speed:	Launched at 410 mph; terminal velocity 570 mph
Maximum altitude:	N/A
Range:	50 miles
Weaponry:	2,643 lb warhead

A Yokosuka MXY-7 seized by the US Army.

"KATYUSHA" BM-8 AND BM-13 MULTIPLE ROCKET LAUNCHER

	BM-8	BM-13	BM-31
Caliber:	3.2 in	5.2 in	11.8 in
Combat weight:	N/A	N/A	N/A
Elevation:	+4° to +45°	+4° to 45°	+4° to 45°
Traverse:	20°	20°	20°
Rocket length:	28 in	56 in	69 in
Rocket weight:	17.6 lb	93.6 lb	203.5 lb
Warhead:	HE: 1.3 lb	HE: 10.8 lb	HE: 203.5 lb
Muzzle velocity:	1,050 ft/s	1,183 ft/s	850 ft/s
Maximum range:	18,350 ft	28,350 ft	14,350 ft

This Soviet rocket launcher was nicknamed "Stalin's Organ" by the German infantry, because of the launching rails, which were arranged next to and on top of each other like organ pipes, as well as the wailing noise it made when fired. The Red Army soldiers, on the other hand, called it "Katyusha," an affectionate diminutive of Katya.

"Stalin's Organ" was one of the best known weapons of the Second World War. It is hard to produce a brief description, as there were numerous different versions with a wide range of different chassis. Essentially, however, they all had several rocket launching pipes (between 16 and 48) with limited traverse, mounted on a truck or a tank, which could all be fired in a matter of seconds. Many of these weapons were launched, and they had a devastating impact on targets on the ground, in spite of their limited accuracy. The shrill noise they made when fired

Loading "Stalin's Organ."

was also a powerful psychological weapon.

The development of the Rs-82 and Rs-132 rockets began in the 1930s, but they were originally intended as aircraft weapons—in fact, they were used in this capacity by almost all Soviet ground attack aircraft and fighter bombers for a long time. In 1938 the Russians began testing ground launchers, and in May 1941 the first of the serial production models, called the BM-13, were finally delivered. They were first deployed on July 14, 1941, against German troops retreating to Smolensk, and seven BM-13s fired 112 rounds into a troop concentration in Orsha, Belarus, inflicting very heavy losses. Nevertheless, the weapon had to remain as well kept a secret as was possible, and only Soviet secret service (NKVD) teams were allowed to use it. During the war, all the different versions of "Stalin's Organ" were dreaded by the enemy and deployed in large numbers: although the exact number produced cannot be established (the only available sources are contradictory), it is clear that over 10,000 of all the different versions were manufactured.

A Studebaker 2.5-tonner with a BM-8-48.

A Studebaker 2.5-tonner with a BM-31-12.

A BM-13 fires a salvo of rockets.

LITTLE BOY AND FAT MAN: THE ATOMIC BOMBS OF HIROSHIMA AND NAGASAKI

	Little Boy	Fat Man
Weight	8,899 lb	10,286 lb
Length	126 in	144 in
Diameter	28 in	60 in
Explosive power:	c.13,000 tons TNT	c. 20,000 tons TNT

Fat Man and Little Boy.

When these bombs were dropped on Japan on August 6 and August 9, 1945, respectively, they heralded not only a new era of weapons technology, but also a new age in history.

Development of these weapons began in 1942, and they were originally intended for use against Germany rather than Japan. The Americans feared that German physicists, who were among the best in the world, would build an atomic bomb for Hitler, and they did not want to be defenseless if the Germans succeeded. So in 1942 in the New Mexico desert, they established a huge secret research complex, which they called Los Alamos, an important part of the Manhattan Project to build an atomic bomb. From 1943 the physicist Robert Oppenheimer led and coordinated thousands of physicists, engineers, and technicians, and within a few years, they achieved their aim. On July 16, 1945, the Trinity Test took place, and the world's first atomic weapon was successfully tested above ground.

The war in Europe had ended on May 8, 1945, but war was still raging in the Pacific, so the Americans decided to deploy the first of these new weapons against Japan. Although by this time the Japanese troops already had their backs to the wall, and defeating them would only have been a matter of time, the Americans wanted to avoid a land invasion of Japan. High casualties would have been unavoidable on both sides, and conventional bombing raids would have continued to inflict terrible devastation without necessarily forcing Japan to surrender. But after two B-29 bombers, "Enola Gay" and "Bocks Car," devastated Hiroshima and Nagasaki respectively with one atomic bomb apiece, killing hundreds of thousands of people, the Japanese Government realized that continuing the war would be pointless, and it acceded to the Allies' conditions of surrender.

If the Manhattan Project had succeeded earlier, or the war in Europe had lasted longer, Germany would also have been hit by an atomic bomb.

Hiroshima after the atomic bomb was dropped.

The crew of "Enola Gay" standing in front of their B-29 bomber.

AIRCRAFT

MESSERSCHMIDT BF 109

The Bf 109 was manufactured in larger numbers than any other military aircraft—around 35,000 were produced—and was the standard plane in the Luftwaffe's fighter squadrons throughout the war. In 1935 the Luftwaffe had only been established relatively recently and was still in need of a single-seat fighter. Four designs were examined, and those from Messerschmidt and Heinkel were short-listed. The first Bf 109 prototype had its maiden flight on May 28, 1935, powered by a Rolls-Royce engine, and the second prototype had a Jumo 210 engine. Other pre-production models had a variety of different weaponry and engines.

The first production model was the Bf 109B-1, which was delivered in early 1937 and soon deployed in the Spanish Civil War. It proved to be the best fighter aircraft in that war, and the German pilots in the Condor Legion, in which fighter aces like Mölders and Galland honed their expertise, experimented with both new aircraft and new tactics. In November 1937 a modified Bf 109 also broke the world speed record for land-based aircraft and won a race around the Alps. As with all Luftwaffe aircraft manufactured in large numbers, a huge number of different versions of the Bf 109 were manufactured, so it is impossible to cover all of them in detail here. But the main

	Bf 109E-7	Bf 109G-10
Type:	Fighter	Fighter
Crew:	1	1
Weight when empty/ max weight at takeoff:	4,436 lb/6,095 lb	4,339 lb/7,709 lb
Length/wingspan/ height:	29.2 ft/32.9 ft/11.3 ft	29.8 ft /33.2 ft/11.3 ft
Engine(s):	One Daimler-Benz DB 601N hanging V12 engine with 1,200 hp	One Daimler-Benz DB 605 hanging V12 engine with 1,475 hp normal performance, and 1,800 hp emergency performance with methanol/water injection
Maximum speed:	359 mph at 12,500 ft	425 mph at 24,650 ft
Service ceiling:	37,085 ft	41,665 ft
Range:	680 miles	350 miles
Weaponry:	1 x 0.8 in MGFF machine gun firing through propeller hub, and 4 x 0.3 in MG17 fixed forward-firing machine guns in the fuselage and wings	1 x 0.8 in MG151/20 machine gun or 1 x 1.2 in MK automatic cannon firing through propeller hub, 2 x 0.5 in MG131 fixed forward-firing machine guns in the fuselage, and various configurations with MG151/20 machine guns or MK108 automatic cannon or an external payload of max. 1,100 lb

model in the fall of 1939 was the Bf 109 E, known as "Emil," whose main advantage compared to the British Spitfires and Hurricanes was that it had a fuel injection pump rather than a carburetor, meaning that fuel could be conserved even with negative G-forces. The Bf 109 F appeared in 1941 and its variants (the F-0 to F-6) are generally regarded as the most attractive of all the Bf 109 models. With a larger

propeller, a new engine cowling, a cantilever tail, and a retractable tail wheel, the Bf 109 F had superior aerodynamics and performance to previous models. The version of the Bf 109 that was manufactured in the greatest numbers was the Model G, which was put into service late in the Summer of 1942. It had a more powerful DB (Daimler-Benz) 605 engine and was better armed, with

A restored Bf 109 G-6 from the Messerschmidt Foundation.

A Bf 109E-4, France, fall 1940.

A Bf 109F-4 Trop of the 53rd German Fighter Wing, Sicily, May 1942.

two 0.5 inch (13 mm) MG131 machine guns above the engine (its large gun cowls were known as "bumps"). Because there were so many different Bf 109 G configurations, it could be used for many different kinds of mission. The next version, the Model H, had a longer wingspan and was only produced in very small numbers. The Model K, based on the Model G, appeared shortly before

A Bf 109G.

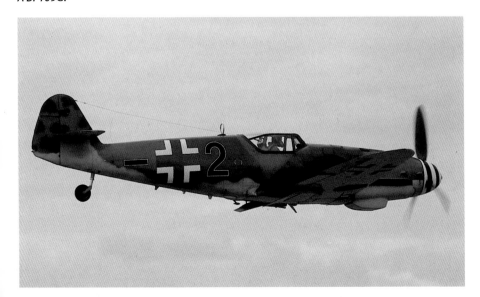

the end of the war, and a few dozen Bf 109T-1s with tail hooks were built for deployment on the *Graf Zeppelin* aircraft carrier, which was never completed. After this project was abandoned, they had their special equipment removed and were put into service as T-2 aircraft. There were other projects, such as the Bf 109 Z, which consisted of two Bf 109 F frames with a

new wing layout, but this version was never put into service.

The Bf 109 was deployed variously as an interceptor, a fighter bomber, and a reconnaissance aircraft. In the early years of the war, it was second only to the Spitfire, but it was later superseded, particularly by the P-51 and the P-47. Its aerodynamics dated back to the 1930s, and it did not have a high-performance engine, so it could not be developed any further. In addition, although its performance easily surpassed that of the Fw 190, it was less robust than the latter. Its landing gear was also very narrow, which led to a number of accidents and could be very dangerous for inexperienced pilots. Nevertheless, production of the Bf 109 was continued after the war. In Spain from 1942 Hispano manufactured it under license as the Ha-1109, Ha-1110, or Ha-1112, installing Hispano-Suiza and, later, Rolls-Royce Merlin engines. The Czech firm Avia also manufactured the Bf 109 under license after 1945, initially installing the original DB 605 engine (Avia 99) and, later, the Jumo 211 F (Avia 199). The Israeli Air Force's first aircraft were Avia 199s donated by Czechoslovakia.

MESSERSCHMIDT BF 110

The German Air Ministry (*Reichsluftministerium*—RLM) ordered the development of a heavy fighter aircraft, and the Bf 110, whose maiden flight took place on 12 May, 1936, was the result. After initial problems with the DB 600, this model was fitted with the Jumo 210 engine, which led to disappointing performance. Consequently, its development was slow, and the first mass-produced model, the C version with twin DB 601 engines, was not delivered to the Luftwaffe until 1939. The D and E versions differed from the C version only in minor respects, while the Bf 110E was fitted with improved DB 610 engines, producing 1,350 hp, and the last models, the G and H, had DB 605 engines.

In the early months of the war, the Bf 110 aircraft were very successful, gaining many aerial victories, but in the late summer and fall of 1940, when they were deployed to escort bombers over England and encountered Hurricanes and Spitfires, they suffered such heavy losses, it seemed that they needed a Bf 109 escort themselves. Nevertheless, on account of their firepower and range, they proved to be valuable aircraft in the Mediterranean area and in the East. They were also very successful as reconnaissance aircraft and fighter bombers, but they were used primarily as night fighters. The earliest tests took place in the winter of 1940–41, but because the aircraft did not yet have radar, they were less than convincing. They fared better when fitted with simple infrared sensors and guided by radar stations on the ground, but the Bf 110 night fighters only really became successful after the installation of on-board radar devices, easily recognizable with their "stag's antlers." Until the very end of the war, the British Royal Air Force and Luftwaffe fought dramatic battles above Germany, in which electronic warfare played an important role for the first time. The Bf 110 was also deployed in daylight against USAAF (United States Army Air Force) bombers in 1943 and 1944, but they suffered heavy losses primarily because of the P-47 and P-51 fighters accompanying the bombers. Until production was halted in March 1945, a total of around 6,050 Bf 110s were produced.

	Bf 110C-4	Bf 110G-4/R3
Type:	Heavy fighter/destroyer	Night fighter
Crew:	2	3
Weight when empty/ max weight at takeoff:	9,912 lb/14,868 lb	11,211 lb/21,784 lb
Length/wingspan/ height:	40.4 ft/54.3 ft/13.9 ft	43.5 ft/54.3 ft/13.9 ft
Engine(s):	Two Daimler-Benz DB 601B-1 hanging V12 engines with 1,020 hp	Two Daimler-Benz DB605B hanging V12 engines with 1,475 hp
Maximum speed:	348 mph at 12,500 ft	342 mph at 23,250 ft
Service ceiling:	33,300 ft	26,700 ft
Range:	800 miles	1,300 miles with 2 additional fuel tanks
Weaponry:	2 x 0.8 in MG/FF and 4 x 0.3 in MG17 machine guns fixed in the nose, 1 x 0.3 in MG15 machine gun in the rear of the cockpit, and an external payload of max. 1,100 lb	2 x 0.8 in MG151/20 machine guns and 2 x 1.2 in automatic cannon fixed in the nose, 1 x MG81Z machine gun in the rear of the cockpit, and 2 x 0.8 in MG/FF machine guns firing diagonally upward from the fuselage. Also fitted with radar

A Bf 110G-4 of the 1st German Night Fighter Wing in mid-1944.

A Bf 110C-4 of the 26th German Destroyer Wing, France, June 1940.

FOCKE-WULF 190 WURGER (STRANGLER)

An Fw 109A-8/R 2 of the 300th German Fighter Wing, Loebnitz, October 1944.

The Focke-Wulf Fw 190 was the best and most versatile piston-engine German fighter aircraft of the Second World War, and it was deployed as a fighter, a fighter-bomber, a ground attack aircraft, a reconnaissance aircraft, a torpedo bomber, and a flight instruction aircraft. The Fw 190 prototype made its maiden flight on July 1, 1939, but at first there were major problems with the new BMW 801 radial engine. This delayed the Fw 190's development, and it was not ready to be put into service until the summer of 1941, when the Fw 190A-1 was delivered to the Luftwaffe. As soon as it was first deployed, the new aircraft proved to be more powerful and versatile than the Me 109; it had superior firepower, but it was less maneuverable than the latter, and could not climb as fast or as high—the BMW 801 engine had been designed for optimum performance at low and medium altitudes. The Fw 190 was dogged by this problem until the introduction in 1944 of the D version with the Jumo 213 V12 engine, which was intended as a high altitude fighter. When it was introduced, the Fw 109A was vastly superior in terms of performance to its Allied counterparts, but as the war progressed, the Allies caught up with and then overtook the Fw 190. The P 51 and P41 in particular clearly outperformed even the D version at altitudes in excess of 4.3 miles (6.9 km) .

Numerous variants and sub-variants of the Fw 190 were produced. The A version was a fighter which could also be deployed as a fighter bomber, and the F and

	Fw 190A-8/R2	Fw 190D-9
Type:	Fighter bomber	Fighter bomber
Crew:	1	1
Weight when empty/ max weight at takeoff:	6,980 lb/10,795 lb	7,685 lb/10,660 lb
Length/wingspan/ height:	29.5 ft/35 ft/13.2 ft	34 ft/35 ft/11.2 ft
Engine(s):	One BMW 901D-2 14 cylinder radial engine with 1,730 hp normal performance and 2,100 hp emergency performance with MW-50 injection	One Junkers Jumo 213A-1 hanging V12 engine with 1,775 hp normal performance and 2,100 hp emergency performance with MW-50 injection
Maximum speed:	407 mph; 425 mph with MW-50 injection	420 mph; 438 mph with MW-50 injection
Service ceiling:	38,000 ft	40,000 ft
Range:	500 miles	520 miles
Weaponry:	2 x 0.3 in MG17 engines fixed above the engine, 4 x 0.8 in MG151/20 machine guns fixed in the wings, and an external payload of up to 2,200 lb	2 x 0.5 in MG131 machine guns fixed above the engine, 2 x 0.8 in MG151/20 machine guns fixed in the wings, and an ext payload of up to 1,100 lb

G versions were fighter bombers and ground attack aircraft with an increased payload and enhanced armor, while the S version was a two-seater flight instruction aircraft. The D version, which was fitted with a liquid-cooled Jumo 213 V12 engine to attain higher altitudes than the other models, is the easiest to distinguish from the rest. The airframe underwent various alterations so that the engine could be installed, and the Jumo's ring-shaped cooler made it look like a radial-engine aircraft. The wings and tail were

no different from the A version, though the horizontal stabilizer was widened, but the fuselage was lengthened to 33 ft 6 inches (10.2 m). As in the later radial-engine models, it was possible to inject the engine with a methanol-water mixture (called MW-50), greatly enhancing the machine's performance.

Until production was halted, around 20,000 of all Fw 190 variants were produced. The Jumo-powered D series was developed further and called the Ta 152, but very few were built.

An Fw 190A-5 of the 51st German Fighter Wing, Eastern Front, July 1943.

MESSERSCHMIDT ME 210 AND 410 HORNISSE (HORNET)

The Me 210 was developed as the successor to the Bf 110 and flew for the first time as early as September 5, 1939, but suffered from severe stability and maneuverability problems. Nevertheless, it went into production after a few modifications, though without great success: production was halted after just 200 models had been manufactured, and the design was completely revised. With the installation of automatic leading-edge slats, a longer fuselage, and more powerful DB 603A engines, its problems were solved. The new model was called the Me 410, and the first aircraft of this kind were delivered in 1943. It was deployed as a fighter (the A-1), a high speed bomber (the A-2), and a reconnaissance aircraft (the A-3). The B series versions were deployed in the same way, but they were fitted with slightly more powerful DB 603G engines and 0.5 inch (13 mm) MG131 machine guns in the nose, instead of the 0.3 inch (7.92 mm)

Me 410B-1	
Type:	Heavy fighter/reconnaissance aircraft/high-speed bomber
Crew:	2
Weight when empty/ max weight at takeoff:	17,467 lb/24,751 lb
Length/wingspan/height:	41.6 ft/54.5 ft/14.3 ft
Engine(s):	Two Daimler-Benz DB 603G hanging V12 engines with 1,900 hp each
Maximum speed:	391 mph
Service ceiling:	31,700 ft
Range:	1,050 miles
Weaponry:	2 x 0.8 in MG151/20 and 2 x 0.5 in machine guns fixed in the nose, 2 x 0.5 in MG131 machine guns in remote-controlled installations (FDSL.131) on the sides of the fuselage, and a payload of up to 2,203 lb in the internal bomb bay; or 2 x 0.8 in MG151/20 machine guns or 1 x 2 in BK5 in the internal bomb bay

MG 17. Until September 1944, a total of 1,160 Me 410s were manufactured, including around 30 different series with different weapon configurations. The Me 410 was used in the bombardment of the English coast and defensively against Allied bombers, but it could never entirely replace the Bf 110, which remained in service as a night fighter until the end of the war. There were plans for an Me 410 C with an increased wingspan and a supercharger for the DB 603 engine, but the project never got past the planning stage.

An Me 410B-3 of the 2nd Group of the 122nd German Long-Range Reconnaissance Squadron, Italy, 1944.

The Me 262B-2a night fighter.

General Galland was so impressed by the Me 262 that after its maiden flight, he likened it to a jet-powered angel. He reckoned that one Me 262 was as effective in combat as five Bf 109s.

MESSERSCHMIDT ME 262 SCHWALBE (SWALLOW)

The Me 262 was the first jet-powered combat aircraft to be put into serial production. Its development began in 1938, when Messerschmidt was contracted by the German Air Ministry to develop a jet-powered fighter aircraft. The air frame had already been designed, but the BMW jet engines were still at the experimental stage. So for its maiden flight on April 18, 1941, the Me 262 had to be fitted with a conventional Junkers piston engine in the nose, but it was already clear that it handled well. Development of the BMW jet engines was still progressing slowly, so the plane was converted to be fitted with Junkers jet engines instead, and the modified version's maiden flight took place on July 18, 1942. It is often claimed that Hitler's wish to use the Me 262 as a high speed bomber slowed down its development, but the main reason for this was that it was difficult to develop jet engines that were both powerful and reliable. Consequently, the Me 262A-1a was not put into service until July 1944. The A-2 was the high speed bomber which Hitler wanted, the A-5 was a reconnaissance aircraft, the B-1a was a two-seater flight instruction aircraft (B-1a), and the B-2a was a night fighter fitted with radar. 1,433 Me 262s were manufactured in total, but there were never more than 250 in service at any given time. Many crashed into the ground, and many more

An Me 262A-1a Swallow.

Me 262A-1a	
Type:	Fighter/fighter bomber
Crew:	1
Weight when empty/ max weight at takeoff:	8,370 lb/14,097 lb
Length/wingspan/height:	35.3 ft/41.6 ft/12.8 ft
Engine(s):	Two Junkers Jumo 004B-1/2/3 jet engines with 1,980 lb thrust each at takeoff
Maximum speed:	540 mph at 20,000 ft
Service ceiling:	38,165 ft
Range:	650 miles
Weaponry:	4 x 1.2 in MK108 machine guns in the nose; 24 R4M 2.2 in rockets could also be carried under the wings

simply could not be flown, as there was not enough fuel, and too few pilots were available.

Although they could attain exceptionally high speeds for the era, many Me 262s were shot down—they were especially vulnerable when landing—so units with Bf 109 and Fw 190 aircraft were stationed at Me 262 airbases. In spite of its limitations, the Me 262 was

heavily armed, with four 1.2 inch (30 mm) MK108 guns in its nose and rocket launchers with 24 rockets under its wings, and it destroyed a number of enemy targets. There were projects to develop it further, but Germany's fortunes in the war meant that these were abandoned.

An Me 262A-2a Albatross.

HEINKEL HE 219 UHU (EAGLE OWL)

He 219A-7/R-4	
Type:	Night fighter
Crew:	2
Weight when empty/ max weight at takeoff:	24,670 lb/33,700 lb
Length/wingspan/height:	51.8 ft/61.7 ft/13.7 ft
Engine(s):	Two DB 603G hanging V12 engines with 1,900 hp each
Maximum speed:	382 mph
Service ceiling:	32,667 ft
Range:	1,150 miles
Weaponry:	2 x 0.8 in MG151/20 machine guns fixed at the wing roots, 2 x 0.8 in MG151/20 machine guns fixed in the underside of the fuselage, 2 x 1.2 in MK108 automatic cannon firing diagonally upward from the fuselage ("diagonal music"). Also fitted with radar

An He 219A-7/R 4 of the 1st German Night Fighter Wing, Westerland (Sylt), early 1945.

The Heinkel He 219 was a Luftwaffe night fighter and, in many respects, a very advanced aircraft. It was the first Luftwaffe aircraft with a three-wheel undercarriage and an ejector seat, and it was fitted with radar as standard, which was apparent from the twin antennae on its nose. This model was originally based on a design for a bomber, which Heinkel altered to meet the requirements of the night fighter, as ordered by the German Air Ministry. The first prototype flew for the first time in November 1942, and in simulated battles with the Do 217N and Ju 88S, it proved to be far superior to both. Yet for no apparent reason, and in spite of its performance, the He 219 was never prioritized, although British RAF bombers were devastating Germany. In mid-1943 the first A-O pre-production models were deployed in the 1st NJG (Night Fighter Wing) in Venlo, Netherlands, and within a few days they had shot down 20 enemy aircraft, including six Mosquito high speed bombers. Yet they were never delivered to the Night Fighter Wings rapidly enough or in sufficient numbers. Eventually, the He 219 was outperformed by new versions of the Mosquito, so a limited series was produced of aircraft with high-performance engines and less weaponry, which could reach 404 mph (650 km/h) at 40,000 ft (12,000m). Only 294 He 219s, including prototypes and pre-production models, were built in total, before production was halted in November 1944 as part of the German Fighter Emergency Program.

MESSERSCHMIDT ME 163 COMET

An Me 163B.

The Me 163 was the world's first rocket-propelled fighter aircraft, and the first machine to fly faster than 621 mph (1,000 km/h). It was designed by Dr Alexander Martin Lippisch, who worked on tailless gliders in the 1930s and joined Messerschmidt in 1939, along with his research team. The first prototype of the Me 163a flew as early as 1941, but its problems were so severe that the improved Me 163B was not delivered until 1944. It shed its undercarriage after takeoff and landed on a skid below its fuselage, but before landing it had to have spent all, or nearly all its fuel, because severe shocks could cause rocket fuel to explode. The Me 163 had a minimal wingspan and was intended to

Me 163B-1a	
Type:	Fighter
Crew:	1
Weight when empty/ max weight at takeoff:	4,196 lb/9,053 lb
Length/wingspan/height:	19.5 ft/31.1 ft/9.2 ft
Engine(s):	One Walther HWK-509A-2 R rocket engine with 37,400 lb thrust
Maximum speed:	622 mph at 30,500 ft
Service ceiling:	40,300 ft
Flight duration:	Around 8 minutes with rocket propulsion
Weaponry:	2 x 1.2 in MK108 machine guns in the wing roots

only a few seconds to aim and fire at the target before the Me 163 had shot past it. In fact, the main Me 163 wing, the 400th Fighter Wing (JG 400), had shot down only nine US bombers by March 1945. Because it flew without an undercarriage, lacked quality, and had such volatile fuel, the Me 163 posed a greater threat to its own crew than to the enemy, so production was halted in February 1945, after only 400 had been produced.

target bombers, taking off only the bombers that were within very close range. With a climbing speed of 16,000 ft/min (4,800m/min), it had no difficulty in reaching its targets, but its speed was also its greatest weakness, as the pilot had

HEINKEL HE 162 SALAMANDER

The He 162 Salamander—also known as the Volksjäger, or "People's Fighter"—was developed and prepared for serial production by Heinkel in a very short time. Heinkel received the contract to build it on September 15, 1944, and just 69 days later, on December 6, 1944, the first prototype flew for the first time. However it crashed due to the lack of raw materials. It was designed to be built with as little scarce raw material (such as aluminum) as possible, and sections of the fuselage and wings were made of wood. In fact, the lack of appropriate construction materials would always be the He 162's main problem and resulted in the imposition of a 373 mph (600 kmh) speed limit, which could only be broken to elude enemy aircraft. Like the Ar 234, the He 162 was equipped with an ejector seat—and because of the aircraft's limitations, He 162 pilots often used it. It is claimed that it shot down an enemy aircraft on April 26, 1945, the day it was put into service. Around 270 He 162s were manufactured until May 1945, and 800 were still under construction at the end of the war. Because the war ended so soon after it was first manufactured, only very few He 162s were actually deployed, and 50 of those in the 1st Fighter Wing were seized by the British at Leck/Schleswig Air Base.

He 162A	
Type:	Fighter
Crew:	1
Weight when empty/ max weight at takeoff:	4,515 lb/5,925 lb
Length/wingspan/height:	30.2 ft/24 ft/8.5 ft
Engine(s):	One BMW-003A-1 jet engine with 1,760 lb thrust at takeoff and 920 kp emergency thrust (deployable for max. 30s)
Maximum speed:	522 mph with normal thrust and 562 mph at 20,000 ft
Service ceiling:	40,000 ft
Range:	560 miles
Weaponry:	2 x 0.8 in MG151/20 machine guns in the fuselage

This He 162A-2 was tested intensively by the US Air Force after the war.

HENSCHEL HS 123

As early as 1933 the Germans wanted a dive-bomber for their air force, which was still being formed. Henschel won the contract with its Hs 123, and the first prototypes were flying in 1935. After two aircraft were destroyed in test dives, the design was completely revised, and the result was an extremely robust aircraft which fulfilled its role superbly. The first serial production machines (Hs 123 A-1) were put into service in 1936 and were first deployed in the Condor Legion in the Spanish Civil War. Production ceased as early as November 1938, as biplanes were considered old-fashioned, yet the Hs 123's deployment in the war belies this evaluation, as it performed very well indeed. Its robust build proved especially valuable for its role as a ground attack aircraft on the Eastern Front, where it was deployed until early 1944.

Hs 123A-1	
Type:	Dive bomber and ground attack aircraft
Crew:	1
Weight when empty/ max weight at takeoff:	3,304 lb/4,879 lb
Length/wingspan/height:	27.8 ft/35 ft/10.7 ft
Engine(s):	One BMW 132Dc 9-cylinder radial engine with 880 hp
Maximum speed:	211 mph
Service ceiling:	30,000 ft
Range:	530 miles
Weaponry:	2 x 0.3 in MG17 machine guns fixed in the fuselage, and an external payload of up to 991 lb – 1 x 550 lb and 4 x 110 lb bombs

An Hs 123A-1.

JUNKERS JU 87 STUKA

Ju 87D-1	
Type:	Dive bomber and ground attack aircraft
Crew:	2
Weight when empty/ max weight at takeoff:	8,590 lb/14,537 lb
Length/wingspan/height:	38.3 ft/46 ft/13 ft
Engine(s):	One Junkers Jumo 211J-1 hanging V12 engine with 1,410 hp
Maximum speed:	255 mph at 12,800 ft
Service ceiling:	24,300 ft
Range:	953 miles
Weaponry:	2 x 0.3 in MG 17 machine guns fixed in the wings, 1 x 0.3 in MG81Z machine gun in rear of cockpit, and an external payload of max. 3,965 lb

The Junkers Ju 87 Stuka (*Sturzkampfbomber*, or dive-bomber) is surely one of the best known aircraft of the Second World War, both because it was a symbol of the Blitzkrieg (literally, "lightning war") of 1939–41, and because of its striking appearance. It was made entirely out of metal, and it had distinctive inverted gull wings and a fixed undercarriage. In 1934 Junkers presented the first prototypes in Dessau, which still had a twin-tail. The first production aircraft (Ju 87 B-1) were delivered to the German Dive-Bomber Wing in 1937 and were soon tested in the Condor Legion in Spain. As long as the Luftwaffe dominated the skies, the Ju 87 proved to be a highly effective weapon, which could attack specific targets in mid-dive. Its intimidating appearance and the wail of its "Jericho sirens" were enough to spread terror and panic on their own. But when it came up against Hurricanes and Spitfires in the Battle of Britain, the tables were turned, and many Stukas were

A Ju 87D-5 of the 3rd Group of the 2nd German Ground Attack Wing, Eastern Front, July 1943.

A Ju 87B-2 during the French campaign in 1940.

destroyed. Consequently, it was no longer deployed on the Western Front, but it continued to enjoy some success in Africa, the Mediterranean, and Russia. At the beginning of the war, the main version was the Ju 87B, but a new model, the Ju 87R, which could carry two additional 300-l fuel tanks under its wings, was introduced especially for anti-naval operations in the Mediterranean. The Ju 87C was to be deployed on the *Graf Zeppelin* aircraft carrier, but the latter was never finished. The most frequently produced version was the Ju 87D, which had a more powerful engine, superior aerodynamics (thanks to the removal of the large cooler on the front of the fuselage, new engine cowling and a new cockpit hood), and a heavy bomb load of 3,965 lb (1,800 kg). There was also a training version with two sets of controls, called the Ju 87H. The final production model was the Ju 87G, which had two 1.5 inch (3.7 cm) guns beneath its wings to fire at tanks, and was the brainchild of Colonel Rudel, who destroyed 519 tanks during the war and is said to have survived being shot down

30 times. From 1944 onward the Ju 87 was frequently deployed at night, as it was too dangerous to fly it during the day.

A Ju 87G-1 with two 1.5 inch (3.7 cm) on-board cannons under its wings.

A total of 5,709 Stukas were manufactured. In spite of its drawbacks, *the Ju 87 was one of the most successful dive-bombers and ground attack aircraft in the war, though its legendary reputation owes more than a little to skillful propaganda.*

HENSCHEL HS 129

Hs 129B-1/R-2	
Type:	Ground attack aircraft
Crew:	1
Weight when empty/ max weight at takeoff:	8,392 lb/11,256 lb
Length/wingspan/height:	32.5 ft/47.3 ft/10.8 ft
Engine(s):	Two Gnome-Rhône 14M-4/5 14-cylinder radial engines with 700 hp each
Maximum speed:	253 mph at 12,650 ft
Service ceiling:	30,000 ft
Range:	348 miles
Weaponry:	2 x 0.3 in MG17 and 2 x 0.8 in MG151/20 machine guns fixed in the fuselage, and 1 x 1.2 in MK-101 automatic cannon in a container under the fuselage or four 110 lb bombs under the wings

The Hs 129 was a ground attack aircraft designed especially to support the ground troops. The first prototypes were presented in 1939, but among other problems, they were underpowered, and the aircraft had to be completely redesigned. In fact, the B-1 version, with a French 700 hp radial engine and front section, was not put into production until late 1941, and Hs 129s were not put into service until mid-1942. They were deployed mostly on the Eastern Front, but also in North Africa and Italy. Because of the nature of its deployment, it was heavily armored (with a cockpit screen

An Hs 129B-2R1 in a Stabskette (a flight of three aircraft) of the 2nd Group of the 1st German Ground Attack Wing, Eastern Front, November 1942.

made of 3 inch (75 mm) reinforced glass) and armed, but its Gnome-Rhône engines were constantly beset with problems, which limited its deployment. As well as infantry support, the Hs 129 was also used as an anti-tank aircraft, which earned it the nickname "the Flying

Can Opener." The Hs 129 came with many different weapons configurations, capable of carrying 30 mm (1.2 inch), 1.5 inch (37 mm) or 3 inch (75 mm) guns under its fuselage, and more than 800 were manufactured in total.

DORNIER DO 17

Like the He 111, the Do 17 was ordered in 1932. It was a very elegant aircraft, earning the nickname, "the Flying Pencil," on account of its slim design, a twin-engine shoulder-wing metal aircraft with an electrically retractable tail wheel. In the Zurich-Dübendorf Air Race in 1937, it easily outstripped fighter planes from other countries. Nevertheless, the earliest combat and reconnaissance models were built only in relatively small numbers. Only the Z version was produced in large numbers (506 in total), but in the early months of the war it was the predominant aircraft in both combat and reconnaissance wings. To give its crew more room, the front section of the Do 17's fuselage was completely redesigned, but the four-seat cockpit spoiled the aircraft's slim appearance. It was also

Do 17Z-2	
Type:	Bomber
Crew:	4
Weight when empty/max weight at takeoff:	11,476 lb/18,921 lb
Length/wingspan/height:	52.7 ft/60 ft/15.1 ft
Engine(s):	Two BMW Bramo 323P 9-cylinder radial engines with 1,000 hp each
Maximum speed:	255 mph at 4,050 ft
Service ceiling:	27,300 ft
Range:	720 miles
Weaponry:	6-7 x 0.3 in MG15 mobile machine guns, with a payload of max. 2,200 lb in the internal bomb bay

deployed as a night fighter, for which it was fitted with an infrared device and fixed weapons—four MG17 and four 0.8 inch (20mm) MGFF guns—towards the front. The Do 17's performance was phenomenal in 1937, but by the time of the Battle of Britain, it was no longer sufficient. Thereafter, the remaining

aircraft were increasingly used for flight instruction or donated to German allies, such as Croatia, or—especially in the case of the E and F versions—put into service as glider tugs.

A Do 17Z.

HEINKEL HE 111

The He 111 prototype flew for the first time in February 1935, and at first it was officially a high speed commercial aircraft (like the Do 17). Some He 111s were indeed put into service by Lufthansa, but the military variant was more important. Because the version with BMW engines was initially a disappointment, a variant with 1,000 hp DB 600A engines was tested in 1936 and performed far better. The first He 111 B-1 aircraft were delivered to the Luftwaffe in late 1936, and very soon they were deployed in the Condor Legion in the Spanish Civil War. The E version and later models were fitted with Junkers Jumo engines, as the Daimler-Benz engines were primarily required for fighter aircraft. The He 111 had elliptical wings, which gave it excellent lift, but they were difficult to manufacture, so the G version had new wings with straight edges front and rear. The most important alteration in its appearance, however, came with the introduction of the P series in 1938, which had a glazed dome rather than a "stepped" cockpit, increasing visibility. This model was replaced by the H series in September 1939, and the latter was the predominant He 111 model throughout the war.

	He 111H-6
Type:	Bomber
Crew:	5
Weight when empty/ max weight at takeoff:	19,199 lb/30,837 lb
Length/wingspan/height:	54.7 ft /75 ft/11.3 ft
Engine(s):	Two Junkers Jumo 211F-2 hanging V12 engines with 1,350 hp each
Maximum speed:	270 mph at 20,000 ft
Service ceiling:	22,300 ft
Range:	1,800 miles
Weaponry:	1 x 0.8 in MG/FF machine gun in the nose, 1 x 0.5 in MG131 or 1 x 0.3 in MG81Z machine gun on the back of the fuselage, 2 x 0.3 in MG81 machine guns in the ventral gondola, 2 x 0.3 in machine guns on the sides, and a combined external and internal payload of max. 6,608 lb

When Germany invaded Poland, 808 He 111s (including all the variants) were deployed. In fact, during the early months of the war, the majority of bomb attacks were carried out by He 111s, and they were constantly in service. In May 1940, they were flown in the campaign on the Western Front, and even as late as the Battle of Britain in the latter part of summer 1940, the He 111 was the Luftwaffe's standard bomber. But it was during the Battle of Britain that its vulnerability to determined fighter attacks was exposed, and many were shot down. Thereafter, the He 111 was instead deployed as a night bomber and for other specialist tasks—for example, as a torpedo bomber, reconnaissance aircraft, transporter, and glider tug. But it still served as a bomber during the day on the Eastern Front.

Until production was halted in the fall of 1944, around 7,300 He 111s were manufactured, and there was a bewildering array of different versions, converted models, and weapons configurations. Another 26 He 111Hs were manufactured under license in Spain and called the CASA 2.111. Ironically, when the supply of Junkers engines had run out, these aircraft were fitted with Rolls-Royce Merlin engines.

An He 111E of the C19 Flight Instruction School in Ohlau, December 1942.

An He 111H-6.

JUNKERS JU 88

A Ju 88G-1.

The Junkers Ju 88 was certainly the most versatile aircraft in the Luftwaffe. Numerous different versions were produced throughout the war, and around 15,000 of all versions were manufactured in total. The first prototype, which was conceived as a high speed medium range bomber, had its maiden flight in December 1936, the fifth prototype set a few world records in March 1939, and soon afterwards the first Ju 88A-1s were delivered to the air force. Even when it was first deployed, it soon became apparent that its defenses were inadequate, so they were considerably improved on the A-4. The main version of the Ju 88A was always the A-4, though later variants (up to the A-17) were also produced, and there was a bewildering array of Ju 88 variants and sub-variants.

While the Ju 88A was designed primarily as a bomber, the Ju 88C was used as a heavy fighter and a destroyer. The D series models were reconnaissance bombers with an increased range, and

	Ju 88A-4	Ju88G-6c
Type:	Bomber/dive bomber	Night fighter
Crew:	4	3
Weight when empty/ max weight at takeoff:	21,718 lb/30,837 lb	20,002 lb/28,855 lb
Length/wingspan/ height:	48 ft/66.9 ft/16.2 ft	51.8 ft/66.9 ft/16.2 ft
Engine(s):	Two Junkers Jumo 211J-1 hanging V12 engines with 1,350 hp each	Two Junkers Jumo 213A-1 hanging V12 engines with 1,750 hp each
Maximum speed:	292 mph at 17,650 ft	388 mph
Service ceiling:	27,000 ft	33,000 ft
Range:	1,696 miles	1,398 miles
Weaponry:	1 x 0.5 in MG131 or 1 x 0.3 in MG81 forward-firing machine gun in the cockpit, 2 x MG81 machine guns in the rear of the ventral gondola, 2 x MG81 machine guns in the rear of the cockpit, and a combined internal and external payload of max. 6,608 lb	4 x 0.8 in MG151/20 machine guns fixed in a ventral gondola, and 2 x MG151/20 machine guns firing diagonally upward from behind the cockpit ("diagonal music")

the G series models served as night fighters with radar. The Ju 88H was a long range reconnaissance aircraft and destroyer, with an extended fuselage for additional fuel tanks. There was also the Ju 88P, with 1.5 inch (3.7 cm), 2 inch

(5 cm) or 3 inch (7.5 cm) anti-tank guns installed in the underside of the fuselage. The more defensive weaponry and equipment the Ju 88 acquired, the slower it became. So in order for it to fulfill its intended role as a high speed bomber,

A Ju 88A-6U with FuG-200 ship locating radar, Mediterranean region.

the Ju 88's aerodynamics were improved on later versions, and they were fitted with more powerful engines. They were the Ju 88S and Ju 88T, a bomber and a reconnaissance aircraft respectively.

Although the earliest examples were still relatively undeveloped and caused a few problems, in the course of the war the Ju 88 became one of the best and most versatile machines on either side. Toward the end of the war, there were attempts to use aging Ju 88s as flying bombs: each plane had its nose removed and replaced with a 6,167 lb (3,800 kg) warhead. An Me 109 or Fw 190 would carry it close to the enemy on a strip on the underside of the fuselage, aim it in the right direction, and release it to fly into its target. Although this was a very promising plan, Ju 88s fired in this way actually hit very few enemy targets, as they could not be relied upon to stay on course when released.

A Ju 88A of the 51st German Bomber Wing (known as "Edelweiss").

DORNIER DO 217

The Dornier Do 217 was best known for firing Hs 293 and Fritz X missiles. The prototype had its maiden flight as early as 1938, having been developed from the Do 17 and fitted with more powerful engines and a greater payload. The A series was conceived as a reconnaissance aircraft, fitted with DB 601 engines, but only eight were ever produced. It was succeeded by the E series, which was fitted with twin 1,600 hp 801 A/B BMW radial engines and used as a bomber, a reconnaissance aircraft, and a torpedo bomber. The E-5 was the first to be equipped with the Hs 293. The K-series was introduced in the fall of 1942 , with a completely altered nose—rounded rather than layered, with a glazed cockpit—and more powerful engines: each BMW 801 G/H engine produced 1,730 hp. In addition, the K-2 had a greater wingspan, so that it could carry Fritz X. The M series was fitted with DB 603 engines

A Do 217E of the 100th German Bomber Wing with Hs 293s (see Special Weapons) under its wings.

Do 217M-1	
Type:	Bomber
Crew:	4
Weight when empty/ max weight at takeoff:	19,471 lb/36,784 lb
Length/wingspan/height:	56.3 ft/63.3 ft/16.7 ft
Engine(s):	Two Daimler-Benz DB 603A hanging V12 engines with 1,750 hp each
Maximum speed:	348 mph at 19,000 ft
Service ceiling:	31,700 ft
Range:	1,335 miles
Weaponry:	2 x 0.5 in MG131 and up to 6 x 0.3 in MG81 mobile machine guns to be fired in various directions in the nose, and a combined internal and external payload of max. 8,810 lb

instead of their BMW counterparts, but the two models are virtually identical in every other respect. As well as bombers and reconnaissance aircraft, there were also night fighters based on the Do 217. The E series bomber was converted to produce the J series, which was equipped with 0.8 inch (20 mm) MGFF and four 0.3 inch (7.92 mm) MG17 guns, as well as a "Lichtenstein" radar in the nose. The N series night fighter was also developed from the M series, and as well as its standard weaponry and radar, these planes often had four additional

guns, MG151/20s firing diagonally upward in the fuselage ("diagonal music"). Because of their long range and stability, the Do 217 J and N excelled as weapons platforms, but were not sufficiently maneuverable to serve as night fighters. There was also a P version, a high-altitude reconnaissance aircraft. With a DB 605 engine in the fuselage driving a supercharger, it could reach altitudes in excess of 10 miles (16 km). Few P series machines were ever produced, but a total of 1,730 Do 217s were manufactured.

JUNKERS JU 188 RACHER (AVENGER)

Junkers began developing a successor to the Ju 88 as early as 1940, but it soon became clear that designing the Ju 288, as it was known, would be hindered by engine trouble, so Junkers decided to produce an interim model. The Ju 88B and E test aircraft had a new fuselage and greater wingspan, and the Ju 188 was developed from them. The prototype of this new model flew for the first time in January 1943, and the first production models were ready just two months later, even though the German Air Ministry had specifically demanded that the new model had to be compatible with both BMW 801 radial and Jumo 213 inline engines. Ju 188s were primarily deployed as reconnaissance aircraft (some of which were equipped with FuG 200 radar to detect ships), bombers, and torpedo bombers. They were maneuverable and handled well, but they appeared two years too late. A high altitude model,

Ju 188E-1	
Type:	Bomber and reconnaissance aircraft
Crew:	4
Weight when empty/ max weight at takeoff:	21,718 lb/33,480 lb
Length/wingspan/height:	49.8 ft/73.3 ft/14.8 ft
Engine(s):	Two BMW 801D-2 14-cylinder radial engines with 1,730 hp each
Maximum speed:	311 mph at 20,000 ft
Service ceiling:	31,150 ft
Range:	1,208 miles
Weaponry:	1 x 0.8 in MG151/20 mobile machine guns in the nose, 1 x 0.5 in MG131 machine gun in the rear of the cockpit, 1 x 0.3 in MG81Z rearward-firing machine gun in the ventral gondola, and a combined internal and external payload of max. 6,608 lb

the Ju 388, was also developed. Only a handful of the latter were ever built,

but 1,076 Ju 188s were manufactured in total.

The Ju 188D-2.

FOCKE-WULF FW 200 CONDOR

The Fw 200 was originally a long haul passenger aircraft. The initial design appeared in 1935, and it successfully completed its first long distance flight in 1937. In fact, the test flight was such a success that the prototype set a few world records, and Lufthansa ordered the first series of production models. In 1940 there were attempts to convert the existing Condors for military purposes, but the test results were unsatisfactory, because the engines were not sufficiently powerful. Instead, two prototypes were converted for use as Hitler's personal transport, and another was converted for Goering. As the war progressed, however, it became clear that Germany required a long range bomber and reconnaissance aircraft, so the German Air Ministry ordered the Fw 200C, which had a reinforced air frame and a ventral gondola with a bomb bay, as well as new 1,200 hp engines. This model was deployed primarily as a sea reconnaissance aircraft and bomber in the Atlantic. Because the sea convoys were poorly defended at first, the Fw 200 enjoyed plenty of success for

Fw 200C-3	
Type:	Sea reconnaissance aircraft and transporter
Crew:	7–8
Weight when empty/ max weight at takeoff:	37,456 lb/54,009 lb
Length/wingspan/height:	78.2 ft/109.5 ft/21 ft
Engine(s):	Four BMW-Bramo 323R 9-cylinder radial engines with 1,200 hp each
Maximum speed:	224 mph at sea level
Service ceiling:	20,000 ft
Range:	2,210 miles
Weaponry:	1 x 0.8 in MG151/20 machine gun in the turret, 1 x 0.8 in MG151/20 machine gun in the front and 1 x 0.3 in MG15 machine gun in the rear of the ventral gondola, 1 x MG15 machine gun on the back of the fuselage, and 1 x MG15 machine gun on each side

a while. They took off from bases in France and Norway, either locating targets for submarines or attacking ships themselves with bombs and Hs 293s. Between August 1940 and February 1941, Fw 200s sank 85 Allied ships, amounting to 363,000 GRT (gross register tons).

An Fw 200C-8 of the 40th German Bomber Wing with Hs 293s under its wings for anti-naval combat.

ARADO AR 234

Ar 234B-2	
Type:	High-speed bomber and reconnaissance aircraft
Crew:	1
Weight when empty/ max weight at takeoff:	11,454 lb/21,696 lb
Length/wingspan/height:	42.1 ft/47 ft/14.3 ft
Engine(s):	Two Junkers Jumo 004B jet engines with 1,960 lb of thrust each
Maximum speed:	460 mph at 20,000 ft
Service ceiling:	33,300 ft
Range:	1,012 miles
Weaponry:	2 x fixed rearward-firing 0.8 in MG151/20 machine guns in the rear, and a payload of up to 4,405 lb under the wings

An Ar 234B-2.

The Arado AR 234 was the world's first jet-powered bomber to be put into service. From 1941 Arado developed a reconnaissance bomber with two jet engines, and the test model was introduced in 1943. To save weight, it shed its undercarriage after takeoff and landed on skids, but this system did not work, so the production model had a three-wheel undercarriage. Not only was the jet engine revolutionary but the AR 234 also had an ejector seat. The reconnaissance version, the Ar 234 B-1, which was fitted with up to four cameras, appeared in 1944, followed by the bomber version, the Ar 234 B-2, which had a three-axle autopilot and a BZA bomb counter, and which could carry 4,405 lb (2,000 kg) of bombs externally. The bomber first came into service with the 76th Bomber Wing in the Ardennes offensive of December 1944, but in April 1945 they could no longer be flown because of the shortage of fuel.

HEINKEL HE 177 GREIF (GRIFFIN)

An He 177A-3 of the 100th German Bomber Wing in Chateaudon, 1944.

An He 177A-5 of the 3rd Group of the 1st German Bomber Wing in East Prussia, summer 1944.

In 1938 the German Air Ministry ordered a heavy bomber with a maximum speed of at least 335 mph (540 km/h), a maximum payload of at least 4,405 lb (2,000 kg), and the capability to dive. So Heinkel developed a technically advanced and innovative aircraft. The He 177 flew for the first time in November 1939 and looked like a twin-engine aircraft, but in fact it had four engines. To reduce air resistance, it was originally supposed only to have two engines, but because no sufficiently powerful engines were available, Daimler-Benz produced a DB 606 engine from two DB 601 engines, and the He 177 had two of the former. But the DB 606 was never reliable and kept overheating, which earned it the nicknames, "Reichsfeuerzeug" (lighter) and "Reichsfackel" (torch). Even at the prototype stage, several aircraft crashed because of engine fires or structural failure. The first He 177s were delivered in mid-1942, though they were still ridden with structural flaws, and the A-3, delivered in late 1942, was the first to be called the "Griffin," but the He 177's main problems would always be its engines. Most He 177s were deployed in air raids

against England or put into service on ships, which made it possible for them to carry Hs 293 or Fritz X flying bombs. The A-5 had a new reinforced structure so that it could carry a heavier payload, and improved DB 610 compound engines, each consisting of two DB 603 engines, but they were still not entirely reliable. The A-7 version was also produced, albeit in small numbers, with a wider wingspan

of 122 ft (36.6 m) to attain higher altitudes. Production of the He 177 was halted in the fall of 1944, after the production of fewer than 900 aircraft. It had the potential to be an excellent aircraft, but because its engines were so unreliable and its manufacturer was bogged down with so many test models and equipment configurations, its effectiveness was severely limited.

	He 177A-5
Type:	Heavy bomber
Crew:	6–7
Weight when empty/ max weight at takeoff:	27,004 lb/68,282 lb
Length/wingspan/height:	68 ft/104.8 ft/21.3 ft
Engine(s):	Two Daimler-Benz DB 610A/B engines (each consisting of two Daimler-Benz DB603 hanging V12s) with 2,950 hp normal power and 3,100 hp emergency power each
Maximum speed:	304 mph
Service ceiling:	26,500 ft
Range:	3,416 miles with two HS 293s
Weaponry:	1 x 0.3 in MG81 machine gun in the nose, 1 x 0.8 in MG151/20 machine gun towards the front, a remote-controlled installation on the fuselage with 2 x 0.5 in MG131 machine guns, 1 x 0.5 in MG131 machine gun in a turning turret on the fuselage, 1 x 0.8 in MG151/20 machine gun in an installation in the rear, and a combined internal and external payload of 13,216 lb

FIESELER FI 156 STORCH (STORK)

	Fi 156C-2
Type:	Liaison and reconnaissance aircraft
Crew:	2
Weight when empty/ max weight at takeoff:	2,048 lb/2,919 lb
Length/wingspan/height:	33 ft/47.5 ft/10.2 ft
Engine(s):	One Argus As10C-3 hanging V8 engine with 240 hp
Maximum speed:	109 mph at sea level
Service ceiling:	15,300 ft
Range:	239 miles
Weaponry:	One mobile rearward-firing 0.3 in MG15 machine gun

The Fieseler Stork.

The Germans required a liaison and observation aircraft that could take off from a very short runway, and the Fieseler Fi 156 was built to meet this requirement. The first of three test aircraft took off on its maiden flight on May 10, 1936, and it was very clear even at this stage that none of the other models could compete with the Fieseler. A slat along the front and flaps along the entire reverse edge of the wings gave it the required landing and takeoff capabilities, and its glazed cabin allowed for excellent downward visibility. After the production of the limited A and B series, the C series went into serial production, and in total around 2,900 Fi 156s were built. The C-1 was soon replaced by the C-2, which had an MG15 gun in a plexiglass bubble (*Linsenlafette*) to defend it against attacks from the rear. The greatest production was of the C-3 , including the C-3 Trop, which was equipped for use in Africa. There was also a D-series (D-0 and D-1), made to transport wounded personnel. Storks were also frequently used for special missions, such as flying Hanna Reitsch into Berlin on April 26, 1945, when the city was beleaguered and lay in ruins.

An Fi 156C-3 in North Africa.

HENSCHEL HS 126

The Hs 126B-1.

	Hs 126B-1
Type:	Short-range reconnaissance aircraft
Crew:	2–3
Weight when empty/ max weight at takeoff:	4,471 lb/6,806 lb
Length/wingspan/height:	36.5 ft/48.3 ft/12.5 ft
Engine(s):	One BMW-Bramo 323A-1 9-cylinder radial engine with 850 hp
Maximum speed:	193 mph
Service ceiling:	27,700 ft
Range:	447 mph
Weaponry:	1 x 0.3 in MG17 fixed machine gun in the fuselage, 1 x 0.3 in machine gun in the rear of the cockpit, and an external payload of 1 x 110 lb or 5 x 22 lb bomb(s)

During the early years of the war, the Henschel Hs 126 was the Luftwaffe's standard short-range reconnaissance aircraft. The earliest prototype was completed in 1936, and in 1937 Henschel built a pre-production series of ten machines. Because these were highly rated, the Hs 126 went into full-scale production, and more than 600 were manufactured. From 1942, however, it was gradually withdrawn from service and replaced by the Fw 189. It was first deployed in the Condor Legion in the Spanish Civil War on the Nationalist side, and the surviving aircraft remained in Spain. The Hs 126 served the Luftwaffe well: it had excellent downward visibility, it was very robust, and there was room for a pilot, a look-out, and/or a gunner.

ARADO AR 196

The Arado Ar 196 was manufactured in larger numbers than any other German seaplane in the Second World War—around 500 were built in total, including 401 A-3 version aircraft. The first prototypes flew in 1938, and the first Ar 196s were deployed in 1939. Ar 196s served as a reconnaissance aircraft on the majority of German cruisers and battleships, from which they were launched by catapult, but they landed next to their carriers and had to be hoisted back on board. They were also used in coastal aviation and sea reconnaissance groups, where their agility and very heavy weaponry made them ideal for sea patrols and reconnaissance missions. Although the Ar 196 was made almost entirely out of metal, the back of the fuselage was covered with fabric. As well as Arado, it was also manufactured by the French firm SNCA and the Dutch company Fokker under German orders (both countries had been occupied), and the last Ar 196s were delivered in August 1944.

	Ar 196A-3
Type:	Ship-based and coastal reconnaissance aircraft
Crew:	2
Weight when empty/ max weight at takeoff:	6,586 lb/ 8,216 lb
Length/wingspan/height:	36.7 ft/41.3 ft/14.8 ft
Engine(s):	One BMW 132K 9-cylinder radial engine with 960 hp
Maximum speed:	193 mph at 13,300 ft
Service ceiling:	23,300 ft
Range:	665 miles
Weaponry:	2 x 0.8 in MGFF fixed machine guns in the wings, 1 x 0.3 in MG17 fixed machine gun in the upper fuselage, and a payload of 2 x 110 lb bombs under the wings

An Ar 196A-3.

HEINKEL HE 115

	He 115-C1
Type:	Reconnaissance aircraft and bomber
Crew:	3
Weight when empty/ max weight at takeoff:	15,112 lb/ 23,491 lb
Length/wingspan/height:	57.7 ft/75.3 ft/21.9 ft
Engine(s):	Two BMW 132K 9-cylinder radial engines with 960 hp each
Maximum speed:	179 mph
Service ceiling:	17,230 ft
Range:	1,730 miles
Weaponry:	1 x 0.3 in MG15 mobile machine gun in the nose, 1 x 0.3 in fixed machine gun under the nose, 1 x 0.3 in machine gun in the rear of the cockpit, 2 x 0.3 in fixed machine guns in the rear of the engine gondolas, and an internal or external payload of max. 1,652 lb—LTF 5 or LTF 6b torpedoes, mines or 3 x 550 lb bombs

The Heinkel He 115 was a twin-engine seaplane with wings attached to the middle of the fuselage and two floats. It made its maiden flight in 1936, and the prototype set six seaplane world records. It was deployed as a mine layer in 1940, with a single magnetic 2026 lb (920 kg) mine. The 106th and 406th Coastal Aviation Groups regularly flew mine-laying missions on the south and east coasts of the United Kingdom. In late 1940 the 115C-1 was introduced with an additional MG151 machine gun in a gondola under the nose, and two rearward-pointing MG17 machine guns in the engine gondolas. There was also a sub-variant with stronger floats for landing on ice and frozen snow. The C-4 was a variant built especially for torpedo attacks, and it was deployed on numerous occasions against convoys in the North Pole. The He 115 flew in coastal aviation groups until the end of the war.

An He 115C-1.

BLOHM AND VOSS BV 138

In 1933 the German Air Ministry invited bids to produce a diesel-engine sea reconnaissance aircraft, and the successful design was submitted by the Hamburg shipbuilders Blohm and Voss. This model was initially called the Ha 138, then later the BV 138. But it soon became apparent that the engines with which it was supposed to be fitted were not available, so the design was altered to accommodate three Jumo 205 engines—the third engine was mounted in a structure attached to the base of the fuselage. Early test results were disappointing, and the design had to be revised again. The first production model

The Bv 138C-1. Because of its somewhat bizarre appearance, this aircraft's crew nicknamed it the "flying clog."

BV 138C-1	
Type:	Reconnaissance seaplane
Crew:	5
Weight when empty/ max weight at takeoff:	17,841 lb/ 32,379 lb
Length/wingspan/height:	66.3 ft/90 ft/22 ft
Engine(s):	Three Junkers Jumo 205D diesel engines with 880 hp each
Maximum speed:	171 mph at sea level
Service ceiling:	16,700 ft
Range:	3,100 miles
Weaponry:	1 x 0.8 in MG151/20 machine gun in a turning nose turret, 1 x 0.8 in MG151/20 machine gun in a turning tail turret, 1 x 0.5 in MG131 machine gun in an open installation behind the central engine gondola, and a payload of up to 6 x 110 lb bombs or 4 x 330 lb depth bombs

(the A-1) was delivered in 1939 with 605 hp Jumo 205C engines. The B-1 version had more powerful Jumo 205D engines and a more robust structure, and it was more heavily armored, and the C-1 model also had its structure reinforced and its weapon load increased. The BV-138 was primarily used as a reconnaissance aircraft during the war, but it was less effective as an air-sea rescue aircraft. There was also a special minesweeping version with an electromagnetic aluminum ring. In total 279 BV 138s were produced, including 127 C-1s.

DORNIER DO 24

In 1935 the Dutch Government required a replacement for its Dornier Whale in the Dutch East Indies, for which Dornier itself submitted a successful bid. They decided to alter the competition design for the BV 138 in accordance with the wishes of the Dutch Government, equipping it with 875 hp Wright radial engines, and in 1937 the Do 24K was manufactured under license by the Dutch company, Aviolanda. When German troops occupied the Netherlands in 1940, three seaplanes of this type were seized and subsequently tested in Germany. As the Do 24 vastly outperformed both the He 59 and the BV 138, its production continued in the Netherlands under German orders, and it became the standard air-sea rescue aircraft. Do 24s were so urgently needed that 48 were also manufactured in France by SNCA from 1942. They continued to manufacture this model even after France was liberated, and 40 were delivered to the French Air Force. In June 1944 12 Do 24s were delivered to Spain, serving in Majorca until the mid-1970s. In total, around 240 Do 24s were produced.

Do 24T	
Type:	Reconnaissance and air-sea rescue seaplane
Crew:	5
Weight when empty/max weight at takeoff:	20,264 lb/40,529 lb
Length/wingspan/height:	66.3 ft/90 ft/22 ft
Engine(s):	Three BMW Bramo 323-R-2 9-cylinder radial engines with 1,000 hp each
Maximum speed:	211 mph at sea level
Service ceiling:	16,700 ft
Range:	1,800 miles
Weaponry:	2 x 0.3 in MG15 machine guns, one in the nose turret, one in the tail turret, and 1 x 0.8 in MG151/20 machine gun in the rear turret

A Do 24N-1 from Dutch stocks, fitted with American radial engines. Because Wright radial engines were no longer available, later Do 24s were fitted with 1,000 hp BMW Bramo 323 R 2 engines.

FIAT C.R.42 FALCO (FALCON)

The Fiat C.R.42 Falcon made its maiden flight on May 23, 1938, but although it was a robust, tidy, and attractive design, it was already dated when it was put into production. Nevertheless, 34 were exported to Belgium, 68 to Hungary, and 72 to Sweden. From the very beginning of the war, the Falcon's weaknesses were exposed: although it was easy to maneuver, it was too lightly armed and too slow, and it was completely out of its depth in the Battle of Britain. It fared rather better, however, in the Mediterranean, where the British also employed outdated aircraft. Once modern fighters such as the M.C. 202 had become available, the Falcon was used as a fighter bomber and a flight instruction aircraft. When the Italians changed sides in 1943, the Luftwaffe took possession of 112 Falcons, and employed them primarily for night raids and anti-partisan missions. In fact, 150 additional C.R.42s specially designed for night raids were manufactured for the Luftwaffe. Until production was halted in late 1944, a total of 1,780 Falcons were produced, and they were still being flown on night missions in May 1945.

	C.R.42
Type:	Fighter
Crew:	1
Weight when empty/max weight at takeoff:	3,925 lb/5,055 lb
Length/wingspan/height:	27.6 ft/32.3 ft/12 ft
Engine(s):	One Fiat A.74-RC-38 14-cylinder radial engine with 840 hp
Maximum speed:	267 mph at 16,700 ft
Service ceiling:	34,000 ft
Range:	481 miles
Weaponry:	2 x 0.5 in Type SAFAT fixed machine guns in the nose, and an external payload of up to 440 lb

A Fiat C.R.42, Sicily, early 1941.

FIAT G.50 FRECCIA (ARROW)

	G.50
Type:	Fighter
Crew:	1
Weight when empty/max weight at takeoff:	4,350 lb/5,319 lb
Length/wingspan/height:	26 ft/36.5 ft/9.9 ft
Engine(s):	One Fiat A.74-RC-38 14-cylinder radial engine with 840 hp
Maximum speed:	293 mph at 16,700 ft
Service ceiling:	32,785 ft
Range:	416 miles
Weaponry:	2 x 0.5 in Type SAFAT fixed machine guns in the nose

A Fiat G.50bis in Libya, summer, 1941.

The Fiat G.50 Arrow was the first Italian single-wing fighter. It was made of metal, and it had an enclosed cockpit and retractable undercarriage. Work began on its design in 1935, and it made its maiden flight in early 1937. It was tested in combat by the *Aviazione Legionaria*, the Italian pilots fighting on the side of the Nationalists in the Spanish Civil War, where it became obvious that it was underpowered. In addition, the Italian pilots greatly disliked the closed cockpit, so it was fitted with an open cockpit based on the 45 version. During the war, the basic G.50sie version was replaced by the G.50bis, which made its maiden flight on September 9, 1940. The latter also had an open cockpit, and was equipped with larger fuel tanks and stronger armor. The Arrow was very agile, but this could not compensate for its underpowered engine or limited weaponry, weaknesses which were a death sentence for many pilots when they were confronted by the British Hurricanes. At diving speeds in excess of 311 mph (500 km/h), it was very difficult to maneuver, and on some occasions, parts of the wings and fuselage would even come loose. In total, around 774 G.50s, including 108 two-seater G.50B training aircraft, were produced.

FIAT G.55 CENTAURO (CENTAUR)

	G.55/I
Type:	Fighter and fighter bomber
Crew:	1
Weight when empty/	5,793 lb/
max weight at takeoff:	8,189 lb
Length/wingspan/height:	31.2 ft/39.5 ft/10.4 ft
Engine(s):	One Fiat RA-1050-RC-58 Tifone hanging V12 engine with 1,475 hp
Maximum speed:	391 mph
Service ceiling:	41,000 ft
Range:	745 miles
Weaponry:	1 x 0.8 in MG151/20 machine gun firing through the propeller hub, 2 x 0.8 in MG151/20 fixed machine guns in the wings, 2 x 0.5 in Type SAFAT machine guns in the nose, and external payload of max. 705 lb

One of the few Fiat G.55s built for the Italian Air Force.

The Fiat G.55 Centaur was a massive improvement on its predecessor, the G.50, mostly because of its superior engine, a DB 605 built under license. It made its maiden flight on April 30, 1942, and it was first tested in combat in March 1943, by which time the Italian Air Ministry had already decided to put it into production. Yet production for the Italian Air Force (*Regia Aeronautica*) was halted in September 1943, after only 16 G.55/0s and 15 G.55/1s had been completed. All 274 Centaurs produced thereafter were delivered to Mussolini's Fascist forces. Thanks to its robust structure, excellent visibility, speed, and good maneuverability, the G.55 was very successful and very popular with its pilots. Early in 1944 two prototypes were fitted with the German DB 603A engine. This model, the G.56, was an aircraft as good as, if not better than, any of its German or Allied counterparts, but the severe shortage of DB 603 engines meant that it could not be put into serial production. From 1944–45 the G.55 was also deployed by the Luftwaffe, which rated it very highly. After the war Fiat used parts left over from the wartime production of the G.55 to produce the G.55A for the Italian and Argentine Air Forces. In 1948 some of the Argentine machines were given to the Egyptians, who deployed them against Israeli Avia 199s that same year.

A Fiat G.55 of the National Republican Air Force (ANR). This was the air force of the northern Italian Fascist republic led by Mussolini after 1943.

MACCHI M.C. 200 SAETTA (LIGHTNING)

	M.C. 200
Type:	Fighter and fighter bomber
Crew:	1
Weight when empty/ max weight at takeoff:	4,174 lb/ 5,605 lb
Length/wingspan/height:	27.3 ft/35.3 ft/11.7 ft
Engine(s):	One Fiat A.74-RC-38 14-cylinder radial engine with 840 hp
Maximum speed:	312 mph at 15,000 ft
Service ceiling:	29,667 ft
Range:	540 miles
Weaponry:	2 x 0.5 in Type SAFAT machine guns in the nose; later models had 2 additional 0.3 in SAFAT machine guns in the wings

The M.C. 200 Lightning had an all-metal layered construction. Its low wings and its tail were cantilevered, and it had a retractable rear wheel. In 1936 Macchi started designing a replacement for the Fiat C.R.32 biplane, and the first prototype, which had an enclosed cockpit, flew in Christmas 1937. Because Italian pilots preferred open cockpits, later models were built in accordance with their wishes, but glazed side shutters were added for wind protection. In 1938 the first series of 99 aircraft was ordered, and in October 1939 the first production aircraft were delivered to the Italian Air Force. By the time the Italians entered the

A Macchi M.C. 200, Libya, June 1941.

war in 1940, they had 156 M.C. 200s, and they were first flown in combat against Malta in the fall that same year. Although the M.C. 200 handled well, its light weaponry and weak radial engine put it at a disadvantage compared to fighters from other countries. M.C. 200s were deployed in Greece, North Africa, Yugoslavia, and later on the Eastern Front, and 23 were flown by free Italian fighter

pilots on the side of the Allies after Italy's surrender in September 1943. The M.C. 200AS variant was built for service in Africa, and the M.C. 200CB was a fighter bomber. In total 1,153 MC 200s were produced.

MACCHI M.C. 202 FOLGORE (THUNDERBOLT) AND M.C. 205 VELTRO (GREYHOUND)

Mario Castoldi was convinced that the M.C. 200 could be more effective with a more powerful engine, which was why its basic design was altered to accommodate an imported Daimler-Benz DB 601 engine. The new machine had a larger fuselage and an enclosed cockpit, but its undercarriage, wing assembly, and tail were practically indistinguishable from the M.C. 200. The M.C. 202 made its maiden flight on August 10, 1940, and Castoldi's convictions were entirely corroborated, so the new model went into production without delay. Nevertheless, because it was not easy to import the DB 601 engine or to manufacture it under license, the M.C. 200 was produced alongside its intended successor. The M.C. 202 was first used in combat in 1941 in North Africa, but it also served on the Eastern Front. Although it still was not sufficiently well armed, Castoldi's new model performed more than well enough to cope with its enemy counterparts. To improve their weaponry, later models in the series were

	M.C. 202	M.C. 205
Type:	Fighter and fighter bomber	Fighter and fighter bomber
Crew:	1	1
Weight when empty/ max weight at takeoff:	5,176 lb/ 6,630 lb	5,685 lb/ 7,507 lb
Length/wingspan/ height:	29.5 ft/35.3 ft/ 10.1 ft	29.5 ft/35.3 ft/ 10.1 ft
Engine(s):	One Alfa-Romeo RA-1000-RC-41-1 Monsone hanging V12 engine with 1,175 hp	One Fiat RA-1050-RC-58 Tifone hanging V12 engine with 1,475 hp
Maximum speed:	370 mph at 16,700 ft	400 mph
Service ceiling:	38,300 ft	37,700 ft
Range:	475 miles	646 miles
Weaponry:	2 x 0.5 in Type SAFAT fixed machine guns in the nose – later models also had 2 additional 0.3 in SAFAT machine guns in the wings— and partial gondolas under the wings with 1 x 0.8 in MG151/20 machine gun each	2 x 0.5 in Type SAFAT fixed machine guns in the nose, 0.3 in SAFAT machine guns under the wings—later models had 0.8 in MG151/20 instead of the 0.3 in MG20 machine guns

An M.C. 205 from the Italian Co-Belligerent Air Force, which fought on the side of the Allies.

An M.C. 202, Sicily, early 1942.

equipped initially with two extra 0.3 inch (7.7 mm) machine guns, and later some of them also had gondolas under their wings, each with one 7.9 inch (20 mm) MG 151/20 machine gun. As with all Italian fighters, there was also a version for the tropics (AS) and a fighter bomber (CB)

with a maximum payload of 705 lb (320 kg). For as long as the M.C. 202 was produced, its engine was difficult to obtain, so only around 1,500 were ever manufactured. The M.C. 205 Greyhound had a more powerful DB 605, producing 1,475 hp, but the body and undercarriage

were almost identical. The prototype made its maiden flight as early as April 19, 1943, but because the DB 605 engine was produced only very slowly under license, the first production models were not delivered to the Italian Air Force until mid-1943. By the time Italy surrendered in September 1943, just 66 Greyhounds had been manufactured, of which only six were put into service by the Italians. After Italy's surrender, 205 more were manufactured under German supervision in northern Italy, some of which were used by the Luftwaffe. Second only to the Fiat G.55, the M.C. 205 was certainly one of Italy's best fighter aircraft.

C.A.N.T. Z.1007 ALCIONE (KINGFISHER)

The Kingfisher was first put into service by the Italian Air Force under the Fascists, and after 1943 it was flown both by Italians fighting on the side of the Allies and by Mussolini's forces. The first prototype of the Z.1007, fitted with three 825 Hp Isotta-Frachini engines, made its maiden flight in March 1937.

Performance was disappointing on account of the underpowered engines, so the Z.1007 was converted to accommodate three Piaggio radial engines, and its fuselage was also made taller and wider in the process. The converted aircraft, called the Z.1007bis, went into production at the C.A.N.T. factory in Monfalcone, Italy, in 1939. The earliest machines had a single tailfin but a twin tail was introduced to give the gunner a better view from his turret. The Z.1007bis was made entirely of wood, which could lead to problems in extreme weather conditions, but it was an excellent bomber, used everywhere from the Sahara to Russia. The Z.1007ter had three 1,150 hp engines and had a maximum speed of 311 mph (500 km/h), but few were ever built, and only 567 Z.1007s, including all the different variants, were manufactured.

	Z.1007bis
Type:	Bomber
Crew:	5
Weight when empty/ max weight at takeoff:	20,694 lb/ 30,000 lb
Length/wingspan/height:	61.2 ft/82.7 ft/17.4 ft
Engine(s):	Three Piaggio P.XI-R2C.40 radial engines with 1,000 hp each
Maximum speed:	289 mph at 13,300 ft
Service ceiling:	27,300 ft
Range:	1,090 miles
Weaponry:	1 x 0.5 in Type SAFAT or Scotti machine guns in a turning turret on the fuselage, two further 0.5 in rearward and downward-firing machine guns of the same type, 2 x 0.3 in Type SAFAT machine guns on the sides, and an internal or external payload of max. 2,643 lb

A C.A.N.T. Z.1007bis from the 95th Group of Italian Squadron 230a in Greece, 1940.

SAVOIA-MARCHETTI S.M. 79 SPARVIERO (SPARROW HAWK)

In October 1934 Savoia-Marchetti introduced the prototype of an eight-seat transport aircraft, which set six world records in September 1935. So the Italian Air Force ordered a new version modified as a bomber, which flew for the first time in October 1936. It had a machine gun installation on top of the fuselage, a ventral gondola for the bombs, and a raised cockpit (hence its nickname, the "hunchback bomber"), but it was not significantly different from the transport version in other respects.

The Sparrow Hawk was first flown in 1937 in the Spanish Civil War, like many other Italian and German aircraft. The Italian Air Force had 594 Sparrow Hawks when the war broke out, and they were soon in use on all fronts. Because it was slightly underpowered, the torpedo bomber version, the S.M. 79-II had more powerful Piaggio engines, producing 1,000 hp each, and in this format it was an outstanding machine. The Sparrow Hawk was very versatile, serving as a high altitude and torpedo bomber, a ground

attack aircraft, and a reconnaissance aircraft. The final version, the S.M. 79-III, appeared in 1943 with higher-performing engines and improved aerodynamics. After the truce between Italy and the Allies in September 1943, the Sparrow Hawk was still used by Mussolini's RSI (*Repubblica Sociale Italiana*) on Germany's side, while the Italian Co-Belligerent Air Force on the Allied side used them only as transporters. A twin-engine version

(the S.M. 79B) was exported to Romania, Iraq, and Brazil. Yugoslavia bought 45 S.M. 79-Is before the war, and between October 1936 and June 1943, around 1,300 S.M. 79s were built.

	S.M.79-I
Type:	Bomber
Crew:	5–6
Weight when empty/	14,978 lb/
max weight at takeoff:	23,084 lb
Length/wingspan/height:	52.7 ft/70.7 ft/14.3 ft
Engine(s):	Three Alfa-Romeo 126-RC.34 radial engines with 780 hp each
Maximum speed:	267 mph at 13,000 ft
Service ceiling:	21,700 ft
Range:	1,180 miles
Weaponry:	1 x 0.5 in Type SAFAT fixed forward-firing machine gun above the cockpit, 1 x 0.5 in rear machine gun, 1 x 0.5 in machine gun in the ventral gondola, 1–2 x 0.3 in Type SAFAT machine guns in the side windows in the central fuselage, and an internal payload of max. 2,753 lb

An S.M.79-III from the ANR, based in Faggioni, 1944.

An early S.M.79-I model being deployed by the Spanish Nationalists.

FIAT BR.20 CIGOGNA (STORK)

The Fiat BR.20's maiden flight took place on February 10, 1936. It had a retractable tail wheel, all-metal wings, and a body made partially out of metal. The first Fiat BR.20s were delivered to the Italian Air Force in the fall of 1936, and 233 were manufactured until 1940. 85 were built for the Japanese, who deployed them in China, but according to some reports, the Japanese pilots were not very impressed by the Stork. Some were also delivered to Venezuela, and others were flown on the Nationalist side in the Spanish Civil War. In 1940 the new BR.20M version, which had a new nose cone and a smoother outer surface, was delivered to the Italian Air Force. Until early 1942, 264 BR.20s were built, and 15 of the final version, the BR.20bis, which had more powerful engines and improved defensive weaponry, were built in 1943. When Italy entered the war in 1940, the Italian Air Force had 172 BR.20s, which were

	BR.20
Type:	Bomber
Crew:	5
Weight when empty/ max weight at takeoff:	14,097 lb/ 21,806 lb
Length/wingspan/height:	53.7 ft/71.9 ft/14.3 ft
Engine(s):	Two Fiat A.80-RC-41 18-cylinder radial engines with 1,000 hp each
Maximum speed:	268 mph at 16,667 ft
Service ceiling:	30,000 ft
Range:	1,865 miles
Weaponry:	1 x 0.5 in Type SAFAT or Scotti machine gun in an installation on the fuselage, 1 x 0.3 in Type SAFAT machine gun in the nose, 1 x 0.3 in machine gun in the lower fuselage, and a payload of up to 3,524 lb

A BR.20 with the Spanish Nationalist emblem—the Italian Aviation Legion fought on the Nationalist side in the Spanish Civil War.

flown in the French campaign and the Battle of Britain.

PIAGGIO P.108

The Piaggio P.108 was the only Italian four-engine long-range bomber in the war, making its maiden flight on November 24, 1939. Four different variants were planned, but only the P.108B (Bombardier) was built in significant numbers. There was a civilian transporter version that could carry 32 passengers, but this was later converted into a military transporter that could carry 56 soldiers. The P.108B was put into service in May 1941, but was not deployed in the 274th Long-Range Bomber Squadron for another year, and even then, on account of technical difficulties, there were never more than seven or eight machines ready

	P.108B
Type:	Bomber
Crew:	6–7
Weight when empty/ max weight at takeoff:	38,161 lb/ 65,826 lb
Length/wingspan/height:	74.3 ft/106.7 ft/20 ft
Engine(s):	Four Piaggio PXII-RC.35 radial engines with 1,500 hp each
Maximum speed:	267 mph at 14,000 ft
Service ceiling:	28,300 ft
Range:	2,185 miles
Weaponry:	Up to 6 x 0.5 in Type SAFAT machine guns in various fuselage positions, 2 x 0.5 in machine guns in remote-controlled installations in the outer engine gondolas, and an internal payload of max. 7,709 lb

Italy's only four-engine bomber, the Piaggio P.108, enjoyed little real success, though it had numerous innovative details.

to be flown at any time. Piaggio bombers carried out night raids on Gibraltar and Algerian ports during the Allied "Torch" land campaign in November 1942. Its remote-controlled gun installations, each of which had a 5 inch (12.7 mm) machine gun, were situated in the rear of each engine gondola. Production was halted in 1943, after only 163 P.108s had been produced, including all the different variants. The P108B's maneuverability was poor, and it suffered from technical problems. By the time Italy surrendered in 1943, more than 95% of P.108s had been destroyed, the remainder serving either in Mussolini's forces or in the Luftwaffe.

NAKAJIMA KI-27 SETSU (NATE)

	Ki-27a
Type:	Fighter
Crew:	1 man
Weight when empty/	2,423 lb/
max weight at takeoff:	3,943 lb
Length/wingspan/height:	25.1 ft/37.7 ft/10.8 ft
Engine(s):	One Nakajima Ha-1b radial engine with 710 hp
Maximum speed:	292 mph
Service ceiling:	34,000 ft
Range:	390 miles
Weaponry:	2 x 0.3 in Type 97 fixed machine guns in the nose

The Ki-27 (Nate).

The Nakajima Ki-27 was an all-metal low-wing aircraft with a fixed undercarriage, and it was put into serial production in 1937. After a few pre-production models, the first variant to be delivered to the Japanese fighter squadrons was the Ki-27a. It was first deployed over northern China in March 1938, where it proved to be very effective against its Chinese counterparts. It was not surpassed until the introduction of the Polikarpov I-16. When the war in the Pacific broke out, the Ki-27a and Ki-27B (a very slightly modified version) represented a large proportion of the Japanese Imperial Army's fighter aircraft.

The Ki-27 was codenamed "Abdul," then later "Nate," by the Allies. From early 1943 onward, the Ki-27 was withdrawn from the front line and served primarily as a flight instruction aircraft, though it was deployed as a kamikaze aircraft toward the end of the war. From 1937–1942, 3,399 Ki-27s were built.

NAKAJIMA KI-43 HAYABUSHA (OSCAR)

	Ki-43IIa
Type:	Fighter/fighter bomber
Crew:	1
Weight when empty/	4,207 lb/
max weight at takeoff:	5,705 lb
Length/wingspan/height:	29.7 ft/36.1 ft/10.9 ft
Engine(s):	One Nakajima Ha-115 radial engine with 1,150 hp
Maximum speed:	329 mph at 13,300 ft
Service ceiling:	37,300 ft
Range:	994 miles
Weaponry:	2 x 0.5 in Type 1 fixed machine guns in the nose, and an external payload of max. 1,100 lb, e.g., two 550 lb bombs under the wings

The Ki-43IIa (Oscar), Burma, mid-1943.

The Ki-43 prototype was an all-metal low-wing aircraft with retractable undercarriage, and it made its maiden flight in January 1939, when its maneuverability was found wanting. So the wings and flaps were altered, and the modified version went into production in early 1941 as the Ki-43Ia, codenamed "Oscar" by the Allies. It was armed with two 0.3 inch (7.7 mm) machine guns, and it was powered by a 975 hp Nakajima-Sakae engine. Although its agility made it very effective in the early stages of the war, it had many faults, which its manufacturers tried to correct in different versions. It was equipped with heavier weaponry (the Ki-43Ic had two 0.5 inch (12.7 mm) machine guns), and the Ki-43II was fitted with a more powerful engine, producing 1,150 hp, protected fuel tanks, and armor for the pilot and the engine. It could also carry a maximum payload of 110 lb (50 kg). Because its successor, the Ki-44, was ineffective, the Ki-43 was kept in production until the end of the war, and 5,919 were produced in total. It was manufactured in larger numbers than any other Japanese fighter aircraft. There was also a Ki-43III, built in 1945, which attained higher altitudes and had a better engine, but it never got past the prototype stage. Like almost all other Japanese aircraft, it was also deployed in kamikaze operations.

KAWASAKI KI-45 TORYU (NICK)

In early 1937, Kawasaki was ordered by the Japanese Imperial Army to design a twin-engine long-range bomber to be deployed in the Pacific. In 1939 a prototype, which had Nakajima-Ha 25 radial engines and was called the Ki-45 Toryu (Dragon Slayer), flew for the first time, but its performance was disappointing. Consequently, its development was delayed until it could be modified to accommodate the more powerful Mitsubishi Ha-102 engine, but even then the latter was ridden with technical problems. So the first Ki-45 models were not produced until September 1941, and further delays meant that they could not be put into service until August 1942. Once they were in service, however, they proved to be effective fighter aircraft (Ki-45Ia), night fighters (Ki-45 KAIc), ground-attack and anti-naval aircraft (Ki-45 KAIb and KAId). The Allies gave the Ki-45 the codename "Nick," and a total of 1,698 were manufactured.

	Ki-45 KAIc
Type:	Heavy fighter/night fighter
Crew:	2
Weight when empty/ max weight at takeoff:	8,811 lb/12,115 lb
Length/wingspan/height:	36.7 ft/50.2 ft/12.3 ft
Engine(s):	Two Mitsubishi Ha-10s radial engines with 1,080 hp each
Maximum speed:	339 mph at 23,300 ft
Service ceiling:	33,300 ft
Range:	1,240 miles
Weaponry:	1 x 1.5 in fixed automatic cannon in the nose, 2 x 0.8 in Type 99 automatic cannon in the fuselage firing diagonally upward, 1 x 0.3 in Type 92 machine gun in the rear of the cockpit, and an external payload of max. 1,100 lb

The Kawasaki Ki-45 KAIa (Nick).

MITSUBISHI KI-46 HEI (DINAH)

	Ki-46II
Type:	Reconnaissance aircraft
Crew:	2
Weight when empty/ max weight at takeoff:	7,187 lb/ 12,775 lb
Length/wingspan/height:	36.7 ft/49 ft/12.8 ft
Engine(s):	Two Mitsubishi Ha-102 radial engines with 1,080 hp each
Maximum speed:	375 mph at 19,333 ft
Service ceiling:	35,730 ft
Range:	1,540 miles
Weaponry:	1 x 0.3 in Type 92 machine gun in the rear of the cockpit

The Ki-46 Hei was one of the best reconnaissance aircraft of its time: it attained high speeds and altitudes, and had a good range. The prototype made its maiden flight in late November 1939, and its performance proved superior to all the other Japanese aircrafts, though it did not quite attain the standards originally expected. It went into production as the Ki-46I but was soon replaced by the improved Ki-46II, which actually surpassed the standards originally set. The Ki-46III performed even better, with a maximum speed of 391 mph (630 km/h) and a range of 2,484 miles (4,000 km/h), but the Ha-112II engines could not be delivered reliably, so Mitsubishi had to continue producing the Ki-46II. In the early years of the war, almost nothing could intercept the Ki-46, and it provided the Japanese with valuable intelligence. Toward the end of the war, some Ki-46IIIs were converted into Ki-46III KAI fighter aircraft, and a total of 1,742 Ki-46s were produced, including 1,093 Ki-46IIs and 611 Ki-46IIIs. It is claimed that the Luftwaffe was interested in manufacturing the Ki-46 under license, but these plans were never realized.

The Mitsubishi Ki-46II (Dinah).

KAWASAKI KI-61 HIEN AND KI-100 GOSHIKI (TONY)

The Ki-61 Hien (Swan) was the only Japanese fighter with an inline engine to be deployed in the Second World War. Like Italian models, it depended upon the transfer of German engine technology, in particular, on the delivery of Daimler-Benz DB 601 V12 engines. The first prototype of the Hien flew for the first time in December 1941 and was immediately put into production, but there were some problems at first with the DB 601, which was built under license by Kawasaki as the Ha-40, and this model was not put into service until April 1943, fitted with Ki-61 engines. Nevertheless, it proved a dangerous opponent for Allied aircraft, and the Allies codenamed it "Tony," initially mistaking it for a German Bf 109 produced under license. Two main variants, the Ki-61 I and II, were built, whose weaponry and maximum altitudes were significantly different, and a total of 2,666 were manufactured. When the Ha-40 manufacturing plants were completely destroyed by US bombers in January 1945, a new engine was

	Ki-61 Ic	Ki-100 Ib
Type:	Fighter/fighter bomber	Fighter/fighter bomber
Crew:	1	1
Weight when empty/ max weight at takeoff:	5,793 lb/ 7,643 lb	5,947 lb/ 8.084 lb
Length/wingspan/height:	29.8 ft/40 ft/12.3 ft	29.3 ft/40 ft/12.3 ft
Engine(s):	One Kawasaki hanging V12 engine with 1,175 hp	One Mitsubishi Ha-112-II radial engine with 1,500 hp
Maximum speed:	348 mph at 13,300ft	366 mph at 33,300 ft
Service ceiling:	33,300 ft	35,700 ft
Range:	1,180 miles	1,240 miles
Weaponry:	2 x 0.5 in Ho-103 machine guns in the nose, 2 x 0.8 in Ho-5 automatic cannon in the wings, and an external payload of up to 1,100 lb, e.g., two 550 lb bombs or two drop tanks	2 x 0.5 in Ho-103 machine guns in the nose, 2 x 0.8 in Ho-5 automatic cannon in the wings, and an external payload of up to 1,100 lb, e.g., two 550 lb bombs or two drop tanks

urgently needed for the existing frames. In an incredible feat of improvisation, in just one month Kawasaki engineers succeeded in converting the Ki-61 to accommodate a radial engine. With a 1,500 hp Mitsubishi Ha-112 II radial engine, the new variant, called the Ki-100 Ia, performed even better than the Ki-61 and was one of the best Japanese fighters. After 275 Ki-61 II air frames were successfully converted, 99 additional converted Ki-100 Ibs, with a new cockpit canopy and rear section, were also produced.

A Ki-100 in the Royal Air Force Museum, Hendon.

NAKAJIMA KI-84 HAYATE (FRANK)

The Nakajima Ki-84 Ia (Frank).

The Allies were fortunate that the Nakajima Ki-84 Hayate (Storm) was not put into service until the summer of 1944, as "Frank"—as the Allies codenamed it—could match the best US fighters at altitudes of up to 30,000 ft (9,000 m) and was one of the Allies' most feared adversaries in Asia and the Pacific. Its low manifold pressure was only a problem at higher altitudes. The Ki-84 had a higher climbing speed and was more agile than its Allied counterparts, as well as being very heavily armed. Right from the start, all Ki-84s were armored and

equipped with self-sealing fuel tanks. Work on this model's design began in early 1942, and after two prototypes had successful test flights, the Ki-84 Ia was put into production in late 1943. Its successors were primarily more heavily armed—for example, the Ki-84 Ib had four 0.8 inch (20 mm) machine guns, and the Ki-84 Ic had two 0.8 inch (20 mm) and two 1.2 inch (30 mm) machine guns. The Ki-84 IIa, b, and c were similar to the K-84 I series models, apart from being partially made of wood to save precious raw materials. In the course of the war, the

Ki-84 suffered from the deteriorating quality of building materials, as well as the declining number of experienced pilots, and its true potential could not be realized. There were various attempts to develop the Ki-84 further, but the war ended before they could get past the testing stage. A total of 3,514 Ki-84s were manufactured.

	Ki-84 Ia
Type:	Fighter/fighter bomber
Crew:	1
Weight when empty/ max weight at takeoff:	5,859 lb/ 8,568 lb
Length/wingspan/height:	33.1 ft/37.5 ft/11.3 ft
Engine(s):	One Nakajima Ha-45 radial engine with 1,900 hp
Maximum speed:	392 mph at 20,300 ft
Service ceiling:	35,000 ft
Range:	1,340 miles
Weaponry:	2 x 0.5 in Type 1 fixed machine guns in the nose, 2 x 0.8 in Ho-103 automatic cannon in the wings, and an external payload of max. 1,100 lb, e.g. two 550 lb bombs under the wings

The Ki-84 was one of the best Japanese fighters in the Second World War.

MITSUBISHI A6M REI-SEN (ZERO OR ZEKE)

The Mitsubishi A6M Rei-Sen Type Zero was (and still is) the best known Japanese fighter aircraft in the Second World War. Its Type Zero designation—hence its name "Zero"—derived from the year in which it was introduced in the Japanese Imperial Navy (2600 according to the Japanese calendar, and 1940 according to the Western calendar). The A6M—codenamed "Zeke" by the Allies—gave the Allies an unpleasant surprise in the early stages of the war in the Pacific, although they had received reports from China about a new fighter. It was fast and agile, and it had a considerable range—at first, none of the other aircraft in the Pacific could touch it. The Zero made its maiden flight in April 1940, and it performed so well that an order was immediately submitted for 15 pre-production A6M1s. They were deployed

A6M5b	
Type:	Fighter/fighter bomber
Crew:	1
Weight when empty/	4,174 lb/
max weight at takeoff:	6,498 lb
Length/wingspan/height:	30.2 ft/40 ft/11.7 ft
Engine(s):	One Nakajima NK1F-Sakae-21 radial engine with 1,130 hp
Maximum speed:	348 mph at 23,300 ft
Service ceiling:	35,700 ft
Range:	1,120 miles
Weaponry:	1 x 0.5 in Type 3 machine gun in the nose, 2 x 0.5 in Type 3 and 2 x 0.8 in Type 99 automatic cannon in the wings, and an external payload of max. 660 lb, e.g., one 550 lb bomb, or an additional fuel tank, or two 130 lb bombs

in China, where they were so successful that the A6M2 was immediately put into production in July 1940. Half a year before war broke out in the Pacific, the A6M3 prototype was tested. Unlike its predecessors, which only had folding wing tips, the A6M3's entire wings could be folded upwards to save valuable space on aircraft carriers. In the early months of the war, the Zero was the undisputed ruler of the Pacific sky. Naturally, however, it did have some weaknesses: although its performance was excellent, this was partly due to its extremely light build and

An A6M5 Zero from one of the kamikaze units based in the Philippines in October 1944.

An A6M2 Zero on the Akagi aircraft carrier in December 1941.

Until mid-1943 the Zero dominated the Asian and Pacific skies. This shows a later model; the original is shown below at an air show.

complete lack of defensive weaponry. Moreover, although it was maneuverable, it could not cope with high speed dives. Once the Allied pilots had discovered these weaknesses, the A6M could no longer dominate them. And when the Americans introduced new, higher performance models (the Hellcat, Corsair, or P-38 Lightning), the tables turned completely. Under pressure because of increasing losses, Mitsubishi strove to improve the Zero with more powerful engines, stronger armor, and heavier weaponry, and the A6M3 was duly replaced in the fall of 1943 by the A6M5. Yet even by mid-1944, this model was barely capable of competing with the enemy, and it was deployed as a kamikaze aircraft and a dive-bomber. Although the Zero was clearly past its prime, Japan continued to manufacture it in large numbers, and there were even new models. The A6M6 was fitted with a more powerful engine, and the A6M7 version was a dive-bomber. The A6M8, powered by a 1,560 hp engine, was Japan's last attempt to catch up with the Allies, but it was only ever built as a prototype. A total of 10,937 Zeros were manufactured, including all the different variants.

The Americans seized numerous A6Ms during the war, some of which (including this one) were subjected to tests in the USA.

AICHI D3A KAUBAKU (VAL)

The Aichi D3A was an all-metal single-wing aircraft with a fixed undercarriage; its development began in 1936 and was heavily influenced by Heinkel designs. The first pre-production models were in service with the Japanese Navy from March 1939. The first models to be deployed still had 1,000 hp Mitsubishi engines, whose power was later increased to 1,070 hp. The D3A1 was the standard bomber on board Japanese aircraft carriers and was in the first wave of attacks on Pearl Harbor. Because its pilots were highly trained and it handled well, "Val" (as it was codenamed by the Allies) was astonishingly successful at first, sinking the British cruisers *Cornwall* and *Dorsetshire* in April 1942 off the coast of Ceylon, followed four days later by the aircraft carrier HMS *Hermes* and the destroyer HMS *Vampire*. The improved D3A2 version had a more powerful 1,300 hp radial engine, a new cockpit, and larger fuel tanks, giving it a range of over 1,500 miles (around 2,500 km). But toward the end of the war, the D3A lagged a long way behind its enemy counterparts, and it was used as a flight instruction aircraft

D3A1 (a later series model)	
Type:	Carrier-borne dive-bomber
Crew:	2
Weight when empty/max weight at takeoff:	5,304 lb/8,040 lb
Length/wingspan/height:	34 ft/47.9 ft/12.8 ft
Engine(s):	One Mitsubishi-Kinsei 44 radial engine with 1,070 hp
Maximum speed:	239 mph at 10,000 ft
Service ceiling:	31,000 ft
Range:	915 miles
Weaponry:	2 x 0.3 in Type 97 fixed machine guns in the nose, 1 x 0.3 in Type 92 machine gun in the rear of the cockpit, and an external payload of up to 815 lb, e.g., one 550 lb bomb under the fuselage and two 132 lb bombs under the wings

The Aichi D3A (Val).

and used in kamikaze operations. Around 1,500 D3As were manufactured, including both series.

YOKOSUKA D4Y SUISEI (JUDY)

D4Y2	
Type:	Carrier-borne dive-bomber
Crew:	2
Weight when empty/ max weight at takeoff:	5,374 lb/ 9,361 lb
Length/wingspan/height:	34.1 ft/38.3 ft/12.5 ft
Engine(s):	One Aichi-Atsuta 32 hanging V12 engine with 1,400 hp
Maximum speed:	348 mph
Service ceiling:	35,670 ft
Range:	910 miles—2,236 miles with additional fuel tanks
Weaponry:	2 x 0.3 in Type 97 fixed machine guns in the nose, 1 x Type 1 0.3 in machine gun in the rear of the cockpit, and a combined internal and external payload of max. 1,233 lb

The D4Y was the only Japanese carrier-borne aircraft with an inline engine.

The Yokosuka D4Y was the only Japanese carrier-borne aircraft with an inline engine. Work began on its design in 1938, and it was fitted with a DB-600 engine, which was built under license. As with many Japanese aircraft designed before the war, its astounding performance figures were achieved at the expense of a solid build, strong armor, and self-sealing fuel tanks. So when it was tested, it became clear that its wing structure was not suitable for dive-bombing, so the first production model, the D4Y-1C, which appeared in late 1942, was flown as a reconnaissance aircraft. In March 1943 a new version, the D4Y1 was introduced with reinforced wings. Various different versions of the D4Y were built either for dive-bombing or for reconnaissance, but they differed only in minor respects. The only exception to this rule was the D4Y3, which was fitted with a 1,580 hp Mitsubishi-Kinsei radial engine. The D4Y2-S version was a night fighter, which had no weaponry in its wings but did have a 0.8 inch (20 mm) machine gun in the fuselage pointed upward. Because it lacked defensive weaponry, and the Allies began to dominate the skies, the Suisei suffered very heavy losses. In the final months of the war, it was also used for kamikaze operations. In total 2,038 Suiseis were built, including all the different variants.

The D4Y (Judy).

NAKAJIMA B5N2 KANKOH (KATE)

	B5N1
Type:	Carrier-borne torpedo bomber/bomber
Crew:	3
Weight when empty/ max weight at takeoff:	1,416 lb/ 9,031 lb
Length/wingspan/height:	34.3 ft/51.7 ft/12.3 ft
Engine(s):	One Nakajima-Sakae 11 radial engine with 1,000 hp
Maximum speed:	230 mph
Service ceiling:	27,530 ft
Range:	1,200 miles
Weaponry:	1 x 0.3 in Type 92 machine gun in the rear of the cockpit, and an external payload of up to 1,760 lb, e.g., one 1,760 lb torpedo or three 550 lb bombs

A B5N (Kate) taking off.

The Nakajima B5N, codenamed "Kate," was the only Japanese carrier-borne torpedo bomber when war broke out in the Pacific. But in late 1941 Kate was already rather dated, as its design dated back to 1935. Nevertheless, it fared rather better than its American counterpart, the Douglas TBD Devastator, and until the introduction of the Grumman Avenger, the B5N2 was the best torpedo bomber in the Pacific. 145 B5N2s, 40 armed with torpedoes and 105 armed with bombs, were employed in the attack on Pearl Harbor, and this model's greatest successes were sinking the American aircraft carriers USS *Yorktown*, USS *Lexington*, and USS *Hornet*. From 1943, however, it was largely superseded by its successor, the B6N, and it was put into service as a flight instruction vehicle, and a target finder, and was used in anti-submarine operations. For the latter role, it was fitted with primitive radar and sensors to detect magnetic disturbances. Kate's last major deployment was in the Battle of the Philippines in October 1944. Around 1,150 B5Ns were manufactured in total.

The Nakajima B5N2 (Kate).

NAKAJIMA B6N2 TENZAN (JILL)

The Nakajima B6N was the B5N's successor and was very similar to the latter, as the Imperial Japanese Navy had stipulated that it must not differ in any significant respect from its predecessor (because of the size of the elevators on Japanese aircraft carriers). Nakajima began designing the new torpedo bomber as early as 1939, but it did not make its maiden flight until the summer of 1941. Contrary to the demands of the navy, which had anticipated a Mitsubishi-Kasei radial engine, the Tenzan prototype was fitted with a Nakajima-Momaru radial engine, which was claimed to offer better fuel economy and greater development potential. It was not, however, very successful in flight tests, and alterations to the engine and tail were unavoidable. Consequently, it was not tested on an aircraft carrier until late 1942, and it was still beset with problems with the engine and the tail hook. An altered version, the B6N1, finally went into production in early 1943, but production was halted after only 135 aircraft had been manufactured, as the navy insisted the model had to be fitted with the Mitsubishi-Kasei engine. So it was converted to accommodate the new engine, and the new model was

	B6N2
Type:	Carrier-borne torpedo bomber/bomber
Crew:	3
Weight when empty/ max weight at takeoff:	6,630 lb/ 12,445 lb
Length/wingspan/height:	36.2 ft/49.6 ft
Engine(s):	One Mitsubishi MK 4T Kasei 25 radial engine with 1,850 hp
Maximum speed:	291 mph
Service ceiling:	30,135 ft
Range:	1,840 miles
Weaponry:	1 x 0.3 in Type 92 machine gun in the rear of the cockpit, 1 x 0.3 in firing rearward and downward in the fuselage, and an external payload of max. 1,760 lb, e.g., one 1,760 lb torpedo or three 550 lb bombs

The Nakajima B6N2 (Jill).

called the B6N2. Even now, however, the Tenzan could only be flown from the largest aircraft carriers, as it required a relatively long runway, and aircraft carriers were not yet equipped with catapults. In fact, by the time it was put into service in mid-1944, most Japanese aircraft carriers had already been sunk, and there was a serious shortage of pilots. Hence, most B6Ns were flown from land bases. By that time, the Allies had won the struggle for the Pacific skies, and the Tenzan enjoyed no real success, even in kamikaze operations. A total of 1,268 B6Ns were manufactured.

MITSUBISHI G4M HAMAKI (BETTY)

The G4M Hamaki, codenamed "Betty" by the Allies, was the best known and most deployed heavy bomber in the Japanese Navy during the war. It was an all-metal single-wing aircraft with retractable undercarriage and powerful engines. Because the Imperial Japanese Navy required a long-range bomber,

The G4M was the standard Japanese twin-engine bomber.

	G4M3
Type:	Bomber
Crew:	7
Weight when empty/ max weight at takeoff:	18,392 lb/27,533 lb
Length/wingspan/height:	65 ft/83.3 ft/20 ft
Engine(s):	Two Mitsubishi MK 4T Kasei 25 radial engines with 1,825 hp each
Maximum speed:	292 mph at 16,667 ft
Service ceiling:	30,735 ft
Range:	2,700 miles
Weaponry:	4 x 0.8 in Type 99 automatic cannon—one each in nose, tail, waist, and rear installations—2 x 0.3 in Type 92 machine guns in the sides, and a combined internal and external payload of max. 2,203 lb, e.g., one 1,760 lb torpedo or four 550 lb bombs

the G4M had a good range, but again this was achieved, in part, by a light frame, a lack of armor, and no protection for the fuel tanks. In 1937 work began on developing a successor for the G3M, and the G4M made its maiden flight in October 1939, and was first deployed in 1941 in the Sino-Japanese War. In the

The Mitsubishi G4M1 (Betty).

early months of the war, this bomber enjoyed some spectacular success, including a major part in the sinking of the British battleships HMS *Prince of Wales* and HMS *Repulse*. It carried the Yokosuka MXYOhka manned bombs, and also on August 19, 1945 transported the Japanese delegation to Iwo Jima, where they officially surrendered.

Betty had really had its day after the summer of 1942. In the Battle of

Guadalcanal in August that year, it became clear that these large, unprotected, and ponderous machines would catch fire as soon as they were hit—a consequence of leaving the fuel tanks unprotected—which earned Betty the nickname, the "One-Shot Lighter." There were four main production models of the G4M: the G4M1 Model 11, the G4M2 Model 22, the G4M3 Model 34, and the G6M1, which differed primarily in

their engine specifications and level of defensive weaponry. In addition, there were a few sub-variants, including the GM61-L2 transporter. A total of 2,479 machines were built, but by the end of the war, only around 160 had survived.

MITSUBISHI KI-21 (SALLY)

	Ki-21 IIb
Type:	Bomber
Crew:	5–7
Weight when empty/ max weight at takeoff:	13,370 lb/ 23,370 lb
Length/wingspan/height:	55.3 ft/75 ft/12.3 ft
Engine(s):	Two Mitsubishi Ha 101 radial engines with 1,500 hp each
Maximum speed:	300 mph at 23,300 ft
Service ceiling:	33,300 ft
Range:	1,675 miles
Weaponry:	4 x 0.3 in Type 92 machine guns—one each in the nose, sides, and waist—1 x 0.3 in Type 92 remote-controlled machine gun in the tail, 1 x 0.5 in tail machine gun (in the rear of the cockpit), and an internal payload of max. 2,203 lb

The Mitsubishi Ki-21 (Sally).

In the early months of the war in the Pacific, the Ki-21, codenamed "Sally" by the Allies, was the Japanese Army's standard bomber, and it remained in front-line service until late 1944. Work began on its design in 1936, and in 1938 the first production model (Ki-21 Ia) was put into service in the Sino-Japanese War. It soon became clear that the Ki-21's defensive weaponry was inadequate, so the improved Ki-21 Ib was ordered to

replace it. The Ki-21 Ic had additional fuel tanks and was intended as a long-range bomber, and the next model, the Ki-22 IIa, had more powerful engines and was better armed. The final model, the Ki-22 IIb, differed only in minor respects from the Ki-22 IIa. One interesting feature was the remote-controlled machine gun in the tail. Given that Sally was meant to be a long-range bomber, its defensive weaponry and payload were insufficient.

Like many other Japanese aircraft, the Ki-21 was also very vulnerable when hit, and from 1943 a large number fell victim to Allied fighters. Hence, it was withdrawn from front-line service in late 1944. Until production was halted, 2,064 Sallys were manufactured, and they were deployed throughout the Pacific.

NAKAJIMA KI-49 DONRYU (HELEN)

	Ki-49 IIb
Type:	Bomber
Crew:	8
Weight when empty/ max weight at takeoff:	14,383 lb/ 25,110 lb
Length/wingspan/height:	55 ft/68.1 ft/14.2 ft
Engine(s):	Two Nakajima Ha 109 radial engines with 1,500 hp each
Maximum speed:	306 mph at 16,700 ft
Service ceiling:	31,000 ft
Range:	1,830 miles
Weaponry:	5 x 0.5 in Type 1 machine guns – one each in the nose, tail, underside, and sides – 1 x 0.8 in dorsal automatic cannon, and an internal payload of up to 2,203 lb

The Nakajima Ki-49 was the Ki-21's successor, flying for the first time in August, but with two 950 hp Nakajima Ha 5 engines, it failed to attain the desired performance, and the second prototype was converted to accommodate two 1,250 hp Nakajima Ha 41 engines. It went into production in this format as the Ki-49 I, and it was deployed in China and in the early battles in the Pacific. Although the Ki-49s performance was supposed to be so good that it did not require a fighter escort, it became apparent that its payload, speed, protection, and range all fell short of the required standards. So in

The Nakajima Ki-49 (Helen).

early 1942 the Ki-49 II was fitted with more powerful Nakajima Ha 109 engines, self-sealing fuel tanks, better armor, and defensive weaponry. But Helen was still no match for its enemies and suffered heavy losses. Consequently, production

was halted in December 1944, after 819 Ki-49s had been manufactured. In the final stages of the war, it was deployed primarily as a transporter, and for anti-submarine and kamikaze operations.

KAWANISHI H8K (EMILY)

The H8K was the highest-performing Japanese reconnaissance seaplane, and probably the best Japanese seaplane, in the Second World War. It was codenamed "Emily" by the Allies, and only 167 machines were ever built. The H8K had considerable reserves of power and a high load-carrying capacity, but its wing load was relatively high (40 lb/sq ft, or 200 kg/m²), so only specially trained pilots flew it. The prototype (H8K1) of this four-engine shoulder-wing aircraft flew for the first time on December 31, 1940, which revealed some weaknesses. In particular, it was very unstable on water. After significant alterations to the model's frame, the first H8Ks went into serial production in 1941 and were put into service in March 1942. The model that was manufactured in the largest numbers was the H8K2 (112 were built), and it had radar, protected fuel tanks, heavier weaponry, and stronger armor. The H8K2-L (of which 36 were built) was a transporter which accommodated 29–64 passengers, and was less heavily armed than the other models. There were also prototypes (the H8K3 and 4) which never

	H8K2
Type:	Reconnaissance seaplane
Crew:	9–10
Weight when empty/ max weight at takeoff:	40,485 lb/ 71,586 lb
Length/wingspan/height:	93.8 ft/126.7 ft
Engine(s):	Four Mitsubishi MK 40 Kasei 22 radial engines with 1,850 hp each
Maximum speed:	293 mph at 16,667 ft
Service ceiling:	28,700 ft
Range:	4,410 miles
Weaponry:	3 x Type 99 automatic cannon—one each in the nose, tail, and rear turrets—2 x 0.8 in automatic cannon in the sides, up to 6 x 0.3 in Type 92 machine guns in the portholes, and a payload (internal or external) of max. 4,405 lb, e.g., two 1,760 lb torpedoes, eight 550 lb bombs or depth charges under the wings

The Kawanishi H8K2 (Emily).

got past the experimental stage. Because it had a considerable range (it could fly for up to 20 hours), was well armed, and was

fitted with radar, Emily was a very successful reconnaissance aircraft.

MORANE-SAULNIER M.S.406

The Morane-Saulnier M.S.406.

	M.S.406C-1
Type:	Fighter
Crew:	1
Weight when empty/ max weight at takeoff:	4,185 lb/ 5,441 lb
Length/wingspan/height:	27.2 ft/35.3 ft/9.3 ft
Engine(s):	One Hispano-Suiza 12Y 31 V12 engine with 860 hp
Maximum speed:	300 mph at 16,700 ft
Service ceiling:	31,300 ft
Range:	4,970 miles
Weaponry:	1 x 0.8 in HS404 automatic cannon firing through the propeller hub, 2 x 0.3 in MAC 1934 machine guns in the wings

The M.S.406 was France's first fighter aircraft with an enclosed cockpit and retractable undercarriage, and its prototype flew for the first time in August 1938. The French Air Force ordered 1,000 slightly altered production M.S.406s, intending that it should be their standard fighter, but production in the newly built state factories was so painfully slow (there were serious shortages of replacement parts and Hispano-Suiza engines) that its competitor, the Bloch M.B.151, which had initially been turned down, was put into production to ensure that the air force would have modern fighter aircraft. By the beginning of the war 572 M.S.406 aircraft had been delivered, but they were outclassed by the German Bf 109s and suffered heavy losses. A total of 1,081 M.S.406s were built, including all the different versions. After France had surrendered, the German and Italian Air Forces took possession of all serviceable M.S.406s and used them as training aircraft. Even in this capacity, however, they were found to be unsatisfactory and given to Germany's allies: Finland received 68, Croatia acquired 48, and 20 were given to Bulgaria. The Finns modified 41 of their machines to accommodate the Klimov engines they had taken from the Russians, calling the new machines the Mörkö Morane, which performed better than the French version. Switzerland also bought the rights to produce the M.S.406 under license in 1938, before renaming it the D-3800 (of which 82 were built) and later replacing it with the improved D-3801, which served as a flight instruction aircraft until 1959.

DEWOITNE D.520

	D.520
Type:	Fighter
Crew:	1
Weight when empty/ max weight at takeoff:	4,465 lb/ 5,896 lb
Length/wingspan/height:	28.7 ft/34 ft/8.6 ft
Engine(s):	One Hispano-Suiza 12Y 45 V12 engine with 935 hp
Maximum speed:	332 mph at 18,300 ft
Service ceiling:	35,000 ft
Range:	950 miles
Weaponry:	1 x 0.8 in HS404 automatic cannon firing through the propeller hub, 4 x 0.3 in MAC 1934 machine guns in the wings

The Dewoitine D.520.

The D.520 was a modern and potentially very effective French aircraft, but it was put into service too late. It made its maiden flight in October 1938, and although there were a few problems with its cooler, it was obviously the best French combat aircraft and a match even for the Bf 109. But because of political disputes and the restructuring of the French air industry (Dewoitne formed part of the state-owned SNCAM company), mass production began only in 1940. Consequently, only a few squadrons were equipped exclusively with D.520s when the Germans invaded. Many units were still phasing in the new fighter, and although it enjoyed some success nonetheless, only 437 had actually been produced, and even fewer (351) had been delivered, so it could not make a difference to the outcome of the invasion. In the last days of the fall of France, some squadrons escaped to North Africa or to the unoccupied areas of France. In 1941 production of the D.520 began under the Vichy Government, which ordered 550 aircraft. Most of the D.520s were seized by the Wehrmacht when it occupied southern France, and they were used as flight instruction aircraft or supplied to Romania, Bulgaria, and Italy.

FRANCE

BLOCH M.B.151 AND M.B.152

In July 1934 Marcel Bloch Aircraft competed for a tender from the French Air Force for an all-metal single-wing aircraft, which was won by Morane-Saulnier. During the competition, Bloch's M.B.150 had serious difficulties—in fact, it did not even manage to take off! Nevertheless, Bloch remained undeterred and radically modified the design. The modified version could actually fly and in fact performed very well, but it was completely unsuited for serial production, so the design had to be fundamentally altered again. The new model, called the M.B.151, flew for the first time in August 1938 and was supposed to be put into production immediately, but only four had been delivered by April 1939. In the intervening period, Bloch had become part of the state-owned SNCASO company, and its engineers had developed a new and improved version, the M.B.152. In total, 160 M.B.151s and 340 M.B.152s were ordered, but production remained very sluggish, and only 120 of both types had been delivered by September 1939. By late November 1939 358 models were finally delivered, but they were nowhere near ready for deployment. At least half the machines had no propeller, no sights, or neither a propeller nor sights. These

Though it was a modern and high-performing aircraft, the Bloch M.B.152 arrived too late to make much difference to France's fate in the war.

	M.B.152
Type:	Fighter
Crew:	1
Weight when empty/ max weight at takeoff:	4,449 lb/ 5,903 lb
Length/wingspan/height:	30.3 ft/35.2 ft/13.2 ft
Engine(s):	One Gnome-Rhône 14N 25 radial engine with 1,080 hp
Maximum speed:	320 mph at 13,300 ft
Service ceiling:	33,300 ft
Range:	375 miles
Weaponry:	2 x 0.3 in MAC 1934 machine guns and 2 x 0.8 in HS404 automatic cannon, or 4 x 0.3 in machine guns

problems were not rectified very quickly, and when the Germans invaded, the French pilots were still not sufficiently well acquainted with the new fighters, potentially very effective though they were, to make any significant impact on the invaders. After France's defeat, six squadrons of the air force under Vichy continued to use the Bloch fighters, and when the Wehrmacht occupied Vichy France in November 1942, the remaining M.B.151s and 152s were given to Romania or used as training aircraft.

The Bloch M.B.152.

POTEZ 63 SERIES

	Potez 63.11
Type:	Reconnaissance and liaison aircraft
Crew:	3
Weight when empty/ max weight at takeoff:	6,905 lb/ 9,978 lb
Length/wingspan/height:	36.4 ft/53.3 ft/10.3 ft
Engine(s):	Two Gnome-Rhône 14M 6/7 radial engines with 700 hp each
Maximum speed:	264 mph at 16,700 ft
Service ceiling:	28,300 ft
Range:	930 miles
Weaponry:	1 x 0.3 in MAC 1934 machine gun fixed in the nose, 2 x 0.3 in machine guns—one in the rear of the cockpit, and one in the fuselage—and a payload of max. 440 lb

The reconnaissance and light ground attack version, the Potez 63.11.

The Potez 63 Series was intended as a stable of heavy twin-engine fighters and reconnaissance aircraft, and the first prototype flew for the first time on April 25, 1936. Serial production began in 1937, but problems with the delivery of engines, propellers, and weapons caused significant delays, and only 291 machines were available when the war broke out. The Potez 630 fighter version was powered by Hispano-Suiza engines, the Potez 631 by Gnome-Rhône engines, but in every other respect the two versions were virtually identical. Their basic design was similar to that of the Bf 110, and they were deployed both as destroyers and night fighters. The 632 was a light bomber, as was the 633; the latter was the export version, but it was requisitioned by the French when the war broke out. The Potez 63.11, which had a glazed nose and shortened cabin, was introduced to modernize the reconnaissance squadrons, and 850 were delivered. The Potez had first-class flight characteristics, but it was underpowered for a fighter. After the fall of France, more than 600 Potez aircraft remained in the unoccupied areas of France and in Algeria, and they were initially put into service by the Vichy Government. More Potez aircraft were also produced under the supervision of the Luftwaffe, who used at least 100 Potez 61.11s as training and liaison aircraft.

BREGUET 690 SERIES

The Breguet Bre. 693.

	Bre. 693
Type:	Bomber
Crew:	2
Weight when empty/ max weight at takeoff:	6,630 lb/ 3,043 lb
Length/wingspan/height:	32.2 ft/51.2 ft/10.6 ft
Engine(s):	Two Gnome-Rhône 14M 6/7 radial engines with 700 hp each
Maximum speed:	305 mph at 16,700 ft
Service ceiling:	31,700 ft
Range:	840 miles
Weaponry:	1 x 0.8 in HS404 automatic cannon and 2 x MAC 1934 machine guns fixed in the nose, 1 x 0.3 in machine gun in the cockpit, 1 x 0.3 in machine gun in the fuselage – later 2 additional 0.3 in fixed machine guns in the motor gondolas—and an internal payload of max. 880 lb

Breguet began designing a two-seater fighter in 1935, and the first prototype, called the Bre. 690, flew for the first time in March 1938. Then the French Air Force wanted an entire stable of aircraft based on this prototype. The first production version, called the Breguet 691, was powered by Hispano-Suiza in-line engines, but because these were at a premium, a decision was made to fit the aircraft with Gnome-Rhône radial engines, and the new version, called the Bre. 693, made its maiden flight in October 1939. This was followed by the 695, which was very similar but was powered by Pratt & Whitney engines. Unfortunately, the combination of a French design and an American engine resulted in inferior performance. The 695 prototype flew for the first time in early 1940, but the Bre. 697 heavy fighter never got past the prototype stage. The first deployment of the 693 took place on May 12, 1940, with catastrophic results: 10 of the 11 aircraft deployed were destroyed or severely damaged. Before France was defeated, half of all the 690 series aircraft were destroyed, but a few were still used by the Vichy regime. In November 1942 the remaining aircraft were confiscated by the Germans and given to the Luftwaffe or the Italians, who used them as training aircraft. Around 300 of the 690 series aircraft were produced in total.

BLOCH M.B.174 AND M.B.175

	M.B.175 B.3
Type:	Bomber
Crew:	3
Weight when empty/	12,467 lb/
max weight at takeoff:	17,672 lb
Length/wingspan/height:	41.4 ft/59.8 ft/11.8 ft
Engine(s):	Two Gnome-Rhône 14N 48/49 radial engines with 1,140 hp each
Maximum speed:	335 mph at 17,300 ft
Service ceiling:	36,700 ft
Range:	995 miles
Weaponry:	2 x 0.3 in MAC 1934 machine guns fixed in the nose, 2 x 0.3 in machine guns in the rear of the cockpit, 3 x 0.3 in waist machine guns, and an internal payload of max. 1,322 lb

Antoine de Saint-Exupéry, author of **The Little Prince,** *flew an M.B.174 in early 1940.*

The Bloch M.B.174 and 175, a light bomber and reconnaissance aircraft respectively, were the best aircraft available for the French in 1940. Bloch began work on the design as early as 1936, and the prototype made its maiden flight in February 1938. After a few alterations, the M.B.174 was created, and it took off for the first time in January 1939. Test flights went well at first, but later there were problems with the engine cooling system, so the first production models were not delivered until March 1940. The 174 proved to be a first-class reconnaissance aircraft, but its bomb bay was too small to carry bombs heavier than 110 lb (50 kg). After 50 machines had been produced, the bomb bay was enlarged, and the new model was called the M.B.175, but only 25 had been delivered when France fell to the Germans. Because the supply of Gnome-Rhône engines dried up, a new version (the M.B.176) was fitted with Pratt & Whitney engines. Most M.B.174s, 175s, and 176s available on June 10, 1940 were destroyed in action, but a few aircraft were withdrawn to the unoccupied area of France. The Luftwaffe took possession of a small number and had a few constructed from existing parts, using them as training aircraft.

BOULTON PAUL P.82 DEFIANT

	Defiant Mk. II
Type:	Night fighter
Crew:	2
Weight when empty/	6,275 lb/
max weight at takeoff:	8,461 lb
Length/wingspan/height:	35.9 ft/40 ft/11 ft
Engine(s):	One Rolls-Royce Merlin XX with 1,280 hp
Maximum speed:	313 mph at 19,300 ft
Service ceiling:	30,835 ft
Range:	465 miles
Weaponry:	4 x 0.3 in Browning machine guns in the rear turret

A Defiant Mark I of No. 410 Squadron, Scotland, fall 1941.

The Defiant was an unusual fighter aircraft, in that it had no fixed forward-firing weaponry, but a motorized gun turret with four 0.3 inch (7.7 mm) machine guns. The idea was to enable the weaponry to be fired in as many directions as possible, enabling the pilot to concentrate on flying the aircraft. Work on its design began in 1935, the prototype made its maiden flight on August 11, 1937, and the Mark I production model was delivered to the Royal Air Force in the summer of 1939. Although it enjoyed considerable success at first, particularly because German pilots mistook it for the Hurricane and did not expect machine gun fire from the turret, the Defiant proved to be an impractical design, as Luftwaffe pilots just began attacking it head on. So from August 1940 the Defiant was only used as a night fighter. The second series model, the Mark II, which had on-board radar, was put into service in September 1941. Until it was replaced by the Beaufighter, the Defiant was flown in 13 night fighter squadrons, and it also served as a target finder and air-sea rescue aircraft. A total of 1,065 Defiants were built.

GLOSTER S.S.37 GLADIATOR

The Gloster Gladiator was the last fighter biplane in the Royal Air Force, and its prototype flew for the first time in September 1934, but the first production models were not delivered until early 1937. 151 Gladiator Mark I aircraft were manufactured for the RAF, and another 147 machines were built to be exported, although the Gladiator was dated in comparison to contemporary single-wing aircraft. The Mark I was soon replaced by the Mark II, which had a triple-blade propeller, an electric starter motor, a dust filter for the engine, and a more powerful engine. Around 100 Mark IIs were converted to create the carrier-borne Sea Gladiator, which served in six squadrons on board British aircraft carriers. When the Second World War broke out, the Gladiator was hopelessly outclassed by modern single-seaters like the Bf 109, so they were only flown by the RAF in less strategically significant areas, such as the Mediterranean. After its involvement in the defense of Norway in 1940, the Sea Gladiator was deployed primarily in the Mediterranean, where both models gave a good account of themselves in defending Malta. A total of 746 Gladiators were produced, including all the different models.

Gladiator Mk. II	
Type:	Fighter
Crew:	1
Weight when empty/ max weight at takeoff:	3,441 lb/ 4,859 lb
Length/wingspan/height:	27.9 ft/32.8 ft/11.8 ft
Engine(s):	One Bristol-Mercury VIIIA radial engine with 850 hp
Maximum speed:	257 mph at 14,800 ft
Service ceiling:	34,035 ft
Range:	440 miles
Weaponry:	6 x 0.3 in Browning fixed machine guns—two in the nose, and two under each lower wing

The Gloster Gladiator.

HAWKER HURRICANE

The Hurricane was initially used as a fighter (day and night), but later it served primarily as a dive-bomber and ground attack aircraft. Its simple (albeit very robust) design and inferior performance meant that it lived very much in the shadow of the famous Spitfire, although it actually shot down more aircraft than the latter in the Battle of Britain. Its prototype took off for the first time on November 6, 1935. The Hurricane's body and wings were mostly made of steel tubing, most of which was covered with fabric, and it was armed with eight 0.3 inch (7.7 mm) machine

A Hurricane Mark IIB with 12 0.3 inch (7.7 mm) machine guns in the wings.

A Hurricane Mark I of No. 1 Squadron, Northolt (Middlesex), August 1940.

	Hurricane Mk. IIB
Type:	Fighter bomber
Crew:	1
Weight when empty/ max weight at takeoff:	5,502 lb/ 7,293 lb
Length/wingspan/height:	32.7 ft/40.6 ft/15.5 ft
Engine(s):	One Rolls-Royce Merlin XX V12 engine with 1,280 hp
Maximum speed:	329 mph at 22,350 ft
Service ceiling:	37,085 ft
Range:	480 miles
Weaponry:	12 x 0.3 in Browning fixed machine guns in the wings, and an external payload of max. 1,000 lb, e.g., two 500 lb bombs

guns in its wings. In 1939 a raft of improvements were introduced, including an improved triple-blade propeller, metal covering on the wings, and the installation of a Rolls-Royce Merlin III engine.

The Hurricane squadrons sent to defend France made little impact on the mighty Luftwaffe, but in the Battle of Britain, 32 Hurricane squadrons completely thwarted the Germans' attempts to take control of the British

skies. While the 19 Spitfire squadrons concentrated on German fighters, the Hurricanes attacked the German bombers. The Hurricane was also deployed in the Mediterranean and North Africa, and throughout the war its

A Hurricane Mark IIC Trop of No. 73 Squadron, North Africa, 1942.

The Hurricane Mark I.

engines and weaponry were constantly upgraded. In addition, the Hurricane's role as a fighter became less important, and Hawker's priority was to improve its capability as a ground attack aircraft—for example, extra features, such as rockets, bombs, additional fuel tanks, and gun installations, were added.

One ground attack model was the Mark IID, which had two 1.5 inch (40 mm) machine guns and was primarily used in anti-tank operations. The Hurricane was also manufactured in Canada, where they had different designations and were mainly fitted with Packard-built Merlin engines. To use it in the Fleet Air Arm (the British Naval Air Force), various versions were converted for use on aircraft carriers. A total of 14,231 Hurricanes were produced, and before the war there were plenty of customers for the export version—among others, it was sold to Yugoslavia, Belgium, Turkey, and Persia. In fact, Hurricanes were still being exported after the war, to countries such as Portugal, Ireland, and Persia. In addition, around 3,000 were delivered to the Soviet Air Force during the Second World War.

The Mark IIC was armed with four 0.8 inch (20 mm) machine guns.

SUPERMARINE SPITFIRE

The Supermarine Spitfire is undoubtedly the best known British fighter aircraft, which enjoys almost legendary status in the United Kingdom, entirely because of its key role in the Battle of Britain. Supermarine had plenty of experience producing record-breaking seaplanes to draw upon for the Spitfire, and the designer Reginald J. Mitchell started work on its development in 1935. Its design included a slender, aerodynamic body and elliptical wings, which guaranteed perfect lift, and it was fitted with a Rolls-Royce V12 engine. The prototype's maiden flight took place on March 5, 1940, and its performance was so impressive that the British Air Ministry immediately ordered 370 Mark I Spitfires. By the time of the Battle of Britain, there were 370 Spitfires in 19 squadrons.

The main version then was the Mark Ia, which was not as heavily armed as the Bf 109E but could climb faster and was more agile. Development and production of the Spitfire continued throughout the war, and there were numerous variants and sub-variants. The first mass-produced model, the Mark V (of which 6,664 were built), was the first to be fitted with variable wing weaponry, which was

The Spitfire's elliptical wings optimized its lift.

Spitfire Mk. VB	
Type:	Fighter
Crew:	1
Weight when empty/max weight at takeoff:	4,993 lb/ 6,412 lb
Length/wingspan/height:	30.4 ft/37.4 ft/10.1 ft
Engine(s):	One Rolls-Royce Merlin XX with 1,480 hp
Maximum speed:	369 mph at 19,815 ft
Service ceiling:	37,085 ft
Range:	1,135 miles
Weaponry:	2 x 0.8 in Hispano-Suiza automatic cannon and 4 x 0.3 in Browning machine guns fixed on the wings

A Spitfire Mark IXB of No. 421 Squadron, Tangmere (Sussex), June 1944.

retained on all the following models. For example, the A model had eight 0.3 inch (7.7 mm) machine guns, the B had two 7.9 inch (20 mm) and four 0.3 inch (7.7 mm) machine guns, the C had four 7.9 inch (20 mm) machine guns, and the E had two 7.9 inch (20 mm) and two 5 inch (12.7 mm) machine guns, as well a payload of up to 1,000 lb (454 kg). The

Mark V was flown across the English Channel in raids against occupied France from early 1941, and by the end of that year 43 squadrons had Mark V Spitfires, though it fell behind the FW 190 from 1942. The version that was most in use in the last three years of the war was the Mark IX, which had a four-blade propeller and a 1,665 hp Merlin engine with a

maximum speed of 409 mph (658 km/h) at an altitude of 25,420 ft (7,626 m). The Mark XIV appeared towards the end of the war, fitted with a five-blade propeller, teardrop canopy, and a new 2,050 Griffon engine which powered it to a maximum speed of 445 mph (717 km/h). A Mark XIV earned the distinction of being the first British aircraft to shoot down the Me 262.

For service in North Africa and the Mediterranean, the Spitfire had large sand filters in front of the air intake in the nose, which spoiled its elegant appearance, as with this Mark VC Trop.

A Spitfire Mark IA of No. 66 Squadron, Kenley (Surrey), September 1940.

The Spitfire Mark VE.

The Spitfire was not only a fighter and a bomber: it was also a photo reconnaissance aircraft (the FR and PR) and took off from aircraft carriers. The latter version, called the Seafire, was first delivered in January 1942, and 2,556 were manufactured, though its narrow gauged, fragile undercarriage was not ideal for service on aircraft carriers. Spitfires flew not only in the RAF, but in practically every Allied air force. By the time production ceased in October 1947, 20,351 Spitfires, comprising of 20 different series, had been manufactured.

HAWKER TYPHOON

To replace the Hurricane, the RAF wanted a fighter powered by the Napier Sabre 24-cylinder H engine or the Rolls-Royce Vulture 24-cylinder X engine, both of which were still being developed. Because the development of the Rolls-Royce engine was halted, the Typhoon prototype which took off for the first time in February 1940 was fitted with a Napier-Sabre engine. But there were major problems with the engine, and the air frame and wings were nowhere near secure enough, so the prototype had to be completely re-engineered. By 1943 most of the defects in the air frame and the engine had been ironed out, but the Typhoon failed to impress either as an interceptor against the Fw 190 or as an escort. Because the Spitfire IX, which was also ready to go into service by then, was a first-class fighter, there was no need to use the Typhoon as a fighter, but the RAF did need an effective dive-bomber, so the existing Typhoons were converted for deployment as low-altitude combat

	Typhoon Mk. IB
Type:	Fighter bomber and ground attack aircraft
Crew:	1
Weight when empty/ max weight at takeoff:	8,793 lb/ 11,390 lb
Length/wingspan/height:	32.5 ft/42.2 ft/15.6 ft
Engine(s):	One Napier Sabre IIA 24 engine in an H-configuration with 2,180 hp
Maximum speed:	405 mph at 18,333 ft
Service ceiling:	34,550 ft
Range:	510 miles
Weaponry:	4 x 0.8 in Hispano-Suiza automatic cannon, and an external payload of max. 2,000 lb

A Typhoon Mark IB of No. 440 Squadron, France, July 1944.

aircraft. They accompanied Allied troops as they advanced into Germany from France, proving to be excellent dive-bombers and ground attack aircraft. With its four 7.9 inch (20 mm) machine guns and eight rockets under its wings, as well as carrying bombs, it terrorized the Wehrmacht. A total of 3,300 Typhoons were produced.

GLOSTER G.41 METEOR

The Gloster Meteor was the Allies' first jet-powered fighter aircraft, and one of only two jet-powered aircraft, along with the Me 262, to be put into service in large numbers in the Second World War. As with German jets, the development of Meteor was severely hindered by technical difficulties with new jet technology, and although work on its design began in 1940, the first prototype did not fly until March 1943. From July 1944 20 pre-

The Gloster Meteor Mark III.

production machines (called the Mark 1), fitted with Rolls-Royce-Welland turbines which produced 1,696 lb of thrust, were in use, but the model's performance was disappointing—it had a maximum speed of only 415 mph (668 km/h) and lacked stability—so they remained in Britain, where they were deployed against the V1s. The first serial production models (Mark III) were fitted with more powerful turbines, which enabled them to attain an acceptable speed. Shortly before the end of the war, some Meteors were flown in Holland and Germany. A total of 3,875 Meteors were manufactured.

	Meteor F. Mk. III (early version)
Type:	Fighter
Crew:	1
Weight when empty/max weight at takeoff:	10,509 lb/13,907 lb
Length/wingspan/height:	41.9 ft/103.7 ft/13.2 ft
Engine(s):	Two Rolls-Royce W.2B/23 Welland 1 jet engines with 1,993 lb thrust each
Maximum speed:	477 mph at 10,000 ft
Service ceiling:	43,700 ft
Range:	685 miles
Weaponry:	4 x 0.8 in Hispano-Suiza automatic cannon fixed in the nose

BRISTOL TYPE 152 BEAUFORT

The Bristol Beaufort was based on the Blenheim but had significantly more powerful engines and a taller and wider body. It made its maiden flight on October 15, 1938, but was not put into service until January 1940, as the Bristol Taurus engines suffered from problems at first. Even when in service the newly developed engines were always temperamental, as they had sleeve valves rather than valve-trains, and at one point all Beauforts had to be grounded. Some were also produced by the Australians, who decided early on to install more reliable American Pratt & Whitney radial engines, and Australian Beauforts were flown in the Pacific from mid-1942 until the end of the war. In spite of all its faults, from 1940–43 the Beaufort was the RAF's standard land-based torpedo bomber and mine layer.

The Bristol Beaufort. Beauforts equipped with radar were flown not only in Britain, but also in the Mediterranean. A total of 1,900 Beauforts were manufactured, including all the different versions.

	Beaufort Mk. I
Type:	Torpedo bomber
Crew:	4
Weight when empty/ max weight at takeoff:	13,095 lb/ 21,211 lb
Length/wingspan/height:	45.3 ft/58.8 ft/12.6 ft
Engine(s):	Two Bristol Taurus radial engines with 1,130 hp each
Maximum speed:	300 mph at 6,100 ft
Service ceiling:	16,765 ft
Range:	1,035 miles
Weaponry:	4 x 0.3 in Browning machine guns—two in the turret, two in a remote-controlled installation under the nose—an internal payload of max. 1,500 lb, and one 1,604 lb torpedo

BRISTOL TYPE 142M, 149, AND 160 BLENHEIM

	Blenheim Mk. I
Type:	Light bomber
Crew:	3
Weight when empty/ max weight at takeoff:	8,392 lb/ 12,489 lb
Length/wingspan/height:	40.4 ft/57.3 ft/10 ft
Engine(s):	Two Bristol Mercury VIII 9-cylinder radial engines with 840 hp each
Maximum speed:	266 mph at 12,000 ft
Service ceiling:	27,735 ft
Range:	1,125 miles
Weaponry:	1 x 0.3 in Browning machine gun, 1 x Vickers K 0.3 in machine gun, and an internal payload of max. 1,000 lb

The Bristol Blenheim Mark I.

The Blenheim was based on one of the first ever commercial aircraft, and on its first flight in 1935, the Bristol Type 142 exceeded all expectations, as it was around 30 mph (48.3 km/h) faster than the fastest RAF fighter at the time. The Air Ministry was interested in the Type 142, and Bristol designed a military version, the 142M. With the exception of the fabric-covered control surfaces, the 142M was made entirely of metal, and it was called the Blenheim Mark I. Its maiden flight took place on June 25, 1936, and the first production machines were delivered to the RAF in March 1943. They were used not only as bombers, but also as night fighters, for which they had a ventral gondola with four 0.3 inch (7.7 mm) guns and were fitted with radar. In July 1940 a Blenheim night fighter became the first aircraft in the world to achieve a radar-guided kill. The Mark I was replaced by the Blenheim Mark IV (the Type 149), which had a longer nose to accommodate the observer and his equipment. At its peak there were 70 Blenheim squadrons in the RAF, and one of its variants, the Bolingbroke, was produced in Canada, though this was used only for training purposes. The final version was the Blenheim Mark V (the Type 160); had additional armor and weaponry but was fitted with the same engine, which made it very slow and ponderous, so it was soon withdrawn from front-line service. The Blenheim was exported to numerous countries, including Finland, Yugoslavia, Romania, and Turkey, and during the war it was flown by the RAF, the RCAF (Royal Canadian Air Force), RSAAF (Royal South African Air Force), the Free French, Portugal, and Greece. A total of 3,983 Blenheims were produced, including the Canadian-built model.

UNITED KINGDOM

BRISTOL TYPE 156 BEAUFIGHTER

The Type 156 was actually developed by Bristol as a heavy long-range bomber, based on the Beaufort and called the Beaufighter, but during the war it was used as a night fighter, a torpedo bomber, and an anti-naval and ground attack aircraft. It made its maiden flight on July 17, 1939 and immediately proved to be an outstanding machine. It was initially mainly used as a night fighter (the Mark IF), as its body was large enough to accommodate very bulky radar equipment. The first production models were delivered to the RAF in September 1940 and made a great impact on the Luftwaffe. As soon as there were sufficient numbers of Mosquitoes for night fighting, Beaufighters were mainly used as heavy fighters and anti-naval aircraft; German transport aircraft on their way to North Africa had some

unpleasant encounters with them. Australia also built the Beaufighter under license and flew it against the Japanese. The different variants differed primarily in their engine specifications and weapon configurations, and numerous models

were fitted with radar. A total of 5,562 were manufactured until production was halted in 1945.

Beaufort Mk. X	
Type:	Heavy (nocturnal) fighter/torpedo bomber/anti-naval aircraft
Crew:	2
Weight when empty/ max weight at takeoff:	13,095 lb/ 21,211 lb
Length/wingspan/height:	42.4 ft/58.8 ft/16.1 ft
Engine(s):	Two Bristol Hercules XVII radial engines with 1,770 hp each
Maximum speed:	303 mph at 1,335 ft
Service ceiling:	15,235 ft
Range:	1,470 miles
Weaponry:	4 x 0.8 in Hispano-Suiza fixed automatic cannon in the nose, 6 x 0.3 in Browning machine guns in the wings, 1 x Vickers K 0.3 in machine gun on the back of the fuselage, and one 1,604 lb/2,128 lb torpedo—also, instead of wing guns, this model could carry eight 90 lb air-to-surface rockets or two 249 lb bombs

A Beaufighter takes off on an anti-naval mission in July 1942.

VICKERS WELLINGTON

The Vickers Wellington was one of the mainstays of British Bomber Command for raids on continental Europe in the first half of the war; it made its maiden flight on June 15, 1936. The

Wellington had an interesting design: its body and wings were fabric-covered, but its geodesic structure, with cantilevered light metal struts like an airship, was pretty well bulletproof, yet the "Wimpey," as it was nicknamed, suffered heavy losses early on. This inspired RAF Bomber Command to use it for night raids instead. Until 1942 Wellington bombers were the main aircraft deployed in bombing raids on Germany, using pioneering electronic target location equipment. In the first 1,000-bomber night bombing raid on Cologne on March 31, 1942, 600 Wellingtons were involved.

From 1943 the Wellington was withdrawn from bomber squadrons but was still used in the Mediterranean and in Coastal Command as a minesweeper, a torpedo bomber, and an anti-submarine aircraft. It was still in service as a training aircraft as late as 1954. Wellingtons flew on 63,977 missions for Bomber Command, and no fewer than 11,461 planes had been manufactured by the time production was halted in October 1945. The various versions mainly differed in their engine specifications (most were powered by Bristol radial engines, but some had Rolls-Royce Merlin or Pratt & Whitney engines), their weapon configurations, and their electronic equipment.

A Wellington B. Mark III of No. 426 Squadron, Dishforth (Yorkshire), early 1943.

	Wellington B.Mk. III
Type:	Medium range bomber
Crew:	6
Weight when empty/ max weight at takeoff:	18,540 lb/ 29,474 lb
Length/wingspan/height:	61.8 ft/87.5 ft/17.7 ft
Engine(s):	Two Bristol Hercules XI radial engines with 1,500 hp each
Maximum speed:	255 mph at 12,700 ft
Service ceiling:	19,300 ft
Range:	1,540 miles
Weaponry:	2 x 0.3 in Browning machine guns in the nose, 4 x 0.3 in machine guns in the rear turret, 2 x 0.3 in machine guns in side installations, and an internal payload of max. 4,496 lb

The Wellington B. Mark II.

DE HAVILLAND D.H. 98 MOSQUITO

The D.H. 98 Mosquito was in a wide variety of roles: as a bomber, a fighter bomber, a night fighter, a reconnaissance aircraft, an anti-naval aircraft, a carrier-borne combat aircraft, and a target finder. On its own initiative De Havilland began work on a design for a high-speed bomber in 1938, and to save raw materials large parts of the plane's design consisted of laminated wood. The British Air Ministry initially turned down De Havilland's offer; only when the war situation became more difficult did a bomber that was not made of light metal become an attractive proposition.

So the first Mosquito prototype took off for the first time on November 25, 1940, achieving an astounding maximum speed of over 390 mph (630 km/h)—which, at the time, made it even faster than the Spitfire. In addition, it could carry the same payload as a contemporary medium-range bomber.

A Mosquito NF Mark II of No. 23 Squadron, Malta, January 1943.

A Mosquito FB Mark VI of No. 418 Squadron, Hendon (Hertfordshire), Fall 1944.

	Mosquito FB Mk. VI
Type:	Fighter bomber
Crew:	2 man
Weight when empty/ max weight at takeoff:	14,286 lb/ 22,280 lb
Length/wingspan/height:	41.6 ft/55 ft/15.5 ft
Engine(s):	Two Rolls-Royce Merlin 25 V12 engines with 1,620 hp each
Maximum speed:	362 mph at 5,583 ft
Service ceiling:	33,567 ft
Range:	1,649 miles
Weaponry:	4 x 0.8 in Hispano-Suiza automatic cannon, 4 x 0.3 in Browning machine guns fixed in the nose, and a combined internal and external payload of max. 2,000 lb, e.g., two 249 lb bombs in the internal bomb bay and eight 90 lb air-to-surface rockets under the outer wings

The Air Ministry had been won over, and ordered three different versions: a photo reconnaissance (PR) model, a bomber (B), and a night fighter (NF). As soon as it was first put in service on July 14, 1941, it lived up to all expectations, and a PR Mark I eluded three Bf 109s over France. From early 1942 the first bomber squadrons with B Mark IV aircraft were ready for service, and they began a series of bombing raids in Germany. The radar-equipped NF Mark II was first deployed in late December 1941. The Mosquito soon showed that, even with its wooden frame, it was very hard-wearing, and it developed into a highly successful aircraft.

As well as the three variants already mentioned, there were numerous other models. The model that was manufactured in the largest numbers and the most important version was the FB (fighter bomber) Mark IV, which was heavily armed with automatic cannon and machine guns in its nose and could also carry bombs and rockets. The Mosquito bombers were increasingly given the role of "scouts" (target finders), marking out targets for Lancaster and Halifax bombers with "Christmas Tree" light bombs. Mosquitoes were also manufactured in Canada and Australia, but their performance was not quite as impressive in the Pacific as in Europe: the warm and humid climate was not good for their wooden parts, and some Mosquitoes literally fell apart in mid-air. A total of 7.781 Mosquitoes were built, including all the different versions, of which 1,134 were built in Canada and 212 in Australia.

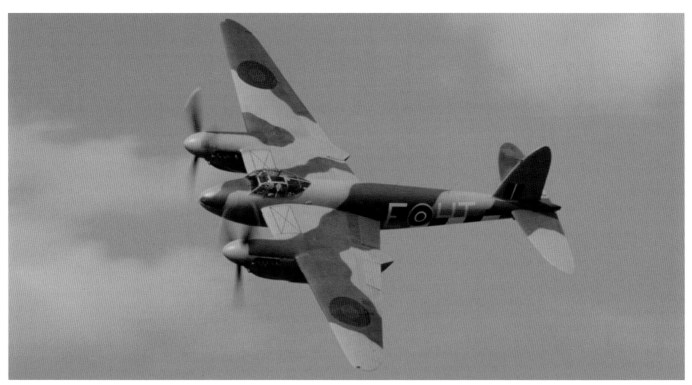

German night fighters found the Mosquito night bomber virtually untouchable.

SHORT S.29 STIRLING

The Stirling Mark III.

	Stirling Mk. III
Type:	Heavy bomber
Crew:	7
Weight when empty/ max weight at takeoff:	43,161 lb/ 69,936 lb
Length/wingspan/height:	89.6 ft/100.7 ft/23.1 ft
Engine(s):	Four Bristol Hercules XVI radial engines with 1,650 hp each
Maximum speed:	270 mph at 14,400 ft
Service ceiling:	16,990 ft
Range:	1,920 miles
Weaponry:	4 x 0.3 in Browning machine guns – two in the nose turret, two in the rear turret— 4 x 0.3 in machine guns in the tail turret, and an internal payload of max. 13,987 lb

The S.29 prototype made its maiden flight on May 14, 1939, and Stirlings flew their first missions for RAF Bomber Command in February 1941. The Mark I was manufactured in large numbers at first, and later the Mark III was used in missions in occupied Europe. In its heyday 11 bomber squadrons were flying the Stirling. It was also deployed as a "scout," a target finder which dropped light bombs above targets. Once there were sufficient numbers of Halifax and Lancaster bombers, the Stirling was restricted to missions of secondary importance, as it could not reach a satisfactory altitude, and its bomb bay could not carry the new 4,000 lb (1.816 kg) bombs. From 1944 it served primarily as a glider tug and a transporter for paratroopers, for which two new versions, the Mark IV and Mark V, were specially built, but in 1946 the Stirling was withdrawn from service even in these capacities. A total of 2,383 Stirlings were produced, including all the different versions.

AVRO LANCASTER

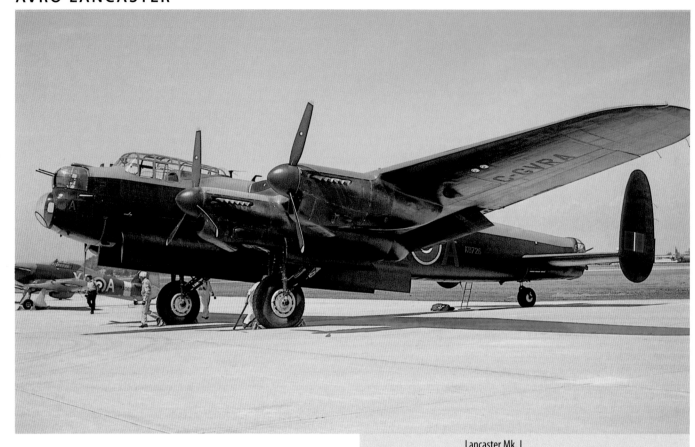

The Lancaster was, by quite some way, the most important and the best British bomber in the Second World War, yet it had its roots in the unsuccessful twin-engine Avro Manchester, which struggled with many different problems for the short time it was in service. To overcome these problems, Avro completely revised its design, equipping the new model with four reliable Rolls-Royce Merlin engines, instead of the problematic Vulture engines. The Lancaster prototype made its maiden flight on January 9, 1941, and in September that same year, bomber crews began training with the first production aircraft. Very little in the basic design was changed at any point during the war, showing how effective it was, and though there were versions other than the Mark I (which was manufactured throughout the war), the differences between them were primarily their engine specifications and weapon configurations. The Mark II had Bristol Hercules engines, and the Mark III was powered by the American-built version of the Merlin, while the

The Lancaster's excellent Rolls-Royce Merlin engines contributed significantly to its success.

Lancaster Mk. I	
Type:	Heavy bomber
Crew:	7
Weight when empty/ max weight at takeoff:	36,868 lb/ 69,936 lb
Length/wingspan/height:	70.6 ft/10.4 ft/20.3 ft
Engine(s):	Four Rolls-Royce Merlin XX V12 engines with 1,280 hp each
Maximum speed:	278 mph at 11,700 ft
Service ceiling:	24,895 ft
Range:	2,530 miles
Weaponry:	4 x 0.3 in Browning machine guns—two in the nose turret, two in the rear turret—4 x 0.3 in machine guns in the tail turret, and normally an internal payload of max. 13,987 lb

Mark X was manufactured in Canada. The Mark VII had a turning gun turret with a 0.5 inch (12.7 mm) machine gun, but special mention should go to the B version of the Mark I, which was modified to carry the 21,980 lb (9.979 kg) "Grand Slam" bomb, which was mainly used against submarine bunkers, and the Mark III B, which carried out the celebrated "Dambuster" raids in 1943, dropping the famous bouncing bombs, which skimmed over the water like stones to destroy the Möhne, Sorpe, and Eder dams

in Germany. The 11,885 lb (5.396 kg) "Tallboy" bomb was also dropped by Lancasters—among other targets, it struck and sank the German *Tirpitz* battleship.

During the war 59 RAF bomber squadrons flew the Lancaster, and it was the main bomber used in night raids on German cities, where a weakness in many Lancasters was exposed which was never eradicated: they lacked defensive weaponry to protect their undercarriages, where many of them carried their ground

*A Lancaster Mark II of No. 426 Squadron,
Linton-on-Ouse (Yorkshire), late 1943.*

A Lancaster Mark X of No. 419 Squadron, Durham, June 1944.

target-finding radar equipment, which gave them no visibility directly downward. German night fighters exploited this weakness by approaching the bombers from below, flying directly beneath them, then opening fire diagonally upward (this was called "diagonal music"). Nevertheless, the Lancaster was by far the RAF's most successful bomber, playing a major role in the Allies' eventual victory. Lancasters flew on more than 156,000 missions and dropped 608,612 tons (618,350 tonnes) of explosives, as well as 51 million firebombs. A new version with an increased range was also planned for deployment in the Far East. Lancasters were not only flown by the RAF: the Canadian (RCAF) and Australian (RAAF) Air Forces also flew them, as did the French Navy. The last of a total of 7,377 Lancasters was completed in February 1946.

*Along with the Halifax, the Lancaster was
the RAF's standard heavy bomber.*

HANDLEY PAGE H.P.57 HALIFAX

	Halifax B. Mk. III
Type:	Heavy bomber
Crew:	7
Weight when empty/ max weight at takeoff:	38,205 lb/ 64,943 lb
Length/wingspan/height:	72.7 ft/105.8 ft/21.1 ft
Engine(s):	Four Bristol Hercules XVI radial engines with 1,615 hp each
Maximum speed:	282 mph at 13,700 ft
Service ceiling:	24,383 ft
Range:	2,529 miles
Weaponry:	8 x 0.3 in Browning machine guns—two in the rear turret, two in the tail turret—1 x 0.3 in machine gun in the nose, and an internal payload of max. 12,989 lb

A Halifax Mark II.

The Handley Page Halifax was one of the RAF's most important heavy bombers in the Second World War, second only to the Lancaster. It was originally meant to be powered by Rolls-Royce Vulture engines, but Handley soon doubted the latter's reliability, so the model was redesigned to take four Rolls-Royce Merlin engines, which resulted in a much larger and heavier machine. The first prototype of the H.P.57 flew on October 25, 1939. So that it could carry a large payload, the all-metal Halifax was built with medium-height wings, and two additional bomb bays were created in the inner wings. From November 1941 the Halifax Mark I, which did not have a machine gun turret on the fuselage, was put into service. Because many bombers were lost in daytime raids, in late 1941 the Halifax was used instead as a night bomber and was successful in this capacity. Halifax bombers were the first machines ever to be equipped with new, top-secret H25 radar installations to locate targets on the ground, and eventually 38 RAF bomber wings put them into service. The Mark II had a machine gun turret on its fuselage, but it no longer had a turret in its nose, while the Mark III was powered by Bristol Hercules radial engines instead of Rolls-Royce Merlins. A total of 6,178 Halifax bombers were produced, including all the different versions.

Although the Halifax was overshadowed by the Lancaster, it was the better multi-purpose aircraft. Until 1945 it flew 75,532 missions and dropped 227,610 tons (231,252 metric tonnes) of bombs. In addition, it was deployed in nine Coastal Command squadrons as a sea reconnaissance and anti-submarine aircraft, towed gliders, carried paratroopers, and flew secret missions to drop spies and parachute weapons and equipment for partisans and resistance fighters.

FAIREY SWORDFISH

The Fairey Swordfish Mark I.

	Swordfish Mk. I
Type:	Carrier-borne torpedo bomber and reconnaissance aircraft
Crew:	2–3
Weight when empty/ max weight at takeoff:	4,725 lb/ 7,531 lb
Length/wingspan/height:	36.3 ft/46.2 ft/12.5 ft
Engine(s):	One Bristol Pegasus III M.3 radial engine with 690 hp
Maximum speed:	138 mph
Service ceiling:	10,865 ft
Range:	543 miles
Weaponry:	2 x 0.3 in Vickers machine guns (one in the nose, one mobile in the rear of the cockpit), and one 1,603 lb torpedo, or an external payload of max. 1,500 lb

In 1930 the Air Ministry required a torpedo bomber and reconnaissance aircraft which could be flown from an aircraft carrier, and the Swordfish was designed to meet this need. But Fairey's first prototype was far from successful—in fact, it even crashed. But the second prototype lived up to expectations, and the Swordfish Mark I went into serial production in 1935. The Swordfish was a fabric-covered biplane with fixed undercarriage, and it wings could be folded so that it could be accommodated on an aircraft carrier. In November 1940 Swordfishes successfully attacked the Italian fleet anchored at the port of Taranto, and in May 1941 a Swordfish carried out a torpedo attack on the *Bismarck*, the famous German battleship. From 1942 it was mostly flown from aircraft carriers in anti-submarine operations. In 1943 the Mark II was introduced, with a more powerful engine and metal-reinforced lower wings, from which rockets could be fired. The Mark III, which was put into service in late 1943, had a radar device in a large dome on its underside, and some Swordfishes (called the Mark IV) had enclosed cockpits for use in extremely cold regions. Until 1944 a total of 2,391 were manufactured.

SHORT S.25 SUNDERLAND

The Short Sunderland was mainly used in sea reconnaissance and anti-submarine operations, but was also an air-sea rescue aircraft and a transporter. It was based on the S.23 civil seaplane, making its maiden flight on October 16, 1937, and the first Sunderlands were put into service by the British Coastal Command in the fall of 1938. From 1940 Sunderlands were equipped with ASV (Air to Surface Vessel) radar to protect Allied

A Short Sunderland Mark III with ASV ship locating radar on the back of the fuselage.

	Stirling Mk. III
Type:	Reconnaissance and anti-submarine seaplane
Crew:	10
Weight when empty/ max weight at takeoff:	32,971 lb/ 57,947 lb
Length/wingspan/height:	86.7 ft/114.6 ft/32.6 ft
Engine(s):	Four Bristol Pegasus XVIII radial engines with 1,065 hp each
Maximum speed:	212 mph at 5,000 ft
Service ceiling:	15,235 ft
Range:	3,000 miles
Weaponry:	4 x 0.3 in Browning machine guns—two in the tail turret, two in the rear turret—4 x 0.3 in machine guns in the tail turret, 2 x 0.5 in Browning machine guns in side installations, 4 x 0.3 in machine guns fixed in the nose, and an internal payload of max. 4,956 lb

convoys and detect and destroy enemy submarines, and it was feared by the Luftwaffe on account of its "porcupine" defensive weaponry. In fact, it is claimed that, when under attack from eight Ju 88s, one Sunderland shot down three enemy planes. Because its undercarriage had to be watertight, its bombs were carried on rails through lateral gaps in the fuselage into the inner wings before being dropped. A total of 749 machines were manufactured, including five series which mainly differed in their engine specifications.

POLIKARPOV I-16

The Polikarpov I-16.

	I-16 Type 24
Type:	Fighter and fighter bomber
Crew:	1
Weight when empty/ max weight at takeoff:	3,249 lb/ 4,537 lb
Length/wingspan/height:	20.1 ft/29.6 ft/8 ft
Engine(s):	One M-62 radial engine with 1,000 hp
Maximum speed:	304 mph
Service ceiling:	31,567 ft
Range:	375 miles
Weaponry:	4 x 0.3 in ShKAS machine guns, or 2 x 0.3 in machine guns and 2 x 0.8 in ShVAK automatic cannon, and an external payload of max 441 lb

The Polikarpov I-16 was the world's first mass-produced single-wing fighter aircraft with retractable undercarriage. Its structure was a composite of wood, steel, and aluminum, covered with fabric. The first prototype flew in late 1933, and serial production of the Type I began in mid-1934. In late October 1936 the first I-16s were delivered to the Spanish Republican forces for deployment in the Civil War, where they were dubbed the "Mosca" (Fly) by the Republicans and the "Rata" (Rat) by the Fascists. A total of 157 machines were sent to Spain, and another 30 were built there under license. At first, the I-16 was the best fighter aircraft in Spain, but later on proved to be inferior to the more modern Bf 109. It was deployed against the Japanese in the border conflict of 1939 and in the Russo-Finnish Winter War of 1939–40, where it was used both as a fighter and as a fighter bomber. But it was so hopelessly outclassed by German aircraft that its pilots often resorted to ramming their enemy, and in late 1943 it was permanently withdrawn from front-line service, as better machines were now available. Until then around 7,000 I-16s were built, including all the different versions.

MIKOYAN-GUREVICH MIG-1 AND MIG-3

The famous aircraft design team of Mikoyan and Gurevich designed their first combat aircraft, the MiG 140, in 1940, but at first no one would have guessed that they would become so successful. The MiG-1 made its maiden flight on April 5, 1940, and 100 aircraft of this type were produced until December 1940. It was certainly fast, reaching 390 mph (628 km/h), but it was only lightly armed, with just two 0.3 inch (7.62 mm) machine guns, and far more seriously, it was very unstable and had a limited range. An improved version, the MiG-3, was notable for its excellent performance, reaching a maximum speed of 398 mph (640 km/h) at 26,000 ft (7,800 m), but below 5,000 m (just over 16,600 ft) its performance was clearly inferior to its German counterparts, and its weaponry—one 0.5 inch (12.7 mm) and two 0.3 inch (7.62 mm) machine guns—was still inadequate. Production of both fighter models was halted in the summer of 1942, after 3,322 machines had been produced, because mass production of the Yak and LaGG fighters had begun in the meantime in the factories behind the Ural Mountains, and new MiGs did not appear until after 1945.

A MiG-3 from an unknown unit in winter camouflage.

	MiG-3
Type:	Fighter
Crew:	1
Weight when empty/ max weight at takeoff:	5,715 lb/ 7,379 lb
Length/wingspan/height:	27.6 ft/34 ft/11.7 ft
Engine(s):	One Mikulin AM 35A V12 engine with 1,350 hp
Maximum speed:	398 mph at 26,000 ft
Service ceiling:	40,000 ft
Range:	740 miles
Weaponry:	1 x 0.5 in UBS machine gun, 2 x 0.3 in ShKAS machine guns fixed in the nose, and an external payload of max. 440 lb, e.g., two 220 lb bombs or eight RS-82 rockets

LAVOCHKIN LAGG-1, LAGG-3, LA-5, AND LA-7

The Lavochkin fighter series was one of the most important Soviet fighter series in the Second World War, second only to the Yak series. All Lavochkin aircraft were made of wood; the company had been developing high performance fighters made entirely of wood since the 1930s. In conjunction with M.I. Gudkov and W.P. Gorbunov, Lavochkin designed a fighter made entirely of laminated Siberian birch wood, and the prototype made its maiden flight on March 30, 1940. But the aircraft was too hastily developed and had many problems, so only 100 LaGGs were manufactured. The improved LaGG-3 had its maiden flight on June 14, 1940, but its engine was both too heavy and insufficiently powerful, so Lavochkin tested several different engines. Furthermore, when Germany went to war with Russia, the LaGG-3 proved to be inferior to the Bf 109, which led to the development of the La-5. By this time, 6,528 LaGG-3 aircraft had been produced.

Instead of the old V12 engine, the new aircraft (the La-5) had to be completely redesigned to take a Shvetsov ASh 82 radial engine, which meant that it was virtually an entirely new aircraft. The La-5 made its maiden flight in April 1942 and went into production in June that same year. It fared especially well in the southern part of the Eastern Front, where it was dubbed "the Wooden Savior of Stalingrad." Once the improved ASh 82FN engine with direct fuel injection was available in early 1943, the La-5FN was introduced. It had a distinctive

	La-7
Type:	Fighter and fighter bomber
Crew:	1
Weight when empty/ max weight at takeoff:	5,782 lb/ 7,489 lb
Length/wingspan/height:	28.7 ft/32.7 ft/9.3 ft
Engine(s):	One 14-cylinder Shvetsov ASh 82FN radial engine with 1,775 hp
Maximum speed:	415 mph
Service ceiling:	39,300 ft
Range:	395 miles
Weaponry:	2–3 x ShVAK or B-20 0.8 in automatic cannon, and an external payload of max. 441 lb, e.g., two 220 lb bombs or eight RS-82 rockets

An La-7 of the 16th Soviet Guard Fighter Wing, Eastern Front, 1945.

forward-facing air intake on the fuselage, as well as a lowered back to allow better rearward visibility. This was the most effective variant of the La-5, helping to turn the tables on the Germans in the summer of 1943. It is claimed that a total of around 10,000 La-5s were built. The La-7 was a further development of the La-5, with a completely protected air frame and a new, more aerodynamically efficient oil cooler under the rear of the cockpit. The front-line forces received their first La-7s in mid-1944, and a total of 5,753 were manufactured.

The LaGG-3.

YAKOVLEV YAK-1, YAK-3, YAK-7, AND YAK-9

	Yak-3
Type:	Fighter
Crew:	1
Weight when empty/ max weight at takeoff:	4,637 lb/ 5,859 lb
Length/wingspan/height:	28.3 ft/30.7 ft/8.1 ft
Engine(s):	One Klimov VK 105PF 2 V with 1,300 hp
Maximum speed:	407 mph at 10,300 ft
Service ceiling:	35,700 ft
Range:	560 miles
Weaponry:	One 0.8 in ShVAK automatic cannon firing through the propeller hub, 2 x 0.5 in UBS machine guns fixed in the nose, and an external payload of max. 440 lb

A Yak-3 in the colors of the Normandy Niemen Squadron—the aircraft pictured is still airworthy today.

The Soviet fighter series that had the largest production in the Second World War was built by the Yakovlev company. The Yak-1 was intended to replace outdated Soviet biplanes. It made its maiden flight on January 13, 1940, and serial production began in December that same year. It was composed of fabric-covered steel rods, with wooden wings and retractable undercarriage. After its first front-line deployment in the summer of 1941, it underwent some improvements: the wing tips were made narrower, and from 1942 the Yak-1B had better all-round visibility, as the back of the fuselage was lowered. Production of the Yak-1 continued until 1943, and

8,721 machines were manufactured. In early 1942 Yakovlev began work on improving the series. Above all, its weight was reduced and it had a more powerful engine, and the Yak-3 was the lightest fighter in the Second World War. Its flight tests took place in April 1943, and in August 1944 the first Yak-3 squadrons were ready for service. The Yak proved to be an outstanding fighter and could also be used as a fighter bomber. In fact, it was so effective that in late 1944 the Luftwaffe High Command ordered its pilots to avoid engaging Yaks in combat at altitudes of around 16,600 ft (5,000m) or less. The Yak was fast, agile, and could climb rapidly, but its range left something

to be desired. A total of 4,848 Yak-3s were manufactured. The Yak-7 was originally developed as a two-seater training version of the Yak-1, but it was also a front-line fighter, and 6,399 were built. The Yak-9 flew for the first time in 1943, and was manufactured in the largest quantities of all the Yak versions: 16,769 machines were built. It was mainly used as a fighter bomber and long-range escort fighter, and was powered by a slightly more powerful 1,600 hp Klimov VK 107A engine, while the two-seater Yak-9UTI served as a training aircraft. Yaks were flown even after 1945; for instance, by the Communists in the Korean War.

Yak-3s of the Free French Normandy Niemen Squadron, East Prussia, early 1945.

Yak 9-T, unknown unit, Kuban, summer 1943.

ILYUSHIN IL-2 AND IL-10 STURMOVIK

The Ilyushin Il-2 was one of the most important combat aircraft in the Second World War, and it is claimed that a total of 36,163 were built, including all the different versions. The first prototype made its maiden flight on October 12, 1940, at which time it was still a single-seater. The first production aircraft were delivered to the Soviet Air Force in May 1941. In the first few months of Germany's invasion of Russia, the Il-2 suffered heavy losses, due to Germany's dominance in the skies. So in 1942 a

A single-seater Ilyushin Il-2.

An Ilyushin Il-2M3 of the 269th Russian Ground Attack Regiment, Kursk, 1943.

	Il-2
Type:	Ground attack aircraft
Crew:	2
Weight when empty/max weight at takeoff:	9,967 lb/ 14,009 lb
Length/wingspan/height:	27.6 ft/34 ft/11.7 ft
Engine(s):	One Mikulin AM 38F V12 engine with 1,700 hp
Maximum speed:	255 mph at 5,000 ft
Service ceiling:	15,085 ft
Range:	475 mph
Weaponry:	2 x 0.9 in VYa automatic cannon, 2 x 0.3 in ShKAS machine guns fixed in the wings, 1 x 0.5 in UBT machine gun in the rear of the cockpit, and a combined payload of max. 1,320 lb

decision was made to introduce the two-seater Il-2M version, in which the observer would be armed with a 0.5 inch (12.7 mm) machine gun to defend against attacks from the rear. The next important new version was the Il-2M3, which had a more powerful engine and V-shaped (therefore, stronger) wing tips.

The Sturmovik's most important task was to attack armored vehicles and ground troops, so it had 0.2–0.5 inch (6–13 mm) thick armor all over—to

protect its engine, pilots, fuel tank, and, in the two-seater version, observer. The German troops nicknamed it "Iron Gustav" or "Black Death," and as well as machine guns and automatic cannon of up to 1.5 inch (37 mm) caliber, it also carried bombs and RS-82 or RS-132 air-to-surface rockets. The Il-2 originally had a composite structure, but was later made entirely of metal. As well as the air force, the navy deployed a torpedo bomber version of the Il-2. An improved version,

called the Il-10, was produced from early 1945. The importance of the Il-2 for the Soviet forces is underlined by a telegram from Stalin about delays in delivering the Il-2: "The Red Army needs Il-2s as it needs air and bread. I demand more machines. That is my final warning!"

POLIKARPOV PO-2

Po-2	
Type:	Light night bomber
Crew:	2
Weight when empty/ max weight at takeoff:	1,696 lb/ 2,793 lb
Length/wingspan/height:	27.6 ft/34 ft/11.7 ft
Engine(s):	One 5-cylinder Shvetsov M-11D radial engine with 125 hp
Maximum speed:	80 mph near ground level
Service ceiling:	4,335 ft
Range:	215 miles
Weaponry:	1 x 0.3 in ShKAS machine gun in the rear of the cockpit, and an external payload of max. 660 lb

Though nondescript to look at, more Po-2s are manufactured than any other aircraft in the world.

The Polikarpov Po-2, originally known as the U-2, was designed in 1927 primarily as a flight instruction aircraft, and its prototype had its maiden flight in January 1928. It proved to be easy to fly and to maintain, as well as being very stable, so it was put into serial production in 1930. The frame was made of wood, the front section of its fuselage was covered with laminated wood, and the rear of the fuselage and the wings were covered with fabric. New versions, in addition to the training model, were produced in very little time, including one to spray crops with insecticide, one to transport the sick, a seaplane, and a passenger aircraft. When Germany attacked the Soviet Union, around 13,000 Po-2s were in service. Out of necessity many new military versions were produced, including liaison and reconnaissance aircraft. They became famous in their capacity as light bombers for harassing German troops in night raids; because of the noise made by its engine, the Germans nicknamed it the "Sewing Machine." It was highly successful, inspiring the Luftwaffe to use dated models which they had seized from the Russians, for similar purposes. It is claimed that around 33,000 U-2s and Po-2s were built; this model was manufactured in the largest numbers of any aircraft in history.

TUPOLEV SB-2

The Tupolev SB-2, also known as the ANT-40, was one of the most modern machines of its kind when it appeared in 1934. With a maximum speed of over 250 mph (400 km/h), it was faster than most contemporary fighters. Development of the SB-2 began in 1933, and the prototype had its maiden flight on October 7, 1934. The second version (hence its SB-2 designation), which was introduced in late December 1934, was put into serial production, and in 1936 the Soviet Union delivered 210 SB-2s to the Republican forces in the Spanish Civil War. The SB-2 also flew missions in the Russo-Japanese border conflict of 1939–40, in the Russo-Finnish Winter War, and on the Chinese side against the Japanese. The SB-2s enjoyed only limited success in these conflicts, and they had almost no success whatsoever against the Luftwaffe. Many were seized by the Germans as they advanced through Russia and passed on to Bulgaria and Finland, and a few were also used for a short time by the Luftwaffe itself. Yet some of the total production of 6,466 remained in front-line service until 1943, after which they served instead as training and liaison aircraft behind the front line. A small number of SB-2 aircraft were also built under license by the Czech firm Avia, which called them B.71s.

A Chinese SB-2 that flew against the Japanese in 1938.

SB-2bis	
Type:	Light bomber
Crew:	3
Weight when empty/ max weight at takeoff:	10,502 lb/ 17,357 lb
Length/wingspan/height:	41.9 ft/67.8 ft/11.4 ft
Engine(s):	Two M-103 V12 engines with 950 hp each
Maximum speed:	280 mph
Service ceiling:	26,000 ft
Range:	1,430 miles
Weaponry:	3-6 x 0.3 in ShKAS machine guns and an internal payload of max. 2,200 lb

ILYUSHIN DB-3 AND IL-4

The DB-3.

The Ilyushin DB-3 and its improved version, the Il-4, were the most important Soviet long-range aircraft in the Second World War. Development began in 1934, and the first prototype made its maiden flight one year later, powered by two M-85 engines, which were actually French Gnome-Rhône engines built under license. A second machine underwent flight tests in May 1936 and set five different net load world records between July and September 1936. The DB-3 attracted international attention when it flew non-stop from

	DB-3M	Il-4
Type:	Medium-range bomber	Medium-range bomber
Crew:	3–4	3
Weight when empty/ max weight at takeoff:	11,608 lb/ 16,872 lb	12,775 lb/ 24,890 lb
Length/wingspan/ height:	47.4 ft/71.5 ft/ 14 ft	49.3 ft/71.5 ft/ 13.7 ft
Engine(s):	Two M-87B radial engines with 950 hp each	Two M-88B radial engines with 1,100 hp each
Maximum speed:	275 mph	265 mph
Service ceiling:	32,300 ft	32,300 ft
Range:	2,360 miles	2,360 miles
Weaponry:	3 x 0.3 in ShKAS machine guns—one in the nose, one in the tail, and one in the waist – and an internal or external payload of max. 3,305 lb	2 x 0.3 in ShKAS machine guns—one in the nose, one in the tail—1 x 0.5 in UBS machine gun in the rear turret, and an internal or external payload of max. 5,505 lb

The Il-4.

Moscow to the USA, a distance of nearly 5,000 miles (8,000 km).

Production of the DB-3b began in 1937. By 1941, 1,528 DB-3s had been manufactured, and there were many different versions including a conventional bomber, a torpedo bomber, and a mine-layer for the navy. The DB-3 was first deployed in the Russo-Finnish Winter War. The Ilyushin Il-4 was an improved version of the DB-3, and the most obvious superficial difference was

its new glazed and pointed nose. It was designed as an all-metal half-shell construction, but later in the war some parts (the outer wings, fuselage, and tail) had to be made of wood, as metal was in short supply. This had a negative effect on its flight, but by using more powerful M-88B engines, its flight weight and payload could be increased. The new machine, originally called the DB-3F, flew for the first time in mid-1939, and serial production began early the following

year. Until 1944, 5,256 machines in the DB-3F/Il-4 series were built. The Il-4 was deployed in all the major battles on the Eastern Front, where they not only flew long-range bombing missions, but also directly supported the troops on the ground, and it remained in service in the Soviet Air Force until 1949.

SOVIET UNION

PETLYAKOV PE-2

The Petlyakov Pe-2 was developed from the unsuccessful VI-100 high altitude fighter prototype. It made its maiden flight in late December 1939, and the first production model took off for the first time in November 1940. The Pe-2 was an all-metal low-wing aircraft with a retractable tail wheel, and proved to be an excellent light bomber, but it did not have a pressurized cabin. When the war broke out, 458 Pe-2s had been delivered, tried, and tested. This model became the Soviet Air Force's standard tactical bomber, but it also served as a ground support and reconnaissance aircraft, and as a day and night fighter. Its robust frame meant that it could also be used as a dive-bomber. Before production was halted, 11,427 planes were produced. There were various versions of the Pe-2, which mainly differed in their weapon configurations

	Pe-2FT
Type:	Light bomber
Crew:	3
Weight when empty/ max weight at takeoff:	13,656 lb/ 18,767 lb
Length/wingspan/height:	42.6 ft/57 ft/11.4 ft
Engine(s):	Two Klimov VK 105PF V12 engines with 1,260 hp each
Maximum speed:	360 mph
Service ceiling:	30,000 ft
Range:	1,100 miles
Weaponry:	2 x 0.3 in ShKAS machine guns fixed in the wings, 1 x 0.5 in UBT machine gun in the rear of the cockpit, 2 x 0.3 in ShKAS waist machine guns, and a combined internal and external payload of 2,200 lb

and VK-105 engine specifications, and the Pe-3M was a fighter version. From late 1944 the Pe-2 was progressively replaced by the Tu-2.

The Pe-2.

TUPOLEV TU-2

	Tu-2
Type:	Medium-range bomber
Crew:	4
Weight when empty/ max weight at takeoff:	16,463 lb/ 25,022 lb
Length/wingspan/height:	46 ft/62.9 ft/15.2 ft
Engine(s):	Two 14-cylinder Shvetsov Ash 82FNV radial engines with 1,850 hp each
Maximum speed:	340 mph
Service ceiling:	31,700 ft
Range:	870 miles
Weaponry:	2 x 0.8 in ShVAK automatic cannon fixed in the wings, 3 x 0.5 in UBT machine guns— and a combined payload of max. 2,484 lb

The Tupolev Tu-2 was an effective medium-range bomber, but it is notable less for its performance than for the fact that it was designed by Andrei Tupolev in prison—he had been incarcerated at Stalin's behest! Work began on designing a twin-engine bomber to outperform the Junkers Ju 88 in 1937, but it was not until January 29, 1941 that the first Tu-2 made its maiden flight. Engine problems were to blame for this, as was the fact that prison did not provide very good working conditions for the designer. In any event, the first production aircraft were delivered to the Soviet Air Force in November 1942. Its design was simple, with classically elegant lines, and it provided all four crew members with good all-round visibility. Between late 1942 and 1945 1,111 Tu-2s were built, and they were deployed on all fronts, where they acquitted themselves well, thanks to their good flying attributes. A total of 2,527 Tu-2s were built before production was halted in 1948, and aircraft of this type remained in service until the late 1950s. Finally, thanks to his successful design, Tupolev was not only released from prison in 1943, but was also awarded the Stalin Prize.

The Tu-2.

LOCKHEED P-38 LIGHTNING

The Lockheed P-38 Lightning is one of the best known and most successful American combat aircraft of the Second World War. The standards required in the tender were so high that in 1937–38 they could be met only by installing two engines. Because a turbocharger was to be installed, the aircraft had an unusual double-fuselage design. The first prototype had its maiden flight on January 27, 1939, and after a few pre-production models and a relatively small number of production models had been built, the P38E was delivered in larger

A P-38J of the 8th US Air Force, England, early 1944.

A P-38L of the 5th US Air Force, the Philippines, December 1944.

	P-38L
Type:	Long-range fighter and fighter bomber
Crew:	1
Weight when empty/ max weight at takeoff:	12,775 lb/ 21,581 lb
Length/wingspan/height:	38.5 ft/52.9 ft/13 ft
Engine(s):	Two Allison V 1710 111 V12 engines with 1,600 hp each
Maximum speed:	415 mph at 25,400 ft
Service ceiling:	44,700 ft
Range:	450 miles without extra fuel tanks, 2,250 miles with them
Weaponry:	1 x 0.8 in Hispano automatic cannon and 4 x 0.5 in Browning machine guns fixed in the nose, and an external payload of max. 4,000 lb

numbers to the US Army Air Force (USAAF). In the Pacific it proved to be a dangerous adversary for the Japanese A6M Zero, and the British took delivery of a number of P-38s, but they were dissatisfied with them as they had no turbochargers. The Luftwaffe first encountered the P-38 in North Africa, and it was deployed as an escort fighter for the 8th USAAF bombers in Germany. In combat with the Bf 109 and Fw 190 the F-38 showed the usual disadvantages expected from a twin-engine fighter, especially limited maneuverability, and in this capacity it was replaced by the P-47 and P-51. But because of the heavy weaponry in its nose, rockets, and a payload of up to 4,000 lb (1,816 kg), it was still a highly effective fighter bomber—after all, the Germans did not give it the nickname "Fork-Tailed Devil," without reason. The P-38 was also used as a photo reconnaissance aircraft, and of the 9.923 P-38s manufactured in total, around 1,400 (called the F-4 or F-5) were converted for this purpose. Shortly before the end of the war, a night fighter version (the P-38M) was introduced, which had a radar device in its nose, but it flew very few missions.

This photo clearly shows the P-38's double fuselage design.

The American pilots with the most kills, Bong and McGuire, both flew P-38s. On April 18, 1943, a P-38 wing based in the Solomon Islands succeeded in shooting down Japanese Admiral Yamamoto's Mitsubishi G4M.

REPUBLIC P-47 THUNDERBOLT

	P-47D
Type:	Long-range fighter and fighter bomber
Crew:	1
Weight when empty/ max weight at takeoff:	9,941 lb/ 17,485 lb
Length/wingspan/height:	36.7 ft/41.4 ft/14.9 ft
Engine(s):	One Pratt & Whitney R 2800 59W Double Wasp 18-cylinder radial engine with 2,535 hp
Maximum speed:	432 mph at 25,400 ft
Service ceiling:	41,650 ft
Range:	1,990 miles with three additional fuel tanks
Weaponry:	8 x 0.5 in Browning machine guns fixed in the wings, and an external payload of max. 2,498 lb, e.g., two 1,000 lb bombs or ten 5 in rockets, napalm tanks or extra fuel tanks

The Republic P-47N Thunderbolt.

The Republic P-47 Thunderbolt was the largest and heaviest single-engine fighter of its time, and its pilots called it the "Jug," short for "Juggernaut," a thoroughly appropriate name. From March 1943 to August 1945, P-47s flew 545,575 missions and destroyed around 7,000 aircraft and 9,000 locomotives, more than 86,000 trucks, and around 6,000 armored vehicles. By contrast, the proportion of P-47s lost in these missions was just 0.7%!

Originally, Alexander Kartveli of the Republic company intended to design a light fighter with two machine guns, but reports from Europe about aerial combat experience forced him to rethink, and he based his design around the most powerful engine available at the time, the Pratt & Whitney R-2800. The P-47 made its maiden flight on May 6, 1941, but the aircraft was afflicted by many different problems, so the P-47C was not deployed in Europe until April 1943. The D version of the P-47 was manufactured in the largest quantity (12,602 aircraft built); initially it had a raised tail section (the

An early P-47 D Razorback.

Razorback) but later this was lowered and the cockpit had all-round visibility, as well as a more powerful engine, and heavier weaponry. The P47-M, of which 130 were produced, was a high-speed version deployed against German jet fighters, and the P-47N was intended for long-range deployment, hence its larger wings and fuel tanks. In its role as an escort fighter the P-47 was rather less effective than the P-51 Mustang, so it was increasingly used as a fighter bomber. It was outstanding in this role, not only because of its firepower, but also because of its robustness and the fact that its Pratt & Whitney engines could withstand even the most severe hits. A total of 15,677 P-47s were manufactured, including all the different versions, and even after 1945 the Thunderbolt remained in service in numerous air forces worldwide for many more years, especially in South America.

A P-47D-30 of the 1st Tactical Air Force, France, fall 1944.

A P-47D-5 (Razorback) of the 8th US Air Force, England, March 1944.

A front view of the colorful "Tarheel Hal."

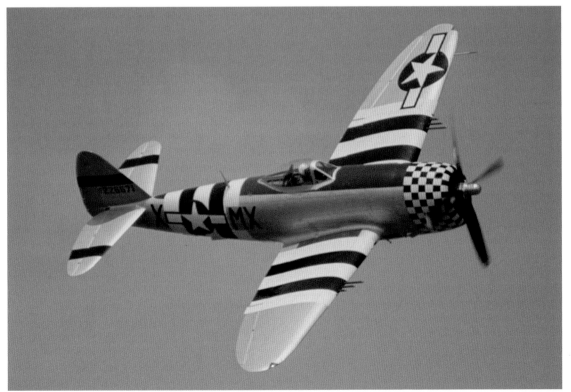

In the final phases of the war, Allied aircraft (like this P-47D) were painted with "invasion stripes" to help troops on their side to recognize them.

NORTH AMERICAN P-51 MUSTANG

A P-51D of the 8th US Air Force, England, November 1944.

The P-51 Mustang was arguably the best and most important fighter aircraft in the Second World War, but as with many large machines, this did not appear likely at first. The British Government approached North American Aviation in early 1940, asking them to produce the P-40 under license for the RAF. But North American Aviation convinced the British that it could produce a much better fighter than the P-40, which was no better than average. After just 117 days of development, the NA-73 took off for the first time on October 26, 1940, powered by an Allison V-1710. The NA-73 was fitted with a special cooler, which not only encountered less air resistance than the P-40 cooler but also produced more thrust, as well as laminated wings which reduced air resistance further. Consequently, the NA-73, which the RAF called the "Mustang," was significantly faster than the P-40, but the RAF was far from satisfied, as the Allison engine's performance above 16,700 ft (5,000m) was not good enough for the aircraft to be deployed as a fighter. So from May 1942 it was used exclusively as a fighter bomber and a low-altitude reconnaissance aircraft. The USAAF ordered this model nevertheless—the fighter was called the P-51 or P-51A, while the dive-bomber was called the A-36A Apache—and from early 1943 tests began to turn the P-51 into a truly first-class fighter by installing the Rolls-Royce Merlin engine. The result was the P-51B, powered by a Merlin built under license by Packard in the USA, and the P-51B and C (an identical model built in a different factory) served from late 1943 as long-range escort fighters, protecting the bombers of the 8th Air Force over Germany. Further improvements were made on the basis of combat experience—the Mustang's back was lowered and it was fitted with a teardrop cockpit, which gave the pilot good all-round visibility. This new model, the P-51D, also had a better engine, stronger

The P-51H.

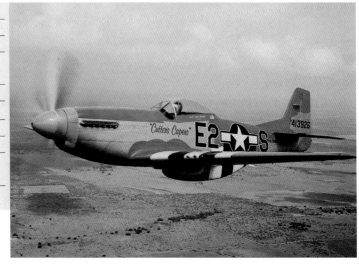

P-51D	
Type:	Long-range fighter and fighter bomber
Crew:	1
Weight when empty/	7,115 lb/
max weight at takeoff:	11,590 lb
Length/wingspan/height:	32.8 ft/37.6 ft/13.7 ft
Engine(s):	One Packard V 1650 7 V12 engine with 1,600 hp
Maximum speed:	437 mph at 25,400 ft
Service ceiling:	41,700 ft
Range:	1,300 miles without extra fuel tanks, and 2,050 miles with them
Weaponry:	6 x 0.5 in Browning machine guns fixed in the wings

Many P-51s are still flying today and can be seen at air shows.

wings, and two additional 0.5 inch (12.7 mm) caliber machine guns in its wings, giving a maximm external payload of 2,000 lb/908 kg). It is impossible to exaggerate the P-51's importance in the US air offensive against Germany. From late 1943 it was a feared opponent at any altitude, and it escorted increasingly large waves of bombers to their targets. Without fighter escorts, the US bombers would have suffered such heavy losses that their missions would not have continued. Although Mustangs were primarily escort fighters, they also

attacked ground targets themselves at low altitudes. Mustangs also escorted Boeing B-29 bombers in Japan, but they were deployed in smaller numbers than in Germany, though their missions there were longer. The Japanese fighters were deployed in typically large numbers, but they were significantly weaker than the technically superior P-51.

In the Second World War the Mustang served almost exclusively as a fighter, fighter bomber, and reconnaissance aircraft, and the A-36 was a dive-bomber. In addition to the P-51D, the P-51H, which

had a 2,200 hp engine, was used in greater numbers toward the end of the war. After 1945 countless air forces put the P-51 into service, as they could be acquired cheaply from US stocks. The Americans themselves used the P-51 again, this time in the Korean War, where it served as a fighter bomber. The Israelis also used P-51s, as in the 1956 Suez War, and the P-51 remained in service in Latin American countries until the 1980s. A total of 15,586 P-51s were produced, including all the different variants, some of which were produced under license in Australia.

A Mustang Mark I of No. 414 Squadron RCAF, Dunsfold (Surrey), early 1943.

A P-51B of the 8th US Air Force, England, June 1944.

NORTHROP P-61 BLACK WIDOW

A P-61A during a test flight in California. At first this model was plagued with serious problems.

The Northrop P-61 Black Widow was the first combat aircraft in the USAAF specifically developed as a night fighter. It was made entirely of metal, and its frame had two long engine gondolas on which the tail was mounted. In 1940, prompted by the German night raids on the United Kingdom, the US Army Air Force ordered a night fighter fitted with radar. By this time, the British had successfully installed an autonomous radar system, the Airborne Intercept (AI) radar, in some of their aircraft. Using data about this device, the Americans developed an improved version which could be installed in the new night fighter.

Northrop introduced a first prototype in May 1942, but various problems prevented serial production until mid-1944. In particular, the machine gun turret on top of the frame caused dangerous vibrations when the guns were fired. But once these problems had been solved, the P-61 proved to be an excellent night fighter, and it was deployed very successfully in Europe and the Pacific. It could also carry an acceptable payload, so it was also deployed as a bomber. Yet, although it had good flying characteristics and shot down a relatively large number of enemy aircraft, only 742 aircraft of this type (including the F-15 Reporter reconnaissance version) were produced, largely because it appeared shortly before the end of the war and was replaced by jet aircraft. The main production model was the P-61B, and there was a P-61C high-speed version, but just 15 of these were delivered to the USAAF. The last P-61s were taken out of service in 1950.

P-61B	
Type:	Night fighter and fighter bomber
Crew:	2–3
Weight when empty/ max weight at takeoff:	23,430 lb/ 36,167 lb
Length/wingspan/height:	50.4 ft/67 ft/14.9 ft
Engine(s):	Two Pratt & Whitney R 2800 65 Double Wasp 18-cylinder radial engines with 2,000 hp each
Maximum speed:	366 mph at 20,300 ft
Service ceiling:	38,300 ft
Range:	2,995 miles with extra fuel tanks
Weaponry:	4 x 0.8 in automatic cannon fixed in the chin (under the nose), 4 x 0.5 in Browning machine guns in a remote-controlled dorsal installation, and an external payload of max. 6,396 lb, e.g., four extra fuel tanks, bombs, or 5 in rockets

CHANCE-VOUGHT F4U CORSAIR

An F4U-1A of the US Navy VF-17 Squadron, Solomon Islands, in December 1943.

	F4U-1
Type:	Carrier-borne fighter and fighter bomber
Crew:	1
Weight when empty/ max weight at takeoff:	8,974 lb/ 13,987 lb
Length/wingspan/height:	33.9 ft/41.7 ft/16.3 ft
Engine(s):	One Pratt & Whitney R 2800 8 Double Wasp 18-cylinder radial engine with 2,000 hp
Maximum speed:	417 mph at 20,300 ft
Service ceiling:	37,490 ft
Range:	1,015 miles
Weaponry:	6 x 0.5 in Browning machine guns or 4 x 0.8 in automatic cannon fixed in the wings, and an external payload of max. 2,000 lb, e.g., two 1,000 lb bombs or six 5 in rockets

An FG-1D Corsair Mark IV of No. 1841 Fleet Air Arm Squadron based on HMS Formidable, the Pacific, August 1945.

The Chance-Vought F4U Corsair is rated by many experts as the best naval combat aircraft in the Second World War. It was deployed by the US Marine Corps and the US Navy, and most Commonwealth countries also flew F4Us. It was designed, above all, for minimal air resistance and maximum speed, using the most powerful engine available at the time. So the Pratt & Whitney R-2800 was installed in the smallest possible air frame. To convert the engine's 2,000 hp into high-speed forward motion, the propeller needed a diameter of more than 13 ft (4 m). The undercarriage (which had a rear wheel) was also very long, making it very unstable, which was hardly ideal for a carrier-borne aircraft. But its designers came up with a ruse to counteract this problem, giving the aircraft its distinctive gull wings. The prototype made its maiden flight on May 29, 1940, but initially it was not possible to fly the aircraft from carriers, as its engine required a large engine cowling in front of the cockpit, which seriously restricted forward visibility, so the cockpit was raised by about 6 inches (152.4 mm) and the F4U was put into service. Even then, the engine created such a high turning moment during takeoff that it was hard to keep the aircraft on track, which was sometimes too much for inexperienced pilots to handle. This earned the F4U the nicknames "Ensign Killer" and "Ensign Eliminator." Nevertheless, once it was airborne, the F4U was a feared combat aircraft, equally suited to aerial combat and ground attack operations. The F4U-1 Corsair was manufactured under license by Goodyear (as the FG-1) and Brewster (which called it the F3A-1), and production continued until 1952. The Corsair was deployed by the Americans in the Korean War and by the French Naval Air Force, and even when they were taken out of service, many smaller air forces acquired them.

A French Navy Corsair, flown until the 1960s.

DOUGLAS TBD DEVASTATOR

The Douglas Devastator.

TBD-1	
Type:	Carrier-borne torpedo bomber
Crew:	3
Weight when empty/max weight at takeoff:	6,176 lb/ 10,185 lb
Length/wingspan/height:	35.6 ft/50.8 ft/15.3 ft
Engine(s):	One Pratt & Whitney R 1830 8 Twin Wasp radial engine with 900 hp
Maximum speed:	206 mph at 7,465 ft
Service ceiling:	20,015 ft
Range:	435 miles with a torpedo/714 miles with a 1,000 lb payload
Weaponry:	1 x 0.3 in or 0.5 in Browning machine gun fixed in the nose, 1 x 0.3 in machine gun in the rear of the cockpit, and a 21 in torpedo or 1,000 lb bomb carried externally below the fuselage

The Douglas TBD Devastator was the US Navy's first single-wing torpedo bomber and the first all-metal aircraft with hydraulically folding wings in the world. The prototype flew for the first time on April 15, 1935, and in 1937 Douglas delivered the first of 129 machines. Until 1941 the Devastator was the standard American carrier-borne torpedo bomber, but by that time it was clearly no longer the navy's ideal choice, and its successor, the TBF Avenger, was already being developed. During the Battle of the Coral Sea, May 7–8, 1942, the Devastator helped to sink a Japanese aircraft carrier, but it was deployed for the last time in the Battle of Midway (June 4–7, 1942) when 41 TBDs launched an attack on a Japanese aircraft carrier, only to be shot down one by one by A6M Zero fighters, so the remaining Devastators were taken out of service immediately afterwards. Nevertheless, because the Zero fighters were preoccupied with the TBDs, high-flying Douglas SBD dive-bombers were able to sink or severely damage three Japanese carriers, while suffering only minor losses.

GRUMMAN TBF AVENGER

TBM-3	
Type:	Carrier-borne torpedo bomber, bomber and reconnaissance aircraft
Crew:	3
Weight when empty/ max weight at takeoff:	10,544 lb/ 18,233 lb
Length/wingspan/height:	133.5 ft/42.2 ft/13.1 ft
Engine(s):	One Wright Cyclone R 2600 20 14-cylinder radial engine with 1,750 hp
Maximum speed:	267 mph at 15,235 ft
Service ceiling:	23,765 ft
Range:	1,130 miles
Weaponry:	2 x 0.5 in Browning machine guns in the wings, 1 x 0.5 in Browning machine gun in the dorsal turret, 1 x 0.3 in Browning waist machine gun, and an internal payload of max. 2,000 lb

The TBM-3 Avenger.

The first TBFs were put into service in January 1942, just one month after Pearl Harbor. Although Grumman had no experience of building them, the company received an order for a torpedo bomber on April 8, 1940. The all-metal prototype flew for the first time on August 1, 1941. Although Grumman were working flat out to produce the TBF, the navy still needed more machines, so General Motors took over some of the production (TBFs produced there were known as TBMs). A total of 9,836 Avengers were built by Grumman and General Motors. The most important model in the series was initially the TBF-1 (or TBM-1), which was delivered to navy squadrons from early 1942. The TBF-3 (or TBM-3), which was put into service in mid-1944, was fitted with radar and could carry 5 inch (127 mm) rockets under its wings. Over 900 TBF/TBM aircraft were delivered to the Royal Navy, which initially renamed them Mark I Tarpoons, only to revert to calling them Mark I Avengers, and 63 were delivered to the New Zealand Air Force. As well as torpedo and bombing raids, Avengers also flew reconnaissance and anti-submarine missions.

DOUGLAS SBD DAUNTLESS

The Douglas SBD Dauntless.

	SBD-6
Type:	Carrier-borne dive bomber and reconnaissance aircraft
Crew:	2
Weight when empty/ max weight at takeoff:	6,529 lb/ 9,511 lb
Length/wingspan/height:	33.5 ft/42.2 ft/13.1 ft
Engine(s):	One Wright Cyclone R 1820 66 radial engine with 1,350 hp
Maximum speed:	255 mph at 14,215 ft
Service ceiling:	25,600 ft
Range:	775 miles
Weaponry:	2 x fixed 0.5 in Browning machine guns, 2 x 0.5 in Browning machine guns, and a payload of max. 1,678 lb under the fuselage, and max. 650 lb under the wings

The Douglas SBD Dauntless was the most successful American dive-bomber. The order was given to put it into serial production in April 1939, and the first squadrons were ready to go into service from late 1940. The Dauntless contributed in part to America's victory over the Japanese Navy, and it served the Americans well until late 1944. It distinguished itself in the Battle of the Coral Sea (May 7–8, 1942) and in the Battle of Midway (June 4–7, 1942), when it managed to sink three Japanese aircraft carriers. Because they could withstand heavy fire, fewer SBDs were lost in the Pacific than any other American aircraft type. The Douglas A-24 Banshee was a land-based version of the Dauntless, and 500 A-24s were delivered to the USAAF from 1940 to 1942, but it proved to be less successful than its carrier-borne counterpart. A total of 5,936 SBDs were manufactured before production was halted in July 1944.

CURTISS SB2C HELLDIVER

The Curtiss SB2C Helldiver was arguably one of the worst aircraft ever to be manufactured in large numbers. The US Navy and Curtiss had expected very good things from this model, but it was beset with developmental problems and was not put into service until November 11, 1943, though the all-metal prototype with folding wings had first flown in 1940! The latter was destroyed in a crash, just days prior to Pearl Harbor, and because the accident was investigated, and the aircraft was redesigned in the light of combat experience, the first production model of the new aircraft did not fly until June 1942. 900 A-25As (as they were now called) were delivered to the USAAF and 26 to the British, but the latter decided that they were unsuitable and never used them. The Helldiver was ponderous and had a few unpleasant characteristics, especially when taking off and landing; unlike the Dauntless, it was far from popular. In spite of this, around 7,000 Helldivers were produced in total, and it remained in service after 1945.

For as long as it was in service, the Helldiver was plagued with problems.

	SB2C-3
Type:	Carrier-borne dive bomber and reconnaissance aircraft
Crew:	2
Weight when empty/ max weight at takeoff:	6,529 lb/ 9,511 lb
Length/wingspan/height:	33.5 ft/42.2 ft/13.1 ft
Engine(s):	One Wright Cyclone R 2600 20 14-cylinder radial engine with 1,900 hp
Maximum speed:	293 mph at 17,265 ft
Service ceiling:	27,135 ft
Range:	1,200 miles
Weaponry:	2 x fixed 0.8 in automatic cannons, 2 x 0.3 in Browning machine guns, and a payload of max. 2,000 lb internally, and max. 1,000 lb under the wings

DOUGLAS A-20 BOSTON/HAVOC

	A-20B
Type:	Light bomber
Crew:	3
Max weight at takeoff:	20,711 lb
Length/wingspan/height:	48 ft/62.3 ft/18.2 ft
Engine(s):	Two Wright Cyclone R 2600 3 14-cylinder radial engines with 1,600 hp each
Maximum speed:	304 mph at 10,165 ft
Service ceiling:	26,700 ft
Range:	1,555 miles
Weaponry:	4 x 0.3 in or 2 x 0.5 in Browning machine guns fixed laterally on the nose, 2 x 0.3 in Browning machine guns in the rear of the cockpit, and an internal payload of max. 2,000 lb

An A-20B in the USAAF. Note the DB-7 series' slender fuselage.

Douglas A-20, known in the factory as the DB-7, was the most important light bomber in the USAAF and was also flown by almost all the Allied air forces. The night fighter developed from the A-20 was called the P-70, and the DB-7 was also used as a reconnaissance aircraft. Its development began in 1937, and the prototype made its maiden flight on October 26, 1938. Although it met all the USAAF's requirements for a new light twin-engine bomber, the air force showed no interest in it at first. France was the first customer for the new aircraft in 1939, placing an order for 100 planes,

which was increased to 170 after the war broke out, but only 70 had been delivered by the time of the German invasion. Some planes were lost, a large number escaped to Britain or formed part of the Vichy regime's air force. But most of the aircraft ordered by the French remained in America or were delivered to the RAF, which urgently required bombers and night fighters and called the Douglas machines the Boston and the Havoc. The first version to be produced in large numbers was the A-208, which was also ordered by the United States Army Air Corps (USAAC). The variant of which

most were manufactured was the A-20G (2,850 were built), which had a fixed nose with six 0.5 inch (12.7 mm) machine guns, a payload of 4,000 lb (1,816 kg), and a motorized machine gun installation on the fuselage.

Until September 1944, 7,385 machines in the DB-7 series were manufactured, including the P-70 night fighter version. Numerous DB-7s were also delivered to the Soviet Union, as part of the two countries' hiring and loaning agreement.

A Douglas A-20B in the USAAF. The A-20 performed superbly for as long as it was in service. But its first-class aerodynamics were to blame for one of this series' main drawbacks: the fuselage was so narrow that crew members could not change positions in mid-flight. If the pilot was hit, this could be fatal. Hence, the glazed-nose A-20 was fitted with rudimentary controls on the bombardier's side.

DOUGLAS A-26 INVADER

	A-26B
Type:	Light bomber
Crew:	3
Weight when empty/	22,830 lb/
max weight at takeoff:	34,949 lb
Length/wingspan/height:	50.8 ft/71.1 ft/18.8 ft
Engine(s):	Two Pratt & Whitney R 2800 27 Double Wasp 18-cylinder radial engines with 2,000 hp each
Maximum speed:	355 mph at 15,235 ft
Service ceiling:	25,600 ft
Range:	1,400 miles
Weaponry:	6 x 0.5 in Browning machine guns fixed in the nose, and 4 x 0.5 in Browning machine guns in remote-controlled installations and a combined payload of max. 4,000 lb

The Douglas A-26 Invader was designed as a successor to the A-20. Its prototype flew for the first time on July 10, 1942, and it was put into serial production in April 1944. The 9th US Air Fleet, which deployed Invaders, flew its first missions in Europe in November 1944, and the Invader was also deployed shortly afterwards in the Pacific. Until the end of the war, the A-26 flew around 11,000 more

The A-26 remained in service in the USAF after 1945.

missions in Europe. It was the most maneuverable US bomber in the war, and its pilots were delighted, claiming that it handled just like a fighter. Two main versions were built during the war: the A-26B, which had a fixed nose and six fixed 0.5 inch (12.7 mm) machine guns, and the A-26C, which had a glazed nose to house a bombardier (bomb dropper). A total of 1,355 A-26Bs and A-26Cs were produced. The Invader was also intensively flown in Korea and Vietnam.

MARTIN B-26 MARAUDER

The Martin B-26 Marauder was the second American medium-range bomber to be put into service. The prototype had its maiden flight on November 25, 1940, and its unusual nose undercarriage, heavy wings, and fast landing speed led to considerable problems. Inexperienced pilots could only control the B-26 with serious difficulty, and it crashed frequently, earning it the nickname "Widow Maker." This was not really fair, as fewer than 1% of all B-26s were lost, the lowest figure for any US bomber. The Marauder specialized in precision attacks on air bases, bridges, railroad installations, depots, and similar targets, proving to be unusually bulletproof and robust. Most B-26 missions were flown in Europe and the Mediterranean, where these machines flew 129,943 missions and dropped 166,706 tons (169,382 tonnes) of bombs. In addition, the Marauder's defensive gunners shot down 402 enemy fighters.

The B-26A Marauder.

As well as the USAAF, the RAF and Free French Air Force flew the B-26. A total of 5,157 B-26s was built, including all the different models (which did not vary significantly).

	B-26B
Type:	Medium-range bomber
Crew:	5–7
Weight when empty/	24,198 lb/
max weight at takeoff:	36,967 lb
Length/wingspan/height:	59.2 ft/72.1 ft/21.8 ft
Engine(s):	Two Pratt & Whitney R 2800 43 Double Wasp 18-cylinder radial engines with 1,920 hp each
Maximum speed:	282 mph at 15,235 ft
Service ceiling:	21,300 ft
Range:	1,150 miles
Weaponry:	5 x fixed and 1 x mobile 0.5 in Browning machine guns in the nose, 6 x 0.5 in Browning machine guns and an internal payload of max. 5,196 lb

NORTH AMERICAN B-25 MITCHELL

	B-25J
Type:	Medium-range bomber
Crew:	5
Weight when empty/ max weight at takeoff:	19,463 lb/ 34,969 lb
Length/wingspan/height:	53.8 ft/68.7 ft/16.6 ft
Engine(s):	Two Pratt & Whitney R 2800 43 Double Wasp 18-cylinder radial engines with 1,920 hp each
Maximum speed:	282 mph at 15,235 ft
Service ceiling:	21,300 ft
Range:	1,150 miles
Weaponry:	5 x 0.5 in fixed machine guns in the nose, 6 x 0.5 in machine guns—two in the dorsal turret, two in the tail turret, and one on each side—an internal payload of max. 2,998 lb, and eight 5 in rockets externally

The B-25J, which was armed with 12 0.5 inch (12.7 mm) machine guns, was the final model in this series.

The North American B-25 Mitchell was the most important American medium-range bomber in the Second World War, and more than 12,000 were deployed in almost all the Allied air forces. The B-25 was developed following an order from the USAAF, and it flew for the first time in January 1939. The first production models were delivered in August 1940, named after General Billy Mitchell, and the B-25's best known mission was Lieutenant Colonel James Doolittle's raid on Tokyo, known simply as the "Doolittle Raid," on April 18, 1942. 16 B-25Bs took off from the USS *Hornet* aircraft carrier, but they were too large to land on it, so they had to reach China, which they almost all managed to do. Although the raid did not cause any severe damage, it ensured that to protect their country from then on, the Japanese kept interceptor fighters on constant standby, which reduced the number which could be used on the front line. All the versions

The prototype of the B-25G, which had a 3 inch (75 mm) cannon and two 0.5 inch (12.7 mm) machine guns in the nose. Because the cannon had to be reloaded manually, this model was unsuccessful. The B-25 was not a convincing anti-naval aircraft until the introduction of the H model, which had an automatic reloading mechanism.

A B-25C from the 9th US Air Force, Tunisia, April 1943.

The B-25B flown by Lieutenant Colonel Doolittle in the Tokyo bombing raid on April 18, 1942.

from A–D were similar, differing only in their engine specifications or their defensive weapon configurations. The B-25G was notable for the heavy weaponry in its nose (one 3 inch (75 mm) cannon and two 0.5 inch (12.7 mm) machine guns), and the B-25H was even more heavily armed, with one 3 inch (75 mm) cannon and eight 0.5 inch (12.7 mm) machine guns, or just 12 0.5 inch (12.7 mm) machine guns, in its nose. This version could also carry 5 inch (127 mm) rockets under its outer wing, and it was especially successful in anti-naval operations in the Pacific. The Mitchell was also deployed in the Mediterranean from mid-1942 and in Western Europe from early 1943. The Soviet Union and the United Kingdom also received relatively large numbers of Mitchells as part of their hiring and loaning agreements with America. The B-25 remained in service beyond the end of the war, and the last USAAF Mitchell was not taken out of service until 1960.

CONSOLIDATED PBY CATALINA

	PBY-5A
Type:	Sea reconnaissance, air-sea rescue and anti-submarine amphibious aircraft
Crew:	9
Weight when empty/ max weight at takeoff:	21,773 lb/ 36,579 lb
Length/wingspan/height:	64.9 ft/105.7 ft/20.5 ft
Engine(s):	Two Pratt & Whitney R 1830 92 Twin Wasp radial engines with 1,200 hp each
Maximum speed:	196 mph
Service ceiling:	13,300 ft
Range:	2,510 miles
Weaponry:	5 x Browning machine guns—2 x 0.3 in, 1 x 0.3 in, and 2 x 0.5 in machine guns—and an external payload of max. 4,000 lb

A Consolidated PBY-5A of the US Coast Guard in 1945 in San Francisco.

The Consolidated PBY Catalina was the Allies' most important sea reconnaissance seaplane, deployed by the US Marines, the Royal Navy, various Commonwealth countries, and the Soviet Naval Air Force. The Catalina made its maiden flight in 1935, and the PBY-1 first flew as a US Navy aircraft in October 1936.

The PBY-4, which was powered by 1,200 hp twin wasp engines and had a moulded perspex cockpit for the observer or gunner on the rear section of the fuselage, was introduced in 1938. The Catalina was made entirely of metal, with very high wings to protect the engine from spray, and it had retractable auxiliary floats in its wings, an unusual feature. The PBY-5, which was introduced in 1940, could also take off and land on land or sea. Because of its considerable range, the PBY was perfectly suited for both long-range reconnaissance and naval convoy protection missions. In May 1941 a Catalina discovered the *Bismarck* and led the Royal Navy to it. More than 3,300 Catalinas were produced in total; it was manufactured in the largest numbers of any seaplane.

BOEING B-17 FLYING FORTRESS

An excellent photograph of a B-17. This one is still airworthy today and features in many air shows. The photograph at the top of the facing page was also taken at an air show.

	B-17G
Type:	Heavy bomber
Crew:	8–10
Weight when empty/ max weight at takeoff:	32,720 lb/ 65,419 lb
Length/wingspan/height:	76 ft/105.4 ft/19.5 ft
Engine(s):	Four Wright R 1820 97 Cyclone 9-cylinder engines with 1,200 hp each
Maximum speed:	300 mph at 15,200 ft
Service ceiling:	39,700 ft
Range:	3,750 miles without bombs, 1,095 miles with maximum payload
Weaponry:	12 x 0.5 in Browning machine guns—two in the chin turret, two in the rear turret, two in the waist turret, and one each in four lateral positions in the nose, in the middle of the fuselage, and in the tail—and an internal payload of max. 12,775 lb

The Boeing B-17 Flying Fortress is one of the best known American combat aircraft of the Second World War, second only to the P-51 Mustang. Along with the B-24, the B-17 carried out the majority of bomber attacks on occupied Europe with the 8th US Air Fleet. The prototype of the B-17 made its maiden flight on July 18, 1935.

This model was originally designed to patrol the American coast, so early models did not really merit the name

"Flying Fortress." At first the designers believed that the model would certainly reach high speeds and altitudes, because it was the first turbocharged bomber in the world. But the RAF's experience in Europe prompted a different approach: the E version (which made its maiden flight on September 5, 1941) was redesigned with stronger armor and heavier firepower, and its side fins were moved further forward. The 8th US Air Fleet's first operation in occupied

Europe was a daylight raid in France on August 17, 1942. The B-17E, of which 512 were built, seated 10 men, and two versions based upon it were built from May 1942 to July 1945 by Boeing, Douglas, and Lockheed. The F-series, of which 3,405 were produced, had even stronger armor and heavier weaponry than its predecessor, and it was first deployed on January 27, 1943. From the fall of 1943, the G version was the most important model in the series, and 8,680

Bei dieser B-17G wurden Kinn- und Unterrumpfturm entfernt, statt-dessen trägt die Maschine eine Radarkuppel unter dem Rumpf.

were manufactured. To protect it from frontal attacks from fighters, it had a third, remote-controlled turret under its nose, and with a total of thirteen 0.5 inch (12.7 mm) Browning machine guns, it was the most heavily armed version of the B-17. Flying Fortresses flew into battle in a tight formation (a "battle box") and welcomed oncoming German fighters with a hail of heavy machine gun fire. But they suffered heavy losses when deployed without a fighter escort. For example, when they raided a ball bearing factory in Schweinfurt and the Messerschmidt factory in Regensburg, 60 out of 376 bombers were shot down, and another 176 were more or less severely damaged. Consequently, the USAAF suspended all unaccompanied bombing raids in the fall of 1943, and they were not resumed until early 1944, when they were escorted by the new Mustang fighters. The Flying Fortress could survive very heavy fire, was easy to maneuver, and was very popular with its crews because it was so reliable.

There were also special variants of the B-17: a photo reconnaissance aircraft, an air-sea rescue aircraft, and a VIP transporter. It also served as a patrol and weather reconnaissance for British Coastal Command, which just called it the "Fortress." The Luftwaffe also flew a few which they had seized for demonstration purposes, to instruct its fighters. It was also called the Do 200 and used as a spy transporter in the 200th German Bomber Wing. 12,731 B-17s were manufactured; when production was at its peak, 16 were being built daily.

A B-17G with open bomb bay.

This B-17G had no chin or ventral turret—instead, it was fitted with radar under the fuselage.

A BIT Ó LACE

The Boeing B-17G was the standard model in the final months of the war.

USA

BOEING B-29 SUPERFORTRESS

	B-29
Type:	Heavy bomber
Crew:	10
Weight when empty/ max weight at takeoff:	70,077 lb/ 123,888 lb
Length/wingspan/height:	100.6 ft/143.5 ft/30.1 ft
Engine(s):	Four Wright R 3350 23 23A 41 97 Cyclone turbocharged radial engines with 2,200 hp each
Maximum speed:	358 mph at 25,400 ft
Service ceiling:	34,000 ft
Range:	3,230 miles
Weaponry:	8 x 0.5 in Browning machine guns—two in each of four remote-controlled installations on the top and bottom of the fuselage—3 x 0.5 in Browning machine guns or two machine guns and one 0.8 in automatic cannon in a manned tail position

The B-29 had an extensive array of defensive weaponry, but its weapons were often removed in 1945, as there was no longer any threat from enemy fighters.

The Boeing B-29 Superfortress was the largest and highest performing bomber to be deployed in the Second World War, and its maximum takeoff weight—including an internal payload of 19,982 lb (9,072 kg)—was more than twice that of the B-17. The origins of the B-29 date back to 1940, when the USA expected the United Kingdom to fall to the Germans, prompting the Americans to develop a long-range bomber that could strike at targets in Europe. Boeing's design for the aircraft broke new ground technologically: it was the first plane in the world to have a pressurized cabin as standard. It also had four aerodynamically efficient weapons installations, which were remote controlled by gunners in the fuselage. B-29s built by Bell even had radar fitted in the rear section. In short, constructing the B-29 was the most complex and comprehensive production program that there had ever been. Thousands of subcontractors contributed components and parts to a complex aircraft, which—as could only have been expected—had to overcome some initial problems. The B-29 prototype made its maiden flight on September 21, 1942.

Its wings had a high aspect ratio and were fitted with enormous Fowler flaps to minimize its landing speed. But initially there were severe problems with the cooler for the Wright radial engines. The first models were delivered in 1943, but they were not deployed in combat until June 1944.

Because of its considerable range, the B-29 was exclusively deployed in the Pacific. At first, it carried out high altitude precision raids on Japanese industrial targets by day, but these were mostly unsuccessful on account of unfavorable weather and wind conditions. After General LeMay took command of the USAAF, however, he changed tactics and deployed B-29s for night raids instead. Because precision raids were even harder by night than by day, they flew at low altitudes and carpet-bombed Japanese cities, which were made largely of wood, killing hundreds of thousands of people. The most devastating of these raids was the bombing of Tokyo, in which more people probably died in one night than in the atomic bomb attack on Hiroshima, which was also carried out by a B-29 (as was the attack on Nagasaki). By the end of the war, 2,132 Superfortresses had been delivered to the USAAF, but production continued after 1945, and a total of 3,790 B-29s were built.

The B-29's clean lines can be seen clearly in this photograph.

CURTISS C-46 COMMANDO

	C-46
Type:	Transporter
Crew:	4
Weight when empty/ max weight at takeoff:	29,300 lb/ 51,000 lb
Length/wingspan/height:	79.9 ft/109.7 ft/22.1 ft
Engine(s):	Two Pratt & Whitney R 2800 34 Double Wasp radial engines with 2,000 hp each
Maximum speed:	245 mph at 13,300 ft
Service ceiling:	28,040 ft
Range:	1,800 miles
Capacity:	Up to 40 people or an equivalent freight load

A Curtiss C-46 flying over the Chinese mountains.

The Curtiss C-46 Commando was the military version of the Curtiss CW-20 civil aircraft. It was unusual in that its fuselage was made up of two circular segments, which meant that there was enough room for passengers and freight. From the front the frame looked like a figure of eight. After Pearl Harbor the USAAF established that it urgently needed transporter aircraft, so it duly ordered the Curtis 200 CW-20B (its military designation was the C-46A Commando). It had a side door for loading freight and a stronger cabin floor, as well as folding seats, and models from the C-46B onward were powered by Pratt & Whitney R-2800 engines. Because of its range and robustness, the Commando was deployed primarily in Asia and the Pacific, and the US Marines called it the RSC-1. The C-46 also served after 1945—for instance, in the Berlin Airlift and the Korean War—and the last C-46s were not taken out of service until 1955. Even nowadays, ex-military C-46 aircraft are flown as civil aircraft in the developing world.

DOUGLAS C-47 SKYTRAIN/DAKOTA

The Douglas C-47 Skytrain was a military version of the Douglas DC-3. The DC-3 made its maiden flight in December 1935 and was a very innovative aircraft for its time; it is still in service (to some extent) today. The C-47 had a stronger cabin floor, more powerful engine, and larger freight doors, than the DC-3, and it was the Allies' most important transporter aircraft in the Second World War. It was used as a transporter, a tug, an air ambulance, and a passenger aircraft, and was also used to release paratroopers. It could carry a freight load up to 5,996 lb (2,722 kg) or 28–35 people. The RAF called their C-47s the "Dakota," and there were also many different designations for this type in the USA—for example, the US Navy called it the R4D. There was also a special freight version with a wider double cargo door to facilitate loading and unloading, and countless other variants. The DC-3 was built under license by the Soviets, who used it intensively during the war, as the Lisunov Li-2, and Nakajima also built a few variants of the DC-3 for military use. Even after 1945, the C-47 remained in service for a long time throughout the world; for instance, the Americans flew them in the Berlin Airlift.

A C47-A of the 9th US Air Force, England, June 1944.

	C-47A
Type:	Transporter
Crew:	4
Weight when empty/ max weight at takeoff:	16,850 lb/ 25,990 lb
Length/wingspan/height:	65.5 ft/96.5 ft/17.2 ft
Engine(s):	Two Pratt & Whitney R 1830 92 Twin Wasp radial engines with 1,200 hp each
Maximum speed:	229 mph at 9,835 ft
Service ceiling:	23,565 ft
Range:	2,125 miles

SHIPS

GERMANY

U-486

U-486 was sunk off Bergen on April 12, 1945.

The 700-plus type VII U-boats built in a number of different versions between 1935 and 1945 formed the backbone of the German Navy's U-boat fleet. The different models were designated A to F of which VIIC was produced in the largest numbers (663) and bore the brunt of the war in the Atlantic and Mediterranean. At first these submarines achieved great success but as Allied countermeasures such as radar and ASDIC/sonar improved, and the seas were more systematically patrolled from the air, losses increased. From 1942–43 onward, the number of anti-aircraft guns carried by the U-boats was significantly increased and the 3.5 inch (88 mm) gun often removed. Numbers of 0.8 inch (20 mm) and 1.5 inch (37 mm) anti-aircraft guns were mounted on the aft of the vessel in single, twin, or sometimes even quadruple configurations. A strengthening of the pressure hull enabled the diving depth to be increased to 660 feet (200 m) and retractable snorkels started to be fitted in 1943. This allowed the batteries to be recharged while the U-boat was submerged and enabled large distances to be covered safely using the diesel engine. In addition, passive radar warning receivers were designed to ensure that threats were identified in good time. Nonetheless, of a total of 40,600 U-boat crew, 30,246 failed to return and 5,338 were taken prisoner. Although 2,882 merchant vessels—for a total of over 14 million GRT (gross registered tonnage)—and 175 warships were sunk by German U-boats, 784 out of 863 submarines were lost.

U-486 went on only two patrols in the North Sea and English Channel, sinking four ships totaling around 20,000 GRT before being sunk by British submarine HMS *Tapir* on April 12, 1945.

	Type VIIC U-boat
Commissioned:	04.22.1944
Fate:	sunk by torpedoes from British submarine HMS *Tapir* off Bergen on 04.12.1945
Displacement:	790 tons/871 tons submerged
Length/beam/draft:	220 ft 2 in/20 ft 4 in/15 ft 9 in
Armor sides/deck:	none
Engines (surfaced/submerged):	two MAN diesel engines delivering 3,200 hp/two electric motors delivering 750 hp
Maximum speed:	17.6 knots (7.6 knots submerged)
Range:	8,500 nm at 10 knots surfaced/80 nm at 4 knots submerged
Crew:	44 (later up to 57 due to increasing number of anti-aircraft guns)
Armament:	4 x forward and 1 x stern 21 in torpedo tubes (14 torpedoes or mines), 1 x 3.5 in gun and 1 x 0.8 in anti-aircraft guns
Diving depth:	330 ft

U-35 was a type VIIA submarine sunk in the North Sea by British destroyers on November 29, 1939.

U-107

U-107 was a type IXB U-boat.

With over 200 vessels in seven different variants, type IX was the second largest class of U-boat in the German Navy. Because of its good seafaring capability and extensive range (initially 10,500 nm and in the later variants 31,500 nm at 10 knots), type IX was deployed predominantly off the US coast, in the South Atlantic and in the Indian Ocean. As with type VII, the different variants represented successive improvements to the original version, even if the differences were slight. Type IX was also equipped with a snorkel and its anti-aircraft capability was steadily increased during the course of the war. *U-107* was built in 1940 and sank 39 ships for a total of 216,795 GRT during its 14 patrols. She was sunk with the loss of her entire crew on August 18, 1944 west of La Rochelle by a British Sunderland.

Type IXB U-boat	
Commissioned:	10.08.1940
Fate:	sunk in the Atlantic on 08.18.1944
Displacement:	1,051 tons/1,178 tons submerged
Length/beam/draft:	250 ft 11 in/22 ft 2 in /15 ft 5 in
Armor sides/deck:	none
Engines (surfaced/ submerged):	two MAN diesel engines delivering 4,400 hp /two electric motors delivering 1,000 hp
Maximum speed:	18.2 knots (7.7 knots submerged)
Range:	12,000 nm at 10 knots surfaced/80 nm at 4 knots submerged
Crew:	48 (later up to 60 due to increasing number of anti-aircraft guns)
Armament:	4 x forward and 1 x stern 21 in torpedo tubes (22 torpedoes or 6 torpedoes and 32 mines), 1 x 4.1 in, 1 x 1.5 in and 1 x 0.8 in anti-aircraft guns
Diving depth:	500 ft

U-2511

Type XXI U-boat	
Commissioned:	09.29.1944
Fate:	surrendered to the United Kingdom at the end of the war
Displacement:	1,610 tons/1,833 tons submerged
Length/beam/draft:	250 ft 11 in/22 ft 2 in/22 ft 7 in
Armor sides/deck:	none
Engines (surfaced/ submerged):	two MAN diesel engines delivering 4,000 hp/two electric motors delivering 5,000 hp and two electric motors for stealth maneuvers delivering 226 hp
Maximum speed:	15.5 knots (17.5 knots submerged)
Range:	14,000 nm at 10 knots surfaced/420 nm at 4 knots submerged
Crew:	57
Armament:	6 x forward 21 in torpedo tubes (23 torpedoes or 17 torpedoes and 12 mines), 4 x 1.2 in or 0.8 in anti-aircraft guns
Diving depth:	660 ft

The type XXI, also known as the *Elektroboot*, was intended to restore the U-boats' command of the seas. In order to achieve a greater underwater speed, the hulls and conning towers of these boats were streamlined and the performance of the electric motors and batteries dramatically increased. Type XXI boats also boasted a fast torpedo reload device and comprehensive sonar and electronics systems. To speed up production, the boats were designed to be pre-manufactured inland and assembled at the coast. Because of their numerous technical innovations, however, there were serious delays in the production program. Although an order for 200 units (later increased to 1,300) was given in June 1943, by the end of the war only 113 had been commissioned. The type XXI pointed the way forward for U-boat construction and many of the features developed for this class of submarine were adopted in post-1945 vessels. *U-2511* completed just one patrol before being captured by the British in Norway.

U-2511.

CLASS S-12 AND S-100 SCHNELLBOOTE (E-BOATS)

The German Navy's torpedo boats (*Schnellboote* or *S-Boote*) were known to the Allies as E-boats (an abbreviation of "enemy boat") and are widely regarded as excellent examples of their type. Because the Versailles Treaty had imposed severe restrictions on the German Navy, considerable energy was devoted to the development of these fast patrol boats as they were not covered by it. Different classes of E-boat, which nevertheless resembled each other closely, were built from 1933 onward. All had a wooden hull and aluminum frame, two forward torpedo tubes, and three diesel (generally Mercedes-Benz) engines. Their anti-aircraft defenses were continually upgraded as aircraft gradually took over as the main threat. The most important type from 1943 onward was the S-100 class, of which 74 had been built by the end of the war. Vessels of the S-100 class had an armored bridge to help them withstand air attack. Around 200 E-boats of all types were built. They were used mainly to attack coastal shipping around the British Isles at night but were also deployed in the Mediterranean and Black Seas. From around 1943 the main burden of the surface war at sea fell to the E-boat fleet as the German Navy's larger ships had either already been destroyed or could no longer operate with any realistic prospect of success. Losses of E-boat crew were correspondingly high although the boats themselves proved extremely robust.

	S12 (S-7 Class)	S-100 Class
Commissioned:	08.31.1935	–
Fate:	surrendered to USA at the end of the war	–
Displacement:	92 tons	122 tons
Length/beam/draft:	104 ft 8 in/16 ft 1 in/3 ft 11 in	114 ft 8 in/17 ft 4 in/5 ft 6 in
Armor sides/deck:	none	bridge, 0.5 in
Engines:	three MB502 diesel engines delivering 3,960 hp	three MB501A/511 diesel engines delivering 7,500 hp
Maximum speed:	37 knots	42 knots
Range:	600 nm	700 nm
Crew:	22	30–32
Armament:	2 x 21 in torpedo tubes, (2 torpedoes), 1 x 0.8 in anti-aircraft gun, 1 x 0.3 in MG	2 x 21 in torpedo tubes (4 torpedoes), 1 x 0.8 in anti-aircraft gun, on the forecastle 1 x 0.8 in double anti-aircraft gun midships and 1 x 1.5 in or 1.6 in anti-aircraft gun aft

An E-boat of the 100 Class. The panther was the emblem of the 4th Schnellboot Flotilla.

S-12 in the Baltic before the war. This vessel survived the war unscathed and went to the Americans as war booty.

Z 4 RICHARD BEITZEN

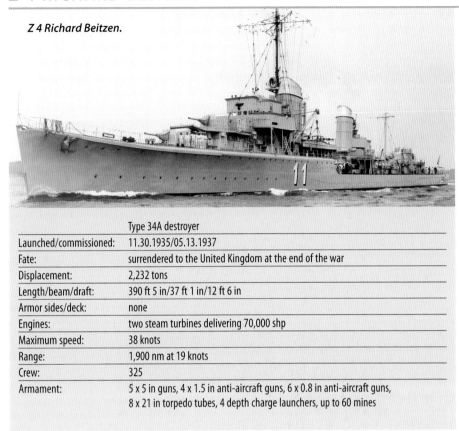

Z 4 Richard Beitzen.

	Type 34A destroyer
Launched/commissioned:	11.30.1935/05.13.1937
Fate:	surrendered to the United Kingdom at the end of the war
Displacement:	2,232 tons
Length/beam/draft:	390 ft 5 in/37 ft 1 in/12 ft 6 in
Armor sides/deck:	none
Engines:	two steam turbines delivering 70,000 shp
Maximum speed:	38 knots
Range:	1,900 nm at 19 knots
Crew:	325
Armament:	5 x 5 in guns, 4 x 1.5 in anti-aircraft guns, 6 x 0.8 in anti-aircraft guns, 8 x 21 in torpedo tubes, 4 depth charge launchers, up to 60 mines

Because such vessels were initially prohibited under the Versailles Treaty, the 16 class 34 and 34A destroyers were the first ships of their type to be built in Germany since the First World War. A new feature was their high-pressure superheated steam technology. Whereas the ship engines of other countries were subject to a maximum boiler pressure of 20 atm, boilers were developed in Germany that could withstand pressures of up to 110 atm in order to generate more power in a smaller space. This system proved very unreliable, however. The high pressure meant that cracked pipes were common, and the ships were also considered not very seaworthy. At the start of the war the *Richard Beitzen* was deployed in the Bay of Danzig but was switched in 1940 to mine-laying operations off the British coast. In 1942 she took part in Operation Cerberus, the breakout of German warships *Scharnhorst*, *Gneisenau*, and *Prinz Eugen* from the Channel. She spent the rest of the war in Norway, where she was severely damaged in an air attack in March 1945. Z 4 was surrendered to the United Kingdom at the end of the war and scrapped in 1949.

Z 25

The type 36 destroyer was a development of the type 34. Reduction of top weight, a flatter superstructure and a widening of the hull resulted in a more seaworthy vessel. The engine was also improved. Type 36A was equipped with 5.8 inch (150 mm) main guns instead of the 5 inch (127 mm) armament. Z 25 served initially in northern Norway but was transferred to France to take part in Operation Cerberus at the beginning of 1942. Afterwards she returned to northern Norway, making up destroyer group Arktis with Z 24 and Z 26. In April 1942, Z 25 and Z 24 damaged British cruiser HMS *Edinburgh* so badly that she had to be abandoned. From March 1943, Z 25 provided U-boats with protection in the Bay of Biscay and in Summer 1944 was moved to the Baltic, where she remained until the end of the war.

	Type 36A destroyer
Launched/commissioned:	03.16.1940/11.30.1940
Fate:	war booty, France
Displacement:	2,232 tons
Length/beam/draft:	416 ft 8 in/39 ft 4 in/12 ft 10 in
Armor sides/deck:	none
Engines:	two steam turbines delivering 70,000 shp
Maximum speed:	38 knots
Range:	2,500–2,900 nm at 19 knots
Crew:	332
Armament:	5 x 5.8 in guns, 4 x 1.5 in anti-aircraft guns, 6 x 0.8 in anti-aircraft guns, 8 x 21 in torpedo tubes, 4 depth charge launchers, ea. 60 mines

The Z 25 was surrendered to France at the end of the war and remained in service as the Hoche *until 1958.*

ADMIRAL GRAF SPEE

	Panzerschiff (pocket battleship) of the *Deutschland* class
Launched/commissioned:	06.30.1934/01.06.1936
Fate:	scuttled in the River Plate, Uruguay, on 12.17.39
Displacement:	12,100 tons
Length/beam/draft:	616 ft 9 in/71 ft 2 in/22 ft 11 in
Armor sides/deck:	max. 3.1 in/1.8 in
Engines:	eight MAN 9-cylinder diesel engines delivering 55,400 hp
Maximum speed:	28 knots
Range:	9,100 nm at 19 knots
Crew:	1,150
Armament:	6 x 11 in guns in two 3-gun turrets, 8 x 5.8 in guns, 6 x 4.1 in anti-aircraft guns, 8 x 1.5 in anti-aircraft guns, 8 x 0.8 in anti-aircraft guns, 8 x 21 in torpedo tubes, 2 Arado AR196 aircraft

The guiding principle behind the **Admiral Graf Spee** *was that she should be "faster than stronger ships and stronger than faster ships."*

In 2004 an initiative was begun to raise parts of the wreck of the **Admiral Graf Spee**, *which lies in shallow water.*

The Versailles Treaty prohibited Germany from possessing warships with a displacement of more than 10,000 tons. As this ruled out the construction of battleships, an alternative was sought. This gave rise to a new type of vessel that was faster than a battleship and more powerful than a cruiser. In the English-speaking world, this concept became known as the "pocket battleship." The idea worked because the major maritime powers were focused on the classes of ship defined in the Washington Naval Treaty. With a maximum speed of 28 knots, the *Graf Spee* and her sister ships the *Admiral Scheer* and the *Deutschland* (renamed the *Lützow* in November 1939) were indeed faster than most battleships

and with six 11 inch (280 mm) guns were more heavily armed than heavy cruisers. An innovative feature was their diesel propulsion, which extended their range and reduced the amount of smoke they generated.

When war broke out the *Graf Spee* was stationed in the South Atlantic fully equipped and immediately began commerce raiding. By December 1939 she had sunk nine merchant ships for a total of 50,089 GRT. On December 13, 1939 she was located by the British heavy cruiser HMS *Exeter* and light cruisers HMS *Ajax* and HMS *Achilles* off the Argentinian coast. During the ensuing battle the *Exeter* was badly damaged and all the other ships were hit too. The *Graf*

Spee was immediately withdrawn to Montevideo (Uruguay). As the German ship could only remain in harbor for 72 hours and the battle damage could not be repaired within this space of time, Captain Langsdorff (who had been tricked into thinking the enemy forces lying in wait outside the harbor were stronger than they actually were) took the decision to scuttle the *Graf Spee* just beyond the mouth of the River Plate on December 17, 1939. The crew were imprisoned in Argentina and Captain Langsdorff took his own life on December 20, 1939.

ADMIRAL HIPPER

The *Admiral Hipper* gave her name to a whole class of heavy German cruisers that included the *Blücher*, the *Prinz Eugen*, the *Seydlitz*, and the *Lützow*. The *Blücher* was lost during the invasion of Norway in 1940, barely three years after launch. The *Prinz Eugen* made a name for herself fighting alongside the *Bismarck* in 1941 and ended her days as a target ship for atomic bomb tests. The *Seydlitz* was due to be converted into an aircraft carrier but the work was never finished. The *Lützow* was sold to the Soviet Union in 1940, towed there in a semi-finished state and never completed. These ships were inadequately armed and armored for their size (nearly 14,000 tons) and did not have sufficient range. Although she had been commissioned at the end of April 1939, the *Hipper* was still not fully operational by the following September. She eventually received her baptism of fire during the invasion of Norway (Operation Weserübung) in April 1940. On April 8 she encountered HMS *Glowworm* and sank the British destroyer during the ensuing battle. In June 1940 the *Hipper* took part alongside the *Scharnhorst* and the *Gneisenau* in Operation Juno, during which three smaller enemy ships were sunk. After this she patrolled the seas between North Cape and Spitzbergen as a commerce raider, sinking one freighter. On November 30, 1940 she broke out to the Atlantic, where she inflicted damage on heavy cruiser HMS *Berwick* and sank 15 freighters during the course of two cruises. She was then moved to Norway (via Germany) and deployed unsuccessfully against convoy PQ17 in July 1941. On November 30, 1942 she set out to attack convoy JW51B in the company of pocket battleship *Lützow* (not to be confused with the *Hipper*-class heavy cruiser of the same name mentioned above) and six destroyers. On New Year's Eve the German flotilla engaged the British escorts, which defended the convoy successfully, sinking a German destroyer and damaging the *Hipper*. Hitler is said to have raged at the failure of Operation Rainbow. The *Hipper* was consequently decommissioned on April 1, 1943, only to be recommissioned as a training ship a year later. On January 30, 1945, she sailed with 1,530 refugees on board from Gotenhafen (present-day Gdynia in Poland) to Kiel, where she was hit by a bomb on April 3. On May 3 she was scuttled in dock.

Heavy cruiser of the *Hipper* class	
Launched/commissioned:	02.06.1937/04.29.1939
Fate:	scuttled in Kiel on 05.03.1945
Displacement:	13,900 tons
Length/beam/draft:	639 ft 9 in/69 ft 11 in /25 ft 3 in
Armor sides/deck:	max. 3.1 in/max. 1.2 in
Engines:	three steam turbines delivering 132,000 hp
Maximum speed:	32.5 knots
Range:	6,800 nm at 19 knots
Crew:	1,600
Armament:	8 x 8 in guns in four double turrets, 12 x 4.1 in anti-aircraft guns, 12 x 1.5 in anti-aircraft guns, 8 x 0.8 in anti-aircraft guns, 12 x 21 in torpedo tubes, 3 Arado AR196 aircraft

*The **Admiral Hipper** was plagued by engine problems throughout her entire operational life.*

BISMARCK

The *Bismarck* and her sister ship the *Tirpitz* were the German Navy's largest vessels and only fully fledged battleships as the artillery of the *Scharnhorst* and the *Gneisenau* was far inferior to that of any likely opponents. The Anglo-German naval agreement of 1935 allowed Germany to build battleships with a displacement of up to 35,000 tons and the *Bismarck* was duly laid down on July 1, 1936. As a result of numerous changes implemented during her construction, however, she ended up displacing 45,950 tons. In their day, the *Bismarck* and the *Tirpitz* were the world's most advanced battleships; the Royal Navy possessed nothing like them as its battleships (with a few exceptions) all dated from before 1918.

After being commissioned on August 24, 1940, the *Bismarck* did not become fully operational until spring 1941. On May 18, 1941 she set out with the *Prinz Eugen* on a merchant shipping raid in the Atlantic. After stopping in Norway, however, the ships were spotted by British reconnaissance airplanes and cruisers and placed under constant surveillance. The battlecruiser HMS *Hood* and the new battleship HMS *Prince of Wales* were sent to the southern exit of the Denmark Strait in order to intercept the German flotilla. The ensuing battle on May 24, 1941 resulted in the sinking of the *Hood* and the disabling of the

The **Bismarck** *in the Atlantic, photographed from the* **Prinz Eugen.**

Prince of Wales, which was forced to disengage. While the *Prinz Eugen* was unscathed, three hits from the *Prince of Wales* destroyed one of the *Bismarck*'s forward tanks causing fuel to leak out. The *Bismarck*'s failure to refuel in Norway now came back to haunt her as it ruled out longer operations. Admiral Lütjens decided to separate the two German ships, leaving the *Prinz Eugen* to hunt merchant ships while the *Bismarck* made directly for St Nazaire in France. A feint succeeded in allowing the two vessels to escape observation by the British cruisers

but an RAF Catalina flying boat later spotted the now unaccompanied *Bismarck*. On May 26, Swordfish torpedo bombers from HMS *Ark Royal* scored a hit to the *Bismarck*'s rudders, rendering her unmaneuverable.

On the morning of May 27 a British battle group comprising battleships HMS *King George V* and HMS *Rodney*, and a number of cruisers and destroyers cornered the *Bismarck*. By the end of a 90-minute battle the German battleship was a floating wreck that ought to have been sunk by torpedoes. Her engines

May 24, 1941: the **Bismarck** *fires a broadside at HMS* **Hood.**

Battleship of the *Bismarck* class	
Launched/commissioned:	02.14.1939/08.24.1940
Fate:	scuttled in the Atlantic on 05.27.1941 after being badly damaged by British units
Displacement:	45,590 tons
Length/beam/draft:	821ft 10in/98ft 5in/34ft 5in
Armor sides/deck:	max. 12.6 in/max. 6.7 in
Engines:	three steam turbines delivering 150,170 hp
Maximum speed:	30.1 knots
Range:	8,100 nm at 19 knots
Crew:	approx. 2,200
Armament:	8 x 15 in guns in four double turrets, 12 x 5.8 in guns, 16 x 4.1 in anti-aircraft guns, 16 x 1.5 in anti-aircraft guns, 20 x 0.8 in anti-aircraft guns, 6 x 21 in torpedo tubes, 4–6 Arado AR196 aircraft

The Bismarck *had large aerial identification markings on her bow and stern.*

Although it is impossible to hide a ship of this size, the Bismarck's camouflage was designed to mislead enemies about her size and speed.

were still working but four hits from close range had penetrated her side armor. It is thought that Admiral Lütjens then ordered the ship to be scuttled with explosives and by opening the sea valves. The *Bismarck* sank at 10.36 with the loss of all but 118 of her crew.

The *Tirpitz*, the *Bismarck*'s sister ship, spent most of her operational life at anchor in Norwegian fjords or unsuccessfully hunting convoys in the North Sea. In September 1943 she was severely damaged by British midget submarines and thereafter became the target of repeated attacks by RAF bombers. On November 12, 1944, Avro Lancaster bombers dropped 6-ton Tallboy bombs on the battleship, two of which scored direct hits while a number of near misses gashed her hull.

The ship capsized with the loss of 1,204 of 2,094 crew.

The Bismarck *in a Norwegian fjord.*

GERMANY

SCHARNHORST

Battleship of the *Scharnhorst* class	
Launched/commissioned:	10.03.1936/01.07.1939
Fate:	sunk by British units in the North Sea on 12.26.1943
Displacement:	31,500 tons
Length/beam/draft:	770 ft 8 in/98 ft 5 in/34 ft 5 in
Armor sides/deck:	max. 13.8 in/max. 3.9 in
Engines:	three steam turbines delivering 160,000 hp
Maximum speed:	31.5 knots
Range:	10,000 nm at 15 knots
Crew:	1,800
Armament:	9 x 11 in guns in three triple turrets, 12 x 5.8 in guns, 14 x 4.1 in anti-aircraft guns, 16 x 1.5 in anti-aircraft guns, 38 x 0.8 in anti-aircraft guns, 6 x 21 in torpedo tubes, 4 Arado AR196 aircraft

The *Scharnhorst* and her sister ship the *Gneisenau* were originally intended to be large *Panzerschiffe* (pocket battleships) but were developed into full battleships in order to match the French *Dunkerque* class. They were the first new ships to significantly exceed the Versailles Treaty limit of 10,000 tons. Political considerations (a desire not to upset the United Kingdom) meant the caliber of the ships' main guns was limited to 11 inches (280 mm). The *Scharnhorst* and the *Gneisenau* were therefore underarmed although it was planned to upgun them to 15 inch (380 mm) main guns at a later stage.

Until 1942, these two ships spent nearly all their time together. In 1939 they sank the British auxiliary cruiser HMS *Rawalpindi* off Iceland. During the invasion of Norway they engaged British battlecruiser HMS *Renown* and both the *Gneisenau* and the *Renown* were damaged. From June 4–10, 1940 the *Scharnhorst* and the *Gneisenau* took part alongside the *Admiral Hipper* and four destroyers in Operation Juno, during which British aircraft carrier HMS *Glorious*, the two destroyer escorts HMS *Ardent* and HMS *Acast*, a tanker, a troop carrier, and minesweeper HMS *Juniper* were all

sunk. The *Scharnhorst* was hit by a torpedo which knocked out its middle and starboard engines and aft triple gun turret. In December 1940 the two battleships switched their attention to merchant shipping in the Atlantic, sinking 22 vessels for a total of 115,600 GRT. Both ships subsequently remained in Brest until February 1942, where they became the targets of repeated bombing by the RAF. On February 11, 1942 they therefore attempted to break out of the Channel for Germany accompanied by the *Prinz Eugen*. The breakout was successful although both the *Scharnhorst* and the *Gneisenau* suffered mine damage. The *Scharnhorst* continued to Norway while the *Gneisenau* was bombed in Kiel and decommissioned. On December 25, 1943, the *Scharnhorst* set out to attack a convoy in the company of five destroyers. Heavy British units, including the new battleship HMS *Duke of York*, located the *Scharnhorst* with their superior radar equipment and sank her on December 26, 1943. All but 36 of her crew perished.

Although classed as such, the Scharnhorst *was not a fully fledged battleship.*

SS EUGENIO DI SAVOIA

The Eugenio di Savoia *in 1939.*

A long with the other ships in the *Duca d'Aosta* class of light cruiser, the *Eugenio di Savoia* was considered well balanced and very seaworthy. Particularly impressive was her speed, which was that of a destroyer. Her armament and armor were on a par with those of other light cruisers. Only her range was limiting but this was not so important as her field of operations was the Mediterranean rather than the Atlantic. The *Eugenio di Savoia* took part in all the major battles fought by the Italian Navy between 1940 and 1943, survived the war unscathed and was awarded to Greece as war reparations. She remained in service as the *Helli* until she was scrapped in 1964.

Light cruiser of the *Duca d'Aosta* class	
Launched/commissioned:	03.16.1935/01.16.1936
Fate:	surrendered to Greece after the war
Displacement:	8,747 tons
Length/beam/draft:	613 ft 2 in/57 ft 5 in/21 ft 4 in
Armor sides/deck:	max. 2.8 in/max. 1.4 in
Engines:	two steam turbines delivering 110,000 hp
Maximum speed:	36.5 knots
Range:	3,900 nm at 14 knots
Crew:	578
Armament:	8 x 6 in guns in four double turrets, 6 x 3.9 in anti-aircraft guns, 8 x 1.5 in anti-aircraft guns, 12 x 0.5 in anti-aircraft MGs, 6 x 21 in torpedo tubes, up to 185 mines, 2 Arado AR196 aircraft

ANDREA DORIA

SS Andrea Doria.

The *Andrea Doria* was a battleship in the *Caio Duilio* class. She had originally been commissioned in 1916 but was comprehensively modernized between 1937 and 1940, receiving new engines and top works. Her hull was also extended by some 33 feet (10 m) and her armament updated (the old 12 inch (305 mm) guns were rebored to 12.6 inches (320 mm) and new secondary and anti-aircraft guns were fitted). Her war was typical of that of most surface vessels of the Italian Navy: other than a number of unsuccessful interventions against British convoys, she saw very little active service. Her operational life ended

Battleship of the *Caio Duilio* class	
Launched/commissioned:	03.30.1913/06.13.1916
Fate:	used as a training ship after the war; scrapped in 1957
Displacement:	29,000 tons
Length/beam/draft:	613 ft 2 in/92 ft 2 in/34 ft 1 in
Armor sides/deck:	max. 2.8 in/max. 1.4 in
Engines:	two steam turbines delivering 85,000 hp
Maximum speed:	27 knots
Range:	3,400 nm at 20 knots
Crew:	1,495
Armament:	10 x 12.6 in guns in two double and two triple turrets, 12 x 5.3 in guns, 10 x 3.5 in anti-aircraft guns, 19 x 1.5 in anti-aircraft guns, 12 x 0.8 in anti-aircraft guns

in March 1942. Following the Italian surrender she was taken to Malta before returning to Italy in June 1944, where she served as a training ship. She was finally scrapped in 1957.

I-400

The *I-400* was a submarine in the *Sen Toku* class. The three vessels hold the record as the largest conventionally powered submarines ever to be built and were designed to attack the Panama Canal. Each of their three Aichi M6A1 airplanes could carry a torpedo or up to 1,763 lb (800 kg) of bombs and was housed in a watertight, pressure-resistant hangar. The planes were launched from a catapult located in front of the tower and all three could be assembled, fueled, armed, and launched within 45 minutes of surfacing. Following the German example, the *I-400* was equipped with a snorkel and was coated with a 0.39 inch (1 cm) thick, rubber-like substance designed to absorb radar and sonar

In 2005 a submarine of the Sen Toku *class similar to the I-400 was discovered off Hawaii.*

signals. The war ended before the *I-400* could be used in combat. She was

surrendered to the USA and was sunk in 1946 during target practice.

Submarine cruiser of the *Sen Toku* class	
Launched/commissioned:	01.18.1944/12.15.1944
Fate:	surrendered to the USA after the war; used as a target ship and sunk in 1946
Displacement:	5,223 tons, 6,560 tons submerged
Length/beam/draft:	400 ft 3 in/39 ft 4 in/23 ft
Armor sides/deck:	none
Engines:	four diesel engines delivering 7,700 hp, two electric motors delivering 2,400 hp
Maximum speed:	18.75 knots (6.5 knots submerged)
Range:	35,000 nm at 14 knots
Crew:	144
Armament:	8 x 21 in torpedo tubes, 1 x 5.5 in cannon, 10 x 1 in anti-aircraft guns, 3 Aichi M6A1 Seiran airplanes
Diving depth:	330 ft

ISOKAZE

The Isokaze shared the same fate as all but one of the Kagero-*class destroyers.*

The *Isokaze* was a Japanese destroyer of the *Kagero* class. Thanks to their combination of seaworthiness, good range, firepower, and speed, the 19 destroyers in this class were regarded as the Japanese Navy's most successful ships of their type although their lack of radar and sonar equipment reduced their effectiveness as the war progressed. Of the 19, 18 were eventually lost, a fate that also befell the *Isokaze*, which sank on April 7, 1945 after taking part in almost all the Japanese Navy's operations in the Pacific. The *Isokaze* was one of the *Yamato*'s escort destroyers. While making for Okinawa, the flotilla was attacked by US carrier planes and the *Isokaze* was so badly damaged that she had to be scuttled by the destroyer *Yukikaze*.

Destroyer of the *Kagero* class	
Launched/commissioned:	06.19.1939/11.30.1940
Fate:	severely damaged by US carrier planes on 04.07.1945 and scuttled near Okinawa
Displacement:	2,490 tons
Length/beam/draft:	388 ft 11 in/35 ft 5 in/12 ft 6 in
Armor sides/deck:	none
Engines:	two steam turbines delivering 52,000 hp
Maximum speed:	35 knots
Range:	5,000 nm at 18 knots
Crew:	240
Armament:	6 x 5 in dual purpose guns, up to 28 x 1 in anti-aircraft guns, 4 x 0.5 in anti-aircraft MGs, 8 x 24 in torpedo tubes, 36 depth charges

KONGO

The *Kongo*, which gave her name to a class of four capital ships, was built in 1912–13 in the United Kingdom. She was the last major Japanese warship to have been

built abroad. Between 1929 and 1931 and 1936 and 1937 the *Kongo*-class ships were comprehensively rebuilt, receiving new engines, reinforced deck armor, torpedo bulges, and additional anti-aircraft guns. Previously classed as battlecruisers, the vessels were reclassified after their refits as fast battleships. The *Kongo* was initially involved in operations against Borneo, Celebes, and Sumatra before heading for Ceylon. In 1942 she took part in the battles of Midway (June) and Guadalcanal

(October) and in 1944 engaged US units during the Battle of Leyte Gulf. She was sunk by US submarine *Sealion* (SS 315) near Taiwan on November 21, 1941. Heavy seas prevented all but 237 members of the crew from being saved.

Note the **Kongo's** *torpedo bulges, which were added later but could not protect her against the USS* **Sealion.**

Battleship of the *Kongo* class	
Launched/commissioned:	05.18.1912/08.16.1913
Fate:	torpedoed and sunk by USS *Sealion* (SS 315) near Taiwan on 11.21.1944
Displacement:	36,600 tons
Length/beam/draft:	728 ft 4 in/101 ft 8 in/31 ft 10 in
Armor sides/deck:	max. 8 in/max. 2–5 in
Engines:	four steam turbines delivering 136,000 hp
Maximum speed:	30 knots
Range:	9,800 nm at 18 knots
Crew:	1,437
Armament (1944):	8 x 14 in guns, 4 x 6 in guns, 4 x 5 in anti-aircraft guns, up to 118 x 1 in anti-aircraft guns, 3 carrier planes

ISE

Battleship of the *Hyuga* class	
Launched/commissioned:	11.12.1916/12.15.1917
Fate:	badly damaged in Kure by US carrier planes and scuttled
Displacement:	35,350 tons
Length/beam/draft:	720 ft 6 in/110 ft 10 in/30 ft 6 in
Armor sides/deck:	max. 12 in/max. 2–4.7 in
Engines:	four steam turbines delivering 80,825 hp
Maximum speed:	25.3 knots
Range:	9,450 nm at 16 knots
Crew:	1,463
Armament:	8 x 14 in guns in four double turrets, 16 x 5 in anti-aircraft guns, up to 104 x 1 in anti-aircraft guns, 22 aircraft

The **Ise** *after her refit, which lasted from September 1942 until September 1943.*

The *Ise* was a battleship of the *Hyuga* class and a veteran of the First World War modernized between 1935 and 1937. After the Battle of Midway in June 1942, the *Ise* and *Hyuga* were converted into carrier battleships in an attempt to compensate for Japan's loss of aircraft carriers. Two of the ships' original six main gun turrets were removed and replaced by a hangar, flight deck, and catapults from where up to 22 airplanes could be launched which would land on "proper" aircraft carriers after carrying out their missions. This plan could not be fully realized as the necessary aircraft could not be delivered and so small numbers of floatplanes were used instead. The *Ise* and *Hyuga* were both hit by bombs in Leyte Gulf on October 26, 1944. They were sent to Kure (Japan) where they were attacked and severely damaged by aircraft from US carriers *Lexington* and *Ticonderoga*. They were then scuttled in shallow water and scrapped on the spot in 1946.

YAMATO

The Yamato *in 1942.*

The Yamato's *anti-aircraft capability was substantially reinforced as late as 1945.*

The *Yamato* and her sister ship the *Musashi* (of her other sister ships the *Shinano* was converted into an aircraft carrier and the *Kii* was never completed) were the largest and most heavily armed and armored battleships the world had ever seen and yet both were sunk by carrier planes. After quitting the League of Nations in 1934 and withdrawing from the Washington Naval Treaty at the end of 1936, Japan started planning a class of super battleship capable of outdoing any imaginable opponent. The plan was designed in particular to force the USA to retaliate by building battleships so large they would not be able to pass through the Panama Canal. As all the US shipyards capable of building and repairing such large vessels were located on the East Coast, this would have given the Japanese an enormous strategic advantage. The designs for the *Yamato* class contained many new features. These included the so-called Kanpon hull line designed to avoid transverse stresses and the extremely unusual shape of the hull itself with its low drag beneath the water line. Its armor was designed to withstand 16 inch (406 mm) shells and one ton (1,000 kg) bombs dropped from a height of over 11,500 feet (3,500 m). Furthermore these ships were regarded as particularly well protected underwater as their side armor was continued all the way down to the bottom of the ship, gradually decreasing in thickness from 410 to 75 mm. For the main armament the designers chose a 18.1 inch (46 cm) L/45 gun, the largest, most powerful weapon ever to arm a ship. The armor-piercing shells fired by these guns weighed 1.6 tons (1,460 kg) and could penetrate 24 inches (60 cm) of steel from a distance of 24 nautical miles (44 km). The *Yamato* was the Japanese flagship at the Battle of Midway but she had no contact with the enemy. On December 25, 1943 she was hit by a torpedo from US submarine *Skate* (SS 305) and put in for repairs at Kure where her 6.1 inch (15.5 mm) side turrets were replaced by extra 4.7 inch (120) mm anti-aircraft guns and a new radar was fitted.

On October 24, 1944 the *Yamato* and *Musashi* took part in the Battle of Leyte Gulf. Together with the *Kongo* they sank US escort carrier *Gambier Bay* and three destroyers. The *Musashi* was sunk by carrier planes later that day while the Yamato was hit by three bombs that caused only minor damage. The repairs were again carried out at the Kure shipyard and her light anti-aircraft defenses were further strengthened. In April 1945 the *Yamato* received orders to attack the US invasion fleet off Okinawa.

Battleship of the *Yamato* class	
Launched/commissioned:	09.08.1940/12.16.1941
Fate:	sunk by US carrier planes on 04.07.1945
Displacement:	69,646 tons
Length/beam/ draft:	864 ft 6 in/127 ft 5 in / 35 ft 5 in
Armor sides/deck:	max. 16.1 in/max. 7.8–9.8 in
Engines:	four steam turbines delivering 165,000 hp
Maximum speed:	28 knots
Range:	7,500 nm at 16 knots
Crew:	3,332
Armament (1945):	9 x 18.1 in guns in three triple turrets, 6 x 6.1 in guns, 24 x 5 in anti-aircraft guns, up to 150 x 1 in anti-aircraft guns, 12 rocket launchers each with 28 x 4.7 in unguided anti-aircraft rockets, 7 aircraft

The construction of the Yamato.

The Yamato *during trials, October 1941.*

The Yamato *caught in a hail of bombs from the attacking US carrier planes. US Navy photographs.*

As it was thought unlikely in the Japanese Navy that she would survive the attack, only enough fuel was taken on board for the outward journey, not for the journey back. On April 7, 1945 she was attacked by 386 US carrier planes on her way to Okinawa and suffered 13 torpedo and eight bomb hits. Her hull was further damaged by numerous near misses. At 14.23 the *Yamato* capsized and an explosion in her forward ammunition store split her in two. Only 269 crew members were saved.

KAGA

Work started on the *Kaga* in 1921. She was originally intended to be a battlecruiser but because of the limitations imposed by the Washington Naval Treaty, she could not be commissioned as such and was converted into an aircraft carrier (completed in 1928). In December 1941 she was part of the Japanese fleet that attacked Pearl Harbor. Along with the *Akagi* she provided support for the invasion of Rabaul in January 1942 and shortly afterward hit a reef and had to be repaired. The following month, aircraft from the *Kaga* and *Akagi* attacked Darwin in northern Australia and sank nine ships including USS *Peary*. At the Battle of Midway the *Kaga* was bombarded by SBD Dauntless dive bombers from USS *Enterprise* causing her to burst into flames and sink shortly afterward.

	Aircraft carrier
Launched/commissioned:	11.17.1921/03.31.1928
Fate:	sunk by US carrier planes at the Battle of Midway on 06.04.1942
Displacement:	38,813 tons
Length/beam/draft:	855 ft 3 in/102 ft 8 in/31 ft
Armor sides/deck:	max. 11 in/max. 4–6 in
Engines:	four steam turbines delivering 127,000 hp
Maximum speed:	31.25 knots
Range:	10,000 nm at 16 knots
Crew:	approx. 2,000
Armament:	10 x 8 in guns in casemate mounts, 16 x 5 in anti-aircraft guns, 22 x 1 in anti-aircraft guns, 72 aircraft (plus 25 dismantled planes in reserve)

The Kaga.

AKAGI

The Akagi.

Like the *Kaga*, the *Akagi* was begun as a battlecruiser and because of the Washington Naval Treaty ended up as an aircraft carrier. After taking part in the attack on Pearl Harbor, she was involved in the invasion of Rabaul and the Bismarck Islands. She also participated in the attack on Darwin in Australia and engaged with Allied naval forces off Sumatra and in the Indian Ocean. During the Battle of Midway she was attacked by dive-bombers from the USS *Enterprise* and *Yorktown* and caught fire. This caused ammunition and aviation fuel to explode and the burnt-out wreck was sunk by torpedoes from Japanese destroyers the following day.

	Aircraft carrier
Launched/commissioned:	22.04.1925/03.27.1927
Fate:	badly damaged by US carrier planes during the Battle of Midway on 06.04.1942 sunk by escort destroyers on 06.05.1942
Displacement:	37,080 tons
Length/beam/draft:	855 ft 3 in/104 ft 4 in/29 ft 10 in
Armor sides/deck:	max. 10 in/max. 4–6 in
Engines:	four steam turbines delivering 133,000 hp
Maximum speed:	31.2 knots
Range:	8,200 nm at 16 knots
Crew:	approx. 2,020
Armament:	6 x 8 in guns in casemate mounts, 12 x 5 in anti-aircraft guns, 28 x 1 in anti-aircraft guns, 66 aircraft (plus 25 dismantled planes in reserve)

SURCOUF

The Surcouf *was a true submarine cruiser and was the largest and heaviest submarine in the world in her day.*

Before the Second World War, the *Surcouf* was the largest submarine in the world. Not only was she armed with torpedoes, she also had two 8 inch (203 mm) cannon mounted in a turret forward of her conning tower and an airplane housed in a watertight, pressure-resistant hangar behind the conning tower. Having avoided falling into German hands by escaping to the United Kingdom, the *Surcouf* fought on the side of the Free French forces during the Second World War. On February 18, 1942 she sank with all hands lost following a collision with a US merchantman in the vicinity of the Panama Canal.

Submarine cruiser	
Launched/commissioned:	11.18.1929/12.15.1932
Fate:	sank as the result of a collision on 02.18.1942
Displacement:	2,880 tons/4,304 tons submerged
Length/beam/draft:	360 ft 11 in/29 ft 6 in/23 ft 7 in
Armor sides/deck:	none
Engines:	two diesel engines delivering 7,600 hp and two electric motors delivering 3,400 hp
Maximum speed:	18.5 knots (10 knots submerged)
Range:	12,000 nm at 10 knots
Crew:	150
Armament:	8 x 22 in torpedo tubes (10 torpedoes), 4 x 16 in torpedo tubes (4 torpedoes), 2 x 8 in guns, 2 x 1.5 in anti-aircraft guns, 4 x 0.5 in anti-aircraft MG, 1 aircraft
Diving depth:	330 ft

RICHELIEU

Battleship of the *Richelieu* class	
Launched/commissioned:	01.17.1939/06.15.1940
Fate:	used as a training ship from 1955; scrapped in 1968
Displacement:	37,832 tons
Length/beam/draft:	813 ft 1 in/108 ft 6 in/32 ft 6 in
Armor sides/deck:	max. 13 in/max. 7.5 in
Engines:	four steam turbines delivering 179,000 hp
Maximum speed:	32.6 knots
Range:	9,836 nm at 16 knots
Crew:	1,550
Armament (nach 1943):	8 x 15 in guns in two quadruple turrets, 9 x 6 in guns, 12 x 3.9 in anti-aircraft guns, 56 x 1.6 in anti-aircraft guns, up to 50 x 0.8 in anti-aircraft guns, 3 aircraft

The *Richelieu* was one of the most advanced ships of her day. An unusual feature was the way her main guns were concentrated into two quadruple turrets on her forecastle and her secondary guns into three triple turrets aft. The reason for this was that it kept the dimensions of the ship—and thus of the areas that needed armor-plating—within limits. Shortly after being commissioned, the *Richelieu* was transferred to Dakar to escape capture by the Germans. As there was no indication at first that she would fight on the side of the Free French forces, she was attacked in Dakar by aircraft from British carrier HMS *Hermes* and later by the battleship HMS *Barham*. In November 1940 she then joined the Free French forces whereupon she was directed to New York for repairs and refitting, which lasted until October 1943. Initially she served in the Mediterranean, later with the British Home Fleet, and ultimately in the Far East. After a brief return to France she remained in Asia until the end of the war.

Note the Richelieu's *unusual concentration of heavy artillery on her forecastle.*

HMS UPHOLDER

The first U-class submarines were built as unarmed practice targets for anti-submarine vessels. They were later fitted with six and then four bow torpedo tubes as it was soon realized that their size made them ideal for operations in the North Sea and Mediterranean. Forty-six U-class vessels and 20 of the very similar V-class submarines were built. Under the command of Lieutenant Commander Wanklyn, HMS *Upholder* sank over 90,000 tons of German and Italian shipping in the Mediterranean. The *Upholder* went missing on April 14, 1942, presumed sunk by an Italian anti-submarine vessel.

HMS Upholder was one of the Royal Navy's most successful submarines.

U-class submarine	
Launched/commissioned:	07.08.1940/10.31.1940
Fate:	lost in action on 04.14.1942
Displacement:	648 tons/730 tons submerged
Length/beam/draft:	195 ft 10 in/15 ft 9 in/15 ft 9 in
Armor sides/deck:	none
Engines:	two Paxman diesel engines delivering 615 hp and two electric motors delivering 825 hp
Maximum speed:	11.75 knots (9 knots submerged)
Range:	4,050 nm at 10 knots (23 nm at 8 knots submerged)
Crew:	33
Armament:	4 x 21 in torpedo tubes (8 torpedoes), 1 x 3 in anti-aircraft gun
Diving depth:	197 ft

HMCS LA MALBAIE

Corvettes of the Flower class performed an invaluable role guarding the convoys that were Britain's lifeline.

When the Royal Navy realized at the outbreak of war that it had a shortage of escort and anti-submarine vessels, it turned to the design for a commercial whaling boat, the main advantages of which were its compact size and simple construction. 145 *Flower*-class corvettes were built by British and 120 by Canadian shipyards. Although conditions on these ships were extremely severe and seasickness was rife, they proved their mettle on arduous and monotonous patrol duties in the North Atlantic. During the first half of the war *Flower*-class corvettes formed the backbone of Britain and Canada's convoy escort fleet. HMCS *La Malbaie*, pictured here, was one of them. She performed her duties steadfastly between mid-1942 and the end of the war, doing her bit to keep a close watch over the North Atlantic.

Corvette of the *Flower* class	
Launched/commissioned:	10.25.1941/04.28.1942
Fate:	decommissioned on 06.28.1945
Displacement:	980 tons
Length/beam/draft:	208 ft 4 in/32 ft 10 in/11 ft 2 in
Armor sides/deck:	none
Engines:	triple-expansion steam engine delivering 2,750 hp
Maximum speed:	16 knots
Range:	3,500 nm at 12 knots
Crew:	85
Armament:	1 x 4.1 in dual purpose gun, 1 x 1.6 in anti-aircraft gun, 2 x 0.8 in anti-aircraft gun, 2 x Hedgehog spigot mortar dischargers, 2–4 depth charge projectors

HMS COSSACK

HMS Cossack *had the distinction of fishing the* Bismarck's *ship's cat (named Oscar) out of the Atlantic.*

HMS *Cossack* was a *Tribal*-class destroyer. This class comprised 27 ships of which 16 were built for the United Kingdom, eight for Canada and three for Australia. As Britain's 16 were among the Royal Navy's most advanced and powerful destroyers, they were used intensively and 12 were lost. HMS *Cossack* was involved in the RN's attempt to prevent Germany's invasion of Norway and was subsequently deployed to protect convoys in the Atlantic. In May 1941 she was part of the battle group charged with sinking the *Bismarck*. On October 24, 1941 she was badly damaged by a torpedo from German submarine *U-563* while escorting a convoy. A tug attempted to tow the *Cossack* to Gibraltar but it ended in disaster when she sank west of Gibraltar three days later with the loss of 159 crew.

Destroyer of the *Tribal* class	
Launched/commissioned:	06.08.1937/06.07.1938
Fate:	torpedoed and sunk by *U-563* west of Gibraltar on 10.24.1941
Displacement:	1,850 tons
Length/beam/draft:	377 ft/36 ft 6 in/9 ft 10 in
Armor sides/deck:	none
Engines:	two steam turbines delivering 44,000 hp
Maximum speed:	36 knots
Range:	5,700 nm at 17 knots
Crew:	190
Armament:	8 x 4.7 in dual purpose guns, 1 x 1.6 in quadruple anti-aircraft gun, 2 x 0.5 in quadruple anti-aircraft MGs, 4 x 21 in torpedo tubes, 1 depth charge rack, 2 depth charge launchers

HMS TRUMPETER

HMS *Trumpeter* was built in the US as a *Bogue*-class escort carrier but was supplied to Britain under the Lend-Lease Agreement, where this type of carrier was known as the *Ameer* class. The *Bogue*-class ships were converted freighters and were used mainly for escorting convoys and hunting submarines. A total of 46 were built in two phases. These and many other escort carriers performed an invaluable service for the Allies as they liberated larger aircraft carriers for more important tasks and provided effective aid in the hunt for German U-boats.

Escort carriers like HMS *Trumpeter helped the Allies avert the U-boat threat.*

Escort aircraft carrier of the *Ameer* class	
Launched/commissioned:	12.15.1942/08.04.1943
Fate:	decommissioned on 06.19.1946
Displacement:	7,800 tons
Length/beam/draft:	495 ft 5 in/69 ft 7 in/25 ft 11 in
Armor sides/deck:	none
Engines:	one steam turbine delivering 8,500 hp
Maximum speed:	18 knots
Range:	not known
Crew:	890
Armament:	2 x 5 in dual purpose guns, 10 x 1.6 in anti-aircraft guns, 20 x 0.8 in anti-aircraft guns, up to 24 aircraft

HMS MANCHESTER

HMS *Manchester* was a powerful, modern ship commissioned on August 4, 1938. She experienced a baptism of fire during the Royal Navy's unsuccessful attempt to prevent the German invasion of Norway and served thereafter mainly as a convoy escort. In 1942 Malta came under siege and needed urgent supplies. A convoy of 14 merchant vessels and several warships including HMS *Manchester* attempted to break through to the island in August 1942 but Italian patrol boats and aircraft spotted the flotilla and attacked. On August 13 two torpedoes fired by the Italian ships disabled the cruiser with the loss of 15 crew. With its engines out of action, HMS *Manchester* drifted toward the Tunisian coast and the order was given to scuttle her. Captain Drew was court-martialed for his decision and was never given another command.

Light cruiser of the *Gloucester* class	
Launched/commissioned:	04.12.1937/08.04.1938
Fate:	scuttled off the Tunisian coast on 08.13.1942 after being torpedoed by an Italian patrol boat
Displacement:	9,650 tons
Length/beam/draft:	590 ft 7 in/64 ft 8 in/20 ft 8 in
Armor sides/deck:	max. 4.9 in/max. 2 in
Engines:	four steam turbines delivering 82,500 hp
Maximum speed:	32 knots
Range:	8,400 nm at 15 knots
Crew:	750
Armament:	12 x 6 in guns in four triple turrets, 8 x 4 in anti-aircraft guns, 8 x 1.6 in anti-aircraft guns, 8 x 0.5 in anti-aircraft MGs, 6 x 21 in torpedo tubes, 2 aircraft

Mounting 12 x 6 inch (152 mm) cannon, HMS Manchester *was heavily armed for a light cruiser.*

HMS EXETER

Heavy cruiser of the York class	
Launched/commissioned:	07.18.1929/07.21.1931
Fate:	sunk by Japanese cruisers in the Java sea on 03.01.1942
Displacement:	8,520 tons
Length/beam/draft:	576 ft 1 in/58 ft 1 in/20 ft 4 in
Armor sides/deck:	max. 3 in/max. 2 in
Engines:	four steam turbines delivering 80,000 hp
Maximum speed:	32 knots
Range:	8,500 nm at 14 knots
Crew:	630
Armament (from 1941):	6 x 8 in guns in three double turrets, 8 x 4 in anti-aircraft guns, 16 x 1.6 in anti-aircraft guns, 6 x 21 in torpedo tubes, 2–3 aircraft

HMS *Exeter*, the fourth Royal Navy ship of that name, was a heavy cruiser in the *York* class. She made a name for herself during the Battle of the River Plate on December 13, 1939. Fighting alongside light cruisers HMS *Ajax* and HMS *Achilles*, HMS *Exeter* succeeded in damaging the far more strongly armed *Admiral Graf Spee* to such an extent that the pocket battleship was forced to take refuge in Montevideo. The *Exeter* sustained such bad damage herself that she only just made it to the Falklands for emergency repairs, which lasted until January 1940. After returning to Devonport for full repairs, which were not completed until March 1941, she was transferred to the Far East, where she was sunk on March 1, 1942 by Japanese cruisers and destroyers while defending the Dutch East Indies (Indonesia).

HMS **Exeter** *made a name for herself during the battle with the* **Graf Spee.**

HMS WARSPITE

HMS Warspite, a veteran of the First World War, was nearly sunk by German Fritz X guided missiles.

HMS *Warspite*, a battleship of the *Queen Elizabeth* class, was built during the First World War and took part in the Battle of Jutland in 1916. Between 1934 and 1937 she underwent extensive modernization, which involved replacing her engines, increasing her armor, and replacing much of her secondary armament with extra anti-aircraft guns. Her superstructure was also modified in order to allow her to accommodate aircraft. At the outbreak of war in 1939 the *Warspite* was on patrol in the Mediterranean and she was immediately ordered to rejoin the Home Fleet. In 1940 she took part in the British attack on Narvik, the Norwegian iron ore port, sinking a number of vessels including a German destroyer. She was then sent back to the Mediterranean, where she was involved with sister ships HMS *Barham* and HMS *Valiant* in the sinking of Italian cruisers *Zara*, *Pola*, and *Fiume* on March 24, 1941. On May 22, 1941 she was badly damaged by German dive-bombers off Crete and sailed to the USA for repairs.

After a short tour of duty in the Pacific, the *Warspite* rejoined the Mediterranean fleet in April 1943, taking part in the Allied landings on Sicily in July and at Salerno in September, where she was seriously damaged by German Fritz X guided missiles. One of the missiles penetrated

Battleship of the *Queen Elizabeth* class	
Launched/commissioned:	11.26.1913/03.19.1915
Fate:	decommissioned in March 1946
Displacement:	31,500 tons
Length/beam/draft:	645 ft 8 in/104 ft/31 ft 10 in
Armor sides/deck:	max. 13 in/max. 4 in
Engines:	four steam turbines delivering 80,000 hp
Maximum speed:	23 knots
Range:	4,200 nm at 14 knots
Crew:	approx. 1,180
Armament:	8 x 15 in guns in four double turrets, 8 x 6 in, 8 x 4 in anti-aircraft guns, 32 x 1.6 in anti-aircraft guns, 15 x 0.8 in anti-aircraft guns, 16 x 0.5 in anti-aircraft MGs, 2–3 aircraft

her deck armor midships and passed through a further six decks before finally exploding and ripping an enormous hole in her hull through which 5,000 tons of water flooded. The outcome was complete engine failure and the loss of power for all systems. The *Warspite* was towed to Malta but the subsequent repairs put her out of action for nine long months.

In June 1944 the battleship supported the Normandy landings. On June 13, 1944, while returning to the United Kingdom to have her worn-out gun

barrels replaced, she struck a mine and was again badly damaged. Following provisional repairs she took part once more in the shelling of coastal positions in France during the Normandy landings. The *Warspite* was decommissioned in March 1946 and eventually scrapped.

HMS HOOD

HMS Hood's thin deck armor proved her undoing

For many years, HMS *Hood* was considered the largest and most powerful battleship in the world. Initially planned as an out-and-out battlecruiser, her armor was strengthened on the basis of lessons learned at the Battle of Jutland in 1916. Her deck armor nevertheless remained relatively weak and ultimately proved her undoing. HMS *Hood* was modernized between 1929 and 1931. She was the pride of the Royal Navy and spent a significant amount of time on official tours to other countries. At the outbreak of war she was with the Home Fleet and took part in the hunt for the *Scharnhorst* and *Gneisenau* in the Atlantic in November 1939. In May 1941 the *Hood* and HMS *Prince of Wales* were given the task of preventing the *Bismarck* and the *Prinz Eugen* from breaking out into the Atlantic. They encountered their opponents in the Denmark Strait south of Greenland on the morning of May 24: two British battleships against a German

HMS PRINCE OF WALES

	Battleship of the *King George V* class
Launched/commissioned:	05.03.1939/03.31.1941
Fate:	sunk by Japanese aircraft east of Malaya on 12.10.1941
Displacement:	38,000 tons
Length/beam/draft:	745 ft/103 ft/35 ft 9 in
Armor sides/deck:	max. 15 in/max. 7 in
Engines:	four steam turbines delivering 110,000 hp
Maximum speed:	28 knots
Range:	14,500 nm at 10 knots
Crew:	1,521
Armament (1941):	10 x 14 in guns in two quadruple and one double turret, 12 x 5.25 in dual purpose guns, 49 x 1.6 in anti-aircraft guns, 8 x 0.8 in anti-aircraft guns, 2 aircraft

HMS Prince of Wales had barely been in service for nine months when she was sunk on December 10, 1941.

Along with her sister ships the *Duke of York*, the *Howe*, and the *Anson*, the *King George V*-class battleship HMS *Prince of Wales* was the Royal Navy's most advanced design of battleship in the Second World War. Opting instead for stronger armor, and not wishing to inflame the naval arms race even further, a decision had been taken during the design phase in the 1930s to arm the battleship with guns no greater than 14 inches (356 mm). Twelve of these were originally planned but it came to be considered more important to strengthen the ship's horizontal protection and so the number of main guns was limited to ten, organized in a brand new configuration of two quadruple turrets and one double. Another innovation was the decision to dispense with secondary armament in favor of a new dual purpose 5.25 inch (13.3 cm) gun designed for use against both air and sea targets.

The *Prince of Wales* had only just been commissioned when she was sent with HMS *Hood* to prevent the *Bismarck* and the *Prinz Eugen* from breaking out into the Atlantic and was badly damaged in the ensuing battle. A hit from the *Bismarck*

	Battlecruiser
Launched/commissioned:	08.22.1918/03.05.1920
Fate:	sunk by the *Bismarck* south of Greenland on 05.24.1941
Displacement:	41,200 tons
Length/beam/draft:	860 ft 2 in/104 ft/29 ft 2 in
Armor sides/deck:	max. 12 in/max. 2 in, 4 in in places
Engines:	four steam turbines delivering 150,000 hp
Maximum speed:	32 knots
Range:	5,200 nm at 18 knots
Crew:	1,419
Armament (1941):	8 x 15 in guns in four double turrets, 6 x 5.5 in guns, 14 x 4 in anti-aircraft guns, 24 x 1.6 in anti-aircraft guns, 20 x 0.5 in anti-aircraft MGs, 5 launchers for unguided anti-aircraft rockets

battleship and cruiser. Six minutes into the battle, the *Bismarck* hit the *Hood's* aft ammunition magazine with the fifth salvo from her 15 inch (381 mm) guns, causing an enormous explosion that swept the *Hood's* main aft turrets and top deck into the sea. The ship sank swiftly with the loss of all but three of her crew.

The reason she succumbed so quickly can be attributed to her original battlecruiser configuration whereby high speeds were achieved at the expense of inadequate deck armor. This meant the *Bismarck's* shells were able to penetrate her ammunition magazines with hardly any resistance.

The damaged *Prince of Wales* disengaged and the subsequent fate of the *Bismarck* and *Prinz Eugen* is described elsewhere in the book.

killed the entire bridge crew with the exception of the captain and a signalman. Other hits took out the forward artillery control station and penetrated the side armor, letting in some 500 tons of water. The ship then disengaged. Once repaired, the *Prince of Wales* carried the British Prime Minister Winston Churchill to Canada in August 1941 for a meeting with President Roosevelt.

In fall 1941 the battleship was transferred to South-East Asia. On December 10, 1941 the *Prince of Wales* and the battlecruiser HMS *Repulse*, sailing out of Singapore, were sunk off the east coast of the Malay Peninsula by bombs and torpedoes from Japanese aircraft. The fate of these two ships made it clear that there was little even modern, well-armored battleships with good anti-

aircraft weaponry could do to defend themselves against a concentrated air attack.

UNITED KINGDOM

HMS ARK ROYAL

HMS *Ark Royal* was the Royal Navy's first modern aircraft carrier. Her flight deck was no longer simply constructed over the hull but was an integral part of the overall structure. The ship had two hangars positioned one above the other which could accommodate a total of 60–72 aircraft (depending on type) and two catapults. Another feature was her side and horizontal armor, without which there would have been more room for airplanes. After the start of the war in September 1939 the *Ark Royal* was sent with other British vessels to try to prevent German warships from breaking out into the Atlantic. During the course of this mission she was torpedoed by German submarine *U-39* and narrowly escaped being sunk. This was because the three torpedoes fired at her detonated prematurely. After taking part in the unsuccessful attempt to thwart the German invasion of Norway, during which aircraft from the carrier sank the German light cruiser *Königsberg*, the *Ark Royal* was transferred to the Mediterranean and then the Atlantic. In

	Aircraft carrier
Launched/commissioned:	04.13.1937/12.16.1938
Fate:	torpedoed by *U-81* east of Gibraltar on 11.13.1941, sinking the following day
Displacement:	22,000 tons
Length/beam/draft:	800 ft/94 ft 9 in/27 ft 1 in
Armor sides/deck:	max. 4.5 in/max. 2.5 in
Engines:	three steam turbines delivering 102,000 hp
Maximum speed:	31 knots
Range:	7,600 nm at 20 knots
Crew:	1,580
Armament (1941):	16 x 4.5 in anti-aircraft guns, 48 x 1.6 in anti-aircraft guns, 32 x 0.5 in anti-aircraft MGs, 60–72 aircraft

May 1941 she joined the Royal Naval flotilla hunting the *Bismarck*. On May 26, Swordfish torpedo bombers from the carrier scored a hit on the *Bismarck*'s rudder machinery, rendering the battleship unmaneuverable. On November 13, 1941 the *Ark Royal* was attacked by German submarine *U-81* and was hit midships. An attempt was made to tow the carrier to Gibraltar but on November 20 the vessel capsized and sank 20 miles from her destination.

One interesting piece of trivia is that the *Ark Royal* was home to Oscar, the *Bismarck*'s cat, after the sinking of destroyer HMS *Cossack*. The animal had thus brought little luck to the three ships that were its home, but survived the sinking of each one and was eventually given a new home by the harbormaster of Gibraltar.

HMS Ark Royal *after being torpedoed by German submarine* **U-81.**

HMS ILLUSTRIOUS

HMS Illustrious.

HMS *Illustrious* gave her name to a class of four aircraft carriers (*Illustrious*, *Victorious*, *Formidable*, and *Indomitable*) that stood out above all for their comprehensive armor. Their hull and hangar sides were 4 inches (102 mm) thick, their flight deck 3 inches (76 mm), and their hangar floor 2 inches (51 mm). The *Illustrious*-class carriers were therefore shorter than the *Ark Royal* and in order to keep the weight to within reasonable limits and improve stability, had no second hangar deck. This meant that at first only 36 (and by parking aircraft on the deck as well up to 54) aircraft could be carried.

HMS *Illustrious* had a turbulent history. Her most famous action was without doubt the attack carried out by her Swordfish torpedo bombers during the night of November 11–12, 1940 on the Italian fleet as it lay at anchor in Tarento, resulting in the sinking of one battleship and the crippling of two others. On January 10 the *Illustrious* was hit eight times by dive-bombers and suffered heavy damage. She then sailed to Malta for repairs, where she was damaged again in another air attack. Once emergency repairs had been carried out, she was moved to Alexandria and then Norfolk, Virginia, where she lay in dock until the beginning of 1942. She then had a tour of duty in the Indian Ocean, where she took part in the invasion of Madagascar, before returning to the Mediterranean and taking part in the Salerno landings in 1943. After yet another spell in the shipyard, the *Illustrious* was stationed in

Aircraft carrier of the *Illustrious* class	
Launched/commissioned:	04.05.1939/05.23.1940
Fate:	decommissioned at the end of 1954
Displacement:	23,100 tons
Length/beam/draft:	734 ft 11 in/95 ft 10 in (waterline)/27 ft 11 in
Armor sides/deck:	max. 4 in/max. 3 in (flight deck), 2 in (hangar floor)
Engines:	three steam turbines delivering 110,000 hp
Maximum speed:	30.5 knots
Range:	11,000 nm at 14 knots
Crew:	1,200
Armament (1941):	16 x 4.5 in anti-aircraft guns, 48 x 1.6 in anti-aircraft guns, 50 x 0.8 in anti-aircraft guns, 36–54 aircraft

The heavy armor of the Illustrious *class proved extremely effective.*

the Far East where she was hit twice in kamikaze attacks but protected from serious damage by the strength of her armor. After the war the *Illustrious* remained in service with the Royal Navy. She was finally decommissioned at the end of 1954 and scrapped in 1956.

USS WAHOO (SS-238)

USS Wahoo *(SS-238)*

The *Gato* class was the backbone of the US submarine fleet and its underwater war against Japan. Over 200 vessels of this highly effective design had been ordered by 1945, achieving a level of success on a par with that of the German U-boat fleet. USS *Wahoo* (SS-238) was one of the most successful of all the US Navy's submarines, sinking 22 Japanese ships for a total GRT of 69,000 during the course of her seven patrols. Nineteen of these sinkings (for a GRT of 55,000) occurred under her second commander, Dudley "Mush" Morton. Morton, however, is a controversial figure as he ordered his men to shoot at the survivors of the troop carrier *Buyo Maru* as they drifted on the sea after the loss of their ship on January 26, 1943. The *Wahoo* was sunk by a Japanese anti-submarine airplane north of Hokkaido in the Sea of Japan on October 13, 1943 during its seventh patrol.

Gato-class submarine	
Launched/commissioned:	02.14.1942/05.15.1942
Fate:	sunk by Japanese aircraft on 10.11.1943
Displacement:	1,525 tons, 2,424 tons submerged
Length/beam/draft:	311 ft 8 in/27 ft 3 in/15 ft 1 in
Armor sides/deck:	none
Engines:	four diesel engines delivering 5,400 hp, four electric motors delivering 2,740 hp
Maximum speed:	20.3 knots (8.75 knots submerged)
Range:	11,000 nm at 10 knots (96 nm at 2 knots submerged)
Crew:	60
Armament:	10 x 21 in torpedo tubes (six forward, four aft, 24 torpedoes), 1 x 4 in dual purpose gun, 2 x 0.8 in anti-aircraft gun
Diving depth:	295 ft

PT-309

During the Second World War the US Navy used two types of fast patrol boat which were produced in large numbers. One was built by the Higgins yard in New Orleans, the other by Elco in New Jersey. Seven hundred boats were built in total and were used mainly in the Pacific, the English Channel, and the Mediterranean. *PT-309* was one of the boats built by Higgins and was commissioned at the end of January 1944. While the boat was in New York awaiting transfer to Europe, her commander, Lieutenant Barker, met Frank Sinatra, who agreed to the vessel being named *Oh Frankie*. While in the Mediterranean, the patrol boat achieved astonishing success without losing a single man. During the course of 75 operations she sank five enemy boats and captured an Italian patrol boat. Today *PT-309* is on display in the Admiral Nimitz Museum in Friedricksburg, Texas.

PT-309: **Oh Frankie.**

Higgins-type motor torpedo boat	
Commissioned:	January 1944
Fate:	decommissioned after the war, now a museum boat
Displacement:	43 tons
Length/beam/draft:	78 ft/19 ft 11 in/5 ft 3 in
Armor sides/deck:	none
Engines:	three Packard gasoline engines delivering 4,050 hp
Maximum speed:	41 knots
Range:	520 nm at 35 knots
Crew:	11
Armament:	4 x torpedoes, 1 x 1.6 in anti-aircraft gun, 2 x 0.8 in anti-aircraft guns, 4 x 0.5 in anti-aircraft MGs

USS DOWNES (DD-375)

USS Downes *(DD-375) before the attack on Pearl Harbor.*

The USS *Downes* was one of 22 *Mahan*-class destroyers built for the US Navy between 1935 and 1937. During the Japanese attack on Pearl Harbor she was so badly damaged that under normal circumstances she would have been scrapped. As destroyers were urgently needed, however, an almost completely new ship was built using every possible reusable part and recommissioned under the same name on November 15, 1943. She then served in the Pacific until the end of the war, when she was decommissioned and broken up.

Destroyer of the *Mahan* class	
Launched/commissioned:	04.22.1936/01.15.1937
Fate:	decommissioned on 12.17.1945
Displacement:	1,500 tons
Length/beam/draft:	341 ft 3 in/35 ft 1 in/9 ft 2 in
Armor sides/deck:	none
Engines:	two steam turbines delivering 49,000 hp
Maximum speed:	37 knots
Range:	6,500 nm at 12 knots
Crew:	158
Armament (1941):	5 x 5 in dual purpose guns, 4 x 0.5 in anti-aircraft MGs, 12 x 21 in torpedo tubes, 2 depth charge racks

USS FLETCHER (DD-445)

USS *Fletcher* (DD-445) gave her name to a class of 175 destroyers built for the US Navy between 1942 and 1944. The *Fletcher* class is held to be the best Second World War destroyer of her type, and after the war many ships of the same extremely successful design were sold to navies all over the world. A number of *Fletcher*-class ships even remained in service into the 1990s. USS *Fletcher* spent the war in the Pacific, taking part in almost every major US operation there. On February 11, 1943 she sank Japanese submarine *RO-102* with depth charges and on February 14, 1945 was slightly damaged by Japanese coastal batteries in Manila Bay. After the war she remained in service with the US Navy until she was decommissioned in 1969.

USS Fletcher *(DD-445).*

Destroyer of the *Fletcher* class	
Launched/commissioned:	05.03.1942/06.30.1942
Fate:	decommissioned in 1969
Displacement:	2,083 tons
Length/beam/draft:	367 ft 5 in/39 ft 4 in/13 ft 9 in
Armor sides/deck:	none
Engines:	two steam turbines delivering 60,000 hp
Maximum speed:	38 knots
Range:	6,500 nm at 15 knots
Crew:	273
Armament (1941):	5 x 5 in dual purpose guns, 4 x 1.1 in anti-aircraft guns, 4 x 0.8 in anti-aircraft guns, 10 x 21 in torpedo tubes, depth charge racks

USS BIRMINGHAM

USS Birmingham.

The USS *Birmingham* was a light cruiser of the *Cleveland* class of which 27 units were built, the largest production run of any class of cruiser ever. Another nine ships in the *Cleveland* class were completed not as cruisers but as *Independence*-class carriers. The *Cleveland* class stood out for the strength of its anti-aircraft armament and was widely regarded as a highly successful, well-balanced design.

USS *Birmingham* was deployed mainly in the Pacific, sustaining damage there on a number of occasions. After being commissioned at the end of January 1943, she was initially sent to the Mediterranean where she supported the Sicily landings in July 1943. The cruiser was then assigned to the Pacific Fleet. On November 8 Japanese aircraft scored hits against her with two bombs and a torpedo off the island of Bougainville, forcing her to retire for repairs, which took until February 1944. After rejoining the Pacific Fleet she took part in numerous operations and survived them all unharmed. During the Battle of Leyte Gulf she was attempting to support the light aircraft carrier USS *Princeton*, which had been badly damaged in a bomb attack, when the carrier was ripped apart by an enormous explosion. The USS *Birmingham* was also badly damaged, suffering 426 fatalities, 237 wounded, and sections of her upper works destroyed. After another spell in the shipyard, lasting until January 1945, she took part in the invasion of Iwo Jima and Okinawa. On May 4, 1945 she was the target of several kamikaze attacks. After shooting down three aircraft, a fourth hit her bow causing serious damage that left 51 dead and 81 wounded. The necessary repairs took until August 1945. After the war the USS *Birmingham* returned to San Francisco where she was mothballed on January 2, 1947.

Light cruiser of the *Cleveland* class	
Launched/commissioned:	03.20.1942/01.29.1943
Fate:	mothballed on 01.02.1947
Displacement:	10,800 tons
Length/beam/draft:	610 ft 3 in/66 ft 3 in/24 ft 11 in
Armor sides/deck:	max. 5 in/max. 2 in
Engines:	four steam turbines delivering 100,000 hp
Maximum speed:	33 knots
Range:	8,000 nm at 15 knots
Crew:	1,200
Armament:	12 x 6 in guns in four triple turrets, 12 x 5 in anti-aircraft guns, 28 x 1.6 in anti-aircraft guns, 10 x 0.8 in anti-aircraft guns, 4 aircraft

The USS Birmingham *after her first spell in the shipyard in February 1944.*

USS INDIANAPOLIS

The captain of the USS **Indianapolis** *was court-martialed and dismissed from the navy after the sinking of his ship.*
He was accused of not taking any measures to protect his ship from U-boat attack.

The USS *Indianapolis* was a cruiser in the *Portland* class (which comprised just two vessels) and spent the entire war in the Pacific. She took part in numerous operations and was flagship of the 5th Fleet of Admiral Spruance. In 1945 the *Indianapolis* took part in the landings on Iwo Jima and Okinawa. On March 31, while pouring pre-invasion fire onto Okinawa, she was hit by a kamikaze pilot and damaged but was able to make it under her own steam to the Mare Island naval shipyards on the west coast of the USA. When the repairs were finished the cruiser was tasked with carrying atom bomb components to Tinian.

After carrying out this mission the *Indianapolis* sailed to Leyte via Guam. On the way there she was hit midships by two torpedoes from Japanese U-boat *I-58* at 00.15 hours on July 30, 1945. The ship capsized within 12 minutes although nearly 900 seamen initially managed to survive the sinking. It had not been possible to put out a distress call and for some obscure reason the ship was not immediately missed by her port of destination. The survivors floated in the sea, mostly without lifeboats or lifejackets, for three days (during which time they were exposed to shark attacks) before being spotted by chance by a patrol aircraft. The last of the 317 shipwrecked seamen were fished out of the Pacific on the fifth day after the sinking.

The USS **Indianapolis** *photographed on April 20, 1942 off the Mare Island Marine Arsenal.*

Heavy cruiser of the *Portland* class	
Launched/commissioned:	11.07.1931/11.15.1932
Fate:	sunk by Japanese submarine *I-58* on 07.30.1945
Displacement:	10,110 tons
Length/beam/draft:	611 ft 3 in/66 ft 3 in/24 ft 3 in
Armor sides/deck:	max. 5 in/max. 2.5 in
Engines:	four steam turbines delivering 107,000 hp
Maximum speed:	32.75 knots
Range:	10,000 nm at 15 knots
Crew:	1,199
Armament:	9 x 8 in guns in three triple turrets, 8 x 5 in anti-aircraft guns, 26 x 1.6 in anti-aircraft guns, 20 x 0.8 in anti-aircraft guns, 4 aircraft

USA

USS MISSOURI BB-63

The USS Missouri.

The USS *Missouri* was a battleship in the *Iowa* class. The original intention was to build six ships in the class but in the end only four were completed (the *Iowa*, *New Jersey*, *Missouri*, and *Wisconsin*).

These were the largest and most powerful battleships ever built in the USA. They were intended mainly as escorts for the US aircraft carrier groups, providing protection against enemy

surface units and air attack, and had a fittingly high top speed of 33 knots—making them the fastest ships of their type in the world. During the design process, greater emphasis was placed

The USS Missouri *firing a broadside from her mighty 16 inch (406 mm) guns.*

on the strength and steadfastness of the vessels than on upgrading their weaponry. Thus the deck armor was 14 inches (355 mm) thick while the lower, 6 inch (152mm) strength deck in the vicinity of the boiler rooms was dispensed with. This was the first time the thickness of a battleship's horizontal armor had ever exceeded that of its side armor. The *Iowa*-class ships were also equipped with quadruple torpedo bulkheads and a triple hull bottom to protect them against mines. The ships' guns could fire 2,650 pound (1,200 kg) shells a distance of 21 nautical miles (39 km). The rapid construction time of these ships (32–41 months) highlights the strength of the US shipbuilding industry during the war.

The USS *Missouri* was commissioned on June 11, 1944 and after crew training she was made flagship of the Pacific Fleet. One of her first missions was to provide covering fire for the invasions of Iwo Jima and Okinawa. On April 11, 1945 a Japanese A6M Zero managed to penetrate the *Missouri*'s anti-aircraft defenses and slammed into the ship. Fortunately this caused only superficial damage as the point of impact was the vessel's side rather than her upper deck. During the attack on Okinawa, the *Missouri* shot down five enemy aircraft and damaged a further six. On July 1945 the ship attacked a section of the Tokyo battle group and shelled industrial targets in Japan. As flagship of the Pacific Fleet, the *Missouri* played a role of historic importance on September 2, 1945 when a Japanese delegation came aboard as the battleship lay at anchor in Tokyo Bay to sign the instrument of surrender. The Second World War in Asia was finally over.

In the years after 1945 the *Missouri*, like the other ships in the *Iowa* class, alternated between reserve status and active service whenever the USA was at war. She and her sister ships took part in the Korean and Vietnam wars, for example, in which their main role was to shell coastal targets. All the ships of this class underwent a thorough refit in the 1980s. Their light anti-aircraft weaponry was stripped out and radar-guided Phalanx anti-aircraft systems, Tomahawk

Battleship of the *Iowa* class	
Launched/commissioned:	01.29.1944/06.11.1944
Fate:	now a museum ship in Pearl Harbor
Displacement:	48,500 tons
Length/beam/draft:	887 ft 2 in/108 ft 2 in/38 ft 1 in
Armor sides/deck:	max. 12.2 in/max. 14 in
Engines:	four steam turbines delivering 212,000 hp
Maximum speed:	33 knots
Range:	16,600 nm at 15 knots
Crew:	2,800
Armament (1945):	9 x 16 in guns in three triple turrets, 20 x 5 in anti-aircraft guns, 80 x 1.6 in anti-aircraft guns, 49 x 0.8 in anti-aircraft guns, 4 aircraft

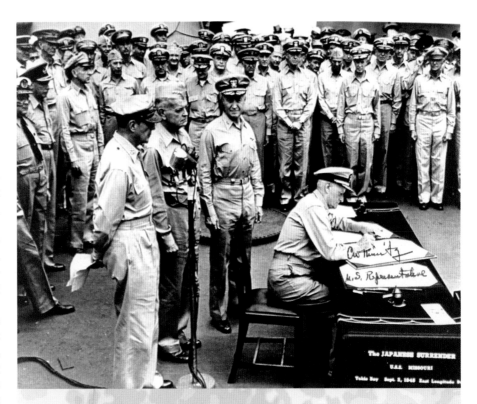

Admiral Nimitz, Commander in Chief of the Pacific Fleet, signing the Japanese surrender on board USS Missouri *on September 2, 1945.*

cruise missiles, and Harpoon anti-ship missiles fitted. Their electronics were also fully upgraded. In this form the *Missouri* took part in the first Gulf War in 1991, during which she launched cruise missiles against Iraq. In 1992 the ship was definitively decommissioned and is now a museum ship in Pearl Harbor. The *New Jersey* and *Wisconsin* have also been transformed into museums although the

second of these has been maintained in a reactivable state. The *Iowa* is part of the US reserve fleet and is currently at anchor in the vicinity of San Francisco.

USS ALABAMA BB-60

Today the USS Alabama *is a floating museum.*

The USS *Alabama* was a battleship of the *South Dakota* class, which comprised four ships (*South Dakota, Indiana, Massachusetts,* and *Alabama*). These ships had been planned even before the Second World War against a background of US rearmament. Their construction, however, was influenced by the Washington Naval Treaty, which was still in force at the time and limited battleships to a maximum 35,000 tons. As a consequence the desired strength and firepower could only be achieved at the expense of speed. In order to save weight, the hull was kept short (681 feet or 297.5 m). This resulted in poor maneuverability but was accepted in exchange for extra armor. The superstructure was also squeezed but this in turn offered the advantage that the ship's silhouette was kept as low as possible.

The USS *Alabama* joined the British Home Fleet in spring 1943, undertaking operations in the North Sea. After returning to Norfolk in August 1943, she set sail for the Pacific, taking part with aircraft carrier groups in the battle for the Gilbert Islands in the Philippine Sea, the Battle of Leyte Gulf, and the battle for the Marshall Islands. In 1945 the *Alabama* was involved in carrier attacks on Formosa (now Taiwan) and Japan itself as well as in the invasion of Okinawa. As the ship and her crew survived all of these combat operations without sustaining any damage, the *Alabama* was nicknamed the "Lucky A." She was decommissioned on January 9, 1947 and remained in reserve in Bremerton until finally being struck from the register of naval vessels on June 1, 1962. On June 16, 1964 she was transferred, fittingly, to the State of Alabama and has lain at anchor near Mobile as a floating museum since September 1964.

	Battleship of the *South Dakota* class
Launched/commissioned:	02.16.1942/08.16.1942
Fate:	now a museum ship near Mobile, Alabama
Displacement:	38,000 tons
Length/beam/draft:	680 ft 9 in/107 ft 11 in/36 ft 1 in
Armor sides/deck:	max. 12.2 in/max. 7.2 in
Engines:	four steam turbines delivering 130,000 hp
Maximum speed:	27.5 knots
Range:	15,000 nm at 15 knots
Crew:	approx. 2,200
Armament (1945):	9 x 16 in guns in three triple turrets, 20 x 5 in anti-aircraft guns, 48 x 1.6 in anti-aircraft guns, 42 x 0.8 in anti-aircraft guns, 3 aircraft

USS COPAHEE CVE-12

	Escort carrier of the *Bogue* class
Launched/commissioned:	10.21.1941/06.15.1942
Fate:	mothballed on 07.05.1946 and struck from the navy register in 1961
Displacement:	7,800 tons
Length/beam/draft:	495 ft 5 in/69 ft 7 in (waterline)/25 ft 11 in
Armor sides/deck:	none
Engines:	one steam turbine delivering 8,500 hp
Maximum speed:	17 knots
Range:	no data
Crew:	890
Armament (1943):	2 x 5 in dual purpose guns, 16 x 1.6 in anti-aircraft guns, 27 x 0.8 in anti-aircraft guns, up to 24 aircraft

The USS *Copahee* was an escort carrier built as part of the first sequence of 46 *Bogue*-class ships. These carriers were based on the hulls of converted freighters and were used mainly for escorting convoys, hunting submarines, and the transportation of aircraft. A number were also lent to the Royal Navy (where they were designated *Attacker* or *Ameer*-class vessels). Their typical complement of aircraft was 12 Grumman Wildcat fighters and nine Grumman Avenger torpedo bombers. The *Copahee* spent the war in the Pacific and survived all her operations unharmed. She was mothballed in 1946.

The USS Copahee transporting captured Japanese aircraft to the USA, July 1944.

USS SAIDOR CVE-117

The USS *Saidor* was an escort carrier in the 46 *Commencement Bay* class, which was intended to comprise 33 ships. As they only started being built shortly before the end of the war, however, only 19 of the vessels were ultimately commissioned. These vessels represented the perfect escort carrier solution and eliminated many of the problems of the other classes. This was largely due to the fact that, although they were based on a large tanker design, thought was given at an early stage to later uses and the carriers of this class were the only ones to remain in service after 1945. USS *Saidor* arrived too late to be used in the Second World War but served as a platform for photographic reconnaissance aircraft during the Bikini Atoll atomic tests. She was mothballed in 1947.

The USS Saidor was finished too late to be used in the Second World War.

	Escort carrier of the *Commencement Bay* class
Launched/commissioned:	03.17.1945/09.04.1945
Fate:	mothballed on 09.12.1947 and struck from the navy register in 1970
Displacement:	11,370 tons
Length/beam/draft:	577 ft 7 in/75 ft (waterline)/30 ft 8 in
Armor sides/deck:	none
Engines:	two steam turbines delivering 16,000 hp
Maximum speed:	19 knots
Range:	no data
Crew:	1,066
Armament (1943):	2 x 5 in dual purpose guns, 36 x 1.6 in anti-aircraft guns, 20 x 0.8 in anti-aircraft guns, up to 33 aircraft

USS LEXINGTON CV-2 AND USS SARATOGA CV-3

The big aircraft carrier USS Lexington *off Hawaii in 1933.*

The USS *Saratoga* and her sister ship USS *Lexington* were the US Navy's first big aircraft carriers. Originally they were both intended to be battlecruisers but could not be completed as such because of the limitations imposed by the Washington Naval Treaty. A decision was therefore taken to convert the ships, on which work had already begun, into aircraft carriers. Both ships escaped the attack on Pearl Harbor as they were on maneuvers in the Pacific at the time.

The *Saratoga* was torpedoed by a Japanese submarine on January 11, 1942 and had to spend several months in the shipyard. Her four double 8 inch (203 mm) gun turrets forward and aft were replaced by 5 inch (127 mm) guns arranged in pairs and her light anti-aircraft weaponry was strengthened at the same time. This work prevented the *Saratoga* from taking part in the Battle of Midway. In August 1942 the carrier was involved in the Guadalcanal landings and shortly afterwards in operations in the Solomon Islands, where she was hit by another submarine torpedo on August 31. Following repairs, the *Sarotoga* was operational again in December 1942 and took part in attacks on Japanese bases on Rabaul and the Gilbert Islands. After the occupation of the Marshall Islands at the beginning of 1944, the carrier was assigned to the British Eastern Fleet, taking part in a number of operations. After this came another spell in the shipyard before the carrier rejoined the US Pacific Fleet. On February 21, 1945 the Saratoga was badly damaged during the assault on Iwo Jima by three bomb

Type: aircraft carrier	USS *Lexington* (1942)	USS *Saratoga* (from 1944)
Launched/commissioned:	10.03.1925/12.14.1927	04.07.1925/11.16.1927
Fate:	damaged by Japanese carrier planes in the Coral Sea and then sunk by US destroyers	sunk on 07.25.1946 while being used as a target ship for atomic bomb tests
Displacement:	33,000 tons	35,000 tons
Length/beam/ draft:	888 ft 1 in/105 ft 8 in/ 31 ft 10 in	901 ft 3 in/129 ft 11 in/ 31 ft 10 in
Armor sides/deck:	6 in/flight deck 1 in strength deck 2 in	6 in /flight deck 1 in strength deck 2 in
Engines:	four steam turbines delivering 210,000 hp	four steam turbines delivering 212,000 hp
Maximum speed:	33.9 knots	34.5 knots
Range:	10,000 nm at 10 knots	10,000 nm at 10 knots
Crew:	2,122	3,300
Armament (1943):	12 x 5 in dual purpose guns, 20 x 1.1 in anti-aircraft guns, 20 x 0.8 in anti-aircraft guns, up to 90 aircraft	16 x 5 in dual purpose guns, 96 x 1.6 in anti-aircraft guns, 32 x 0.8 in anti-aircraft guns, up to 80 aircraft

USS Lexington, 1938.

USS Lexington *around 1934.*

and as many kamikaze hits and again once more had to spend a substantial period of time in dock.

After these repairs she did not return to active service, however, but was initially mothballed and then used as a target ship during the atomic tests in the vicinity of Bikini Atoll and sunk on July 25, 1946.

Shortly after Pearl Harbor the *Lexington* took part in the defense of Wake Island and then had a spell in the shipyard,

where she also swapped her 8 inch (204 cm) guns for dual purpose 5 inch (127 cm) guns. In May 1942 the carrier was tasked with preventing the Japanese landings at Port Moresby and a battle with Japanese carriers ensued in the Coral Sea. Although the *Lexington*'s aircraft had played an important part in the sinking of the Japanese aircraft carrier *Shoho*, she

was so badly hit by carrier planes on May 8, 1942 that she caught fire and had to be abandoned by her crew. The survivors were rescued by the destroyer USS *Phelps*, which then sank the *Lexington* with four torpedoes. The USS *Lexington* was thus the first aircraft carrier to be lost by the USA.

The USS Saratoga *before her major refit in 1942. Her 0.8 inch (20.3 cm) guns can still be seen forward and aft of her island.*

The call sign "SARA" is clearly discernible in the view from above.

USS HORNET CV-8

	Aircraft carrier of the *Yorktown* class
Launched/commissioned:	12.14.1940/10.21.1941
Fate:	badly damaged by Japanese carrier planes off the Santa Cruz Islands on 10.26.1942 and sunk by Japanese destroyers the next day
Displacement:	20,200 tons
Length/beam/draft:	828 ft 5 in/113 ft 10 in/28 ft 10 in
Armor sides/deck:	4 in/2 in
Engines:	four steam turbines delivering 120,000 hp
Maximum speed:	32.5 knots
Range:	10,500 at 15 knots
Crew:	2,919
Armament (from 1943):	8 x 5 in dual purpose guns, 16 x 1.1 in anti-aircraft guns, 24 x 0.5 in anti-aircraft MGs, up to 96 aircraft

USS **Hornet** *on October 27, 1941, shortly after her completion.*

The USS *Hornet* (CV-8) was one of the *Yorktown* class of four aircraft carriers, the others being the *Yorktown*, *Enterprise*, and the smaller *Wasp*. The reason the *Wasp* was smaller was that anything over 14,000 tons would have exceeded the upper limit for the US carrier fleet under the Washington Naval Treaty. Overall, these vessels are regarded as having been highly successful, versatile carriers. During the early part of the war they bore the brunt of the bitter fighting in the Pacific with the result that by the end of 1942, all of them other than the *Enterprise* had been lost.

The *Hornet* was commissioned on October 20, 1941 and sailed out of port just a few months later with two large B-25 Mitchell bombers on board. To the astonishment of the crew, the bombers took off out at sea from the ship, the first time any aircraft of this size and weight had ever achieved such a feat. By the beginning of April, training was complete and the *Hornet* set sail with a complement of 16 B-25 bombers for Japan. Its mission was the famous raid on the Japanese mainland of April 18, 1942 led by Lieutenant Colonel James Doolittle. The *Hornet* also took part in the Battle of the Coral Sea and the Battle of Midway. Although her aircraft did not hit any Japanese carriers, they sank a destroyer and inflicted serious damage on two cruisers as well as inflicting lighter damage on a number of other ships. Following this the *Hornet* took part in the fighting in the Solomon Islands, where her aircraft severely damaged the Japanese ships *Shokaku*, an aircraft carrier, and *Chikuma*, a cruiser. The *Hornet* came under such severe attack herself from Japanese dive-bombers and torpedo bombers that she had to be abandoned, with the loss of 111 lives. Japanese destroyers sank the drifting wreck with torpedoes on October 27.

USS FRANKLIN (CVE-13)

The USS *Franklin* was one of the 23 vessels of the *Essex* class. This was the largest class of aircraft carrier ever built, although not all its number were used during the war. These ships formed the core of the US fast carrier battle groups of the second half of the war and played an important role in the victory over Japan. The *Essex* class was a direct development of the *Yorktown*-class carriers, though freed from the constraints of the Washington Naval Treaty, which meant they could be bigger and heavier. An innovation that has survived to this day was the deck-edge aircraft elevator, which interferes far less with flight operations. These aircraft carriers were

The burning *USS* **Franklin** *photographed from the USS* Santa Fe.

considered the best of their day. Most of them were modernized after the war and remained in service for decades. The USS *Lexington* (CV-16) served as a training ship until 1991.

The USS *Franklin* was commissioned on January 31, 1944 and after testing and training joined the Pacific Fleet in June that year. There she took part in numerous landing operations and assaults on Japanese bases. On September 13 the carrier narrowly escaped serious damage when she was missed by two torpedoes, while a kamikaze pilot hit her at such a flat angle that his burning aircraft glanced off the flight deck and skidded into the sea. While supporting the assault on the Philippines a bomb hit the deck elevator, causing light damage to the ship, and during the Battle of Leyte the carrier was hit again by kamikaze bombers—this time so badly that she had to return to the USA for repairs.

Aircraft carrier of the *Essex* class	
Launched/commissioned:	10.14.1943/01.31.1944
Fate:	decommissioned in 1964
Displacement:	27,100 tons
Length/beam/draft:	869 ft 1 in/147 ft 6 in/34 ft 1 in
Armor sides/deck:	4 in/flight deck 1.5 in, strength deck 2.5 in
Engines:	four steam turbines delivering 150,000 hp
Maximum speed:	33 knots
Range:	15,000 at 15 knots
Crew:	3,448
Armament (from 1943):	12 x 5 in dual purpose guns, 32 x 1.6 in anti-aircraft guns, 46 x 0.8 in anti-aircraft guns, 80–100 aircraft

In March 1945 the *Franklin* was just 50 nautical miles (approximately 90 km) from Japan. On the morning of March 19 a single Japanese airplane broke through the cloud cover and hit the carrier with two 550 pound (250 kg) bombs, which passed through the flight deck and set fire to fuel and ammunition in the hangar below. The ship went up in flames and all her power failed; 724 of the company were killed and 264 wounded. Despite listing chronically, the *Franklin* was prevented from sinking—in part thanks to USS *Santa Fe* (CL-18), which had sped onto the scene to help.

Although the aircraft carrier was repaired, she never again saw active service, remaining instead in reserve until 1964, when she was struck from the ships register.

INDEX

PICTURE CREDITS

2 Corbis Corporation, 6b Corbis Corporation, 7t US Air Force, 7b Deutsches Wehrkundearchiv, Herford, Germany, 8–9 Shutterstock, Inc., 10t Corel Stock Photo, 10b Corel Stock Photo, 11mr Deutsches Wehrkundearchiv, Herford, Germany, 11b Vincent Bourguignon, Rochefort, Belgium, 12t Public Domain, 12b Corel Stock Photo, 13m Deutsches Wehrkundearchiv, Herford, Germany, 13b Public Domain, 14m Vincent Bourguignon, Rochefort, Belgium, 14bl Deutsches Wehrkundearchiv, Herford, Germany, 14br Deutsches Wehrkundearchiv, Herford, Germany, 15m Deutsches Wehrkundearchiv, Herford, Germany, 15m Public Domain, 15b Vincent Bourguignon, Rochefort, Belgium, 16mr Deutsches Wehrkundearchiv, Herford, Germany, 16b Vincent Bourguignon, Rochefort, Belgium, 17b Corbis Corporation, 18t Deutsches Wehrkundearchiv, Herford, Germany, 18b Vincent Bourguignon, Rochefort, Belgium, 19t Paul Scarlata, Asheboro, USA, 19b Vincent Bourguignon, Rochefort, Belgium, 20t Paul Scarlata, Asheboro, 20b Vincent Bourguignon, Rochefort, Belgium, 21t Akira Takizawa, Tokyo, Japan, 21b Akira Takizawa, Tokyo, Japan, 22t Vincent Bourguignon, Rochefort, Belgium, 22b Paul Scarlata, Asheboro, USA, 23t Vincent Bourguignon, Rochefort, Belgium, 23t Vincent Bourguignon, Rochefort, Belgium, 23b Vincent Bourguignon, Rochefort, Belgium, 24t Vincent Bourguignon, Rochefort, Belgium, 24b Corel Stock Photo, 25t Corel Stock Photo, 25b Vincent Bourguignon, Rochefort, Belgium, 26t Vincent Bourguignon, Rochefort, Belgium, 26b Vincent Bourguignon, Rochefort, Belgium, 27t Vincent Bourguignon, Rochefort, Belgium, 27b Vincent Bourguignon, Rochefort, Belgium, 28t Vincent Bourguignon, Rochefort, Belgium, 28b Vincent Bourguignon, Rochefort, Belgium, 29t Vincent Bourguignon, Rochefort, Belgium, 29b Vincent Bourguignon, Rochefort, Belgium, 30t Public Domain, 30b Oliver Missing, Vallendar, 31t Vincent Bourguignon, Rochefort, Belgium, 31b Corbis Corporation, 32t Corel Stock Photos, 32b Corel Stock Photos, 33t Vincent Bourguignon, Rochefort, Belgium, 33b Paul Scarlata, Asheboro, USA, 34 Corbis Corporation, 35mr stock.xchng, 35ml Oliver Missing, Vallendar, 35b Vincent Bourguignon, Rochefort, Belgium, 36t Corel Stock Photo, 36b Corel Stock Photo, 37t Vincent Bourguignon, Rochefort, Belgium, 37br Oliver Missing, Vallendar, 38 Corbis Corporation, 39t Corbis Corporation, 40–41 Shutterstock, Inc., 42t Shutterstock, 42b Deutsches Wehrkundearchiv, Herford, Germany; artist: Grzegorz Jackowski, 43t Vincent Bourguignon, Rochefort, Belgium, 43b Deutsches Wehrkundearchiv, Herford, Germany, 44t Deutsches Wehrkundearchiv, Herford, Germany; artist: Grzegorz Jackowski, 44b Deutsches Wehrkundearchiv, Herford, Germany; artist: Grzegorz Jackowski, 45t Deutsches Wehrkundearchiv, Herford, Germany; artist: Grzegorz Jackowski, 45b Vincent Bourguignon, Rochefort, Belgium, 46m Vincent Bourguignon, Rochefort, Belgium, 47t Deutsches Wehrkundearchiv, Herford , 47m Deutsches Wehrkundearchiv, Herford, Germany, 47b Vincent Bourguignon, Rochefort, Belgium, 48t Vincent Bourguignon, Rochefort, Belgium, 48b Vincent Bourguignon, Rochefort, Belgium, 49t Vincent Bourguignon, Rochefort, Belgium, 49b Vincent Bourguignon, Rochefort, Belgium, 50t Vincent Bourguignon, Rochefort, Belgium, 50b Jaap Meijer, Assen, the Netherlands, 51t Oliver Missing, Vallendar, 51b Jaap Meijer, Assen, the Netherlands, 52t Jaap Meijer, Assen, the Netherlands, 52b Oliver Missing, Vallendar, 53t Deutsches Wehrkundearchiv, Herford, Germany, 53b Vincent Bourguignon, Rochefort, Belgium, 54m Deutsches Wehrkundearchiv, Herford, Germany, 54b Deutsches Wehrkundearchiv, Herford, Germany, 55t Oliver Missing, Vallendar, 55b Oliver Missing, Vallendar, 56ml Shutterstock, Inc., 56mr Oliver Missing, Vallendar, 56b Oliver Missing, Vallendar, 57t Vincent Bourguignon, Rochefort, Belgium, 57b Oliver Missing, Vallendar, 58b Vincent Bourguignon, Rochefort, Belgium, 59b Jaap Meijer, Assen, the Netherlands, 60–61 Deutsches Wehrkundearchiv, Herford, Germany, 62t Deutsches Wehrkundearchiv, Herford, Germany; artist: Grzegorz Jackowski, 62b Vincent Bourguignon, Rochefort, Belgium, 63t Deutsches Wehrkundearchiv, Herford, Germany; artist: Grzegorz Jackowski, 63b Vincent Bourguignon, Rochefort, Belgium, 64or Deutsches Wehrkundearchiv, Herford, Germany, 64b Deutsches Wehrkundearchiv, Herford, Germany; artist: Grzegorz Jackowski, 65m Deutsches Wehrkundearchiv, Herford, Germany; artist: Grzegorz Jackowski, 65b Deutsches Wehrkundearchiv, Herford, Germany; artist: Grzegorz Jackowski, 66t Deutsches Wehrkundearchiv, Herford, Germany; artist: Grzegorz Jackowski, 66m Deutsches Wehrkundearchiv, Herford, Germany; artist: Grzegorz Jackowski, 66b Deutsches Wehrkundearchiv, Herford, Germany, 67t Deutsches Wehrkundearchiv, Herford, Germany, 67m Deutsches Wehrkundearchiv, Herford, Germany; artist: Grzegorz Jackowski, 67b Deutsches Wehrkundearchiv, Herford, Germany; artist: Grzegorz Jackowski, 68m Deutsches Wehrkundearchiv, Herford, Germany, 68b Deutsches Wehrkundearchiv, Herford, Germany; artist: Grzegorz Jackowski, 69t Deutsches Wehrkundearchiv, Herford, Germany, 69b Deutsches Wehrkundearchiv, Herford, Germany; artist: Grzegorz Jackowski, 70t Deutsches Wehrkundearchiv, Herford, Germany, 70m Deutsches Wehrkundearchiv, Herford, Germany; artist: Grzegorz Jackowski, 70b Deutsches Wehrkundearchiv, Herford, Germany; artist: Grzegorz Jackowski, 71t Deutsches Wehrkundearchiv, Herford, Germany; artist: Grzegorz Jackowski, 71b Deutsches Wehrkundearchiv, Herford, Germany, 72t Deutsches Wehrkundearchiv, Herford, Germany; artist: Grzegorz Jackowski, 72m Deutsches Wehrkundearchiv, Herford, Germany; artist: Grzegorz Jackowski, 72b Deutsches Wehrkundearchiv, Herford, Germany, 73t Vincent Bourguignon, Rochefort, Belgium, 73m Vincent Bourguignon, Rochefort, Belgium, 73b Public Domain, 74t Vincent Bourguignon, Rochefort, Belgium, 74m Deutsches Wehrkundearchiv, Herford, Germany; artist: Grzegorz Jackowski, 74b Deutsches Wehrkundearchiv, Herford, Germany; artist: Grzegorz Jackowski, 75t Deutsches Wehrkundearchiv, Herford, Germany, 75bl Deutsches Wehrkundearchiv, Herford, Germany, 75br Deutsches Wehrkundearchiv, Herford, Germany, 76t Vincent Bourguignon, Rochefort, Belgium, 76b Vincent Bourguignon, Rochefort, Belgium, 77t, 77b Vincent Bourguignon, Rochefort, Belgium, Deutsches Wehrkundearchiv, Herford, Germany; artist: Grzegorz Jackowski, 78mr Vincent Bourguignon, Rochefort, Belgium, 78bl Deutsches Wehrkundearchiv, Herford, Germany, 79tl Vincent Bourguignon, Rochefort, Belgium, 79b Vincent Bourguignon, Rochefort, Belgium, 80m Deutsches Wehrkundearchiv, Herford, Germany, 80b Deutsches Wehrkundearchiv, Herford, Germany; artist: Grzegorz Jackowski, 81t Deutsches Wehrkundearchiv, Herford, Germany; artist: Grzegorz Jackowski, 81b Deutsches Wehrkundearchiv, Herford, Germany, 82t Deutsches Wehrkundearchiv, Herford, Germany, 82b Vincent Bourguignon, Rochefort, Belgium, 83t Vincent Bourguignon, Rochefort, Belgium, 83bl Deutsches Wehrkundearchiv, Herford, Germany, 83br Vincent Bourguignon, Rochefort, Belgium, 84mr Vincent Bourguignon, Rochefort, Belgium, 84bl Deutsches Wehrkundearchiv, Herford, Germany, 84br Deutsches Wehrkundearchiv, Herford, Germany, 85t Deutsches Wehrkundearchiv, Herford, Germany; artist: Grzegorz Jackowski, 85b Deutsches Wehrkundearchiv, Herford, Germany; artist: Grzegorz Jackowski, 86m Vincent Bourguignon, Rochefort, Belgium, 86b Vincent Bourguignon, Rochefort, Belgium, 87t Deutsches Wehrkundearchiv, Herford, Germany, 87ml Vincent Bourguignon, Rochefort, Belgium, 87mr Deutsches Wehrkundearchiv, Herford, Germany; artist: Grzegorz Jackowski, 86t Deutsches Wehrkundearchiv, Herford, Germany, 86b Deutsches Wehrkundearchiv, Herford, Germany; artist: Grzegorz Jackowski, 87t Vincent Bourguignon, Rochefort, Belgium, 87b National Archives and Record Administration, USA, 90t Vincent Bourguignon, Rochefort, Belgium, 90b Vincent Bourguignon, Rochefort, Belgium, 91t Corbis Corporation, 91b Vincent Bourguignon, Rochefort, Belgium, 92t Vincent Bourguignon, Rochefort, Belgium, 92bl National Archives and Record Administration, USA, 92br National Archives and Record Administration, USA, 93t Corbis Corporation, 93b Vincent Bourguignon, Rochefort, Belgium, 94t Deutsches Wehrkundearchiv, Herford, Germany, 94b Vincent Bourguignon, Rochefort, Belgium, 95t Vincent Bourguignon, Rochefort, Belgium, 95b Vincent Bourguignon, Rochefort, Belgium, 96t Vincent Bourguignon, Rochefort, Belgium, 96b Vincent Bourguignon, Rochefort, Belgium, 97t Vincent Bourguignon, Rochefort, Belgium, 97b Vincent Bourguignon, Rochefort, Belgium, 98t Vincent Bourguignon, Rochefort, Belgium, 98b Vincent Bourguignon, Rochefort, Belgium, 99t Jaap Meijer, Assen, the Netherlands, 99b Vincent Bourguignon, Rochefort, Belgium, 100t Jaap Meijer, Assen, the Netherlands, 100b Vincent Bourguignon, Rochefort, Belgium, 101t Vincent Bourguignon, Rochefort,

201t Deutsches Wehrkundearchiv, Herford, Germany; artist: Grzegorz Jackowski, 201b Vincent Bourguignon, Rochefort, Belgium, 202t Deutsches Wehrkundearchiv, Herford, Germany, 203t Deutsches Wehrkundearchiv, Herford, Germany; artist: Grzegorz Jackowski, 203b Deutsches Wehrkundearchiv, Herford, Germany, 204t Vincent Bourguignon, Rochefort, Belgium, 204b Vincent Bourguignon, Rochefort, Belgium, 205t Vincent Bourguignon, Rochefort, Belgium, 205b US Air Force, 206t Deutsches Wehrkundearchiv, Herford, Germany; artist: Grzegorz Jackowski, 206m Deutsches Wehrkundearchiv, Herford, Germany; artist: Grzegorz Jackowski, 207tr Corel Stock Photo, 207m Deutsches Wehrkundearchiv, Herford, Germany; artist: Grzegorz Jackowski, 207b Mikhail Bykov, Moscow, Russia, 208t Vincent Bourguignon, Rochefort, Belgium, 208b Vincent Bourguignon, Rochefort, Belgium, 209m Deutsches Wehrkundearchiv, Herford, Germany; artist: Grzegorz Jackowski, 209b Di Freeze, Westminster, USA, 210t Vincent Bourguignon, Rochefort, Belgium, 210b Vincent Bourguignon, Rochefort, Belgium, 211t Mikhail Bykov, Moscow, Russia, 211b Public Domain, 212t Corel Stock Photo, 218b Corel Stock Photo, 219tr Public Domain, 219b Mikhail Bykov, Moscow, Russia, 220t Corel Stock Photo, 220b Mikhail Bykov, Moscow, Russia, 221t Corel Stock Photo, 221b Public Domain, 222m Deutsches Wehrkundearchiv, Herford, Germany; artist: Grzegorz Jackowski, 222b Vincent Bourguignon, Rochefort, Belgium, 223t Vincent Bourguignon, Rochefort, Belgium, 223b Vincent Bourguignon, Rochefort, Belgium, 218t Akira Takizawa, Tokyo, Japan, 218b Corel Stock Photo, 219t Vincent Bourguignon, Rochefort, Belgium, 219b Vincent Bourguignon, Rochefort, Belgium, 220b Corel Stock Photo, 220b Thomas Genth, Münster, Germany, 221t Vincent Bourguignon, Rochefort, Belgium, 221b Public Domain, 222m Corel Stock Photo, 222b Corel Stock Photo, 223t Corel Stock Photo, 223b US Air Force, 224t Vincent Bourguignon, Rochefort, Belgium, 224b Public Domain, 225t Akira Takizawa, Tokyo, Japan, 225m Akira Takizawa, Tokyo, Japan, 225b Mikhail Bykov, Moscow, Russia, 226t Mikhail Bykov, Moscow, Russia, 226b Public Domain, 227t Vincent Bourguignon, Rochefort, Belgium, 227mr Akira Takizawa, Tokyo, Japan, 228t Vincent Bourguignon, Rochefort, Belgium, 228b Vincent Bourguignon, Rochefort, Belgium, 229t Vincent Bourguignon, Rochefort, Belgium, 229b Vincent Bourguignon, Rochefort, Belgium, 230t Vincent Bourguignon, Rochefort, Belgium, 230b Public Domain, 231t Vincent Bourguignon, Rochefort, Belgium, 231b Vincent Bourguignon, Rochefort, Belgium, 232t Vincent Bourguignon, Rochefort, Belgium, 232b Corel Stock Photo, 233b Corel Stock Photo, 234t Corel Stock Photo, 234b Corel Stock Photo, 235t Corel Stock Photo, 235m Royal Air Force, 235b Shutterstock, Inc., 236t Corel Stock Photo, 236b Corel Stock Photo, 237t Corel Stock Photo, 237m Corel Stock Photo, 237b Royal Air Force, 238t Corel Stock Photo, 238b Vincent Bourguignon, Rochefort, Belgium, 239t Vincent Bourguignon, Rochefort, Belgium, 239b Vincent Bourguignon, Rochefort, Belgium, 240b Royal Air Force, 241t Corel Stock Photo, 241b Royal Air Force, 242t Corel Stock Photo, 242b Corel Stock Photo, 243t Corel Stock Photo, 243b Vincent Bourguignon, Rochefort, Belgium, 244t Corel Stock Photo, 245t Corel Stock Photo, 245m Corel Stock Photo, 245b Corel Stock Photo, 246t Royal Air Force, 246b Royal Air Force, 247t Vincent Bourguignon, Rochefort, Belgium, 247b Vincent Bourguignon, Rochefort, Belgium, 248t Corel Stock Photo, 248b Vincent Bourguignon, Rochefort, Belgium, 249t Corel Stock Photo, 249b Vincent Bourguignon, Rochefort, Belgium, 250t Public Domain, 250m Corel Stock Photo, 250b Deutsches Wehrkundearchiv, Herford, Germany; artist: Grzegorz Jackowski, 251t Mikhail Bykov, Moscow, Russia, 251b Deutsches Wehrkundearchiv, Herford, Germany; artist: Grzegorz Jackowski, 252t Mikhail Bykov, Moscow, Russia, 252b Vincent Bourguignon, Rochefort, Belgium, 253t Mikhail Bykov, Moscow, Russia, 253b Mikhail Bykov, Moscow, Russia, 254t Vincent Bourguignon, Rochefort, Belgium, 254b Vincent Bourguignon, Rochefort, Belgium, 255t Corel Stock Photo, 255m Corel Stock Photo, 255b US Air Force, 256t Corel Stock Photo, 256b Corel Stock Photo, 257t Corel Stock Photo, 257b Corel Stock Photo, 258t US Air Force, 258b US Air Force, 259t Corel Stock Photo, 259mt Corel Stock Photo, 259mb stock.xchng, 259b Corel Stock Photo, 260t Corel Stock Photo, 260b US Air Force, 261t Corel Stock Photo, 261m Corel Stock Photo,

261b Corel Stock Photo, 262t US Air Force, 263t Corel Stock Photo, 263m Corel Stock Photo, 263b Corel Stock Photo, 264t Mikhail Bykov, Moskau, 264b Corel Stock Photo, 265t Corbis Corporation, 265b Vincent Bourguignon, Rochefort, Belgium, 266t US Air Force, 266b US Air Force, 267t Corel Stock Photo, 267b Vincent Bourguignon, Rochefort, Belgium, 268t Shutterstock, Inc., 268b US Air Force, 269t Corel Stock Photos, 269m Corel Stock Photos, 269b Corbis Corporation, 270t Shutterstock, Inc., 270b US Air Force, 271t Corel Stock Photo, 271m US Air Force, 271b Vincent Bourguignon, Rochefort, Belgium, 273tl US Air Force, 273tr US Air Force, 273b US Air Force, 274t Vincent Bourguignon, Rochefort, Belgium, 274b US Air Force, 275t US Air Force, 275b Corel Stock Photo, 276–277 Corbis Corporation, 278t Vincent Bourguignon, Rochefort, Belgium, 278b Deutsches Wehrkundearchiv, Herford, Germany, 279t Vincent Bourguignon, Rochefort, Belgium, 279b Vincent Bourguignon, Rochefort, Belgium, 280m Vincent Bourguignon, Rochefort, Belgium, 280b Deutsches Wehrkundearchiv, Herford, Germany, 281t Deutsches Wehrkundearchiv, Herford, Germany, 281b Deutsches Wehrkundearchiv, Herford, Germany, 282t Deutsches Wehrkundearchiv, Herford, Germany, 282m Vincent Bourguignon, Rochefort, Belgium, 283b Deutsches Wehrkundearchiv, Herford, Germany, 284t Deutsches Wehrkundearchiv, Herford, Germany, 284b Deutsches Wehrkundearchiv, Herford, Germany, 285t Vincent Bourguignon, Rochefort, Belgium, 285m Vincent Bourguignon, Rochefort, Belgium, 285b Deutsches Wehrkundearchiv, Herford, Germany, 286b Deutsches Wehrkundearchiv, Herford, Germany, 287t Corbis Corporation, 287b Vincent Bourguignon, Rochefort, Belgium, 288t Vincent Bourguignon, Rochefort, Belgium, 288b Vincent Bourguignon, Rochefort, Belgium, 289t Vincent Bourguignon, Rochefort, Belgium, 289b Vincent Bourguignon, Rochefort, Belgium, 290t Vincent Bourguignon, Rochefort, Belgium, 290m Vincent Bourguignon, Rochefort, Belgium, 291tl Public Domain, 291tr Public Domain, 291ml US Navy, 291mr US Navy, 292t Vincent Bourguignon, Rochefort, Belgium, 292b Vincent Bourguignon, Rochefort, Belgium, 293t Vincent Bourguignon, Rochefort, Belgium, 293b Vincent Bourguignon, Rochefort, Belgium, 294t Vincent Bourguignon, Rochefort, Belgium, 294b Department of National Defence/National Archives of Canada, 295t Vincent Bourguignon, Rochefort, Belgium, 295b Vincent Bourguignon, Rochefort, Belgium, 296t Vincent Bourguignon, Rochefort, Belgium, 296b Vincent Bourguignon, Rochefort, Belgium, 297t Vincent Bourguignon, Rochefort, Belgium, 298t Vincent Bourguignon, Rochefort, Belgium, 299b Vincent Bourguignon, Rochefort, Belgium, 300b Corbis Corporation, 301t Vincent Bourguignon, Rochefort, Belgium, 301b Royal Navy, 302t Vincent Bourguignon, Rochefort, Belgium, 302b Vincent Bourguignon, Rochefort, Belgium, 303t Corbis Corporation, 303b Vincent Bourguignon, Rochefort, Belgium, 304t Vincent Bourguignon, Rochefort, Belgium, 304b US Navy, 305t Corbis Corporation, 305b US Navy, 306t Vincent Bourguignon, Rochefort, Belgium, 306b Corbis Corporation, 307m US Navy, 308t Vincent Bourguignon, Rochefort, Belgium, 309t US Navy, 309b US Navy, 310t US Navy, 311tl US Navy, 311tr US Navy, 311m Vincent Bourguignon, Rochefort, Belgium, 311b Vincent Bourguignon, Rochefort, Belgium, 312t US Navy, 312b Corbis Corporation, 313b Corbis Corporation

Vincent Bourguignon's website: http://ww2drawings.jexiste.fr

Jaap Meijer's website: http:// www.armymotorcars.com

Oliver Missing's website: http://www.o5m6.de

Akira Takizawa's website: http://www3.plala.or.jp/takihome

t = top	mr = middle right	tl = top left
m = middle	ml = middle left	br = bottom right
b = bottom	tr = top right	bl = bottom left